Also in the Variorum Collected Studies Series:

NEHEMIA LEVTZION
Islam in West Africa
Religion, Society and Politics to 1800

RICHARD M. FRANK (Ed. Dimitri Gutas)
Philosophy, Theology and Mysticism in Medieval Islam
Texts and Studies on the Development and History of Kalām, Vol. I

RICHARD M. FRANK (Ed. Dimitri Gutas)
Early Islamic Theology: The Mu`tazilites and al-Ash`ari
Texts and Studies on the Development and History of Kalām, Vol. II

ANDREW RIPPIN
The Qur'an and its Interpretative Tradition

DIMITRI GUTAS
Greek Philosophers in the Arabic Tradition

MICHAEL BRETT
Ibn Khaldun and the Medieval Maghrib

M.J. KISTER
Concepts and Ideas at the Dawn of Islam

G.H.A. JUYNBOLL
Studies on the Origins and Uses of Islamic Hadith

DAVID AYALON
Islam and the Abode of War
Military Slaves and Islamic Adversaries

GEORGE MAKDISI
Religion, Law and Learning in Classical Islam

FRANZ ROSENTHAL
Muslim Intellectual and Social History
A Collection of Essays

WILFERD MADELUNG
Religious Schools and Sects in Medieval Islam

VARIORUM COLLECTED STUDIES SERIES

Islam in Africa and the Middle East

Nehemia Levtzion

Nehemia Levtzion

Islam in Africa and the Middle East

Studies on Conversion and Renewal

Edited by Michel Abitbol
and Amos Nadan

ASHGATE
VARIORUM

Published in the Variorum Collected Studies Series by

Ashgate Publishing Limited
Gower House, Croft Road,
Aldershot, Hampshire
GU11 3HR
Great Britain

Ashgate Publishing Company
Suite 420
101 Cherry Street
Burlington, VT 05401–4405
USA

Ashgate website: http://www.ashgate.com

ISBN 978–0–86078–988–8

British Library Cataloguing in Publication Data
Levtzion, Nehemia
Islam in Africa and the Middle East : studies on conversion and renewal. – (Variorum collected studies series; no. 844)
1. Conversion – Islam 2. Islam – Africa 3. Islam – Middle East 4. Islamic renewal – Africa 5. Islamic renewal – Middle East
I. Title
297.5'74'096

ISBN 978–0–86078–988–8

Library of Congress Control Number:
Levtzion, Nehemia.
Islam in Africa and the Middle East : studies on conversion and renewal / by Nehemia Levtzion ; edited by Michel Abitbol and Amos Nadan.
p. cm. – (Variorum collected studies series; 844)
Includes index.
ISBN 978–0–86078–988–8 (alk. paper)
1. Islam – Africa – History. 2. Islam – Middle East – History. 3. Muslim converts – Africa – History. 4. Muslim converts – Middle East – History. 5. Islamic renewal – Africa – History. 6. Islamic renewal – Middle East – History. I. Abitbol, Michel. II. Nadan, Amos. III. Title.

BP64.A1L48 2007
297.096–dc22 2006034263

The paper used in this publication meets the minimum requirements of the American National Standard for Information Sciences – Permanence of Paper for Printed Library Materials, ANSI Z39.48–1984. ∞ ™

Printed by TJ International Ltd, Padstow, Cornwall

VARIORUM COLLECTED STUDIES SERIES CS844

Contents

This volume contains xxx + 304 pages

Introduction
The Legacy of Nehemia Levtzion 1935–2003

The scholarly work of Nehemia Levtzion, published in a variety of books and articles, has been widely acclaimed by scholars and students of Islam, Africa and the Middle East. The present book contains a representative group of Professor Levtzion's essays, including four hitherto unpublished ones, dealing with various aspects of Islam in Africa and the Middle East. In addition to his academic achievements, Levtzion dedicated much time and effort to developing higher education in Israel, and in the last six years of his life was chairperson of the Planning and Budgeting Committee of the Israeli Council for Higher Education. Because the different chapters in this book speak for themselves, our focus here is on the writer's biography.

Nehemia Levtzion was a modest man who was reluctant to talk about himself. At his 60th birthday celebration, however, when asked to speak to friends and family about his life, he gave the following account (translated from Hebrew), which sums up his life story:

* * *

I was born in Be'er-Tuvia on 24 November 1935, to Pnina (nee Perlow) and Aron Lubetski; this name was later changed to Levtzion. My sister Hanna was three years older than me.

At that time Be'er-Tuvia was the southernmost Jewish settlement in Palestine, and was surrounded by Arab villages. The moshav[1] of Be'er-Tuvia was established in 1930, a few months after the destruction of the moshavah[1] of Be'er-Tuvia during the [Arab] Disturbances of 1929 and the expatriation of its inhabitants. We did not have a farm. My father worked as the secretary and accountant of the moshav and we lived in the workers' neighbourhood, but participated fully in village life.

---

[1] A moshav was a Jewish village with some collective agricultural assets, yet with private farms and residences. A moshavah was only based on private ownership, unlike a kibbutz which was based on collective, Marxist-style ownership.

The events that we experienced were the activities of the British Army; first with much admiration during the Second World War, and later with much tension, when the British searched for weapons, or on the night when a ship with [illegal Jewish] immigrants landed on the coast at Nitzanim. During the War of Independence [1947–48] the village was bombed by the Egyptian Army and we, the children, were evacuated to the centre of the country.

In 1949, after the War of Independence, my family moved to Tel Aviv, and a new chapter began of five years of school (one year in the Ledogma primary school and four years in the 'Ironi Alef high school) and in the naval division (Yamiya) of the United Youth Movement (Hatno'a Ha-meuhedet). Until 10th grade we were occupied in sea activities, including participating in (and winning) the Cities' Sailing Competition from Haifa to Tel Aviv. In the 11th and 12th grades my focus was the youth movement, in its guidance of pupils and its fostering of the *gar'in*.[2]

In December 1953 we [the members of the youth movement] enrolled in the Nahal,[2] after three months of training in Kibbutz Tzora. At the end of this basic training, the *gar'in* moved to Kibbutz Ayelet Ha-shachar, and I was sent for *hadracha* [guidance] to Hatno'a Ha-meuhedet. I was posted to Haifa, and although the youngest leader, I was appointed coordinator of the movement in Haifa, and soon became a member of the national secretariat. In 1954 I coordinated the national summer camp in the Hulda forest.

In 1955, when the *gar'in* went to 'advanced [military] manoeuvres' in the Nahal, my request to leave the *hadracha* and join the military practice in Camp Natan next to Beersheba was approved. In July the *gar'in* joined as 'members' of Kibbutz Ma'ayan Baruch. It was a new chapter lasting two years, until July 1957. During this time I was a member of the Kibbutz's secretariat and in the second year I was also in charge of the sheep pen. In August and September 1956 I travelled to Holland and England with a delegation of leaders of the Habonim youth movement's summer camps.

In October 1957 I started my studies at the Hebrew University, at the Department of Arabic Language and Literature and the Department of Middle Eastern History. Three months after my arrival in Jerusalem I began to work at the Israeli Information Center as editor-in-chief of their publications, and continued there until 1961.

---

[2] *Gar'in*, literally nucleus, refers to a group aimed at founding a settlement in a certain locality, or future locality, immediately after high school. This was done through the Nahal or Fighting Pioneer Youth, a scheme for Israeli youth that combined active military service with civilian service – especially the promotion of Jewish settlement in Israel.

In all I have achieved, I am grateful to my teachers Baneth, Plessner, Shamosh, Ashtor, Heyd and Baer, all of blessed memory, and to Ayalon and Shinar, may they live long. My interest in Islam was apparent in all my seminar papers during my BA studies: on the Khawāridj sects (for Baneth), Moḥammad ʻAbdūh (for Baer) and on Ibn Taymiyya (for Ayalon). But beyond these individual studies, I was fascinated by the phenomenon of the spread of Islam – or Islamization.

In the first year of my MA course, around Hanukah 1961, I was invited to the home of the late Professor Uriel Heyd, head of the Institute for Humanities Studies. He spoke about the university's plan to enlarge the scope of the Center for African and Asian Studies. He said, 'since you are interested in process of Islamization, go and study this process in Africa.' The university, he promised, 'would pay for your studies, and afterwards you would be able to establish a department for African Studies.'

On 4 May 1961, the Gindel and Levtzion families celebrated our marriage [Nehemia Levtzion to Tirtza Gindel]. Tirtza had to finish teaching in a high school in Tiv'on, and a year later moved to teach at the regional school of Mate Yehuda in Kibbutz Kiriyat ʻAnavim. I was then an assistant in the department, and invested much effort into completing all my obligations for the MA, including a thesis and final exam, by July 1962.

At the beginning of November that year Tirtza and I travelled to London for my Ph.D. studies in the history of Africa at the School of Oriental and African Studies (SOAS), University of London. During the first year I decided that my doctoral topic would be the expansion of Islam in Northern Ghana and neighbouring areas (the Volta River Basin). In July 1963 we spent a month in Paris, working in archives, and then travelled to Rome, via Switzerland and Italy, and at the beginning of September 1963 flew from Rome to Accra.

I dedicated about three months to studying the Arabic scripts collected at the University of Ghana, and in November we went north to Tamale. Tirtza decided to teach in a Ghanaian high school in Tamale, instead of at the Israeli school. Therefore we rented a house in Tamale. This was a base from which I travelled every Sunday to visit Muslim communities in Ghana, Togo and Upper Volta, returning to Tamale at the weekend. In all my travels in a Volkswagen 'Beetle' I was joined by a translator, Hajj Ibrahim, with whom I spoke Arabic and who translated the local languages into Arabic.

In January 1964 Tirtza and I went on a long and adventurous journey via Upper Volta, south to Dahomey, north to Nigeria up to Niger on the Sahara border, and from there back to Ghana. We returned to London in August 1964, after visiting Austria, Prague and Copenhagen. In Copenhagen I worked on Arabic scripts from Kumasi, from the beginning of the 19th century, which had been seized by the Danes in Accra.

On 12 November 1965 our oldest son, Moshe, was born in London. He went to Israel with Tirtza in June 1965. I submitted my Ph.D. in August 1965, and until it was read by the examiners, I participated in a conference on the history of Africa in Dar-es-Salaam, Tanzania, and also visited Kenya and Uganda. In November I defended my Ph.D. thesis, and returned to Jerusalem as a lecturer in African and Islamic Studies at the Hebrew University.

On the eve of the Six Day War [1967] the faculty's board approved the proposal to establish a Department of African Studies for postgraduate students. Robert Shershevsky, who had partnered me in the preparatory work for it, died in that war, and I was appointed to coordinate the new department. Shmuel Eisenstadt, the dean of the Department of Social Science, was of great assistance at that time (the department came under the two faculties [Humanities and Social Sciences]).

The academic year 1967–68 was the department's first year, and we succeeded in getting an excellent group of students, among them Victor Azarya, Binyamin Neuberger and Michel Abitbol. We encouraged them to complete their Ph.D. studies outside the country. Their first degrees were from different departments, so that the new department was, as planned, interdisciplinary, with a historical approach as its integrative basis. After a year Naomi Chazan, who came with an MA in African Studies from Columbia, commenced her Ph.D. thesis in the department.

On 22 February 1968 our daughter Osnat was born.

In 1968 my first book, based on my doctoral thesis, was published. Jan Vansina, a prominent historian of Africa, wrote in 1994, in a book that explored the development of African Studies in the field of Islam in Africa: 'Less dismissive views became dominant after 1968, when Nehemia Levtzion published his *Muslims and Chiefs in West Africa*.'

My MA thesis at the Hebrew University (supervised by Peesah Shinar). was on the empire of Mali in the Middle Ages according to Arabic sources. Already, before coming to London, I had published an article in the very important *Journal of African History*, where I pointed out a mistake in the understanding of Ibn Khaldūn's text, which had caused confusion concerning the genealogy of Mali's rulers. Following the completion of [my] book on Northern Ghana, I then wrote a history of Ghana and Mali. In 1973 *Ancient Ghana and Mali* was published, and during the 1970s I wrote several chapters for the *Cambridge History of Africa* series on the history of Western Sudan up to 1800; I completed my contribution to a book on the *History of West Africa in the Middle Ages*. In 1981 the volume that I edited with John Hopkins [*Corpus of Early Arabic Sources for West African History*], which includes the translation into English of Arabic texts up to the 16th century, was published. This volume, known to researchers of Africa by the abbreviation '*Corpus*', gave historians who do not read Arabic access to the sources. It is one of the most cited publications in the research literature.

In 1969 we went on our first sabbatical and got to know the United States.

On 2 June 1970 our daughter Noga was born.

In 1972–73 we went on sabbatical to Cambridge [UK]; I was a Fellow at St John's College. That year I had the opportunity to broaden my interest in the processes of Islamisation, and to return from the history of Islam in Africa to Islam in general. In the same year I ran a seminar at SOAS, with that institution's best researchers, on the process of Islamization. The fruits of that seminar were published in a book that I edited, *Conversion to Islam*, 1979.

On 5 July 1974 our son Avner was born.

In 1974 I was appointed head of the research committee of the Faculty of Humanities. In order to make better use of the limited resources for research, and after checking the needs of most researchers in the faculty, I set out new regulations that enabled every researcher to have access to printing and editing for his publications, and removed limitations on the number of photocopies. These arrangements exist today, with almost no changes, more than 20 years later.

In those years I dealt, for the first time, in a modern subject, as well as paying attention to the rising power of Islam in international relations. Thanks to a grant from the Leonard Davis Institute [for International Relations, Hebrew University] I completed some research, published in 1980 as *International Islamic Solidarity and its Limitations*.

In 1977 we again went on sabbatical to England, first to Oxford and then Manchester. While at Manchester I was chosen to be the Dean of the Faculty of Humanities at the Hebrew University and took up that position when I returned in September 1978. These were three fascinating years that I am not able to cover in this framework.

In Passover 1980 we lost our eldest son, Moshe, in a car accident.

After my term as dean, we went on sabbatical to Boston in 1981–82. I belonged simultaneously to the Center for Middle Eastern Studies at Harvard; the Center of African Studies in Boston; and the Department of Political Science at Brandeis. Between these, we managed to advance a joint endeavour of 20 years standing between myself and Ivor Wilks, which was published in 1986: *Chronicles from Gonja: a Tradition of West African Muslim Historiography*. Another [colleague] who greatly contributed to this work was Bruce Haight, a former student of Ivor's and mine.

After my return to Israel in August 1982 I was asked to become director of the Ben Zvi Institute, and hence to continue with the advancement of studies on the traditions of Judaism in the 'East'. It was also a first opportunity for me to dedicate effort to the field of Judaism.

In those five years, 1982–87, I was also the academic principal of a new programme, funded by the Rothschild Fund, to assist young diplomats from the Israeli Foreign Ministry to do two years study at the Hebrew University.

Simultaneously, I became a member of the Planning and Budgeting Committee of the Israeli Council for Higher Education [PBC], after a previous term in 1980–81. As a member of the PBC I was the head of two committees, the committee for regional colleges and the committee for overseas students.

In 1983 we ran an international workshop at the Truman Institute for the Advancement of Peace [Hebrew University], on rural and urban Islam in Africa, which led to publication of the volume, *Rural and Urban Islam in West Africa* (1986).

In 1985 I coordinated a research group at the university's Institute for Advanced Studies, focusing on eighteenth-century renewal and reform movements in Islam. At the end of that year we held an international conference on the subject, leading to a book that I edited with John Voll, *Eighteenth Century Renewal and Reform in Islam* (1987).

In May 1987 I was chosen to be president of [Israel's] Open University, which opened a chapter of the five most fascinating years of my life. I received into my hands a well-established university, and I set a personal target to materialize its great potential. It seems to me that this was achieved in the doubling of the number of students to 20,000; in the establishment of colleges in which intensive studies could be conducted; in concentrating the studies in social sciences around occupations that were more in demand; and in presenting of the university as a valued alternative to other universities for youngsters finishing their military service. With this, the economic standing of the university was widened and stabilized.

In August 1992 we celebrated the marriage of Osnat and Amit, and in July 1993 the marriage of Noga and Amos.

Immediately after ending my term as president of the Open University, I agreed to replace Professor Moshe Davis as the academic chairperson of The International Center for the University Teaching of Jewish Civilization. This took me back to dealing with Jewish Studies.

From January 1994 I was the head of the Van Leer Institute in Jerusalem. I was asked to take this position after the institute had fallen into severe economic crisis and there were also personal difficulties. After a few months the institute was rehabilitated, and it gradually achieved a level of activity above what it had experienced in the past. The institute's emphasis is on continual intellectual dialogue.

In my research these days I focus on understanding the organisational and structural changes that took place in Sufi brotherhoods during the eighteenth century. These contribute to a more comprehensive understanding of the movements of reform and renewal. Simultaneously, I am cooperating with two archaeologists, Roderick and Susan McIntosh, and with an historian of oral traditions, David Conrad, in rewriting the book on Ghana and Mali, a book that has still not been superseded after 20 years. I am also engaged in another project, the Cambridge *History of Islam in Africa*, together with Randall Pouwels.

Since I live in an age where people gather things that they wrote, in 1994 a collection of essays of mine was published by Variorum under the title, *Islam in West Africa: Religion, Society and Politics to 1800*. On 23 June our first grandson, Yoav Moshe, was born to Osnat and Amit Korach.

* * *

Nehemia Levtzion passed away three months before his 68th birthday. If he had spoken to his friends and family on his 67th birthday, he would probably have added to the above that he chaired the Planning and Budgeting Committee of the Israeli Council for Higher Education (1997–2003) and was president of the Israel Oriental Society (1997–2003); he would have mentioned his new publications, especially the book he co-authored with J. Spaulding, *Medieval West Africa: Views from Arab Scholars and Merchants* and the book with M. Hoexter and S. N. Eisenstadt, *The Public Sphere in Muslim Societies*. Also, in September 1998 the family celebrated Avner and Tal's marriage; and by that time he had five grandchildren and another on their way.

The aim of the present book – the second volume of Professor Levtzion's essays – has been to give a more comprehensive understanding of the author's views, as well as of the process by which he developed them. The essays appear in two broad sections: 'History, Culture and Societies' and 'Revivalism, Sufism and Fundamentalism'. The four previously unpublished essays have been lightly edited, and it is important to mention that they were working papers and that Levtzion would probably have made some changes.

Nehemia Levtzion: Bibliography

Note: This list, including the different categories, was prepared by Professor Levtzion.

1. Conversion to Islam

Books

1.1 *Muslims and Chiefs in West Africa: A Study of Islam in the Middle Volta Basin in the Pre-Colonial Period*. Oxford: Clarendon Press, 1968, 256 pp.

1.2 (editor) *Conversion to Islam*. New York: Holmes & Meier, 1979, 270 pp.

Articles and Chapters

1.3 "Patterns of Islamization in West Africa", in *Aspects of West African Islam*, edited by D.F. McCall and N.R. Bennett. Boston: Boston University Press, 1971, pp. 31–39. Reprinted in *Conversion to Islam*, edited by N. Levtzion, New York: Holmes & Meier, 1979, pp. 207–216 (reprinted in 4.2).

1.4 "Conversion to Islam: Some notes towards a comparative study", *Actes de 29e Congrès International des Orientalistes: Etudes Arabes et Islamiques*, edited by C. Cahen. Paris: L'Asiathèque, 1975, pp. 125–129.

1.5 "Towards a comparative study of Islamization", in *Conversion to Islam*, edited by N. Levtzion, 1981, pp. 1–23 (see no. 1.2; reprinted in this present volume as essay I).

1.6 "Conversion under Muslim domination: a comparative study", in *Religious Change and Cultural Domination*, edited by David N. Lorenzen. Mexico City: El Colegio de México, 1981, pp. 19–38; reprinted in this present volume as essay II.

1.7 "Shari'a and custom in the process of Islamization and sedentarization", *Cathedra*, vol. 20 (1981), pp. 78–80 (Hebrew).

1.8 "Migration and settlement of Muslim nomads and conquerors: their contribution to Islamization", in *Emigration and Settlement in Jewish and General History*, edited by A. Shinan. Jerusalem: Zalman Shazar Center, 1982, pp. 95–107 (Hebrew).

1.9 "Slavery and Islamization in Africa", in *Slaves and Slavery in Muslim Africa*, edited by J.R. Willis. London: Frank Cass, 1985, vol. 1, pp. 182–198 (reprinted in 4.2).

1.10 "Aspekte der Islamisierung: Eine kritische Wurdigungder Beobachtungen Max Webers", in *Max Weber Sicht des Islam: Interpretation und Kritik*, edited by W. Schluchter. Frankfurt: Suhrkamp, 1987, pp. 142–155.

1.11 "Conversion to Islam in Syria and Palestine, and the survival of Christian communities", in *Conversion and Continuity: Indigenous Christian Communities in Medieval Islamic Lands*, edited by M. Gervers and R.J. Bikhazi. Toronto: Pontifical Institute of Mediaeval Studies, 1990, pp. 289–312; reprinted in this present volume as essay III.

1.12 "Conversion and Islamization in the Middle Ages: how did Jews and Christians differ?", *Pe'amim*, vol. 42 (1990), pp. 8–15 (Hebrew).

1.13 "Islamisierungmuster: Die Begegnung des Islam mit Achsenzeitreligionen", in *Kulturen der Achsenzeit II: Ihre institutionelle und kulturelle Dynamik*, edited by S.N. Eisenstadt. Frankfurt: Suhrkamp, 1992, vol. 3, pp. 226–241.

1.14 "Aspects of Islamization: Weber's observations on Islam reconsidered", in *Max Weber and Islam*, edited by T.B. Huff and W. Schluchter, New Brunswick, NJ: Transaction Publishers, 1999, pp. 153–161 (an English translation of 1.10; reprinted in this present volume as essay IV).

2. Renewal, Reform and Sufi Brotherhoods in the Eighteen Century

Book

2.1 (co-editor with J.O. Voll), *Eighteenth Century Renewal and Reform in Islam*. Syracuse, NY: Syracuse University Press, 1987, 200 pp.

Articles and Chapters

2.2 "Notes on the Origins of Islamic Militancy in the Futa Jallon", *Notes Africaines* (Dakar), no. 132 (October 1971), pp. 94–96 (reprinted in 4.2).

2.3 "Eighteenth-century renewal and reform movements in Islam", in *Renewal (tajdid) and Reform (islah) in Islam*, a special issue of *Hamizrah Hehadash*, vol. 31 (1986), pp. 48–70 (Hebrew).

2.4 (with J.O. Voll), "Eighteenth-century renewal and reform movements in Islam: an Introductory Essay, in *Eighteenth Century Renewal and Reform in Islam*, edited by Levtzion and Voll, 1987 (see 2.1), pp. 13–20.

2.5 "The Eighteenth Century: Background to the Islamic Revolutions in West Africa", in *Eighteenth Century Renewal and Reform in Islam*, edited by Levtzion and Voll, 1987 (2.1), pp. 21–38 (reprinted in 4.2).

2.6 "Eighteenth-century renewal and reform in Islam: the role of Sufi turuq in West Africa", in Levtzion, *Islam in West Africa* (no. 1.10) 1994 (from a collection of papers entitled *The Cloth of Many Colored Silks: Papers on History and Society Ghanaian and Islamic in Honor of Ivor Wilks).*

2.7 "al-Tijani, Ahmad", *Oxford Encyclopedia of the Modern Islamic World*, edited by J.L. Esposito. New York: Oxford University Press, 1995.

2.8 (with Gideon Weigert), "Khalwatiyya", *Oxford Encyclopedia of the Modern Islamic World*. New York: Oxford University Press, 1995.

2.9 (with Gideon Weigert), "Religious Reform in Eighteenth-century Morocco", *North African, Arabic and Islamic Studies in Honor of Pessah Shinar*, published as *Jerusalem Studies in Arabic and Islam* 19 (1995), pp. 173–197; reprinted in this present volume as essay X.

2.10 "Eighteenth-Century Sufi Brotherhoods: Structural, Organizational and Ritual Changes", in *Essays on Scripture, Thought and Society. A Festschrift in*

Honour of Anthony H. Johns, edited by P.G. Riddell and T.Street. Leiden: Brill 1997, pp. 147–60; reprinted in this present volume as essay XI.

2.11 (with Gideon Weigert), "The Muslim holy cities as foci of Islamic revivalism in the eighteenth century", in *Sacred Space: Shrine, City, Land,* edited by B.Z. Kedar and R.J. Zwi Werblowsky. The Israel Academy and Macmillan (UK), 1998, pp. 259–77; reprinted in this present volume as essay XII.

2.12 (with Gideon Weigert), "Renewal and reform of the Khalwatiyya in Egypt in the 18th century". Unpublished paper presented to the Middle East Studies Association annual meeting, San Antonio, TX, November 1990.

2.13 'The Dynamics of Sufi Brotherhoods', in *The Public Sphere in Muslim Societies*, edited by M. Hoexter, S.N. Eisenstadt and N. Levtzion. Albany: SUNY series in Near Eastern Studies, 2002, pp. 109–118; reprinted in this present volume as essay XIII.

3. Studies on Islam

Books

3.1 *International Islamic Solidarity and its Limitations*. Jerusalem: Magnes Press for the Leonard Davis Institute for International Relations, 1980, 65 pp.

3.2 (with Daphna Ephrat and Daniela Talmon-Heller), *Islam: A History of the Religion.* The Open University of Israel, Volumes 1 and 2, 1998; Volume 3, 2000 (in Hebrew).

3.3 (co-editor with M. Hoexter and S.N. Eisenstadt), *The Public Sphere in Muslim Societies.* Albany, NY: SUNY Press, 2002, 191 pp.

Articles and Chapters

3.4 "The Integration of the Muslim Northern Region into the Federation of Nigeria", *Hamizrah Hehadash*, vol. 12 (1962), pp. 28–46 (Hebrew).

3.5 "Sects in Islam", in *Studies in the History of the Arabs and Islam*, edited by H. Lazarus-Yafeh. Tel-Aviv: Reshafim, 1967, pp. 176–198 (Hebrew).

3.6 "Non-Arab Islam and the Middle East Conflict", in *Islamic Aspects of the Middle East Conflict.* Jerusalem: Truman Research Institute, 1974, pp. 17–23 (Hebrew).

3.7 "Between *'ulama'* and rulers in the Muslim State", in *Priesthood and Monarchy: Studies in the Historical Relations of Religion and State*, edited by I. Gafni and G. Motzkin. Jerusalem: Zalman Shazar Center, 1985, pp. 115–121. (Hebrew).

3.8 "The Spirit of the Mediterranean: Cultural Exchanges in Trade and War", *DOMUS: International Review of Architecture, Design, Art, Communication* no. 813 (March 1999), pp. 4–6.

3.9 "Islam and politics: lessons from the past", *Hamizrah Hehadash* 40 (1999), pp. 5–8 (in Hebrew); *Prajna Vihara: Journal of Philosophy and Religion* (Assumption University, Bangkok), vol. 1; no. 2 (July–December 2000), pp. 111–120.

3.10 "Tolerance in Islam", in *Education for Human Values, Tolerance and Peace*, edited by J. Iram. School of Education, Bar-Ilan University 2000, pp. 15–19.

3.11 "Islam in African and Global Contexts: Adventures in Comparative Studies of Islam", paper presented to the conference on Islam in Africa: A Global, Cultural and Historical Perspective, Binghamton University, NY, April 19–22, 2001.

4. Islam in Africa

Books

4.1 (co-editor with H.J. Fisher) *Rural and Urban Islam in West Africa*. Boulder, CO: Lynne Rienner, 1987, 176 pp.; first published as a special issue of *Asian and African Studies*, vol. 20, no. 1 (1986).

4.2 *Islam in West Africa: Religion, Society and Politics to 1800*. London: Variorum, 1994, 300 pp.

4.3 (co-editor with R.L. Pouwels), *The History of Islam in Africa.* Athens, OH: Ohio University Press, 2000, 591 pp.

Articles and Chapters

4.4 "Islam in Africa: some central issues for research and teaching", *Hamizrah Hehadash*, vol. 17 (1967), pp. 1–17 (Hebrew).

4.5 “The long march of Islam in the Western Sudan”, in *The Middle Age of African History*, edited by R. Oliver. London: Oxford University Press, 1967, pp. 13–18.

4.6 “Reflections on the Muslim historiography in Africa”, in *Emerging Themes of African History*, edited by T.O. Ranger. Nairobi: East African Publishing House, 1968, pp. 23–27.

4.7 “L‘Islam et le commerce chez les Dagomba du Nord Ghana”, *Annales: E.S.C.*, vol. 23 (1968), pp. 723–743.

4.8 “Islam in Coastal West Africa”, in *Islam in Tropical Africa*, edited by J. Kritzeck and W.H. Lewis. New York: Van Nostrand, 1969, pp. 301–318.

4.9 “The *‘ulama’* of the Western Sudan before the fifteenth century”, in *The ‘Ulama’ and Problems of Religion in the Muslim World: Studies in Memory of Uriel Heyd*, edited by G. Baer. Jerusalem: Magnes Press, 1971, pp. 52–62 (Hebrew).

4.10 “Islam in West African politics: accommodation and tension between the *‘ulama’* and the political authorities”, *Cahiers d‘Etudes Africaines*, vol. 18 (1979), pp. 333–345.

4.11 “Sociopolitical roles of Muslim clerics and scholars in West Africa”, in *Comparative Social Dynamics: Essays in Honor of S.N. Eisenstadt*, edited by E. Cohen, M. Lissak and U. Almagor. Boulder, CO: Westview Press, 1985, pp. 95–107.

4.12 “Islam and religious pluralism in West African states”, *Revue Française d‘Histoire d‘Outre Mer*, vol. 68 (1981), pp. 154–155.

4.13 “Rural and urban Islam in West Africa”, in *Rural and Urban Islam in West Africa*, edited by N. Levtzion and H.J. Fisher, Boulder, CO: Lynne Rienner, 1987 (4.1 above), pp.1–20 (reprinted in 4.2).

4.14 “Merchants vs. Scholars and clerics: differential and complementary roles”, in *Rural and Urban Islam in West Africa*, by N. Levtzion and H.J. Fisher, Boulder, CO: Lynne Rienner, 1987 (1.8 above), pp. 21–37 (reprinted in 1.10).

4.15 “Islam in Sub-Saharan Africa”, *Encyclopaedia of Religion*, edited by M. Eliade et al. New York: Macmillan, 1987, vol. 7, pp. 344–357.

4.16 "Islam and state formation in West Africa", in *The Early State in Africa*, edited by S.N. Eisenstadt, M. Abitbol and N. Chazan. Leiden: E.J. Brill, 1987, pp. 98–108.

4.17 "Muslim *'ulama'* and human rights in pre-colonial West Africa", in *Human Rights in Developing Countries: Problems and Prospects*, edited by C.E. Welch. Buffalo, NY, 1989. pp. 122–138.

4.18 "Islam in Africa to 1800", *The Oxford History of Islam*, edited by J.L. Esposito. New York: Oxford University Press, 1999, pp. 475–507.

4.19 (with R.L. Pouwels), "Introduction: Patterns of Islamization and varieties of religious experience among Muslims of Africa", in *The History of Islam in Africa*. Athens: Ohio University Press 2000, edited by N. Levtzion and R.L. Pouwels (see above 4.3), pp. 1–18.

4.20 "Islam in the Bilad al-Sudan to 1800", in *The History of Islam in Africa*. Athens, OH: Ohio University Press 2000, edited by N. Levtzion and R.L. Pouwels (see above 4.3), pp. 63–91; reprinted in this present volume as essay V.

5. History of West Africa

Books

5.1 *Ancient Ghana and Mali*. London: Methuen, 1973, 283 pp. (hardcover and paperback); 2nd edition, New York: Holmes & Meier, 1980 (hardcover and paperback).

5.2 *An Introduction to African History*. Tel Aviv: The Open University of Israel, 1980, 147 pp. (Hebrew).

Articles and Chapters

5.3 "Salaga – a nineteenth century trading town in Ghana", *Asian and African Studies*, vol. 2 (1966), pp. 207–244.

5.4 "Oral traditions and historical consciousness in Africa", in *Awareness of the Past in the Consciousness of the Nations and of the Jewish People*. Jerusalem: Zalman Shazar Center, 1969, pp. 124–134 (Hebrew).

5.5 "The early states of the Western Sudan to 1500", in *History of West Africa*, edited by J.F.A. Ajayi and M. Crowder. London: Longman, 1971, vol. 1, pp. 120–157. (Several later editions)

5.6 "Notes sur les états Dyula de Kong et de Bobo", *Bulletin de Liaison. Centre Universitaire de Recherches de Dévelloppement*. (Abidjan), vol. 1 (1971), pp. 61–62.

5.7 "Northwest Africa: from the Maghrib to the fringes of the forest in the seventeenth and eighteenth centuries", *Cambridge History of Africa*, vol. 4, edited by J.R. Gray. Cambridge, 1975, pp. 142–222.

5.8 "North Africa and the Western Sudan from 1050 to 1590", *Cambridge History of Africa*, vol. 3, edited by R. Oliver. Cambridge, 1977, pp. 331–462.

5.9 "The Sahara and the Sudan from the Arab conquest of the Maghrib to the rise of the Almoravids", *Cambridge History of Africa*, vol. 2, edited by J.D. Fage. Cambridge, 1979, pp. 628–674.

5.10 "Abdallah ibn Yasin and the Almoravids", in *Studies in West African Islamic History*, vol. 1, edited by J.R. Willis. London: Frank Cass, 1979, pp. 78–112 (reprinted in 4.2).

5.11 "Kotoko", *Encyclopaedia of Islam* , vol. 5 (1980), pp. 278–279.

5.12 "Cad", *Encyclopaedia of Islam* (1981), 2nd edition, supplement, pp. 163–167.

5.13 "The Jews of Sijilmasa and the Saharan trade", in *Communautés juives des marges sahariennes du Maghreb*, edited by M. Abitbol. Jerusalem: Ben-Zvi Institute, 1982, pp. 253–263 (reprinted in 4.2).

5.14 "Mamluk Egypt and Takrur (West Africa)", in *Studies in Islamic History and Civilization in Honour of David Ayalon*, edited by M. Sharon. Leiden: E.J. Brill, 1986, pp. 183–207 (reprinted in 4.2).

5.15 "Mali", *Encyclopaedia of Islam*, vol. 6 (1987), pp. 257–261.

5.16 "Berber nomads and Sudanese states: the historiography of the desert–Sahel interface", in Levtzion, *Islam in West Africa*, 1995 (no. 4.2).

5.17 "Kingdoms of the Western Sudan", Encyclopedia of Africa, edited by J. Middleton. Simon & Schuster (forthcoming).

6. Textual Studies

Books

6.1 (with J.F.P. Hopkins) *Corpus of Early Arabic Sources for West African History*. Cambridge, UK: Cambridge University Press, 1981 (Fontes Historiae Africanae: Series Arabica IV), 493 pp.

6.2 (with I.G. Wilks and B.M. Haight) *Chronicles from Gonja: A Tradition of West African Muslim Historiography*. Cambridge, UK: Cambridge University Press, 1986 (Fontes Historiae Africanae: Series Arabica IX), 258 pp.

6.3 (with Jay Spaulding), *Medieval West Africa: Views from Arab Scholars and Merchants*. Princeton, NJ: Markus Wiener 2002, 126 pp.

Articles and Chapters

6.4 "The thirteenth and fourteenth century kings of Mali", *Journal of African History*, vol. 4 (1963), pp. 341–353 (reprinted in 4.2).

6.5 "Early nineteenth-century manuscripts from Kumasi", *Transactions of the Historical Society of Ghana*, vol. 8 (1965), pp. 99–119 (reprinted in 4.2).

6.6 "Ibn Hawqal, the cheque and Awdaghust", *Journal of African History*, vol. 9 (1968), pp. 223–233 (reprinted in 4.2).

6.7 "Mahmud Ka'ti fut-il l'auteur de *Ta'rikh al-Fattash*?", *Bulletin de l'IFAN* (Dakar), vol. 33 (1971), pp. 665–674. Published also in English in *Research Bulletin: Centre of Arabic Documentation* (Ibadan), vol. 6, nos. 1–2 (1970), pp. 1–12.

6.8 "A Seventeenth-Century Chronicle by Ibn al-Mukhtar: a critical study of *Ta'rikh al-Fattash*", *Bulletin of the School of Oriental and African Studies*, vol. 34 (1971), pp. 571–593 (reprinted in 4.2).

6.9 "Was royal succession in ancient Ghana matrilineal?", *International Journal of African Historical Studies*, vol. 5 (1972), pp. 91–93.

6.10 "Oral traditions and Arabic documents in the Muslim historiography of Africa", *Congrès International des Africanistes*. Paris, 1972, pp. 47–59.

6.11 "Ancient Ghana: a reassessment of some Arabic sources", *Revue Française d'Histoire d'Outre-Mer*, vol. 66 (1979), pp. 139–147 (reprinted in 4.2).

6.12 "The twelfth-century anonymous *Kitab al-Istibsar*: a history of a text", *Journal of Semitic Studies*, vol. 24 (1979), pp. 201–217 (reprinted in 4.2).

6.13 "Muslim Travellers and Trade", *Trade, Travel and Exploration in the Middle Ages: An Encyclopaedia*, edited by John B. Friedman Kristen M. Figg. New York and London: Garland Publishing, 2000, pp. 418–25.

6.14 "Arab geographers, the Nile, and the history of *Bilad al-Sudan*", in *The Nile: Histories, Cultures, Myths*, edited by H. Erlich and I. Gershoni. Boulder, CO: Lynne Rienner, 2000, pp. 71–76; reprinted in this present volume as essay VI.

6.15 "The Almoravids in the Sahara and *Bilad al-Sudan:* A Study in Arab Historiography", *Jerusalem Studies in Arabic and Islam (*JSAI), vol. 25 (2001), pp. 133–152; reprinted in this present volume as essay VIII.

Nehemia Levtzion: Curriculum Vitae

Note: written by Levtzion in 2002

Positions

Bamberger and Fuld Professor of the History of the Muslim Peoples. The Hebrew University of Jerusalem (1982–August 2003)

President, Israel Oriental Society (1998–August 2003)

Chair, Planning and Budgeting Committee, the Council for Higher Education (March 1997–March 2003)

President, Open University of Israel (1987–1992)

Dean, Faculty of Humanities, The Hebrew University of Jerusalem (1978–1981)

Executive Director, Van Leer Jerusalem Institute (1994–1997)

Academic Chairman, International Center for University Teaching of Jewish Civilization (1992–1997)

Director, Ben-Zvi Institute for the Study of Jewish Communities in the East (1982–1987)

Chairman of the Executive Committee, Israel Oriental Society (1979–1998)

Personal Honours

Honorary Fellow, the Open University, Israel (1995)

Honorary Fellow, Jerusalem Academy of Music and Dance, Israel (2003)

Honorary Fellow, Tel Hai Academic College, Israel (2003)

Honorary Fellow, Shenkar College of Engineering and Design, Israel (t.b.a. 2004)

The Bublik Prize of the Hebrew University of Jerusalem (t.b.a. 2004)

Education

1957–1960: BA, The Hebrew University, in Islamic History and Arabic

1961–1962: MA, The Hebrew University, in Islamic History

1962–1965: PhD, University of London, School of Oriental and African Studies, History (Islam in Africa)

Hebrew University

Lecturer, 1965–1969

Senior Lecturer, 1969–1973

Associate Professor, 1973–1978

Professor, from 1978

Visiting Appointments

Visiting Associate Professor, Northwestern University, Evanson, Ill. (1969)

Fellow, St John's College, Cambridge (1972–73)

Visiting Professor, University of California, Los Angeles (1975)

Fellow, St Antony's College, Oxford (1977)

Simon Senior Fellow, University of Manchester (1977–78)

Fellow, Center for Middle Eastern Studies, Harvard University (1981–82)

Fellow, Wissenschaftskolleg: Institute of Advanced Studies, Berlin (1996, 1997)

Visiting Professor, Ecole des Hautes Etudes en Sciences Sociales, Paris (1998)

Visiting Professor, Michigan State University, East Lansing, Michigan (2000)

Personal

Born 24 November 1935, in Israel (then Palestine)

Parents: Penina (nee Perlow) and Aron (formerly Lubetski)

Married to Tirtza (nee Gindel)

Children: Moshe (1965), Osnat (1968), Noga (1970), Avner (1974)

Acknowledgements

Grateful acknowledgement is made to the following persons, journals, institutions and publishers for their kind permission to reproduce the essays included in this-volume: Holmes & Meier, New York (for essay I); El Colegio México, Mexico City (II); Pontifical Institute of Mediaeval Studies, Toronto (III); Transaction Publishers, New Brunswick, NJ (IV); Ohio University Press, Athens, OH (V); Lynne Rienner Publishers, Boulder, CO (VI); Tirtza Levtzion (VII, IX, XIV, XV); *Jerusalem Studies in Arabic and Islam*, Jerusalem (VIII, XII); Brill, Leiden (XI); Macmillan, Basingstoke (XII); SUNY, Albany, NY (XIII).

Publisher's Note

The articles in this volume, as in all others in the Variorum Collected Studies Series, have not been given a new, continuous pagination. In order to avoid confusion, and to facilitate their use where these same studies have been referred to elsewhere, the original pagination has been maintained wherever possible.

Each article has been given a Roman number in order of appearance, as listed in the Contents. This number is repeated on each page and is quoted in the index entries.

I

Toward a Comparative Study of Islamization

The spread of Islam from its emergence in the Arabian Peninsula in the seventh century to its current expansion in Africa is a fascinating and intriguing topic. Across the barriers of climate and culture in Asia and Africa, Islam won converts and was adopted by entire ethnic groups. Indonesia and Morocco, West Africa and India are worlds apart; yet in all these regions Islam was so assimilated into the local cultures as to be considered an indigenous religion. Diversity, however, did not break the unity of Islam, and the many local forms should be considered as variations of one universal religion.

The expansion of Islam in different cultural contexts and historical circumstances is a subject which lends itself to a comparative study. But, for that purpose one needs the cooperation of scholars who are acquainted with the source material, languages, history, and cultures of the major Islamic regions. This volume is the product of such a cooperative effort. The twelve essays span the thirteen centuries of Islamic history and deal with the spread of Islam in the Arab lands, Iran, Anatolia, India, Indonesia, China, the Sudan, and East and West Africa. Methodologically, the essays range from analyses of historical processes of Islamization to a review of modern European and Muslim interpretation of conversion to Islam. They include also an anthropological study and two expositions on the theme of conversion in local myths, chronicles, and didactic literature.

This introductory essay attempts a comparative approach to the study of Islamization based on evidence from different parts of the Muslim world. For this purpose I refer mainly to the material presented and analyzed in the essays of this volume.*

* In this reprinting, see the bibliography following p. 23.

Earlier comprehensive studies of conversion to Islam, such as Thomas Arnold's *The Preaching of Islam* (first published in 1896) or Xavier de Planhol's *Les fondements géographiques de l'histoire de l'Islam* (1968) did provide comparative insights, but the basis for their analysis was regional. The present essay utilizes a thematic, rather than a regional, approach. We shall deal with such themes as conversion under Muslim political rule; the role of nomads, traders, and *ṣūfīs* as agents of Islamization; the encounter of Islam with other religions; individual and communal conversions; and reform or the perfection of the initial adhesion to Islam.

There is enough material for separate essays on each of these themes. In this introductory essay, however, references will be limited mainly to contributions presented here. In this way, it is hoped that the volume will be rendered more cohesive.

Any comparative analysis is exposed to criticism on errors of fact and interpretation by scholars who are experts on those areas from which examples have been taken. Some readers may also question the validity of certain generalizations or express doubts about patterns discerned and parallels drawn. Such criticism, questions, and doubts can in themselves be scholarly contributions to the study of conversion to Islam. Indeed, the author wishes no more than that this comparative essay stimulates further discussion and debate about Islamization in its widest topical and geographical context.

Source Material on Conversion to Islam

The absence of contemporary local Islamic sources for the earliest period of the spread of Islam is a problem common to all parts of the Muslim world. This is hardly surprising, since Muslim historiography developed only after Islam had been established in a region and a class of literati had emerged. Moreover, works written more than two centuries after the initial spread of Islam sometimes had legal rather than purely historical implications, because the status of people and property was, at least theoretically, determined by methods of conquest and patterns of conversion. In the Arab lands and in Iran this approach created some intricate historiographical problems, stemming from attempts to connect conversion, taxation, and the role of the *mawālī*. It was left to modern historians to distinguish historical realities from fictions.[1]

In Egypt, Syria, and Anatolia, where Christian communities survived the first impact of the Muslim conquest, records and chronicles bring evidence on conversion to Islam from the viewpoint of the declining Christian

1. Cf. D. C. Dennett, *Conversion and Poll-Tax in Early Islam* (Cambridge, Mass., 1950); M. Brett, "The spread of Islam in Egypt and North Africa," in M. Brett, ed., *Northern Africa: Islam and Modernization* (London, 1973), p. 9.

communities.[2] In other parts of the Muslim world the advent of Islam brought about the impoverishment of whatever literary resources that region had possessed before. Ricklefs (chap. 6) says that the early period of Islamization in Java, between the fourteenth and sixteenth centuries, "coincides with one of the most poorly documented eras in Javanese history."

Gradually the Islamized society began to articulate its own perception of the process of Islamization, which is represented in historical traditions. These traditions ought to be dealt with according to the methodology for the study of oral literature. West African chronicles (from Timbuktu, Kano, Gonja, and elsewhere) incorporate traditions on conversion to Islam.[3] If correctly interpreted, such traditions may yield evidence on the agents of Islamization, the nature of conversion, or the reaction of different sections of the society to these processes.

An external view of Islamization is provided by Muslim and Christian travellers. Ibn-Faḍlān of the tenth century reported on the conversion of the Bulgars on the Volga. In the fourteenth century Ibn-Baṭṭūṭa visited China, Sumatra, India, East and West Africa. Observations of this pious Moroccan Muslim at the court of the king of Mali provide the first eyewitness evidence on the role of Islam in an African kingdom (Levtzion, chap. 11). Though few Muslim travellers wrote their own accounts, reports of many others—including traders and seamen—were included in the works of Arab geographers. In this respect, Arab geographical literature is perhaps the most important single category of source material for the study of the spread of Islam. Though this literature has been extensively used by modern historians, it ought to be reexamined for more information and new interpretations.

Europeans visited Asia Minor when the process of Islamization and Turkicization was in progress. They described the conditions of the Christian communities under the rule of the Turks, and recorded cases of conversion to Islam.[4] The Portuguese reached Indonesia in time to witness the results of the first phase in the spread of Islam there. The account of

2. E.g., *Chronique de Jean, Eveque de Nikiou*, pub. and trans. by Zotenberg (Paris, 1883); Severus ben el Moqaffa', *Historia Patriarcharum Alexandrinorum*, ed. by C. F. Seybold (Bertyi, 1904); *Chronique de Michael le Syrien, patriarche jacobite d'Antioche (1116–1199)*. ed. by J. B. Chabot (Paris, 1899–1901). These and other Christian sources were extensively used by T. Arnold, *The Preaching of Islam* (3rd edition, London, 1935); for references to Christian sources on the Islamization of Anatolia, see S. Vryonis, *The Decline of Medieval Hellenism in Asia Minor and the Process of Islamization from the Eleventh through the Fifteenth Century* (Los Angeles, 1971).

3. Oral traditions on Islamization are incorporated in such chronicles as *Ta'rīkh al-Fattāsh*, ed. by O. Houdas and M. Delafosse (Paris, 1913); "The Kano Chronicle" in H. R. Palmer, *Sudanese Memoirs* (Lagos, 1928), vol. 3; "The Gonja Chronicle," MS at the Institute of African Studies, Legon, Ghana.

4. S. Vryonis, *The Decline*, p. 183 and *passim*.

Tomé Pires (1512–15) is perhaps the earliest contemporary evidence on Islam in Indonesia (Ricklefs, chap. 6).

Narrative sources, though not yet exhausted, will surely leave many gaps in the study of Islamization. We need the imagination and ingenuity of researchers to seek new methods and propose original interpretations. Archaeological evidence, inscriptions, gravestones and old mosques may indicate some landmarks in the process of Islamization.[5]

In his essay on Anatolia, Ménage (chap. 4) refers to two studies, by O. L. Barkan and by W. C. Brice, that suggest interpretative evidence from two sorts of data. Barkan's study of the Ottoman tax registers, in which religious affiliation is recorded, gives some idea of the religious composition of the population at different stages in the process of Islamization.[6] W. C. Brice studied toponyms in Anatolia in order to discern patterns of Turkicization. The survival of pre-Turkish names, mainly in Eastern Anatolia, might imply that the local population had remained on the land and experienced a gradual ethnic, cultural, and religious change. In Western Anatolia, on the other hand, the prevalence of Turkish toponyms might be explained by the depopulation of old villages and the settlement there of Turkish nomads. Such an interpretation is in agreement with other evidence which suggests that the tribal Turks who swept over eastern Anatolia operated most intensively and for a longer period in its western portion near the frontier of Byzantium.[7]

Richard Bulliet (chap. 3) suggests that personal names may be used for the study of religious change in Iran. On the basis of the biographical literature on Iranian Muslims he proposes an interesting correlation between the recurrence of four categories of names (Arab, Old Testament/Qur'ānic, Persian, and Muslim names) and successive phases in the progress of conversion to Islam in Iran. Bulliet has also attempted quantitative techniques to produce a "curve of conversion" which he relates to the development of Islamic institutions in Iran, with special reference to Islamic schools of law (*madhāhib*). In the seventh and eighth centuries, Bulliet argues, most converts were Ḥannafīs, whereas in the ninth century converts were mainly Shāfi'īs and Ḥanbalīs.

The distribution of the schools of law over the Muslim world suggests routes of the spread of Islam. The predominance of the Ḥanafī school in northern India indicates Turkish influence from Central Asia, whereas on the coast of southern India the Shāfi'ī school was brought directly from Arabia. The prevalence of the Shāfi'ī school in Indonesia may suggest that Islamic influence came mainly from Arabia and southern India (and not as

5. For inscriptions on gravestones in Indonesia, see Ricklefs (chap. 6); in Africa, see J. Sauvaget, "Les épitaphes royales de Gao," *Bull. IFAN* 12 (1950), pp. 418–440.

6. O. Barkan, "Essai sur les données statistiques des registres de recensement dans l'empire ottoman aux XVe siècle," *JESHO* 1 (1958), pp. 7–36.

7. W. C. Brice, "The Turkish colonization of Anatolia," *Bulletin of the John Rylands Library* 38 (1955), p. 63.

previously suggested from Bengal, which is Ḥanafite). In Ethiopia one may distinguish two lines of Islamic penetration, the Maliki from the Sudan, and the Shāfi'ī from Arabia.

In his essay on dreams and conversion Humphrey Fisher (chap. 12) suggests a new line of investigation. His argument that common patterns of dreaming and dream-interpretation provide an excellent point of contact between Islam and African traditional religions may be extended to other parts of the Muslim world. "The very dream," Humphrey Fisher says, "may be an avenue for the acceptance of new ideas or objects, or even of new religious beliefs, being thus in itself a channel of conversion." Indeed, in two myths from Indonesia (Russell Jones, chap. 7) the crisis involved in conversion to Islam was eased by dreams. A myth from Pasai, the first state to become Muslim, tells that the king saw the Prophet in a dream (and according to Muslim oneirology, Fisher shows, "if the Prophet himself appears in a dream, that dream must be true"). By spitting into the king's mouth the Prophet taught him "the two statements of the profession of the faith" as well as "all the thirty sections of the Qur'ān". When he woke up from his sleep the king realized that he was circumcised. In this way the king was spared the agony of circumcision and the tedious study of the Qur'ān. Also the Prophet foretold the arrival of a ship with missionaries from Mecca and thus paved the way for the acceptance of their message. A similar theme appears also in a myth from Malacca. According to a tradition from Malabar in South India, the king converted to Islam after he had seen the Prophet's miracle of splitting the moon.[8]

Ancestors, Humphrey Fisher says, appear in dreams to sanction a religious change. He gives the example of a West African Muslim "whose father had forbidden him to leave orthodox Islam for the Aḥmadiyya; but, after the father died he returned, now a posthumous Aḥmadī himself, to his son in a dream encouraging the young man to change also." For Java there is the story of Raden Patah (the first Muslim king of Damak), who saw his dead father (the last king of the Hindu state of Majapahit) in a dream. The practice of Islam was permitted to Raden Patah by his father provided he maintained the Javanese royal traditions.

Humphrey Fisher's examples for the connection between dreams and conversion in Africa are concerned with Christianity and Aḥmadiyya. He admits that he has not yet found evidence on conversion to Islam from an African religion which was motivated or eased by dreams. But his methodological and theoretical considerations, and their relevance to Indonesia, suggest that more research may yield evidence of this kind for Africa and for other parts of the Muslim world.

In concluding this section on the sources for the study of conversion to Islam, it is necessary to emphasize the importance of field research. The anthropologist's approach is represented in this volume by Murray Last's

8. Y. Friedmann, "*Qiṣṣat Shakarwatī Farmād*: A Tradition Concerning the Introduction of Islam to Malabar," *Israel Oriental Studies* 5 (1975), pp. 233–258.

contribution (chap. 13) which presents an analysis of a current process of religious change. In Africa historians have followed the lead of the anthropologists in the use of field research. I had myself the experience of working among Muslim communities in present-day Ghana. By recording traditions and by tracing genealogies back to the ancestor who had converted to Islam, it was possible to propose some patterns for the spread of Islam in that part of Africa between the sixteenth and the nineteenth centuries.[9] Though field research has been pursued most profitably in the periphery of the Muslim world, it ought to be attempted also in regions with a longer Islamic history, perhaps by exploring the religious history of individual villages or families.

The Militant Expansion of Islam: The Role of the Nomads

The first distinction which suggests itself in a comparative study of Islamization is that between conversion under Muslim political rule, established by conquest, and conversion beyond the military expansion of Islam.

Conversion to Islam as the immediate result of conquest or political submission (*islām*) was limited to a small number of cases, and mainly to two tribal societies, the Bedouins of Arabia and the Berbers of Maghrib. By paying allegiance to the Prophet Muḥammad, Arab tribes were assumed to have accepted Islam. Therefore, when after the death of the Prophet many tribes withdrew their allegiance, their political secession—the *ridda*—was interpreted as a religious apostasy. The Berbers, Muslim traditions say, had apostasized twelve times before they finally accepted Islam.[10] Those traditions refer to the fierce resistance of the Berbers to the Arab occupation, and to their successive revolts which forced the Arabs to withdraw from the Maghrib on several occasions. Political insubordination was described as apostasy in religious terminology, using the word *irtaddū* which is derived from the same root as *ridda*. Significantly, when toward the end of the seventh century Ḥassān ibn-al-Nuʻmān consolidated the Arab conquest of the Maghrib he is said to have returned to Qayrawān "after the *islām* of the Berbers had been made good (*baʻda mā ḥasuna islām al-barbar*)."[11] In other words, the Berber tribes (like the tribes of Arabia) were

9. E.g., N. Levtzion, *Muslims and Chiefs in West Africa: A Study of Islam in the Middle Volta Basin in the Pre-Colonial Period* (Oxford, 1968); see also, P. Ferguson, "Islamization in Dagbon: A Study of the Alfanema of Yendi," unpublished Ph.D. dissertation, Cambridge; J. L. Triaud, "Lignes de force de la penetration islamique en Côte d'Ivoire," *Revue des Etudes Islamiques* 42 (1974), pp. 123–160.

10. Ibn Khaldūn, *Kitāb ta'rīkh al-duwal al-islāmīya bi'l-Maghrib*, ed. M. G. de Slane (Paris, 1847), vol. 1, p. 136; *Histoire des Berberes*, trans. by M. G. de Slane (Paris, 1925), vol. 1, p. 215.

11. Ibn ʻIdhārī, *al-Bayān al-mughrib fī akhbār al-Andalus wa'l-Maghrib*, ed. by G. S. Colin and É. Lévi-Provençal (Leiden, 1948), vol. 1, p. 38.

assumed to have become Muslims after their political submission.

The Islamization of lands conquered by the Muslims continued for a few centuries, and in some regions was never completed. In the Fertile Crescent and in Egypt significant Christian and Jewish minorities survived; in India the majority of the population remained Hindus. If the military conquest did not in itself bring about conversion to Islam, it did pave the way for two processes which were more directly related to Islamization: colonization of the conquered lands by nomads and the evolution of a Muslim government and Islamic institutions.

The militant expansion of Islam was closely associated with nomads of the desert (Arabs) and of the steppes (Turks). Even in Africa the few cases of Islamic militancy were linked to nomads, such as the Almoravid movement among the Ṣanhāja of the southwestern Sahara and the *jihāds* of the eighteenth and nineteenth centuries in which Fulani, cattle pastoralists, played an important role.

Conquest by tribal nomads was followed, where geographical conditions permitted, by the migration and settlement of the conquerors and their kin. As a result, cultural and ethnic changes (Arabization or Turkicization) were at least as important as, and perhaps even more marked than, the process of religious change (Islamization). The impact of the nomads was expressed either through the violent disruption of sedentary life or through intensive social contacts with the settled population (or, evidently, via various combinations of the two). Generally speaking, the latter pattern evolved where the conquest and the creation of the Muslim state preceded the migration of tribal nomads (as in the Fertile Crescent and Egypt), whereas the former occurred where the nomads in their tribal formations were engaged in the military occupation of the land (as in Anatolia, the Sudan, and perhaps also in the case of the Hilālian invasion of the Maghrib).

In the Fertile Crescent and in Egypt the military conquest had been accomplished within a short period and caused little destruction. Though nomads themselves, the Arab conquerors had an urban leadership (from Mecca) which imposed regimentation and discipline. The Arab warriors (*muqātila*) were segregated in the *āmṣār*, garrison towns, such as Kūfa and Baṣra in Iraq and al-Fusṭāṭ in Egypt. Under these conditions, Shaban says (chap. 2), contacts between the Muslims and the local population were very limited and there was little to invite or encourage conversion. The change came about when Kūfa and Baṣra became flourishing towns and centers of trade and administration. Local people from the countryside migrated to the *amṣār* as artisans, traders, laborers and domestics. Thus, the *amṣār*, strongholds of Arab segregation, became centers of acculturation in which the indigenous population adopted the Arabic language and converted to Islam.[12]

12. See also R. Blachère, "Regards sur l'acculturation des Arabo-Musulmans jusque vers 40/661," *Arabica* 3 (1957), pp. 254–255.

A similar process took place in al-Fusṭāṭ and in Qayrawān. In the Maghrib the Arab army was augmented by the recruitment of human levies imposed upon the local population. Berber recruits thus joined the ranks of the Muslim army in the Maghrib, which was evidently short of manpower. These newly recruited Berbers were taught the ways of Islam, as ritual observances formed part of their military training.[13]

Compared to the Fertile Crescent and Egypt, the process of religious and cultural change in Anatolia was more violent and thorough. Whereas in the Arab lands the conquest was immediately followed by the creation of the state, with its offer of protection for life and property, in Anatolia tribal nomads carried on a piecemeal conquest which wrought destruction and displacement for more than four centuries. Even the Balkans fared better, and were conquered by the Ottomans in a series of decisive campaigns fought by a disciplined army. The Seljuk sultans of Rūm extended their authority only over part of Anatolia, and after the destruction of their sultanate by the Mongols, Anatolia of the fourteenth and fifteenth centuries became a mosaic of states until the consolidation of the Ottoman rule there. In the Balkans, on the other hand, the efficient state-apparatus of the Ottomans was established soon after the conquest. Also, migration of Turkish tribal nomads to the Balkans was restricted. In the first quarter of the sixteenth century, the nomads formed only three and a half percent of the population in the Balkans, compared to about sixteen percent of the population in Anatolia. All these factors help explain why Islamization in the Balkans was limited and why they did not undergo any significant process of Turkicization.[14]

The migration and settlement of the conquerors raise some questions regarding the composition of the Muslim population in the conquered lands. What, some researchers ask, was the proportion of those who were descendants of the foreign incomers to those who were descendants of local converts?

Osman Turan estimates that about 70 percent of the population of Anatolia consists of the Turkish ethnic element, and only 30 percent are descendants of local converts.[15] These figures, which are only conjectural, imply that the cultural and religious change in Anatolia involved a demographic process in which the invading nomads replaced a diminishing local population. In India, according to Hardy (chap. 5), the apparently purely academic problem of whether the majority of the Muslims in India

13. M. Brett, "The Spread," pp. 3–5.

14. S. Vryonis, *The Decline*, pp. 69, 112–118, 144–145, 164, 356; S. Vryonis, "Religious changes and patterns in the Balkans, 14th–16th centuries," in H. Birnbaum and S. Vryonis, eds., *Aspects of the Balkans: Continuity and Change* (The Hague and Paris, 1972), pp. 151–176. For another authoritative interpretation of the impact of the Turkish invasion of Anatolia, see C. Cahen, *Pre-Ottoman Turkey* (London, 1968).

15. O. Turan, "L'Islamisation dans la Turque de moyen âge," *Studia Islamica* 10 (1959), p. 152.

are descendants of local converts or of immigrant Iranians, Afghans, Arabs, and Mughals has had political and emotional implications.

Conversion under Muslim Rule

The imposition of Muslim rule is, according to the political theory of Islam, sufficient to change the status of a country and make it part of *dār al-Islām*. The *sharī'a* recognizes the existence of a non-Muslim population within the Muslim state. A military conquest was not, therefore, necessarily followed by widespread conversion. The process of Islamization progressed and matured over decades and centuries largely as a result of the creation of an Islamic ambience and the development of Muslim religious and communal institutions.

Richard Bulliet (chap. 3) postulates that precisely such a process explains the growth of the Muslim community in Iran from a handful of Muslims, almost all of them Arabs, to the encompassing of perhaps 80 percent of the population by the beginning of the eleventh century. As the number of converts grew, so did opportunities for human contacts and social interaction, which seem to have been principal factors in the process of Islamization. This process was aided further by the fact that once conversion to Islam took place, there was no backsliding. In most instances, moreover, intermarriages were between Muslim men and non-Muslim wives, and their offspring were always brought up as Muslims. The conversion of the bulk of the population can also be explained by other factors. One should, however, seek more specific motivations for the earliest converts. There are reports that shortly after the defeat of the Iranian imperial army, the *asāwira*—officers of the Iranian cavalry—converted, joined the Muslim army, and were given a high stipend. Also, some *dahāqīn*—members of the Iranian landed aristocracy—converted and were exempted from the poll tax.[16] By their conversion the *dahāqīn* avoided the humiliation associated with the payment of the poll tax, whereas the *asāwira* maintained their privileged status as warriors. By the beginning of the second century of the *hijra*, bureaucrats had been induced to convert in order to retain governmental positions.

Conversions carried out to preserve or promote economic, social and political interests were recorded in most regions under Muslim rule. Ménage (chap. 4) and Hardy (chap. 5) refer to the conversion of fief holders—*timariots* in the Ottoman empire and *zamīndārīs* in Mughal India. They may have adopted Islam in order to hold on to their offices and property or in order to secure official forbearance after they had failed to pay their dues to the treasury.

16. On the *dahāqīn*, al-Baladhurī, *Kitāb futūḥ al-buldān*, ed. by M. J. de Goeje (Leiden, 1863–1866), pp. 265, 357–358; on the *asāwira*, see *ibid*., pp. 280, 373–375.

A liberal policy towards the local non-Muslim population aided the consolidation of Muslim rule and helped to maintain the administrative structure. Non-Muslims performed useful services in the economy and in the administration of the state. The situation began to change when the proportion of the Muslims in the population increased and the influence of the *'ulamā'* over the people and the rulers was consequently enhanced. In their pragmatic approach Muslim rulers often avoided the strict application of the discriminating regulations against their non-Muslim subjects. But the *'ulamā'* viewed such a policy as an affront to Islam, in particular when non-Muslims were given governmental positions and allegedly exercised authority over the Believers. The *'ulamā'* generated the common people's resentment against the non-Muslims and built up pressure on the political authorities. The latter sometimes yielded to this pressure and enforced the regulations against non-Muslims as stipulated by the *sharī'a*. During such periods of distress, which became more frequent in the late Middle Ages, people converted to escape humiliating conditions. In some extreme situations, in an atmosphere of religious fanaticism, non-Muslims were subject to physical assaults by the masses, to official persecution, and to forced conversions.

Such pressures were particularly apparent in Egypt, where a strong Christian community survived into the late Middle Ages. The Coptic community in Egypt sharply decreased (almost to its present proportion in the population) in the fourteenth century—a period of increasing intolerance—when the Mamluk sultans gave in to the pressure of the *'ulamā'* and to popular resentment against what was considered the privileged position of the Copts.[17]

Almost all the evidence about forced conversions in Anatolia comes from Christian sources. Vryonis assumes that the prevalence of Crypto-Christianity, which was tolerated by the Greek church, indicates conversion to Islam under duress.[18] Without dismissing this explanation, Ménage (chap. 4) considers the possibility that many Christians were torn between the promise of material benefits given to converts and their anxiety to secure Christian salvation. There is, however, an obvious example of forced conversion in the Ottoman empire. In the *devshirme* system, boys levied from among the non-Muslim population were converted to Islam and recruited into the army.

Traditions about forced conversions were recorded in different regions of India, and many of them are associated with Aurangzīb (1658–1707), who is remembered as the most fanatic of the Mughal emperors. The authenticity

17. E. Ashtor, *A History of the Jews in Egypt and Syria* (Jerusalem, 1944, in Hebrew), *passim*; D. Richards, "The Coptic bureaucracy under the Mamluks," *Colloque International sur l'Histoire du Caire* (Cairo, 1972), pp. 373–381.

18. S. Vryonis, *The Decline*, pp. 177–178; F. W. Hasluck, *Christianity and Islam under the Sultans* (London, 1929), vol. 2, pp. 470–473.

of such accounts is not always certain, but even Sir Thomas Arnold, who in *The Preaching of Islam* portrays Islam as a peaceful missionary religion, could not escape the conclusion that "it is established without doubt that forced conversions have been made by Muhammadan rulers."[19]

Although it is difficult to assess the relative importance of forced conversions in the general process of Islamization, they seem to have weighed less than is implied in non-Muslim sources and more than is admitted by Muslims. Modern Muslim historians in India were particularly uneasy about forced conversions. They were inclined to emphasize the spiritual appeal of Islam, but could not ignore the impact of political authority. Peter Hardy (chap. 5) says that these historians found a solution of sorts by stressing not the bare pressure of the Muslim authorities, but "the role of temporal power in creating a total Islamic environment as a precondition of the fostering of the right attitude and state of mind in individuals."

In a paper presented to the seminar on conversion to Islam (and not included in this volume) Mervin Hiskett says that "military conquest cannot, of itself, force men to abandon their beliefs and ideas. But the Muslim political authorities can set up the institutions which, given time, will persuade them or pressure them into doing so." Hiskett had in mind the Islamic state created by the Fulani conquest of northern Nigeria. The modern successor of that state, the government of the Sardauna of Sokoto (1960–1966), became directly involved in promoting conversion. The Sardauna, according to Murray Last (chap. 13), "led an official campaign against 'paganism', and groups were massed for ceremonial conversion."

The Encounter with Other Religions

The Arabs' pride in their race, their language, and their tribes was vindicated by their military victories and by the creation of a powerful Arab empire. Their political success strengthened their conviction that their religion—Islam—was undoubtedly superior. On the other hand, defeat, humiliation, and political subjugation sapped the confidence of the conquered in their own religion and values. Conversion was greatly advanced by the political and military predominance of the Muslims. In all cases of conversion from Christianity, Muslims had a political superiority, achieved by military conquest. The same was true in the case of Iran and the northern parts of India. But in other areas, in the further lands of Islam, Muslims were considered to be superior because of their literacy, magical and healing efficacy, and their wealth.

Jan Knappert (chap. 9) explains that "since many Muslims in East and Central Africa are successful businessmen, one may begin to wonder whether there is after all something in their amulets." He goes on to say that

19. T. Arnold, *The Preaching*, p. 261.

"Islam had the prestige of the successful men's religion." Swahili literature, which is explicitly didactic, tells how the successful victories of Muḥammad and his successors led to the acceptance of Islam by his enemies. Success is Islam's advertisement.

In Africa and Indonesia Islam challenged syncretistic and latitudinarian religions and infiltrated into the religion of the politically dominating group in a process which eventually led to the Islamization of the state and its society.

In China the Muslims had neither political nor cultural superiority. There was, according to Raphael Israeli (chap. 8) "a confrontation between two very self-confident cultures, both having a long history of swallowing others rather than being swallowed up." For the Muslims in China it was not so much the problem of spreading their religion but rather that of surviving. Because the outside pressure was more cultural than religious, the Muslims accepted the influence of Chinese civilization but maintained an Islamic spiritual identity. They adopted what Israeli calls a double standard of behavior, by being Chinese in public and Muslim in private.

The pace of conversion was influenced by the spiritual, material, and institutional conditions of the former religions at the time of their encounter with Islam. Where the preexisting religion had been interlocked with the defeated imperial system, it suffered more from the Muslim conquest. The collapse of the Sāsānian empire (226–651) caused the destruction of the upper echelons of the Zoroastrian hierarchy. In Asia Minor the Muslim conquest had a devastating effect on the Greek Orthodox Church, which had been an integral part of the Byzantine structure. Christian communities under Turkish rule were cut off from the center of the church in Constantinople and were left without ecclesiastical leadership.[20] Conditions changed after the conquest of Constantinople in 1454, when the Greek Patriarchate was given official status within the Ottoman empire. Christian communities under Ottoman rule enjoyed the pastoral care of an organized clergy, and as Ménage (chap. 4) points out, this goes some way in explaining why conversion to Islam decreased in comparison with the earlier period.

The schism in the Greek Orthodox church in Syria and Egypt and the hostility of the Monophysites to Byzantium had eased the military conquest of those lands by the Arabs. But because those churches had already undergone a religious and political alienation from their rulers, their communal institutions were not at first adversely affected by the Arab conquest. Indeed, under the more tolerant rule of the Arabs, the Syriac and Coptic churches even became more cohesive. Communal solidarity among the Copts contributed to restricting the rate of conversion. Over the centuries, however, domination by an alien religion had a wearing effect on the churches; their property dwindled and the spiritual and moral standards of their clergy declined. Christian sources often blamed the ignorance and

20. S. Vryonis, *The Decline*, pp. 288–350.

corruption of the clergy for defections of Christians to Islam in Syria and in Egypt, as well as in Asia Minor.[21]

The Muslim conquest of India eliminated the Chhattri, the Hindu political-military dominating class, but the Hindu religious hierarchy survived. The Muslim conquerors confirmed the superior and privileged status of the Brahmans.[22] Hindu society, Peter Hardy says (chap. 5), "remained a highly stratified society, in which even after the Muslim conquest prestige did not belong exclusively to the possessors of physical power (i.e. the Muslims), but also to those, the Brahmans, who were the guardians of 'a cultural vision' and that a non-Muslim one." The cohesion of Hindu society is important in explaining the limited success of Islam in Delhi and Agra, where Muslims comprised no more than a quarter of the population even at the centers of Muslim power.

In his review of European and Muslim interpretations of conversion to Islam in India, Peter Hardy quotes conflicting views about the relevance of "the caste system" to the spread of Islam. To refute the view that members of low castes were tempted to convert in order to improve their social status, it is claimed that the social position and the family status of a convert did not change with conversion. In any case, there were no mass conversions among the low castes. Individual conversions, from all levels of the Hindu society, might have occurred in order to repair the social consequences of ritual pollution caused by the breaking of the laws or taboos of the caste.

Richard Bulliet (chap. 3) touches upon a similar problem when he argues that individuals do not willingly change religions unless their existing social status is either threatened or can be maintained or improved through conversion. During the Umayyad period (661–750) converts became *mawālī* and assumed a legally and socially subordinate position in the Arab-Muslim society. As a result it seems that most of the non-Arab converts at that period were either from the lowest echelon of Sāsānian society or prisoners of war. In other words, converts were of such low status that being a *mawlā* was superior to what they had previously been. Because of their inferior status the *mawālī* were attracted to revolutionary millenarian movements, such as Khārijīya, small Shī'ī groups and the 'Abbāsid *da'wa*. On the other hand, those members of the upper classes, such as the landed aristocracy and the bureaucrats, who were accorded privileged status after conversion, adhered to the religion of the rulers, to Islamic orthodoxy.

Neo-Zoroastrian and Islamic revolutionary movements in Iran were defeated by the conservative alignment of the Arab rulers and the Iranian elite. The latter converted, maintained their socio-economic positions, and were able to exploit the weakness of the Caliphate to create independent

21. T. Arnold, *The Preaching*, pp. 79, 166–187; C. R. Haines, *Christianity and Islam in Spain, 756–1031* (London, 1889), pp. 78–80; G. Wiet, *L'Egypte arabe* (Paris, 1937), pp. 41–42.

22. Y. Friedmann, "A Contribution to the Early History of Islam in India," *Studies in Memory of Gaston Wiet*, ed. M. Rosen-Ayalon (Jerusalem, 1977), 327.

Muslim Iranian dynasties. Richard Bulliet notes that it was under those dynasties—between the middle of the ninth and the second half of the tenth century—that "Iran had become a predominately Muslim country." The timely conversion of the Iranian upper classes helped maintain the structure of Iranian society and its cultural heritage within Islam.

Generally speaking, where Islam had been adopted first by the upper classes and only later permeated other levels of the society, the revolutionary impact of Islamization was mitigated and pre-Islamic structures survived. "There is some evidence," Ricklefs (chap. 6) says, "to suggest that Islam may have found favor among some members of the upper classes of Javanese society, and that it may have spread at least in some areas, particularly in the interior of the island, through the patronage of the traditional elite. . . . The introduction of Islam brought few important changes to the religious life of the interior of Java." Both in Indonesia and in West Africa (Jones, chap.7; Levtzion, chap.11) traditional accounts emphasize the centrality of the rulers as the early recipients of Islamic influence and the subsequent continuity of these ruling dynasties from the pre-Islamic to the Islamic periods.

The link between political continuity and the nature of the Islamization of a ruler is admirably illustrated in one version of a Javanese tradition about Raden Patah, the first Muslim king of Damak, who was the son of the last king of the Hindu state of Majapahit. Though Raden Patah possessed all the concomitants of royalty, he was prevented by a certain supernatural power from attaining the kingship. He was advised to seek permission from his father, who had already turned into a spirit. His father gave him leave to ascend the throne, provided he abandoned the dress of a *haji* and wore the robes appropriate to a Javanese ruler. In other words, the practice of Islam was permitted to him provided he maintained the royal traditions. A balance had to be restored because a Javanese king is not allowed excessive conformity to Islam.[23]

Evidence from West Africa (Levtzion, chap. 11) suggests that in the evolutionary process of Islamization, African rulers (whose legitimacy derived from the traditional pre-Islamic heritage) did not become unqualified Muslims. There seems to have been a clear distinction between being a chief and being a Muslim. Rex O'Fahey (chap. 10) observed that the sultans of Dār Fūr retained traits and cults of divine kingship long after their conversion to Islam. About 1730 Sultan 'Umar Lel, who had been brought up in the more orthodox milieu of the *fuqarā'*, sought to abdicate

23. This version of a tradition has been reported in a paper by A. Christie, "Temple to Mosque: Islam to Java," which was submitted to the seminar on Conversion to Islam, but is not included in this volume. The historical value of traditions of this kind is disputed, but they are important in presenting the Javanese idea of a continuity between Majapahit and its successor Islamic states. Pertinent methodological and historiographical problems are discussed by M. C. Ricklefs, "A Consideration of Three Versions of the *Babad tanah Djawi*, with Excerpts on the Fall of Madjapahit," *BSOAS* 35 (1972), pp. 285–315.

because he could not rule justly. Similarly, the fourteenth century ruler of Kano, 'Umaru, who is said to have been associated with the *mallams*, resigned "and spent the rest of his life in regret for his actions while he had been *sarki* (king)." [24] Both in Dār Fūr and in Kano those orthodox kings were exceptional; other rulers lived comfortably in the two worlds of tradition and Islam.

Traders as Carriers of Islam

If nomads carried the burden of the militant extension of Islam, traders served as vehicles for the propagation of Islam beyond the boundaries of the military expansion. They carried Islam across the steppes to Central Asia, and as far as China, through the desert to sub-Saharan Africa and over the ocean to Indonesia and East Africa.

Islam developed in the urban milieu of Mecca where, claims Shaban (chap. 2) "trade and religion were inseparable." The garrison towns (*amṣār*), we have already noted, were foci for Arabization and Islamization. In Iran Bulliet (chap. 3) says that the influx of people from the outlying areas made the towns the initial centers of conversion. Other areas converted later and the Islamic institutions which had found their original forms in urban milieus were extended to the rural areas.

From Mecca and the early garrison towns of the Arab conquerors to the modern cities of Africa, Islamization was thus closely linked to urbanization. In Islam, migration to the town is considered meritorious because it is in the urban milieu that one can fully practice the Muslim way of life.[25] Also, the mobility of the traders stands in stark contrast to the stability of the peasants. The latter are more strongly attached to local spirits and to the deities of nature, whereas traders are more susceptible to the adoption of a universal and abstract religion. One may even say that, in the non-Christian fringes of the Muslim world, traders are almost universally identified as Muslims.

Trade across cultural and ethnic boundaries is more conveniently conducted among people who share a common faith and a lingua franca. Murray Last (chap. 13) shows that, even within the same ethnic group, religious adherence plays an important role in commerce. A non-Muslim Hausa who desires to expand his trade beyond a certain limit must convert in order to be admitted to the credit system. A trader's credit is higher if he exhibits orthodoxy and strictly observes the precepts of Islam.

Trade, therefore, contributes not only to the spread of Islam but also to the development of religious conformity. Rex O'Fahey (chap. 10) associates

24. "The Kano Chronicle" in Palmer, *Sudanese Memoirs*, vol. 3, p. 108; see also Levtzion (chap. 11).

25. G. E. Von Grunebaum, *Medieval Islam* (Chicago, 2nd ed., 1953), pp. 173–174.

the growing orthodoxy at the court of the sultan of Dār Fūr with the development of trade in the sultanate, which also brought about the establishment of a capital and the emergence of "new and Islamically inspired bureaucratic forms." On the other hand, O'Fahey remarks, the Fūr farmers have as yet hardly moved beyond an undifferentiated and formal religious commitment. Similarly, M. C. Ricklefs (chap. 6) underlines the distinction in Java between the less commercial society of the interior, where "Islam was certainly not of an exclusive nature," and the trading communities of the north coast, where "Islam struck deeper roots . . . superseded and to some extent even put an end to what they had believed before." Through trade the coastal Javanese therefore had constant access to knowledge about Islam.

Significantly, not only did peasants who had become traders turn to Islam, but the reverse is also true. Documented cases exist of traders who experienced a process of de-Islamization after they had settled down among peasants and became isolated from other Muslim communities.[26] Trade and trade routes are, therefore, important as lines of communication between remote Muslim communities and the centers of Islam. In China, Raphael Israeli (chap. 8) observes, the process of Sinicization among the Muslims intensified after contacts with the heartland of the Muslim world had been seriously reduced with the decline of Muslim trade across the steppes and over the Indian Ocean. Those Muslims who had become isolated from other Muslim communities inside China were more thoroughly assimilated into the Chinese culture and society, even to the point of total rejection of Islam.

Saints and Ṣūfīs as Agents of Islamization

Historians assign great importance to the role of traders as carriers of Islam, but indigenous traditional accounts hardly mention traders as agents of Islamization. Conversion myths from Indonesia (Jones, chap. 7) describe the arrival of Muslims by sea from Arabia via southern India. But on board these ships there were saints, men of religion not traders. Similarly traditions about the origin of Muslim groups in the Volta Basin in West Africa rarely, if at all, mention trade as the reason for the migration of their ancestor, and often describe him as "a *mallam* who used to wander about."[27]

There is more than simply a bias in these traditions. Traders did open routes, expose isolated societies to external cultural influences, and maintain communications. But it seems that traders were not themselves engaged in the propagation of Islam. They were accompanied or followed

26. Y. Person, "Les ancêtres de Samori," *Cahiers d'Etudes Africaines*, vol. 8 (1963), pp. 133–134, 139–140, 147–152; Levtzion, *Muslims and Chiefs*, p. 144.

27. N. Levtzion, *Muslims and Chiefs*, p. xxiii.

by Muslim divines, professional men of religion, who rendered religious services to the traders in the caravans or to the newly established commercial communities. Some of these men of religion were tempted to stay behind at the court of a chief who sought their services, and initiated the process of Islamization in that chiefdom.

The *fuqarā'*, as those divines are known in the eastern Sudan, had been responsible for the southern thrust of the Islamic frontier between the fourteenth and the sixteenth centuries. From the Nile, O'Fahey (chap. 10) says, the *fuqarā'* were attracted to new lands in the west, which were in extreme perplexity and error (*al-dalāl*), simply because of the lack of scholars there. They brought to the sultan of Dār Fūr and to the provincial rulers their skills in literacy, divination, and magic and were given in return land and privileges. As more *fuqarā'* settled under the auspices of the rulers, Islamic influence on the sultanate increased.

The frontiers of Islam were extended not through the work of the learned urban *'ulamā'*, but by the efforts of the rural rustic divines, many of whom were mystics and often also members of institutionalized *ṣūfī* orders. Mystics of different religions meet at two levels of the religious experience: at the speculative level in search of unity with the Highest of all, and at the level of magic in recruiting supernatural aid. Common people often seek the services of divines of another religion, especially after their own theurgist has failed to bring relief. Murray Last (chap. 13) quotes the words of a Hausa Muslim scholar saying: "without non-Muslims, Muslim scholars would starve." By the use of Muslim amulets and under the influence of the Muslim divines, non-Muslims were drawn into the orbit of Islam, and set out on the long course of Islamization. This process was greatly aided by the latitudinarian attitude of Muslim divines who were willing, at least temporarily, to accommodate themselves to other people's customs and beliefs.

Until the tenth century, conversion to Islam occurred only within the Muslim dominions. The growth of trade in Central Asia after the Muslim conquest of Iran and Transoxiana at first helped the spread of Manichaeism and Nestorian Christianity rather than of Islam. Only heterodox sects (Khārijīs, Shī'īs and Ismā'ilīs) propagated their creeds without the support of the state, and in this respect, as well as in working among the urban lower classes and rural and tribal societies, they preceded the *ṣūfī*s. It was only after the tenth century, and the growth of the *ṣūfī* movement, that Islam spread beyond the frontiers of the Muslim states. Mystics of different sorts carried the main burden of the spread of Islam in the further Islamic lands, but they also played an important role in promoting conversion to Islam in lands under Muslim rule, especially those conquered after the tenth century such as Anatolia, India, or the Sudan.

Speros Vryonis analyzed the contribution of two *ṣūfī* orders to the Islamization of Anatolia: the Mevlevis of Jalāl al-Dīn al-Rūmī, who won converts in the towns, and the Bektashis who worked in the rural and tribal milieu. Ménage (chap. 4) dwells upon the role of the non-institutionalized *baba* or 'holy man'. The 'holy man' was in fact the old Turkish shaman of Central Asia, who acquired a veneer of Islam. He interpreted dreams, induced rain, cured diseases, and ensured fertility. It was to this brand of Islam, 'Islam of the babas', that the Christians of Asia Minor were exposed.

"In the rural districts of Asia Minor," Ménage says, "the credal gap between the ill-instructed Christian and the ill-instructed Muslim became narrower and easier to cross, as 'the Islam of the babas', already diluted by the tolerance of pagan Turkish beliefs and customs, became still further diluted by the adoption as popular cult-centers of the Christian (and pre-Christian) sacred sites and the accretion of Christian feastdays, saints, and even rituals."

In India, as in Asia Minor, traditions ascribe the conversion of individuals, groups, or districts to saints. The *ṣūfīs* helped to increase social interaction which had otherwise been rather circumscribed, between Muslims and Hindus. Mysticism also furnished Islam's philosophical contact point with Hinduism. It was through such contacts, fostered by the simplicity and broad humanism of the *ṣūfīs*, that Islam gained converts. *Ṣūfīs* were particularly important in achieving the almost total conversion in eastern Bengal. They established their *khānaqāhs* on the sites of Buddhist shrines, and fitted well into the religious situation in Bengal, as depicted by Peter Hardy (chap. 5): "Medieval Bengal was a world of shifting beliefs and social allegiances . . . of a genuine syncretism of belief and conduct, to which the institutions and teachings of formalist Islam did not penetrate."

Javanese traditions hold that Islam was brought by the *wali sanga*, or the nine *walīs* (saints). The adoption of Islam, according to Ricklefs (chap. 6), may have been no extraordinary matter for the Javanese elite, who had long been able to adopt various Hindu-Buddhist cults without any apparent sense of conflict. The new faith may have been a means of tapping another source of supernatural energy. Javanese Islam was mystical, a natural development given the predominately mystical thrust of previous religions in Java. Being by nature committed to mysticism, Javanese Muslims were relatively unconcerned with personal practice. Islam became the religion of nearly all the Javanese largely because it adapted successfully to the main configurations of preexisting Javanese religions. It gave greater richness to Javanese religion without requiring the abandonment of older ideas. Islam was added as another element to a syncretic complex.[28]

Syncretism appears to be a key term in the study of Islamization in three different regions, Anatolia, Bengal, and Java (of which two came under Muslim rule by conquest, and one experienced a peaceful penetration of Islam). In these three regions Islamization was not so much a process of individual conversions, but what might be described as a religious transmutation of the society, in which nearly the entire population became Muslim, or was assumed to be Muslim.

28. Ricklefs (chap. 6); A. Christie "Temple to Mosque."

Communal and Individual Conversion

The process of Islamization in Anatolia, Bengal, Java, and West Africa involved what might be termed a communal or group conversion. Islam was adopted by ethnic groups in their own milieu, while maintaining their own cultural identity. There was hardly a break with past traditions, and pre-Islamic customs and beliefs survived. In this process more people came under the influence of Islam, but they took longer to cover the distance from the former religion to Islam, viewed as a continuum from nominal acceptance of Islam to greater conformity and commitment.

Some of the differences between the Islamization of Bengal and Northwest India, or between the spread of Islam in West Africa and the East African coast, might be explained by the distinction between communal and individual conversion. In Northwest India the representatives of Islam were Turks and Afghans, who proudly retained their foreign identity. The terms "Muslim" and "Turk" were synonymous, and Hindus who converted "became Turks" as they had to join a new society with a foreign ethnic element at its core.[29] The convert accepted not only a new religion but also a new cultural and ethnic identity. A similar pattern evolved on the East African coast, where for centuries Islamization implied Swahilization, as converts left their own tribes and joined the only known Muslim community, that of the Swahili.

This was a process of individual conversions. Every convert had the personal experience of breaking off from his own society against social and moral pressures. Along this pattern, conversion was a rather slow process, involving individuals and small groups. There was a limited territorial expansion (into the hinterland of East Africa or into the Hindu countryside) as new converts tended to migrate to live in existing Muslim communities. Although fewer people accepted Islam at each stage, their conversion was often more meaningful and closer to Nock's definition of conversion as "reorientation of the soul, . . . a turning which implies a consciousness that a great change is involved." Communal conversion, on the other hand, might fit Nock's definition of adhesion, where there is "no definite crossing of religious frontiers" and "the acceptance of new worships as useful supplements and not as substitutes."[30]

So far we have analyzed the two patterns of conversion in the abstract. Murray Last's account (chap. 13) of conversions among the Maguzawa is in fact a case study of individual conversions. There is no doubt that the converts undergo a meaningful change, but at the same time there is an

29. I. H. Qureshi, *The Muslim Community of the Indo-Pakistani Subcontinent (610–1947)* (The Hague, 1962), p. 50; A. Schimmel, "Turk and Hindu: A Poetical Image and Its Application to historical Fact," in S. Vryonis, ed., *Islam and Cultural Change in the Middle Ages* (Wiesbaden, 1975), pp. 107–126.

30. A. D. Nock, *Conversion: the Old and the New in Religion from Alexander the Great to Augustine of Hippo* (Oxford, 1933), p. 7.

important element of continuity. The break is signalled by the building of a new house. The wife, however, continues her offerings. The transition from using "pagan" to using Muslim supernatural safeguards is gradual, as is the loosening of kin ties. During the transitional period the process may be, although seldom is, reversed. But once the conversion had "caught," the convert easily assimilated into the Muslim Hausa society.

The two patterns of communal and individual conversion might be discerned already at the time of the Prophet. When a man from the Juhayna tribe came to pay allegiance to Muḥammad he was asked what kind of a pledge he had in mind, namely *bay'a 'arabiya* or *bay'at al-hijra.*[31] *Bay'a 'arabiya*, or the Bedouins' pledge, was offered by those Arabs who returned to their tribes to follow their former way of life. *Bay'at al-hijra* was taken by those Arabs who left their tribes to join the Muslim community in Medina. Their conversion implied a break with the past and unqualified commitment to Islam.

The majority of the Arab tribesmen accepted Islam collectively, in what might be described as a passive adhesion to Islam. The significance of the religious change became evident only when they emerged from the Arabian Peninsula. In a paper presented to the seminar on conversion to Islam (and not included in this volume), Patricia Crone discussed the meaning of the term *muhājirūn*, or the *moagaritai* of the papyri, which refers to the Muslim Arab conquerors in the Fertile Crescent and Egypt. One notion behind this term is *hijra*, not the famous one of the Prophet but a second *hijra*, the exodus from the desert.[32] Those tribes who remained behind in the wastes of the Arabian Peninsula maintained their previous way of life, which was not very different from that of the pre-Islamic period. For some of them a meaningful conversion to Islam was delayed perhaps until the rise of the Wahhābī reform movement.

In the Fertile Crescent and in Egypt, Islamization was largely a process of individual conversions, in which people left their communities and cut themselves off from their kin to become Muslims. In the Maghrib the early converts were those who were individually recruited to the Muslim army or migrated to Qayrawān and other Arab towns. This process, however, involved only a small proportion of the population. The bulk of the Berber tribesmen, like the Bedouins of Arabia, were assumed to have become Muslims, collectively, after the military and political submission. This nominal acceptance of Islam was only the beginning of a long process of Islamization, which was accomplished through the work of missionaries of heretic sects (Ibāḍīs and Fāṭimids), the influence of the *marabouts*, and the impact of Arabization.

31. Ibn Sa'd, *Kitāb al-ṭabaqāt al-kabīr*, ed. by Julius Lippert (Leiden, 1908), vol. 4, part 2, p. 66.

32. P. Crone, "The *mawālī* and *islām*," unpublished paper submitted to the seminar on conversion to Islam, but not included in this volume.

Reform or the Perfection of the Initial Adhesion to Islam

We have already referred to Nock's categories of "conversion" and "adhesion". Conversion, according to Nock, is limited to the prophetic religions which are exclusive and require unqualified commitment. Adhesion, on the other hand, is typical of nonprophetic religions which are often pragmatic in seeking "to satisfy a number of natural needs, to set a seal on the stages by which life is marked and to ensure the proper working of the natural processes and sources of supply on which its continuance depends." [33]

Islam is a prophetic religion, and conversion, according to Nock's definition, is certainly needed to become a Muslim. Yet, the successful spread of Islam may be explained only by the fact that whole societies embraced Islam in a process which Nock would have called adhesion.[34] One might even say that in its first encounter with peoples of other religions Islam was not presented in all its vigor (and prophetic exclusiveness). Its representatives, mainly popular divines, emphasized what was common to Islam and the local religions, using prayers, amulets, and other charms to recruit supernatural aid. Also, initial demands on the new Muslim were minimal. Only after Islam had gained a foothold in a society did the exclusive nature of this prophetic religion gradually become more manifest.

Islamization of a social or ethnic group is not a single act of conversion but a long process toward greater conformity and orthodoxy. The growth of Islamic learning, communications with the central lands of the Muslim world through the pilgrimage to Mecca, socioeconomic changes, all these led to improved observance of the precepts of Islam in worship and law. Rex O'Fahey (chap. 10) points out an evolutionary process in Dār Fūr in which the expansion of the sultanate and closer commercial ties with Egypt added strength to Islam at the expense of "the old order of belief, [until] by the nineteenth century the sultans were encompassed by the full panoply of Islamic orthodoxy." But elements of the pre-Islamic heritage survived in Dār Fūr as well as in other societies across the Muslim world, from the Bedouins of Arabia and the Berbers of the Maghrib, to Africa and Indonesia. There and in other parts of the Muslim world the perfection of the initial adhesion to Islam required a reform movement.

In Java, according to Ricklefs (chap. 6), the reform movement provoked a reaction. As militants began to claim "that their more zealous and demanding teachings contained what it really meant to be a Muslim, some of the elite felt they wanted no part of it. . . . But as Javanese *santri* have pressed for greater conformity . . . the risk has grown that they may purge Islam of just those elements which have enabled it to become a part of the Javanese cultural environment." Under the influence of the reformists in

33. A. D. Nock, *Conversion*, p. 8.

34. H. J. Fisher, "Conversion reconsidered: Some Historical Aspects of Religious Conversion in Black Africa," *Africa* 43 (1973), p. 33.

the nineteenth century the concept "bad Muslims" became important in Java. But, as Ricklefs says, "if some visitor or teacher told the Javanese that their neglect of the daily prayer or other formal transgressions required reform, most Javanese would probably have taken the view that each finds his own way to God." In other words, many Javanese viewed the syncretistic system, their own Islam, as an authentic faith and refused to admit failure; such an admission is a prerequisite for reform.

O'Fahey (chap. 10) explains the survival side by side of two belief systems—Islam and the traditional religious culture—by the Fur's ability to compartmentalize their culture.

Similarly West African Muslims who continued to espouse pre-Islamic beliefs, rituals, and customs were often conscious that these were remnants of the past. Preachers could instill a guilt consciousness among those who mixed Islam with the traditional religion. Though they did not necessarily conform in practice to the teachings of the reformers, they did admit failure. The success of the reform thrust in West Africa was achieved, however, mainly by the triumphant *jihād* movements of the eighteenth and nineteenth centuries. Whereas the old Islamized kingdoms of West Africa could not disengage themselves from their pre-Islamic heritage, Islam became the raison d'être of the states which had emerged as a result of the *jihād*. Not only did the *sharī'a* become the only recognized law, but there was also a greater conformity of individuals to Islam in belief and in practice. Murray Last's study (chap. 13), presented in this volume, deals with conversion directly to the level of a reformed (or, post-*jihād*) Islam—hence also the high economic cost of conversion.

Just as Islam succeeded in penetrating into the religious life of the Africans because of its leniency, so too were Muslims integrated into African kingdoms because Islam did not challenge the existing political order. The reform movement which sought to change the parochial and particularistic nature of African Islam also brought about a politicization of Islam in Africa. This is true of the militant *jihād* movements in which Muslims took over political authority and of the modern reform movements, such as the Wahhābiyya in West Africa. In Senegal there is a religious and political conflict between the old *marabouts* and the reformists.[35] Similarly, in Indonesia, according to Ricklefs (chap. 6), there is a conflict between two groups of *'ulamā'* or *santri*; the *santri-kolot* (the old traditional *'ulamā'*) and the *santri-moderen* (the modernist *'ulamā'*). The latter became active in militant Islamic political movements.

In China, according to Raphael Israeli (chap. 8), Islamic revivalism, which emerged as a vigorous reaction to an extreme anti-Muslim oppression under the Ch'ing dynasty, developed into a *mahdist* or a millenarian

35. L. Kaba, *The Wahhabiyya: Islamic Reform and Politics in French West Africa* (Evanston, Ill., 1974); L. C. Behrman, *Muslim Brotherhoods and Politics in Senegal* (Cambridge, Mass., 1970).

movement with clear political implications. There was no great concern for orthodoxy and conformity in the Muslim "New Sect" of China, but the movement arrested, or even reversed, the process of Sinicization to which Muslims had been subjected for four centuries.

Throughout the Muslim world local forms gave way to greater uniformity under the persuasive or militant pressure of the reformists. Accommodation and reform are the two facets of Islam that helped to achieve both variety and unity over such extensive areas.

BIBLIOGRAPHY
CHAPTER I

Arnold, T. *The Preaching of Islam*. London, 3rd edition, 1935.

Ashtor, E. *A History of the Jews in Egypt and Syria*. Jerusalem, in Hebrew, 1944.

al-Baladhurī, Aḥmad ibn Yaḥya ibn Jābir. *Kitāb futūḥ al-buldān*, edited by M.J. de Goeje. Leiden: Brill, 1866.

Barkan, O. "Essai sur le données statistiques des registres de recensement dans l'empire ottoman aux XVe siècle." *Journal of the Economic and Social History of the Orient*, Vol.1, 1958, pp.7–36.

Behrman, L.C. *Muslim Brotherhoods and Politics in Senegal*. Cambridge: Harvard University Press, 1970.

Blachère, R. "Regards sur l'acculturation des Arabo-Musulmans jusque vers 40/661." *Arabica*, Vol. 3, 1957, pp. 254–255.

Brett, M. "The spread of Islam in Egypt and North Africa", in *Northern Africa: Islam and Modernization*, edited by M. Brett. Portland: International Scholarly Book Services, 1973.

Brice, W.C. "The Turkish colonization of Anatolia." *Bulletin of the John Rylands Library*, Vol. 38, 1955.

Chabot, J.B. (ed.) *Chronique de Michael le Syrien, patriarche jacobite d'Antioche (1116–1199)*. Paris: Leroux, 1899–1901.

Cahen, C. *Pre-Ottoman Turkey*. New York: Taplinger, 1968.

Denenett, D.C. *Conversion and Poll-Tax in Early Islam*. Cambridge: Harvard University Press, 1950.

Fisher, H.J. "Conversion Reconsidered: Some Historical Aspects of Religious Conversion in Black Africa." *Africa*, Vol. 43, 1973, pp. 27–40.

Friedmann, Y. "Qiṣṣat Shakarwatī Farmād: A Tradition Concerning the Introduction of Islam to Malabar." *Israel Oriental Studies*, Vol. 5, 1975, pp. 233–58.

Friedman, Y. "A Contribution to the Early History of Islam in India," in *Studies in Memory of Gaston Wiet*, edited by M. Rosen-Ayalon. Jerusalem, 1977.

Von Grunebaum, G.E. *Medieval Islam*. Chicago: University of Chicago Press, 2nd edition, 1953.

Haines, C.R. *Christianity and Islam in Spain*, 756–1031. London, 1889.

Hasluck, F.W. *Christianity and Islam under the Sultans*. Oxford: Clarendon Press, 1929.

Houdas, O. and Delafosse, M. (eds). *Ta'rīkh al-Fattāsh*. Paris, 1913.

Ibn 'Idhārī. *Al-Bayān al-mughrib fi akhbār al-Andalus wa'l-Maghrib*, edited by G.S. Colin and E. Lévi-Provençal. Leiden, 1948.

Ibn Khaldūn, Abu Zayd. *Kitāb ta'rīkh al-duwal al-Islāmīya bi'l-Maghrib*, edited by M.G. De Slane. Paris, 1847.

Kaba, L. *The Wahhabiyya: Islamic Reform and Politics in French West Africa*. Evanston: Northwestern University Press, 1974.

Levtzion, N. *Muslim and Chiefs in West Africa: A Study of Islam in the Middle Volta Basin in the Pre-Colonial Period*. Oxford: Clarendon Press, 1968.

Nock, A.D. *Conversion: the Old and New in Religion from Alexander the Great to Augustine of Hippo*. Oxford: Clarendon Press, 1933.

Palmer, H.R. (ed.), "The Kano Chronicle," in his *Sudanese Memoirs*. Lagos: Government Printer, 1928.

Person, Y. "Les ancêtres de Samori". *Cahiers d'Etudes Africaines*, Vol. 8, 1963.

Qureshi, I.H. *The Muslim Community of the Indo Pakistani Subcontinent*. The Hague: Mouton & Co., 1962.

Rickklefs, M.C. "A Consideration of Three Versions of the Babad tanah Djawi, with Excerpts on the Fall of Madjapahit". *Bulletin of the School of Oriental and African Studies*, Vol. 35, 1972, pp. 285–315.

Sauvaget, J. "Les épitaphes royales et Gao," *Bull. de l'IFAN*, Vol. 12, 1950, pp. 418–40.

Seybold, C.F. Severus ben el-Moqaffa'. *Historia Patriarcharum Alexandrinorum*. Bertyi, 1904.

Schimmel, A. "Turk and Hindu: A Poetical Image and Its Application to Historical Fact," in *Islam and Cultural Change in the Middle Ages*, edited by S. Vryonis. Wiesbaden, 1975, pp.107–26.

De Slane, M.G. translator, *Histoire des Berberes*. Paris, 1925.

Turan, O. "L'Islamisation dans la Turquie de moyen âge". *Studia Islamica*, Vol. 10, 1959.

Vryonis, S. *The Decline of Medieval Hellenism in Asia Minor and the Process of Islamization from the Eleventh through the Fifteenth Century*. Los Angeles: University of California Press, 1971.

Vryonis, S. "Religious changes and patterns in the Balkans, 14th–16th centuries," in *Aspects of the Balkans: Continuity and Change*, edited by H. Birnbaum and S. Vryonis. The Hague and Paris: 1972, pp. 151–76.

Wiet, G. *L'Egypte arabe*. Paris, 1937.

Zotenberg, H. (translator) *Chronique de Jean, Eveque de Nikiou*. Paris, 1883.

Conversion Under Muslim Domination: A Comparative Study

The present essay is part of a comprehensive study of Islamization in which I am engaged.[1] It is based on a view of the Muslim world as a whole, in spite of its regional diversity, and on the assumption that the particular and the universal in the process of Islamization may be better appreciated through a comparative study. There are, I know, many pitfalls in such a venture, and mainly because no one can pretend to have an intimate knowledge of the history and culture of all the regions which are brought into a comparative study.

In this paper I shall, of course, expose myself to criticism not only for spreading the net extensively over all the lands under Muslim domination, but also for choosing such a general title. In fact I shall deal here, perhaps too briefly, with several topics, each deserving a more detailed treatment and a more careful examination of the evidence. I have done so in order to raise a number of comparable themes and to suggest some general patterns of religious change under political domination.

1. *Military conquest and conversion to Islam*

The expansion of Islam as a religion is sometimes too narrowly associated with the military expansion of Islam. An analytical distinction between the two processes is necessary, not only because Islam as a religion spread beyond the limits of the Muslim military expansion (to Africa. Indonesia and China); but also because military conquest itself was not immediately followed by widespread conversion to Islam.

According to the political theory of Islam, the imposition of Mus-

[1] See N. Levtzion, "Conversion to Islam: Some Notes towards a Comparative Study," *Actes du 29ᵉ congrès international des orientalistes. Études arabes et islamiques: I. Histoire et civilization*, vol. 3 (Paris, 1975), pp. 125-9. See also the introductory essay to the forthcoming volume *Conversion to Islam*, edited by N. Levtzion.

lim rule was sufficient to change the status of a country and make it part of *dār al-Islām* ("the abode of Islam"), even if the population of that country was entirely or predominantly non-Muslim. The *sharīʿa* recognizes the existence of a non-Muslim popularion within the Muslim state. In other words, both in practice and in theory, the principal aim of the military conquest was territorial expansion rather than conversion.[2]

The Fertile Crescent and Egypt, Iran and Spain were conquered after the Arabs had defeated imperial armies. The civilian population, which had not taken part in the military struggle, passively changed allegiance, and was left undisturbed. In fact, the lack of religious pressure made it easier to consolidate Muslim rule, and by refraining from antagonizing the local population, the authorities obtained its cooperation by maintaining the administrative structures of the former empires. Institutional continuity and minimal social and economic disruption were not conductive to religious change.

Beyond the frontiers of the former empires, as in Transoxania, or outside the effective control of those empires, as in the Berber hinterland of the Maghrib, larger sections of the population were involved in resisting the Arabs' encroachment. Such regions had to be reconquered several times after recurring revolts had forced the Arabs to retreat. In Muslim historiography the revolts in Bukhara and in the Maghrib, which brought about a temporary regression of dār al Islām, are presented as apostasy *(ridda)*, the same term being used as in the case of the political and religious secession of the Arab tribes after the death of the Prophet.[3] It was therefore in these regions that the Muslim conquerors sought to consolidate their political domination by promoting religious adherence to Islam among the local populations.

In Bukhara, the Arab conqueror Qutayba b. Muslim destroyed fire-temples, built mosques and rewarded those who attended the Friday prayer at the mosque with a grant of two dirhams.[4] In another remote

[2] G.E. von Grunebaum, "The First Expansion of Islam: Factors of Thrust and Containment," *Diogenes* 53 (1966): 65-66.

[3] Narshakhī, *The History of Bukhara*, trans. R.N. Frye (Cambridge, Mass., 1954), p. 48, [translated from a Persian abridgement of the Arabic original].
Ibn Khaldun, *Kitāb ta'rīkh al-duwal al-islāmiyya min Kitāb al-'ibar*, ed. M.G. de Slane, vol. 1 (Paris, 1947), p. 136; translated by M.G. de Slane as *Histoire des Berbères et des dynasties musulmanes de l'Afrique septentrionale*, vol. 1 (Paris, 1925), p. 215.

[4] Narshakhī, *History of Bukhara*, p. 49.

and intractable province, Sijistan, the governor al-Rabīʿ b. Ziyād (651-2) initiated a systematic policy of Islamization. Local chronicles describe him as a righteous ruler, who brought in *ulamā,'* compelled the local population to study the Koran and converted many Zoroastrians.[5] In the fourteenth and fifteenth centuries the Muslim rulers of Bengal sought to strengthen their hold over the country by encouraging conversion. They supported the missionary work of Sufi saints, but they also intervended directly by dispensing favors and applying pressure.[6]

Throughout the Muslim world and at different periods, there were other examples of measures taken by the Muslim authorities to promote conversion to Islam in order to bolster their political control. Let us dare a giant's leap in time and space from the early centuries of Islam in the eastern provinces of Iran to contemporary Africa. In northern Nigeria, Muslim political domination was imposed by conquest in the early nineteenth century. The creation of Muslim state and the development of Islamic institutions accelerated a process of Islamization, which had begun many centuries earlier. As elsewhere, converts to Islam benefited from material advantages by joining the religious community of the rulers. But, as long as Muslim rule in northern Nigeria depended on its own military and political strength (in the precolonial period) or on the support of the British administration (during the colonial period), there was no evidence of any official policy to encourage conversion.

During the decolonization and post-independence periods, the Muslim ruling elite in northern Nigeria felt that its hold over the country was challenged through the competition of rival parties in parliamentary elections inside and outside the northern Region. The ruling elite decided to make Islam the corner-stone of a united northern front. For this purpose, they sought to bring more ethnic groups of the north into the fold of Islam, and the premier of the region, the Sardauna of Sokoto, headed an official campaign of conversion which reached its peak in 1964-65, when the political struggle in Nigeria was the most intense.[7]

[5] C.E. Bosworth, *Sistan under the Arabs; 651-864* (Rome, 1968), p. 23.

[6] K.S. Lal, *Growth of Muslim Population in Medieval India* (Delhi, 1973), pp. 174-9.

[7] C.S. Whitaker, *The Politics of Tradition: Continuity and Change in Northern Nigeria: 1946-1966* (Princeton, 1970), pp. 349-50; J. Gilliland, "African Traditional Religion in Transition: The Influence of Islam on African Traditional Religion in

In recent years, there is some evidence that Iddi Amin of Uganda exploits the power of the regime to advance the cause of Islam and to promote conversion. According to the official census of 1959, Muslims formed only 5.4 percent of the population of Uganda.[8] But Iddi Amin, who has discovered the political potential of Islam, seeks to widen the public basis of Islam in Uganda by increasing the number of Muslims.[9]

Conversion under the direct impact of military conquest or through the pressure of political domination often proved to be ephemeral and reversible after the pressure had been removed. Following the conquest of Sind in 711-2, some Indian princes adhered to Islam. But soon after the Arab conqueror Muhammad b. al-Qasim had left Sind with most of the Arab troops, and the Arabs' hold over the country had weakened, many Indian princes regained their independence and renegaded.[10] In West Africa, many of those who had been nominally converted under the domination of the Tijani Empire of Segu reverted to their traditional religions when this empire was destroyed by the French conquest.[11] In the same manner, many of those who had registered as Muslims under the Sardauna of Sokoto in 1964-65 ceased to be Muslims shortly after the fall of the Sardauna, as a result of the coup d'état of January 1966.

In all the examples given above, the pressure to induce conversion had not been kept up long enough to enable Islam to take root. Generally speaking, the process of Islamization progressed and matured over a long period in a Muslim ambience created by the development of Muslim religious and communal institutions, and not as the direct and immediate consequence of Muslim political domination.

Our comparative excursion in search of examples for an official policy to promote conversion has taken us to the frontiers of the militant

Transition: The Influence of Islam on African Traditional Religion in North Nigeria," (Ph. D. diss., The Hartford Seminary Foundation, 1971), pp. 274-6; M. Last, "Some Economic Aspects of Conversion to Islam in Hausaland (Nigeria)," *Conversion to Islam*, ed. N. Levtzion (forthcoming).

[8] J. Cuaq, *Les Musulmanes en Afrique* (Paris 1975) p. 436.

[9] Reports on mass conversion in Uganda were reported in the *Voice of Uganda*, 11 December 1972 and 7 March 1973.

[10] Y. Friedmann, "A Contribution to the Early History of Islam in India", in the forth coming *Gaston Wiet's Memorial Volume*; See also K.S. Lal. *Growth*, p. 99.

[11] J.S. Trimingham, *A History of Islam in West Africa* (London, 1962), p. 163; B.O. Oloruntumin, *The Segu Tukulor Empire* (London, 1972,) pp. 316-7.

expansion of Islam. In the central provinces of the Arab Empire there were also cases of conversion promoted for political aims. In 696, an Arab who led a rebellion against the governor of Khurasan promised an exemption from taxation to those who would embrace Islam. He did so in order to win the support of the local population.[12] A similar promise was made in 744 by a deposed governor of Egypt seeking to regain his former position with the aid of the local population.[13] The very fact that such promises were made only proves that, in general, the Arab authorities did not encourage conversion and were reluctant to exempt converts from paying the tax to which non-Muslims were liable.

2. *The position of non-Muslims in the Muslim state: from tolerance to compulsion*

Exemption from the poll tax was demanded by the *mawālī,* the non-Arab converts to Islam, and became a central issue in the politics of the Ummayyad period. It became closely connected to the question as to whether non—Arab Muslims should be granted equal status to that of the Arabs, and whether mutual assimilation should be allowed. The issue was decided by the Abbasid revolution, which was initiated by the assimilated society of Khurasan. It marked the shift from an Arab identity to a Muslim identity, and eliminated the ambiguity in the official policy of the Muslim state towards conversion.

As the distinction between Arabs and non—Arabs within the Muslim society became blurred, differences between Muslims and non—Muslims within the Muslim state became more marked. By the ninth century, the proportion of Muslims in the population had increased and the doctrinal and legal framework of Islam had been established. The influence of the 'ulamā' —exponents of the religious law— increased, over both the rulers and the people. Growing religious consciousness bred intolerance towards the non-Muslims.

Under the Abbasid caliph al-Mutawwakil (847-61), the discriminating regulations against non-Muslims, as stipulated in the sharī'a, were officially and strictly applied for the first time. On this occasion,

[12] H.A.R. Gibb, *The Arab Conquests in Central Asia* (London, 1923), p. 24. D.C.

[13] D.C. Dennett Conversion and Poll Tax in Early Islam (Cambridge, 1950). p. 86: I.M. Lapidus, "The Conversion of Egypt to Islam," *Israel Oriental Studies* 2 (1972): 252.

and in the following centuries, the strict enforcement of these regulations resulted in the conversion of many wishing to escape humiliation or to retain their high positions.

One may discern two major trends in the attitude towards non-Muslims: one reflecting the views of the political authorities, and the other, the view point of the 'ulamā'. The rulers, guided by the pragmatic demands of government, needed the services of the non-Muslims and were inclined to refrain from enforcing the discriminatory regulations. The 'ulamā' considered this policy an affront to Islam and a violation of the sharī'a. The 'ulama' generated the masses' resentment of the non-Muslims, in particular of those who held governmental positions. With the economic decline of the Muslim world in the late Middle Ages, intolerance increased.

The rulers submitted to the combined pressure of the 'ulamā' and the masses, and enforced the discriminatory regulations. During such periods of duress, which became more frequent between the tenth and fourteenth centuries, more individual and group conversions were reported. In this atmosphere of religious fanaticism non-Muslims were sometimes exposed to physical harm, and many converted to save their lives and property.[14]

Such pressures were particularly strong and effective in Egypt since, more than any other land under Muslim rule, it had a strong and fairly cohesive Christian community in the late Middle Ages —an era of increasing intolerance. Also non-Muslims were more prominent in public service there than in other countries. Under the Mamelukes, in the first half of the fourteenth century, official pressure and popular persecutions brought about a sharp drop in the number of Copts.[15]

The attitude toward the non-Muslims, and in particular the Christians, was influenced by external political events. The Crusades increased the animosity toward Christians, and the Christians' support of

[14] For the development of official policies and popular attitudes towards the non-Muslims, see A.S. Tritton, *The Caliphs and Their Non-Muslim Subjects* (London, 1930); E. Strauss (Ashtor), "The social isolation of *ahl al-dhimma*." in *Etudes orientales à la mèmorire de P. Hirschler* (Budapest, 1950); S.D. Goitein, *Jews and Arabs: Their Contacts through the Ages* (New York, 1955), pp. 67-9; C. Cahen, "*Dhimma*", in *EI*, vol. 2, pp. 227-230.

[15] E. Ashtor, A. *History of the Jews in Egypt and Syria*, vol. I (Jerusalem, 1944) [in Hebrew]; D. Richards, "The Coptic Bureaucracy under the Mamluks," *Colloque international sur l'histoire du Caire* (Cairo, 1972), pp. 373-81.

the Mongols provoked violent reactions. The reconquest of Spain fanned Muslim fanaticism in that country.

The Seljuk sultans of Rum generally pursued a liberal policy towards their non-Muslim subjects. Both the sultans and the dervishes combined a zealous missionary spirit with tolerance towards non-Muslims. Broad-mindedness and leniency proved effective in promoting conversion.[16] Christian sources, however, record cases of forced conversions. The existence of crypto-Christians, who could expect absolution from the Church, may have been the result of forced conversions. But one cannot rule out the possibility that those Christians were torn between the lure of material benefits promised to converts and their anxiety to secure Christian salvation.[17]

Muslim historiography in India emphasizes the nonviolent, missionary aspects of conversion to Islam.[18] But Hindu traditions record cases of forced conversions, which are associated with certain rulers such as Sikandar of Kashmir (1389-1413), Jalal al-Din of Bengal (1414-31) and, in particular, with the Mughal sultan Aurangzib (1658-1707).[19]

The latter's reign marked the ascendency of Islamic orthodoxy in India in reaction to the latitudinarian policy of al-Akbar (1556-1605). Whereas al-Akbar sought a rapprochement between Muslims and Hindus, the orthodox 'ulamā' demanded a strict application of the rules of the sharī'a in relation to non-Muslims.[20]

Hindu bankers and traders dominated important sectors of the eco-

[16] O. Turan, "Les souveraines Seldjukides et leurs sujets non-musulmans," *Studia Islamica* 1 (1953): 66-8.

[17] F.W. Hasluck, *Christianity and Islam under the Sultans*, vol. 2 (Lodon, 1929), pp. 470-3; S. Vryonis, *The Decline of Medieval Hellenism in Asia Minor and the Process of Islamization from the Eleventh through the Fifteenth Century* (Berkeley and Los Angeles, 1971), pp. 177-8, 360-1; V.L. Ménage, "The Islamization of Anatolia," in N. Levtzion (ed.), *Conversion to Islam* (forthcoming).

[18] P. Hardy, "Modern Europeans and Muslim interpretation of conversion to Islam", in *Conversion to Islam*, ed. N. Levtzion (forthcoming). Peter Hardy refers to such modern Muslim historians as I.H. Qureshi and S.M. Ikram.

[19] T.W. Arnold, *The Preaching of Islam* (Lahore, 1914), pp. 261-5; I.H. Qureshi, "Muslim India before the Mughals," in *The Cambridge History of Islam*, vol. 2 (Cambridge, 1970), p. 25.

[20] T.H. Qureshi, *The Muslim Community of the Indo-Pakistan subcontinent: 610-1947*. (The Hague, 1962). pp. 149-63; Y. Friedman. *Shaykh Ahmad Sirhindi: An Outline of His Thought and a Study of His Image in the Eyes of Posterity* (Montreal, 1971). pp. 73-5, 85.

nomy in the Mughal Empire, and had considerable influence over the government's finances. Hindus served in prominent positions in the administration. Even the 'ulamā' often found themselves depending on Hindu officials, bankers or merchants, which exacerbated their resentment towards non-Muslims.[21] But in India, the Muslims always remained a minority, and therefore did not reach the stage at which religious intolerance generates popular animosity whithin the majority against a dominated religious minority.

We have dealt at some length with the role of the Muslim state in promoting conversion, but it appears that, in spite of the many examples given, direct intervention of the political authorities in exerting pressure or bestowing favors was somewhat limited and sporadic. It certainly cannot explain the conversion of the majority of the people in territories under Muslim rule.

More important, perhaps, is the support given by the Muslim state to Islamic institutions. The establishment of mosques, *madāris, zawāya*, and *caravanserais* created a Muslim city, even when the majority of its population still adhered to its former religion, and created that Islamic ambience which induced people to convert.

Prominent among the Islamic institutions as active agents of Islamization were the sufi orders. Whereas the established 'ulamā' acted mainly within the Islamic society, the sufis went out to establish contacts with non-Muslims and penetrated other societies. By emphasizing the common religious experiences (such as the belief in healing and the worship of shrines and saints, they encouraged the rural and tribal masses to embrace Islam. In Anatolia and India the political authorities supported the missionary work of the dervishes.[22] The latter also played an important part in spreading Islam in the Sudan after the creation of the Muslim states of Sennar and Darfur.[23] In the Maghrib, the *marabouts* ("sufi saints") offered a more meaningful

[21] S.A.A. Rizvi, "The Breakdown of Traditional Society [in India]," in *The Cambridge History of Islam*, vol. 2, pp. 67-8.

[22] S. Vryonis, *The Decline of Hellenism*, pp. 352-4; J.S. Trimingham. *The Sufi Orders in Islam* (Oxford, 1971), pp. 20-4; A. Rahim, "The Saints in Bengal," *Journal of the Pakistan Historical Society* 8 (1960): p. 206.

[23] Y.F. Hasan, *The Arabs and the Sudan* Edinburgh, 1967), pp. 179-80; P. Holt, "The Islamization of the Nilotic Sudan," in *Northern Africa: Islam and Modernization*, ed. M. Brett (London, 1973), pp. 16-8; R.S. O'Fahey and J.L. Spaulding, *Kingdoms of the Sudan* (London 1974), pp. 72-3, 123-4.

religious experience in the tribal hinterland and improved on the earlier nominal adhesion of the Berbers to Islam.[24] But the role of the Sufis was by no means specific to conversion under Muslim rule. They also played an important part in spreading Islam beyond the limits of its militant expansion in Indonesia and in Africa.

3. *Stratification, social classes and religious change*

People do not willingly change their religion unless their social status is threatened or conversion helps to maintain or improve it. During the first century of the *hijra,* the Arabs were reluctant to extend any of their own privileges to the conquered peoples and, therefore, did not generate any motivation for conversion. But a closer examination of the evidence suggests that the Arabs adopted a different policy towards selected groups.

Members of an elite corps of the Iranian cavalry, the *asāwira,* converted after the defeat of the Sasanid imperial army. They were incorporated into the Arab army and were allocated the same pension *('ata')* as the Arab *muqātila* ("warriors"). The Arabs, it appears, were concerned as much with the status of the converts as with their ethnic affiliation. The *dahāqīn,* members of the Iranian landed aristocracy, who converted, were exempted from the poll tax. In the Sasanid Empire, the poll tax was levied only from the masses and denoted a low social status. The dahaqin converted in order to evade the poll tax, not because of the fiscal burden it represented, but because they considered it humiliating.[25]

At the risk of a sweeping generalization, one may say that, in many cases, people maintained their social status when they went through the process of religious change. Warriors were concerned with maintaining their status, as were members of the conquered nobility and officials in public service. The conquerors were willing to integrate, into their respective classes, those likely to be useful to the Muslim state. Conversion could facilitate integration, although it was not always a condition.

[24] G.H. Bousquet, *L'islam maghrebin* (Alger, 1954), pp. 64 160-1 ; M. Brett, "The Spread of Islam in Egypt and North Africa," in *Northern Africa*, ed. M. Brett, pp. 7-9.

[25] D.C. Dennett, *Conversion and Poll Tax,* p. 15, 31-3; M.G. Morony, "The effects of the Muslim Conquest on the Persian Population of Iraq" (forthcoming).

In Spain, Christian families of the upper classes who had converted to Islam maintained their status within the Muslim society.[26]

Members of the Christian military elite in the Balkans were incorporated into the military-administrative establishment of the empire while still adhering to their own religion. But as they became socially isolated from the Christian communities, they gradually were assimilated with the Turks.[27]

Whereas conversion to Islam to preserve social status, property or office occurred mainly among the upper classes of the dominated society, conversion to improve economic conditions occurred among the lower clases. It was among the poor that the poll tax may have been a serious economic burden, and they, more than members of the middle classes, may have converted to ease this burden.[28] When Qutayba b. Muslim promised two dirhams to all those who would attend the Friday prayer at the mosque, he attracted converts from among the poor people of Bukhara. Material privileges were often used to promote conversion, as a European visitor to Anatolia reported at the end of the fourteenth century: "The great lords shew particular honour to him [the new convert] and make him rich; this they do that Christians may be more willing to be converted to their faith."[29]

The relation between social stratification and religious change has a special significance in India, because of the caste system. Some historians contrasted the egalitarian nature of Islam with the rigid stratification of Indian society and concluded that Islam may have attracted members of the lower classes who hoped to improve their social status.[30] Without entering into a detailed discussion of this complicated issue, one may say that some of the basic facts do not support such a simplistic explication. First, there was no widespread conversion among the lower classes, and second, the Muslim society in India is more rigidly stratified than other Muslim societies. Converts

[26] H. Terrasse, "L'Espagne musulmane et l'heritage visigothique", *Etudes d'orientalisme dediées à la mémoire de Lévi-Provençal,* vol. 2 (Paris, 1962), p. 762.

[27] H. Inalcik, "Ottoman Methods of Conquest," *Studia Islamica* 2 (1954), 113-117; T.W. Arnold. *The Preaching of Islam.* p. 195.

[28] Cf. S.D. Goiten, "Evidence on the Muslim Poll Tax from Non-Muslim Sources," *Journal of the Economic and Social History of the Orient* 6 (1965).

[29] Report by Schiltberger, quoted in S. Vryonis, *The Decline of Hellenism,* pp. 357-

[30] See T.W. Arnold, *The Preaching of Islam*, pp. 270-2, 291-4. Views of other historians are discussed in P. Hardy, "Modern European and Muslim Interpretation" (forthcoming).

seem to have moved from the Hindu to the Muslim society while maintaining their social status.[31] (One should add, however, that social stratification in Muslim society did not have the religious sanction it did in Hindu society).

The progress of Islamization in India was slower than in almost all other territories which were under Muslim rule for several centuries. In Delhi and Agra, close to the centers of Muslim power, the Muslims formed no more than a quarter of the population. It appears, therefore, that in India one has to explain the slow place of conversion and its limitations, rather than a successful process. Many factors must be taken into account, and we shall refer to these in other sections of this paper. In the present context, however, one may say that rigid social structures may have hampered the spread of Islam . Since the time of the first Arab conqueror, Muhammad b. al-Qasim, at the beginning of the eighth century, Muslim rulers ratified the eminent position of the Brahmans. In India, therefore, prestige did not exclusively belong to those who possessed political power but also to the Brahmans, custodians of the spiritual heritage.[32]

The survival of a stratified society almost intact halted the progress of Islam in India. In places like Iran and the Balkans, where Islam had first been adopted by the upper classes and only later penetrated other levels of society, religious change had only a limited affect on the sctructure of the dominated society and allowed the survival of the pre-Islamic cultural heritage. By retaining their positions of leadership the upper clases shielded the dominated society from the penetration of the dominating society. Such a penetration, with its disruptive consequences, occurred mainly in regions where nomads played an active role.

4. *The role of the nomads*

One of the salient features of the militant expansion of Islam is the role of the nomads. In the seventh and eighth centuries the Arabs,

[31] A.C. Mayer, "Hind [Ethnography]," in *EI*, vol. 3, p. 411.

[32] Such an explanation is offered by P. Hardy, "Modern European and Muslim Interpretation" (forthcoming). On the position of the Brahmans following the Arab conquest, see Y. Friedmann, "Contribution to the Early History of Islam in India" (forthcoming).

nomads from the hot deserts, established Muslim domination from Iran to Spain. From the eleventh century, the Turks, nomads from the cold steppes, extended the rule of Islam to India and Asia Minor.[33] Even in West Africa, where Islamization progressed through the work of trades and men of religion, militant expressions of Islam were associated with nomads. The sanhaja of the Sahara created the Almoravid movement in the eleventh century, and the Fulbe herdsmen fought the *jihads* of the eighteenth and nineteenth centuries.

Conquest by nomads was followed, where geographical and political conditions permitted, by migration and settlement of the conquerors and their kin in the conquered territories. Such a process, which has demographical and ecological implications, effectuates an intensive penetration into the dominated society and brings about a religious change (Islamization) as well as a cultural and ethnic change (Arabization or Turkification). The depth of the penetration and the extent of the cultural and religious changes were conditioned by the nature of the conquest and the character of the nomads' invasion.

In his study of the Islamization of Anatolia, Speros Vryonis compared the Arab conquest of the Fertile Crescent to the Turkish conquest of Anatolia.[34] The Arab conquest was accomplished within the relatively short period of a few years and was immediately followed by the creation of a Muslim state which provided protection of life and property, and exercized control over the movements of the nomad tribesmen. The Turkish conquest of Anatolia, on the other hand, extended over a long period of time, since wars, invasions and tribal migrations continued from the second half of the eleventh century until the consolidation of Ottoman rule over Anatolia in the fifteenth century. Unlike the Arabs, the Turks upset the existing Byzantine administration, replacing it with the Seljuk sultanate of Rum in one part of the conquered territory only, the rest being held by nomad tribesmen. The piecemeal conquest by the nomads wrought the destruction of rural life and the displacement of populations. It was in the areas held by the nomads that the process of Turkification was the most intensive.

In the first quarter of the sixteenth century, nomad Turks still formed

[33] The role of the nomads in the spread of Islam is a central theme in X. de Planhol, *Les fondements géographiques de l'histoire de L'Islam* (Paris, 1968).

[34] S. Vryonis, *The Decline of Hellenism*, pp. 143-194.

about sixteent percent of the population of Anatolia. At the same time, they accounted for only approximately three and a half percent of the population of the Balkans[35]. The Balkans had been conquered by the Ottoman army and were immediately ruled as a Muslim state. The migrations of the nomads were controlled by the Ottoman authorities and, here, penetration into the conquered society was limited. Islamization in the Balkans was more restricted and there was no significant process of Turkification.

Paradoxically, the creation of a Muslim state softened the impact of the nomads and curbed a more drastic process of religious and cultural change. The Arab conquerors of the Fertile Crescent, Egypt and the Maghrib were concentrated in garrison towns, the *amṣār,* and this allowed little opportunity for social interaction. However, the garrison towns soon developed into centres of trade and administration and attracted people from the countryside: servants, traders, artisans and officials. In the service of the Arabs, the newcomers to the towns adopted the Arab language and way of life, and converted to Islam. The garrison towns, which had begun as strongholds of Arab segregation, turned into centers of assimilation.[36]

This process, however, affected only a fraction of the local population, as conversions were individual and involved only those who chose to leave their own society and join the Muslim community in the towns. The demilitarization of the garrison towns progressed not only as a result of the influx of local civilian population, but also by the gradual removal of Arabs from the register of warriors (muqātila). Deprived of their pensions *('atā')* some of these Arabs settled in the villages among the local peasants. They were joined by Arab nomads whom the Umayyad authorities had directed to certain regions. It was in one of these areas of Arab settlement, in the Hawf region of the delta in Egypt, that conversion among the Copts progressed, and it was there also that the Copts' rebellions in the first half of the ninth century were the fiercest.[37] Even limited contacts with Arab settlers created upheavals which in many ways led to Islamization.

[35] S. Vryonis, "Religious Changes and Patterns in the Balkans, fourteenth to sixteenth centuries," in *Aspects of the Balkans: Continuity and Change,* ed. H. Birnbaum and S. Vryonis (The Hague, Paris, 1972), p. 172.

[36] R. Blachère, "Regards sur l'acculturation des Arabo-Musulmans jusque vers 40/661," *Arabica* 3 (1957), 254-5.

[37] I.M. Lapidus, "The Conversion of Egypt to Islam," *Israel Oriental Studies* 2

Khurasan provides another example of the consequences of social interaction between the Arabs and the conquered population. The Arab tribesmen, who had been sent to Khurasan by the Umayyads, were not settled in garrison towns but in villages around Merv, near and among the local population. As a result, there were more conversions —in particular among the common people— than in most, if not all, other lands conquered by the Arabs in that early period. Here the early contacts between the Arabs and the local population did not occur in the amṣār, where the Arabs were a majority and which were *foci* of Arabization, but in the countryside, where the dispersed Arabs were a minority. Consequently, the Arab settlers were culturally absorbed by the local population, and by the middle of the eighth century, had adopted the local Iranian dialect. This twofold process of assimilation —Islamization of the Iranians and Iranization of the Arabs— precipitated the crisis which brought about the 'Abbāsid revolution.[38]

In Anatolia the Muslim conquest coincided with the influx and settlement of the nomadic tribes. In the Arab lands there were two phases of Arab penetration, which are most clearly seen in the Maghrib. Many of the Arab conquerors of the Maghrib in the seventh century returned to the East, others proceeded to Spain, and those who remained gathered in the garrison towns, mainly in Qayrawan. Only those Berbers who migrated to the towns or enlisted in the Muslim army came into direct contact with the Arabs. The tribal Berbers of the hinterland had been only nominally Islamized, and there was hardly any change in their way of life. The second phase began in the eleventh century with what is known as the Hilalian invasions, when Arab nomads in tribal formations entered the Maghrib. They brought about the Arabization of the steppes and the lowlands, partly by displacing the Berbers and partly by assimilating them. By adopting the Arab language and customs, the Berbers lost their ethnic uniqueness and became more deeply commited to Islam.[39]

(1972): 256-7; M. Shaban, *Islamic History* (Cambridge, 1971), pp. 112-3, 146; M. Brett, "Conversion to Islam in Egypt and North Africa: The Early Centuries." (Paper discussed at the Seminar on Conversion to Islam, SOAS, University of London. 29 January 1973).

[38] M. Shaban, *The Abbāsid Revolution* (Cambridge, 1970), *passim;* M. Sharon, "The Advent of the 'Abbāsids," (Ph. D. diss., The Hebrew University of Jerusalem, 1970), pp. 32-5 [in Hebrew].

[39] For different, sometimes conflicting, views of the role of the Hilalians in the

A similar process, though on a smaller scale (and which remained almost unnoticed, perhaps because there was no Syrian Ibn Khaldūn to magnify it!), occurred in Syria and Palestine. The Umayyad rulers successfully prevented the migrations of Arab nomads to Syria in order to avoid disturbing the administration and life of the local population. When security in Syria and Palestine weakened under the 'Abbāsids, the Bedouins penetrated the valleys, pressing the settled population into the mountains and towns. During the tenth and eleventh centuries, under the impact of the nomads, agricultural production declined, the settled population decreased, and the process of Arabization and Islamization intensified.[40]

The nomads, Arabs, Turks and Fulbe, were not themselves piously committed to Islam. They did not, therefore, contribute directly to Islamization in the religious sphere, but as conquerors and settlers under a sophisticated and urbane leadership, they accomplished the cultural change toward Arabization which, eventually, led to a deeper Islamization.

In the case of the Fulbe of West Africa, their contribution as fighters of the jihād movements was not followed by the same cultural and ethnic transformation caused by the Arabs and the Turks. The eighteenth century jihād in Futa Jallon (Guinea) did make those highlands the domain of the Fulbe, not by assimilating the former population but rather by displacing and subjugating it. In Adamawa (northern Cameroon), the Fulbe occupied the grasslands of the valleys, while the Kirdi and other local tribes lived in the less accessible parts. They accepted the political rule of the Fulbe, but were little affected by Islam. In northern Nigeria, the jihād had a more widespread influence over the inhabitants. In the Fulbe emirates, the Islamization of the Hausa, which had begun long before the jihād, was almost complete. But the Hausa culture still prevailed. Whereas the Fulbe pastoralists continued their transhumance, they retained a distinct Fulbe culture. Those Fulbe who became immersed in the political and religious

Maghrib, see H. R. Idris, *La Berbéries orientale sous les Zīrides* (Paris, 1962): J. Poncet, "Le mythe de la catastrophe hilalienne," *Annales: ESC 22* (1967), 1099-1120; M. Brett, "Ifrīqiya as a Market for Sharan Trade from the Tenth to the Twelfth Century," *Journal of African History* 10 (1968): 347-64; See also X. de Planhol, *Les fondements géographies, pp. 146-8.*

[40] M. Sharon, *Palestine under Muslim rule* (Jerusalem, 1973) [in Hebrew].

affairs of the emirates were, to a large extent, culturally assimilated by the Hausa.[41]

5. The cultural balance

Military power and political authority instills a sense of superiority in conquerors, whereas defeat and subjugation saps the self-confidence of the conquered. The psychological implications of this confrontation could lead members of the conquered society to identify with their rulers by assimilation. Yet human history has witnessed quite a few cases —that of the Germanic tribes is the most famous— in which victorious invaders had asserted their political dominion, but assimilated the superior culture and the more coherent religion of the defeated.

The cultural and material achievement of the Arab nomads of the desert did not reach the level of their neighbors' in Egypt, Syria and Iran. But even before their military and political success, the Arabs felt superior to their neighbors because of the inherent contempt of the nomad for the peasant and because of the Arabs' pride in their language, their tribe and their status. Such feelings were inculcated by doctrines of Islam which made the Arabs convinced that their religion was the most perfect. This sence of superiority was vindicated by their military victories and the creation of a mighty Arab Muslim empire.[42]

In the eastern provinces, Egypt, Syria and Iran, the local populations did not immediately accept the cultural and religious superiority of the conquerors. This was even more so because the Arabs retained Persian and Greek for some time as the official languages for administration. It was only towards the end of the seventh century and at the beginning of the eighth century that Arabic was introduced as the official language, and local officials had to learn Arabic in order to keep their government positions.

For reasons which will be discussed later in this paper, the Christians of Syria and Egypt maintained their religious and communal cohesion over a longer period. In Iran, on the other hand, the military defeat and the collapse of the empire created a temporary sense of frustration

[41] V. Azarya, "Traditional Aristocracy Facing Change: A Comparative Study of Fulbe Adjustment to Social Change in Guinea, Nigeria and Cameroon," (Ph. D. diss., the University of Chicago, 1973).

[42] G.E. von Grunebaum, "The First Expansion," pp. 67-70.

which opened the way for large scale conversions. Yet, by the end of the second century of the hijra, a cultural revival within Islam and on its fringes gave expression to Iranian national pride. The development of the Iranian language and of the national heritage was associated with a political reassertion which led to the rise of Iranian national dynasties. It was under these dynasties, between the middle of the ninth and the second half of the tenth centuries, that Iran became a predominantly Muslim country. The pace of Islamization increased owing to the elimination of resistance to political domination by alien Arabs which had been sustained by adherence to residual Zoroastrian traditions.[43]

Religious and political reactions against Arab domination in the Maghrib found expression in Ibadite and Shī'ite dissent and gave rise to Berber dynasties in the tenth century. But there was nothing similar to the Iranian *shu 'ūbiyya* among the Berbers, who seem to have resigned themselves to accepting their cultural and ethnic inferiority, as the Arabs maintained.

The Christian civilization of Spain was at a low point at the time of the Muslim conquest in the eighth century. Admiration for Arab culture led not only to conversion, but also to the adoption of Arabic and of some aspects of the Arabs' way to life by those who remained Christians. Arabized Christians, known as *Mozarabs,* were sometimes assimilated by conversion, but many upheld the distinction between the religious and the cultural spheres. Some or them were even religious fanatics and supported the Christian kingdom in its confrontation with the Muslims in Spain.[44]

The Turks, uncouth people of the steppes, relied on military prowess in their confrontation with the Christian population of Anatolia. The rural population came under the influence of the "babas" who preached an Islam impregnated with shamanist elements. This appealed to peasants whose folk religion was, in turn, imbued with pre-Christian beliefs and customs. The Turks had less to offer from their cultural heritage to the more sophisticated urban Christians. In the towns,

[43] R. Bulliet, "Conversion to Islam and the Emergence of a Muslim Society in Iran," in *Conversion to Islam,* ed. N. Levtzion (forthcoming).

[44] E. Lévi-Provençal, m *Histoire de l'Espagne musulmene,* vol. 3 (Paris, 1953), pp. 214-7; H. Pérès, "Les elements ethiques de l'Espagne musulmane et la langue arabe au 5e/IIe siècle," *Etudes d'orientalisme dediée à la mémoire de Lévi-Provençal,* vol. 2 (Paris, 1962), p. 726.

the cultural dimension of Muslim domination was provided by the Persian civilization, which prevailed in the court of the Seljuk sultans of Rum.[45] In India, under rulers of Turkish or Afghan origin, it was again the Persian culture that represented Islam in the confrontation with the high Hindu civilization.[46]

6. *The preexistent religions in their encounter with Islam*

The process of Islamization was greatly influenced by the organizational, material and spiritual position of the religious systems encountered by Islam. Among the more important factors was the relationship between the preexistent religious and political systems. The religious hierarchy suffered more from the Muslim conquest whenever it was tied to the defeated imperial institutions and depended on them.

The Zoroastrian religious establishment was an integral part of the Sasanid imperial structure, and the collapse of the empire almost destroyed the upper echelon of the religious hierarchy. Spiritual decadence and sterility in the Zoroastrian "church" during the last decades of the Sasanid Empire had already caused widespread disaffection among the upper clases of Iranian society. However, defection (mainly to the Nestorian church) was prevented by pressure from imperial authorities, who practically equated religious conformity with political loyalty. Following the Muslim conquest and the relaxation of these constraints, members of the upper classes converted to Nestorian Christianity. But when more opportunities arose for the integration of members of the upper classes into the Muslim society, the conversions to Islam increased.

Both the Zoroastrian church and Iranian society had been affected earlier at the top. In the villages the *mobads* maintained their influence and sustained the opposition to Arab domination and to Islam. Because of the ineffectiveness of Zoroastrian "orthodoxy", religious opposition to Islam developed neo-Zoroastrian syncretic and heretic movements. These movements contributed to the cultural

[45] O. Turan, "L'islamization dans la Turquie du moyen âge," *Studia Islamica* 10(1959): 139.

[46] Aziz Ahmad, "Hind [Islamic Culture]," in *EI,* vol. 3, p. 349.

and political revival which, as we have seen above, paved the way for Islamization.[47]

In Asia Minor the Muslim conquest had a devastating influence on the Greek Orthodox church because the latter had been closely integrated into the Byzantine Empire. Regions conquered by the Turks were cut off from the centre of the Church in Constantinople. Moreover, because of the protracted conflict between the Turks and the Byzantines, members of the Greek clergy were suspected of being agents for the enemy. Bishops could not reach their sees. The Christian population in Asia Minor remained without religious leadership while submitted to the political and fiscal pressures of the Muslim state and to the influence of Muslim men of religion.[48]

In explaining the successful expansion of the Arabs into the Fertile Crescent and Egypt, historians often refer to the religious schism of the Byzantine Empire, and to the tension betwen the official church and the Monophysitic sects which attracted a major part of the local population. Indeed, this rift explains why the local Christian communities, who had been persecuted by the official church and the Byzantine authorities, did not resist the Arab conquest and sometimes even welcomed it. But, on the other hand, the lack of any affinity between the Monophystic churches and the Byzantine Empire contributed to their survival under Muslim domination. These churches had already been accustomed to religious and political alienation from their rulers, and because the Muslim conquerors were more tolerant than the Byzantines, the Monophysite communities even revived after the Arab conquest and improved their cohesiveness. Such communities in Egypt and Syria fought the temptations to convert by exerting social and moral pressure on their members.

This, however, was true mainly in the first period after the Muslim conquest. Over the years the political domination of another religion had a deteriorating effect on the conquered religious community. Skepticism began to creep in and the intellectual resources waned. Many of the economic resources of the church had been appropriated during the conquest or gradually sapped by the rulers.

The church was unable to maintain its communal services, and its

[47] M.G. Morony, "The Effects of the Muslim Conquest on the Persian Population of Iraq," (forthcoming); M. Azizi, *La domination arabe et l'épanouisement du sentiment national en Iran* (Paris, 1938), pp. 289-90.

[48] S. Vryonis, *The Decline of Hellenism*, pp. 194-216, 288-350.

poorer members were tempted to seek aid from Muslim welfare institutions which were supported by the political authorities.

The intellectual and material impoverishment of the church bred corruption of the clergy, who also became dependent on the Muslim authorities. The community lost its cohesion, and its members did not have to overcome strong social constraints on the road to conversion. Such descriptions and criticism of the deterioration of the Christian communities to explain the defection of Christians to Islam appear in Christian sources, both local and European.[49] Different religious conditions in the regions of India during the encounter with Islam produced different patterns of Islamization. At the beginning of the eight century, when the Arabs invaded Sind, Buddhism retreated before the aggression of the Brahmans, who were supported by the Indians princes. It is likely that conversion to Islam was more common among the Buddhists than among the Hindus. By the eleventh century, when the Muslims established their domination over the principal regions of northern India, Hinduism had already been well implanted and could better resist the impact of Islam. Eastern Bengal, on the other hand, was in a stage of religious transformation at the time it was conquered by the Muslims. The majority of the population was still Buddhist, but it was pressed by the Brahmans. Muslim rulers and preachers seem to have found the population there disposed to embrace Islam.[50]

It is significant that in the lands of ancient civilizations and in their encounter with coherent religions —Christianity, Hinduism and Zoroastrianism— conquest and the imposition of Muslim rule preceded conversion to Islam. But in the more remote lands of Islam —in Africa and Indonesia— where Islam challenged syncretistic and latitudinarian religions, it was spread by the work of traders and clerics. There one has to deal not with conversion to Islam under Muslim political domination but with the penetration of Islam into the religion of the politically dominant society, which is another fascinating aspect in the comparative study of Islamization.

[49] T.W. Arnold, *The Preaching of Islam*, pp. 79, 166-187; C.R. Haines, *Christianity and Islam in Spain: 756-1031* (London, 1889), pp. 78-80; G. Wiet, *L'Egypte arabe* (Paris, 1937), pp. 41-2.

[50] I.H. Qureshi, *The Muslim Community of the Indo-Pakistan Sub-Continent: 610-1947* (The Hague, 1962), pp. 39-40, 70, 75; S.M. Ikram, *Muslim Civilization in India* (New York, 1963); K.S. Lal, *Growth*, pp. 179-81.

III

Conversion to Islam in Syria and Palestine and the Survival of Christian Communities

Introduction

Conversion to Islam in Syria and Palestine was a long and slow process that left few traces in the literary and documentary sources. It is only through a survey of nine centuries of demographic, cultural, ethnic and religious changes that one can discern some patterns of the process.

The Byzantine period in Palestine and Syria was one of growth and prosperity. Beyond its economic and strategic significance, Palestine was also important to the Byzantine emperors as the cradle of Christianity. The emperors and the church contributed to the expansion of old towns and to the development of new ones. Irrigation projects were constructed and a measure of security helped an unprecedented settlement of the Negev in the desert fringes of Palestine.[1]

Though figures on population in the middle ages are problematic,[2] one may use some that are not controversial. At the end of the sixth century the population of the whole of Syria, including Palestine, is estimated at about four to five millions, whereas Palestine itself had a population of at least one million.[3] In the country as a whole Christians were in the majority, but in some areas other groups were predominant: the Jews in the Galilee and the Samaritans in Samaria. Over nine centuries later, at the beginning of the Ottoman period in the sixteenth century, the population of Palestine was estimated at about 300,000.[4] If

[1] Dan, pp. 294-96.

[2] See, for example, the warning in Ayalon "Population".

[3] Poliak, p. 43; Broshi, p. 450; Tsafrir, p. 70.

[4] Lewis *Archives*, p. 10.

Reprinted from *Conversion and Continuity: Indigenous Communities in Islamic Lands, Eighth to Eighteenth Centuries*, ed. Michael Gervers and Ramzi J. Bikhazi, pp. 289–312, by permission of the publisher.

these figures are even approximately correct, the population of Palestine was reduced during that period to about one third of its size, and the Christians to a small minority.

The period of the crusades was about half way in time between the Arab and the Ottoman conquests. Though this period is better documented, there is no agreement among scholars how far conversion to Islam had advanced before the eleventh century, and what was then the proportion of Muslims and Christians in the population. Moshe Gil asserts that the Christians were still in the majority among the rural population of Palestine.[5] But, according to Joshua Prawer, the Muslims were in the majority in the local population, "certainly to the south of Lebanon."[6] In Syria as a whole the distribution was not equal in the different regions. In northeastern Syria, in the Jazīrah, Diyār Bakr and Diyār Muḍar, the Muslims were predominant; but in northwestern Syria, in the regions of Antioch and Edessa, Christians were numerous, and were probably still in the majority at the time of the crusades. In southern Syria and in Palestine the Christian population became scantier, except in Lebanon and in towns close to the Christian holy places like Jerusalem, Bethlehem, Nazareth and the villages in their vicinity. There were also Christian communities on the main road to Nablus and around Gaza.

Syria and Palestine experienced three processes between the seventh and the sixteenth centuries; one, a religious change through islamization; second, a cultural-ethnic transformation of arabization; third, a demographic decline.

The present contribution is an attempt to analyze these processes within the framework of comparative studies of conversion to Islam.[7] The three sections of this paper address three problems central to the study of conversion to Islam. First, the role of the nomads as conquerors and raiders, on the one hand, and as migrants and settlers, on the other. Second, the impact of Muslim rule on conversion to Islam. Third, the internal dynamics within the Christian communities that might have influenced their resilience.[8]

In writing this paper only the most important original sources, like al-Balādhurī and Michael the Syrian, were consulted. Otherwise this study is a reinterpretation of earlier and current scholarly studies. In line with the general topic of this volume, our discussion will be limited to the two largest Christian communities in Syria and Palestine, namely the Jacobites and the Greek Orthodox. We have not dealt with the two other

[5] Gil *Palestine*, vol. 1, p. 142.

[6] Prawer *Kingdom*, pp. 48-57; Prawer "Minorities" p. 65.

[7] Levtzion "Islamiz."

[8] Levtzion "Migration"; Levtzion "Conversion"; Levtzion "Patterns".

important communities in the area, the Jews and the Samaritans; nor with two other Christian communities, the Nestorians and the Armenians, that were represented in Syria, but had their centers and most of their adherents elsewhere.

THE ROLE OF THE NOMADS

The militant expansion of Islam in different parts of the world was closely associated with nomads of the desert (Arabs, Berbers or Somalis) and nomads of the steppes (Turks). As conquerors, tribal nomads could bring about more severe disruption of life than ordinary armies. Also, conquest by nomads could open the way for later invasions from the same direction. But perhaps more important was the role of the nomads as migrants and settlers in the conquered lands, where they developed intensive social and cultural contacts within the local population. They not only added to the number of Muslims and accelerated the process of religious change (islamization), but also brought about cultural and ethnic transformations (arabization or turkification). Because nomads became assimilated into the local population, it is often difficult to ascertain what was the proportion of the descendants of the invading nomads when compared to the descendants of the local converts.[9]

The conquest of Syria and Palestine was the outcome of a series of battles between the Byzantine imperial armies and Arab tribal forces, followed by the surrender, peacefully or after a siege, of the principal towns. For the local population that remained mostly passive, the Arab conquest seems to have been only a matter of transferring allegiance from one foreign power to the other. In a Jewish apocalypse of the mid-eighth century, "The Secrets of Rabbi Simon Ben Yohay," the Arab invasion which terminated Roman rule in Palestine is represented as a positive event in an eschatological drama.[10] The Jacobite patriarch Michael the Syrian, who wrote in the twelfth century but relied on contemporary sources, considered the Arab conquest a delivery from the tyranny of the Byzantines: "... to avenge them God brought the sons of Ishmael from the south to save us from the hands of the Romans."[11]

Beyond political and eschatological expectations, the actual encounter with the Arab conquerors was far from idyllic. Sophronius, the Greek patriarch of Jerusalem, in his Christmas sermon, probably in 637 before the Arab conquest of Jerusalem, complained that the advancing Muslims had left behind a trail of destruction; they spoiled the crops, burnt towns, set fire to churches and attacked monasteries. Other

---

[9] Levtzion "Islamiz.," pp. 7-9; Levtzion "Migration".

[10] Crone & Cook, p. 3; Kedar "Agriculture," pp. 3-5.

[11] Michael the Syrian, vol. 2, p. 412.

contemporary Greek sources have detailed accounts of pillaging, burning, destruction, killing and enslavement of many thousands during the conquest of towns in Palestine.[12]

Greek sources might be suspected because the fortunes of their church changed completely with the Muslim conquest. But Jacobite writers, who were generally sympathetic to the Arab conquerors, also reported acts of violence. The same Jacobite patriarch Michael the Syrian related how Mu^{c}āwiyah, as the military commander of Syria, ravaged the countryside of some provinces in northern Syria and led many people to slavery.[13]

Acts of violence and destruction were probably more frequent when the Arab nomads first entered the lands of civilization, and when warriors inspired by their new faith first saw the flourishing centers of Christianity. The Patriarch Michael the Syrian reported that "when the sons of Haggar entered the town [Caesarea of Cappadocia] and saw the beauty of the buildings, the churches and the monasteries, they regretted the treaty [they had earlier made with that town]."[14]

The injunction of the Caliph Abū Bakr to the Muslim warriors to abstain from the destruction of trees, fields and livestock suggests that such acts of violence were common. The visit of the Caliph ^{c}Umar to Palestine in 638 seems to have been a turning point in disciplining the Arab tribal armies to ensure a more orderly government of the conquered territories and more leniency towards the local population.

Another objective of ^{c}Umar's visit was to supervise the division of the captured lands among the Muslims. During the conquest many local people, mainly the more wealthy Greek-speaking townsmen, chose to follow the retreating Byzantine army. When the Muslims entered Damascus, Aleppo, Bālis and Qāṣirīn they found many vacant houses.[15] In some towns – such as Tiberias, Homs and Aleppo – the inhabitants accepted as part of the treaty made with the conquerors to hand over to the Muslims part, often half, of the property.[16] Only those houses and lands that had been abandoned by their occupants were given to Muslims.[17] The authenticity of the texts of the treaties might be suspect,[18] but there is no reason to question the historical facts that Muslims settled in the conquered towns.

---

12 Constantelos, pp. 330-32, 338; Kaegi, pp. 140-44.

13 Michael the Syrian, vol. 2, pp. 431, 441.

14 Michael the Syrian, vol. 2, p. 441.

15 Baladhuri, pp. 123, 147, 150.

16 Baladhuri, pp. 116, 131, 147.

17 Baladhuri, pp. 152, 170.

18 Donner, pp. 245-47.

As long as the Byzantines had naval superiority, the coastal towns of Syria and Palestine were under threat. Tripoli, Caesarea and Ascalon were raided from the sea. The Muslims fortified the coastal towns and settled military guards there.[19]

Al-Balādhurī refers also to the distribution of grants of lands (*qaṭā'i^{c}*) to Arabs. These could have been lands abandoned by rich landowners, in all probability Greek-speaking, who had left with the Byzantines. On the other hand, very few peasants seem to have left. The rural Christians, mostly Syriac-speaking monophysites, had no reason to flee before the Arab conquerors.[20]

In Iraq, Egypt and Ifrīqiyyah the Arab conquerors settled in the *amṣār* that later developed into towns and became foci for the islamization and arabization of those lands. In Syria and Palestine there was no large scale settlement of Arabs, and those who stayed behind settled in existing towns, where dwellings were available.[21]

The limited settlement of Arabs in southern Syria and Palestine immediately after the conquest is explained also by the inclination of the nomad warriors to move towards new battlefronts. Arabs who had participated in the conquest of Syria and Palestine moved on to Egypt or farther north to the Jazīrah. The instructions of the Caliph ^{c}Uthmān to Mu^{c}āwiyah, governor of Syria and the Jazīrah, to settle nomads (*a^{c}rāb*) in places far from the cities and villages[22] refer mainly to the Jazīrah. Indeed the Jazīrah seems to have been arabized and islamized more intensively than any other part of Syria.

There are no records of any large scale migration of Arab tribesmen into Syria and Palestine, in the decades following the conquest, similar to the influx of tribesmen into Iraq.[23] The Arab tribes provided most of the recruits to the Muslim army, but always as individuals, who had left their tribal formations and never as groups that continued their tribal way of life. Also their commanders came from the urban center of Makka.

During the Byzantine period Arab tribes settled on the fringes of Palestine, but did not penetrate inland. The Byzantine authorities recruited the services of those tribes, but protected the settled population. Immediately after the conquest those tribes entered the settled lands, but were restrained by Mu^{c}āwiyah and other Umayyad rulers, who sought to maintain the prosperity of the land and the flow of income from taxation.[24]

---

19 Baladhuri, pp. 117-18, 126-28, 143-44; El'ad; Gil *Palestine*, vol. 1, pp. 48, 66-67, 89.

20 Baladhuri, pp. 151-52; Donner, pp. 248-50.

21 Donner, p. 245.

22 Baladhuri, p. 178.

23 Donner, pp. 149-50.

24 Hasson, p. 61.

Moreover, tensions that accompany the encounter of nomads with sedentaries might have been mitigated by the fact that most of the Arabs who settled in Syria and Palestine were from among the Christian Arab tribes, who had joined the conquerors and converted to Islam. They had contacts with the settled population of Syria and Palestine for a long time.

Hence, during the first phase, the impact of the Arab nomads in Syria and Palestine was limited. Even cases of killing and brigandage seem to have come under control. The Muslims who settled in the towns soon mixed and came into social contact with the local population, but the rural countryside was hardly affected at that stage.

For the Umayyads, Syria and Palestine were the core area of their empire. They improved roads, maintained irrigation projects, and protected the cultivated lands from the bedouins.[25] The change came about after the fall of the Umayyads and the transfer of the capital from Damascus to Baghdad. Under the Abbasids, Syria and Palestine became neglected provinces, and from the end of the eighth century their frontiers were open to the bedouins in their tribal formations, uncontrolled by state authorities.

Settlements in the Negev which had flourished under Byzantine rule were among the first victims of the nomads. The Nessana papyri stopped after 700, an indication that the settlements in that area were deserted.[26] By the end of the eighth century most of the area south of a line from Gaza to Hebron had been desolated, as people sought security farther north.[27] According to archaeological surveys and excavations many synagogues and churches from the late Byzantine period were destroyed or left to decay not long after the Arab conquest. This might have taken place in the late eighth or early ninth century.[28]

Al-Balādhurī reported that during the caliphate of Hārūn al-Rashīd estates in Palestine were abandoned.[29] In the years 807-15, during the reign of Hārūn and his successors, there were tribal revolts of Arabs against the Abbasids. Greek sources report that in 796 monasteries in Ascalon and Gaza were attacked. In 809, the war between al-Amīn and al-Ma'mūn caused great sufferings to the Christians; churches and monasteries in the environs of Jerusalem were abandoned. In 813 the riots erupted again, and many Christians – monks, priests and laymen – sought refuge. In the first half of the ninth century Christians from urban settlements in Palestine and Syria migrated to Byzantine lands in Asia

---

25 Planhol, p. 76; Sharon.

26 Gil *Palestine*, vol. 1, p. 141.

27 Prawer "Intro.," p. 11.

28 Gil *Palestine*, vol. 1, pp. 51, 133.

29 Baladhuri, p. 144.

Minor and Cyprus. Jews also left for neighboring countries.[30]

Emigration is to be considered as an important factor in the depopulation of Syria and Palestine. Many left when they felt insecure. Others had to leave during periods of persecutions, such as those under the Fatimid caliph al-Ḥākim, when many Christians are reported to have migrated from Palestine.[31]

In the tenth century the Middle East saw another wave of migration of tribal nomads from the Arabian peninsula. Its main thrust brought the Banū Hilāl and related tribes to Egypt, and from there farther west to North Africa and south to the Sudan, where these nomads contributed to the arabization of the Maghrib and the Sudan. This large scale migration agitated smaller tribes in the Syrian desert that easily penetrated the defenseless frontiers of Palestine. The nomads took possession of the low lands and pushed the settled population to the mountains. In the tenth century, income from the taxation of Syria and Palestine was reduced by half compared to the Umayyad period.[32] This could have been the result of depopulation and the disruption of agricultural production, but also could have been the outcome of conversions among the local people, as the new Muslims ceased to pay the *jizyah*.

In the tenth century the region was raided by the Qarmāṭians, who were often in alliance with the bedouins. As the Fatimids extended their rule to Syria and Palestine, they failed to assert their authority. The bedouins, led by the Banū al-Jarrāḥ, were in open revolt and virtually dominated most of Palestine, causing more destruction.[33]

The bedouins who revolted against the Fatimids enjoyed the sympathy of the local Christians and the support of the Byzantines, who sought to weaken the Fatimids. Gil suggests that the anti-Fatimid attitude of the Christians might have brought about the persecutions by the Caliph al-Ḥākim (996-1021).[34] This may be supported by Goitein, who learned from the Geniza that the great persecution under al-Ḥākim had first been directed against the Christians alone, and only at a later juncture were the Jews affected as well.[35]

In the last three decades of the eleventh century, immediately before the coming of the crusaders, the raiding bedouins were replaced by the invading Turkomans, who wrought destruction on villages and towns from Antioch to Jerusalem, and caused deprivation to the settled

---

30 Gil *Palestine*, vol. 1, pp. 392-93; Constantelos, pp. 343-44; Browne, pp. 49-50.

31 Linder, p. 116.

32 Planhol, p. 76; Sharon, p. 18.

33 Fraenkel "Bedouins"; Gil *Palestine*, vol. 1, pp. 315-28.

34 Gil "Jerusalem," pp. 20-21.

35 Goitein *Society*, vol. 2, pp. 283-84.

population, Muslim and non-Muslim alike. Though there is disagreement among historians about the influence of the rule of the Turkomans on the local Christian population, there is no doubt about the adverse results of the coming of those nomads, except perhaps for the fact that they pushed the bedouins back to the desert. No Turkomans, however, remained within the frontiers of the Latin states of the crusaders.[36]

Following the reconquest of Syria and Palestine by the Muslims, the Mamluks systematically destroyed the coastal towns to prevent another Christian invasion from the sea. The most devastated part of the shore was the section stretching south of Sidon to al-ᶜArīsh, that is the entire coast of Palestine.[37] In 1326 Ibn Baṭūṭah visited Ascalon, Acre and Tyre, and saw those towns in ruins.[38]

The results are evident when one compares patterns of settlement in the Byzantine period with those of later periods. In a map of Palestine from 1931, there were 934 settlements, but no less than 1790 ruins. In the Saron plains there were 93 settlements during the Byzantine period, but only 52 at the time of the crusades, and no more than 21 ca. 1800. A survey from 1938 of the region immediately to the south of Lydda and Ramla showed that of the 293 settlements in the Byzantine period 193 were deserted. Human devastation was followed by soil erosion, the blocking of rivers and the appearance of marshes. This in turn caused additional depopulation.[39]

During the Mamluk period, in the fourteenth and fifteenth century, incursions by the bedouins became more frequent and more devastating. Bedouins raided villages, attacked travellers and threatened even the urban centers. The decline of the population of Palestine during the Black Death in the middle of the fourteenth century left many villages deserted and large tracts of agricultural lands uncultivated. The resultant vacuum further encouraged the bedouins to take control of lands that had formerly been settled.[40] Was not the decline of agriculture the cause for bedouinization more often than the latter the cause for the former?

Bedouins settled in the valleys that cut across the mountains west of the River Jordan. It was at that period that the Samaritans, who had been until then masters of the area, were reduced to a small minority in their own territory.[41] The Christian communities survived immediately

---

36 Cahen "Crusade," p. 15; Fraenkel "Seljuks"; Gil *Palestine*, vol. 1, p. 346; Prawer "Minorities," p. 62.

37 Ayalon "Naval," pp. 8-9.

38 Battutah, vol. 1, pp. 126, 129-30.

39 Planhol, p. 73.

40 Drori, pp. 24, 28.

41 Poliak, p. 56.

north and south of Jerusalem, not only because they clustered around the holy places of Christianity, but also because the highlands were less accessible to nomads than the plains.

Damascus and northern Syria suffered more than Palestine from the Mongol invasion in the thirteenth century, and from the raids of Timur Lang in 1400, that left many villages and towns in ruins, with many thousands dead or captive. The whole population suffered, but it seems that the Christians suffered just a bit more, and the rural monophysites more than the urban Greek Orthodox.

There is no doubt that the population of Syria and Palestine was adversely affected by wars of conquest, revolts and raids of nomads. The decline of the population was the result of several factors, such as emigration, plagues and epidemics, deterioration of diet, and a decrease in the rate of natural growth. Many of those who survived physically converted to Islam, for reasons that will be discussed below.

Both Prawer and Gil, though not always in agreement, assert that there was no significant settlement of bedouins in Palestine before the coming of the crusaders, and that the Muslims of the country were predominantly descendants of local converts (Christians, Jews and Samaritans).[42] According to Prawer, the bedouins pressed on the frontiers of the Latin kingdom of Jerusalem, but very few of them lived within the kingdom.[43] The descendants of the bedouins who had entered Palestine between the ninth and the eleventh centuries might have retreated before the Turkomans or were chased out by the crusaders. Still, it is possible that many of them had by then been assimilated among the local peasantry.

Whatever the fate of those earlier bedouins, other waves of Arab tribesmen entered during the late Mamluk period. They settled in the valleys and in the mountains of Samaria and the Galilee and contributed to the process of arabization and islamization, not only by adding to the number of Muslims, but also by interacting with the local population.

THE IMPACT OF MUSLIM RULE: PRESSURES AND TEMPTATIONS

A country becomes part of *Dār al-Islām* by the imposition of Muslim rule, irrespective of the number of Muslims or their proportion in the population. The *sharīᶜah* recognizes the existence of a non-Muslim population within the Muslim state. Conversion of the subjects of the Muslim state is not even considered among the politico-religious obligations of the Muslim ruler. But he has to apply strictly the stipulations that regulated the status and behavior of the non-Muslims.

---

[42] Prawer *Kingdom* p. 56; Gil *Palestine*, vol. 1, pp. 141-42.

[43] Prawer *Kingdom*, p. 50; Prawer "Minorities," pp. 64-5.

There were from time to time forced conversions to Islam, but these seem to have weighed less than non-Muslims claim and more than what Muslims admit. Moreover, the recorded cases of forced conversions cannot explain the islamization of vast territories and millions of people.[44]

Significantly, conversion to Islam from Christianity occurred only under Muslim rule. The process was a long one, that extended over many centuries. The creation of an Islamic ambiance and the development of Muslim religious and communal institutions, as the Christian ones became impoverished, provided the context for the main gradual process, that was accentuated by recorded cases of individual conversions. These cases were the outcome of temptations and persuasion to join the privileged Muslim society, or pressures that made the inferior position of non-Muslim less bearable.

Non-Muslims were free to practice their own religions with a few restrictions. The assumption was that the poll tax (*jizyah*) imposed on the non-Muslims, though higher than the tithe paid by Muslims, was not an intolerable fiscal burden. But the late S.D. Goitein changed his mind as he moved from literary to documentary Geniza sources. He realized that a very considerable section of the non-Muslim population, that experienced poverty and privation, must have been unable to pay the *jizyah*, and often suffered humiliation on its account.[45] The "season of tax" was one of horror, dread and misery. Among the lower classes people might have converted to Islam in order to evade the *jizyah*. It is, however, difficult to assess how significant were such conversions in the long process of islamization.

Among the higher circles there were Christian officials in the administration who converted to Islam in order to retain their positions. Muslim rulers employed Christians and Jews, who thus held authority over Muslims and also had access to wealth. This was resented by the ulama, who exerted pressure on the rulers to dismiss Christian and Jewish officials. Indeed a change of policy towards the non-Muslims often began with a decree that called for the conversion of non-Muslim officials or their dismissal. But the fact that such decrees had to be renewed from time to time clearly indicates that the rulers needed those non-Muslim officials, and reappointed them.

The Jacobite patriarch Michael the Syrian recorded cases of outbursts of all sorts against Christians during the Umayyad period, such as the order to knock down the crosses in the reign of ᶜAbd al-Malik, the destruction of churches at the time of al-Walīd, or the tearing up of all the paintings and statues from the temples and other buildings under

[44] Levtzion "Islamiz.," pp. 9-11; Levtzion "Conver.," pp. 19-27.

[45] Goitein *Society*, vol. 2, pp. 380-81, 392-93.

Yazīd II (720-24).[46] Records of such cases for later periods become less frequent in the *Chronicle* of Michael the Syrian. All sources, however, refer to the three most famous reigns, during which heavy pressure was put on Jews and Christians; those of the Umayyad ᶜUmar b. ᶜAbd al-ᶜAzīz (717-20), the Abbasid al-Mutawakkil (847-61) and the Fatimid al-Ḥākim (996-1021).

On these occasions the rulers, instigated by the ulama, applied more strictly the discriminating regulations against non-Muslims. Not only were Jews and Christians dismissed from official positions, but they also had to put on those signs that distinguished them from the Muslims. New churches, said to have been built after the Muslim conquest, were destroyed. Non-Muslims were attacked, their houses sacked and their wealth pillaged by the Muslim mob in waves of fanaticism.

The extent to which such persecutions brought about conversion to Islam, depended not only on their intensity and frequency, but also on the resilience of the Christian communities. Communal cohesion and leadership could have exerted moral pressure on individuals not to break away, whereas deterioration of the societal texture of the community opened the way for conversion to those who sought to retain office or to escape hardship. More will be said on these aspects in the last section of the paper.

Under the crusaders, the conditions of the indigenous Christians changed little. Their legal status was not different from that of their Muslim neighbors, as all non-Franks were non-privileged subjects. By that time the Christians, who wore beards and spoke Arabic, were closer in their way of life to the Muslims than to the Latin Christians. The crusaders had little respect for all the eastern Christians, but they recognized the differences among the denominations. Greek Orthodoxy was considered a schism which could be healed by replacing Greek bishops with Latins, and by subordinating the lower, Arabic-speaking, clergy, to Latin prelates. The monophysite creed, on the other hand, was considered a heresy to be left alone. The Jacobites, therefore, retained their own hierarchy. From the political point of view the crusaders had greater sympathy towards the monophysites than towards the Greek Orthodox, because the latter looked to the unfriendly Byzantium. Yet, the crusaders succeeded in alienating all the eastern Christians, who once again – as in the seventh century – greeted the Muslim reconquest in the twelfth century as a delivery from religious coercion by their coreligionists.[47]

---

[46] Michael the Syrian, vol. 2, pp. 475, 481, 489.

[47] Cahen *Syrie*, pp. 333-34; Prawer *Kingdom*, pp. 219-23; Prawer "Minorities," pp. 73-84.

Nevertheless, after the crusaders had been expelled from Syria and Palestine, the indigenous Christians stayed on to be avenged. The long jihad against the crusaders cultivated religious fanaticism among the Mamluks, which in turn brought about a radical change in the policy towards the non-Muslims. As Hitti says, "The Christian military venture left Islam more militant, less tolerant, and more self-centered."[48]

Historians of eastern Christianity attributed that change of policy to the decline in power of the Arabs and the rise of the Turks. The latter, as the "Barbarians" who brought to an end the "Classical Age," were fanatic and narrow minded.[49] This is a rather simplified explanation for an historical process that needs some elaboration.

The Turks ruled over large parts of the Muslim world as military elites, ethnically and culturally alien to the people of the land. The religion of Islam was the only link between the rulers and the ruled. The Turks therefore sought to add legitimacy to their authority by stressing their role as the guardians of Islam in defending *Dār al-Islām* against crusaders and Mongols and in supporting Muslim institutions. The Mamluks cultivated close relations with the ulama, who were the intermediaries between the rulers and the local population. The Mamluks established mosques, *madrasahs* for the teaching of the Islamic sciences and *khānaqāhs* for the lodging of sufis. They created *waqfs* to support these institutions and appointed ulama to administer the endowments. The ulama used their increased influence over the rulers to press for harsher policies against non-Muslims.

In the late middle ages employment of Muslims in the administration became a more acute problem than ever before. By that time Muslims formed the majority of the population, and with the development of the *madrasahs* the number of educated people increased. Because all military and political offices were open only to Mamluks, local Muslims, as well as sons of Mamluks, could advance only in the administration, where the non-Muslims were conspicuous.

In the thirteenth and fourteenth centuries militant ulama produced treatises against the non-Muslims. The most famous among them was Ibn Taymiyyah (1263-1328). He represented not only the militancy of the Ḥanbalī school, but also the fanaticism of Syria. The Syrian Muslims, more than the Egyptians, experienced the two traumatic, nearly catastrophic, threats to Islam, from the crusades and the Mongols. Not only the crusades, but the Mongols as well, generated anti-Christian sentiments among Muslims in Syria, because many Christians collaborated with the invaders and behaved arrogantly during the brief period that the Mongols ruled over Syria.

---

[48] Hitti "Crusades," p. 49.

[49] J.-B. Chabot, "Introduction", in Michael the Syrian, vol. 1, p. vii; Atiya, p. 200.

During the second half of the thirteenth and the first half of the fourteenth centuries, under the influence of the ulama, the Mamluk rulers were compelled, often against their own will, to reintroduce time and again the decrees against non-Muslim officials in the administration, that usually carried with them the other discriminating stipulations. Muslim fanatics destroyed churches and attacked those non-Muslims who, in their opinion, did not fully comply with the regulations. Destruction and loss of life and property often followed. Persecutions were only partly and temporarily mitigated by the intervention of the Christian kings in Europe or Byzantium in favor of the local Christians.[50]

In Egypt, the pressure on the Copts was heavier and more effective than in any other period. As a result, conversion accelerated. It was during the thirteenth and the fourteenth century that the number of the Copts in Egypt was reduced radically, almost to their present proportion.[51] The Copts were closer to the seat of government and the Egyptian chronicles of the time are concerned more with the events in Egypt. But it is clear from the same sources that any new decree issued in Cairo was immediately dispatched to Damascus and read there before the governor, the amirs and the religious dignitaries.[52] Considering the anti-Christian atmosphere in Damascus, such decrees were undoubtedly implemented promptly. Though we lack the detailed evidence available for Egypt, it is likely that many Christians converted also in Syria. Those events, together with other factors, such as the loss of life caused by the invasion of Timur Lang and the deterioration of morality in the churches, contributed to reduce the number of Christians in Syria during that period, probably to their present proportion in the population.

The Monophysite and the Orthodox Churches: Internal Dynamics

The Arabs' pride in their race, their language, and now their new religion, was vindicated by their military victories and their political ascendancy. On the other hand, defeat, humiliation and political subjugation sapped the confidence of the conquered peoples in their own religion and values.

At the time of the Arab conquest the majority of Christians in Syria and Palestine were monophysites, mainly Jacobites. Under Byzantine rule the monophysites had been severely persecuted by the Greek Orthodox church in league with the imperial authorities. For the monophysites, who had neither a tradition of their own government nor aspirations for political sovereignty, liberation meant freedom of

[50] For a detailed and amply documented account see Strauss. This study on the Jews under the Mamluks has many references to Christians as well.

[51] Little "Coptic"; Richards.

[52] Strauss, vol. 1, pp. 79-80, 86 and *passim*.

worship. This they enjoyed more under Muslim rule than when governed by Christians.[53] The Jacobites were always more numerous in Muslim lands than in countries under Christian rule. They had no allies outside the Muslim lands, and were not suspected of treachery.[54]

Because the Greek Orthodox church was closely associated with the Byzantine empire, an erstwhile enemy of the Muslims, the Arabs were more sympathetic to the monophysites. Some churches that had been seized from the monophysites by the Byzantines were returned by the Arabs. Later, however, the Muslim authorities changed their policy to be more even-handed. This was perhaps due also to the influence of Constantinople, with whom the Muslim state had diplomatic dealings in spite of continuous warfare.

There are no records of mass conversions of Christians to Islam in Syria and Palestine, though as mentioned above, there were periods of hardship when more people chose to accept Islam. The process of islamization was slow and gradual, involving individuals and small groups, over many centuries. In fact it has never been complete as evidenced by the survival of the Christian communities. The parallel process of arabization, on the other hand, was faster and complete.

Greek as the higher cultural language of the Byzantine empire had not made much progress in Syria and Palestine; its use remained limited to the small Hellenistic elite in the towns. The rest of the population spoke Syriac, a west Aramaic dialect. The spread of Christianity added some strength to Greek as the official language of the church. But the religious schism made Syriac the ritual language of the Jacobites and the Nestorians. Yet even in the Greek Orthodox church many members of the lower clergy spoke only Syriac, and Greek priests often needed interpreters. The change from Syriac to Arabic, from one Semitic language to another, was relatively easy.

Arabic became the language of the administration in the Umayyad state during the reign of ᶜAbd al-Malik (685-705). The numerous Christians who served as government officials had to learn the language. With the flourishing of Arab civilization from the latter part of the eighth century, Christian intellectuals played an important role in the transmission of the Greek sciences to the Arabs, mainly through translations from the Syriac. Literary Arabic became the language of the intelligentsia. The vernacular spread through contacts of the local inhabitants with the Arabs.

The process of arabization in the Greek Orthodox community since the end of the eighth century is attested by the translation of religious

---

53 Prawer *Kingdom*, p. 216.

54 Cahen *Syrie*, p. 191.

tracts into Arabic. Because Greek remained the official language of the Church, in use by the higher priesthood, it is likely that Arabic replaced Syriac as the language of the lower classes in the Greek Orthodox population.[55]

In the Jacobite and Nestorian churches Arabic was adopted for daily use, but Syriac remained the liturgical language. By the eleventh century, and certainly before the crusades, Arabic became the dominant language, both written and spoken. Syriac literature had been in decline since the tenth century, though there was a "Syriac Renaissance" in the twelfth and thirteenth centuries, represented by Michael the Syrian and Bar Hebraeus, the two greatest writers in Syriac.[56]

Cultural assimilation through arabization, though a separate process from islamization, might have accelerated the pace of the latter. The loss of the indigenous language and what might be called, in modern terms, the "national identity" of the Syrian Christians, prepared the ground for the next phase, that of religious change. It has been suggested, in contrast, that the survival of the "national languages" among the Armenians and the Georgians, helped their resistance to islamization.

Without even the remnants of political institutions the Jacobites had no socio-political elite of laymen. The senior ecclesiastical offices of the Jacobite church were open only to monks. Hence ascetics rather than congregations represented the church, consequently it did not develop strong communal institutions.[57] In Jerusalem, the Jacobite bishop was always appointed from monasteries in Syria, Mesopotamia and Asia Minor, and the monks in the monasteries around Jerusalem also came from distant places. This may demonstrate the weakness of the Jacobite lay community in Jerusalem that had been excluded from Jerusalem by the Byzantines before the Arab conquest.[58] In contrast, the Greek Orthodox had a strong local community in Jerusalem, and their patriarch often came from the ranks of Palestinian priests and monks.[59]

The Jacobite ecclesiastical hierarchy was torn by dissension and intrigue, as amply documented in the *Chronicle* of the Patriarch Michael the Syrian. As early as the reign of Mu^{c}āwiyah the Jacobite bishops challenged the authority of the patriarch and his claim to the exclusive right to ordain new bishops.[60] The patriarch received a diploma from the caliph that officially recognized him as the head of the Jacobite

---

[55] Linder, pp. 117-20.

[56] Atiya, p. 204; Haddad *Syrian*, p. 15; Anawati "Factors," p. 40; Brock, p. 10.

[57] Crone & Cook, p. 68.

[58] Linder, p. 126.

[59] Linder, pp. 103, 109.

[60] Michael the Syrian, vol. 2, p. 457.

community. But instead of using this privilege to add cohesion to the church, the bishops became jealous of the patriarch. They sought to undermine his position, going even as far as accusing him before the caliph.[61] High ranking priests paid the caliph and Muslim officials to gain favor, and as a result the Muslim authorities became deeply involved in the affairs of the church, even applying pressure to appoint to the patriarchate a candidate that they favored.[62] During the reign of the Abbasid caliph al-Mahdī, the bishops who refused to accept the authority of the patriarch accused him of being friendly with the Byzantines and hostile to the caliph. In retribution the caliph ordered the destruction of churches.[63] Ecclesiastical dignitaries who had failed to obtain a desired office in the church, or those who had been deposed, avenged it by converting to Islam.[64]

A church "full of confusion and troubles," as described by its patriarch Michael the Syrian,[65] had no moral resources to hold its adherents together. In addition the church was losing its economic assets, not only through confiscations and pillaging by the Muslim rulers, but also by mismanagement and simonism.

European historians explained the defection of Christians to Islam by the "debased condition – moral and spiritual – of the Church ... torn asunder by internal discords, wavering in its fundamental dogmas."[66] Such a view reflected the arrogance of western Christianity in the nineteenth century towards the eastern churches. Significantly, modern Arab historians of eastern Christianity blame the crusaders as "possibly the decisive factor in the alienation of the Muslim from the older spirit of fellowship with his Christian neighbor. Following this, the position of the eastern Churches greatly deteriorated."[67] The crusaders were indeed a cause of increased Muslim fanaticism towards Christians, but earlier attitudes of Muslims to Christians had not been exactly in a "spirit of fellowship."

The period immediately after the Arab conquest was one of growth and expansion for the Nestorians, who successfully propagated their faith in the eastern provinces of the new Muslim empire, and beyond its frontiers among the nomad Turks of the Eurasian steppes. Though not as successful as the Nestorians, the Jacobites also experienced moments of progress and prosperity during the early centuries of Islam. Some of

---

[61] Ibid., vol. 2, p. 506.

[62] Ibid., vol. 2, p. 524.

[63] Ibid., vol. 3, pp. 19-20.

[64] Ibid., vol. 3, pp. 153-57.

[65] Ibid., vol. 2, p. 529.

[66] Arnold, pp. 70-71, quoting Milman, Canon Taylor and Caetani.

[67] Atiya, p. 194.

them amassed great wealth from trade or from holding high office. Part of this wealth was directed to the building of new churches or the restoration of old ones.[68] They also contributed to monastic foundations, to schools and libraries.[69]

By the tenth century the energies of the Jacobite community had been exhausted, and they entered a period of decline. At that stage the Jacobites and the Nestorians began to suffer from the fact that they had been cut off spiritually and politically from the main stream of Christianity. Their provincial character and marginality forced them to close up and to turn inward to preserve whatever cultural achievements they had had in the past. Their moral, spiritual and creative resources eroded and dwindled. It was at that period, as mentioned above, that the literary output in Syriac declined.[70]

At the time of the Arab conquest, and for some centuries thereafter, the Jacobites were more numerous than the Greek Orthodox. They were stronger in the north, in Syria, even in the region of Antioch, which was a stronghold of the Greek Church. But there were Jacobite communities also in the south, in Palestine.[71] The Jacobites had the allegiance of the rural population in the countryside, which was more exposed to the pressure of the bedouins and suffered more from the process of destruction and nomadization as described above. As a result, the Jacobites declined in numbers more than the Greek Orthodox, who were strongly represented in the towns, and who received moral, spiritual, political and material support from Byzantium.[72]

Immediately after the Arab conquest the Greek Orthodox suffered more than the monophysites because they were deprived of the privileged status they had enjoyed under the Byzantines. Also, there is evidence that the Greek Orthodox were exposed to more intensive persecutions whenever warfare between the Muslims and the Byzantines escalated.[73] The Muslim authorities delayed the appointment of new Greek Orthodox patriarchs, and their sees remained vacant: Jerusalem during 638-705, Antioch during 702-742. Patriarchs were exiled and even executed.[74]

In the long run, however, the fact that the Greek Orthodox clergy were not isolated outweighed what they suffered as allies of Byzantium. The Greek Orthodox church remained a great landowner in Syria and

---

68 See Michael the Syrian, vol. 2, pp. 457-77.

69 Atiya, pp. 193-99.

70 Atiya, pp. 200, 204; Haddad *Syrian*, pp. 4-5, 9-10; Anawati "Factors," pp. 38-40.

71 Prawer "Minorities," p. 67.

72 Haddad *Syrian*, pp. 7-9.

73 Gil *Palestine*, vol. 1, pp. 245, 267-68, 390; Constantelos, pp. 328, 336.

74 Constantellos, pp. 345-47.

Palestine even after centuries of Muslim rule. The Christian peasants on church estates, especially in the neighborhood of Christian shrines such as Bethlehem, Nazareth and Mount Tabor, were shielded in some ways from direct confrontation with the Muslim authorities. This might have helped them to survive longer in their faith.[75] In the eleventh century the Orthodox patriarch was recognized by the Muslim authorities as the head of the community, and was given an official status within the administrative structure of the state. It certainly added strength and cohesion to the community.[76]

In the tenth century the Byzantines reconquered the northern part of Syria and ruled there for almost 120 years (969-1084). It was during this period that there were large scale conversions in southern Syria and Palestine. The fact that northern Syria was then under Byzantine rule goes a long way to explain why Christians had remained a majority in this area until the coming of the crusaders, and why those Christians were mainly Greek Orthodox.[77] For the second half of the tenth century, when the political power of Byzantium was growing, there is evidence that monophysite priests and laymen joined the Greek Orthodox church.[78]

By the beginning of the Ottoman period the Jacobites and the Nestorians remained, in the words of Haddad, "numerically insignificant remnants of once proud tradition."[79] The Greek Orthodox survived relatively better, though they suffered a serious schism when almost half of their numbers turned into "Greek Catholics," as they followed those who entered into union with Rome.

In conclusion, we may do well to refer very briefly to the only Christian community that grew in numbers and in communal cohesion since the middle ages. The Maronites numbered about 40,000 in the twelfth century, and ten times more in the middle of the twentieth century.[80] They survived and grew more vigorous mainly because of the relative security of the mountains. Mount Lebanon seems to have been sparsely inhabited before the seventh century, when the Maronites began to migrate from their previous habitations in the plains of the Orontes.

Among all the eastern Christians the Maronites were the closest allies of the crusaders. After the crusaders had been expelled from the Lebanese coast, the Mamluks sent several expeditions, between 1300 and 1305, to subdue the Maronites and their heterodox Muslim neighbors.

---

75 Prawer *Kingdom*, p. 57.

76 Linder, pp. 101-102.

77 Prawer *Kingdom* p. 52.

78 Gil *Palestine*, vol. 1, pp. 369-70.

79 Haddad *Syrian*, p. 10.

80 Hitti *Syria*, pp. 521-22.

Another punitive expedition was sent against the Maronites in 1367, after an attempted invasion by the Latin king of Cyprus. Following that, however, the Mamluks consolidated their hold over the coast, but left the Maronites to administer their own affairs provided they paid the tribute.[81] In their mountains the Maronites were free from direct intervention by the Muslim authorities and also from harassment by the bedouins. But perhaps no less important is the fact that they developed their own individualism, and did not look for employment in the Muslim administration.[82]

Bibliography

Anawati "Factors"	G.C. Anawati, "Factors and Effects of Arabization and Islamization in Medieval Egypt and Syria," in *Islam and Cultural Change in the Middle Ages*, ed. S. Vryonis, Wiesbaden, 1975, pp. 17-41.
Arnold	T.W. Arnold, *The Preaching of Islam: A History of the Propogation of the Muslim Faith*, London, 1913 (rpt. 1935).
Atiya	Aziz S. Atiya, *A History of Eastern Christianity*, London-Notre Dame, 1968.
Ayalon "Naval"	D. Ayalon, "The Mamluks and Naval Power," *Proceedings of the Israeli Academy of Sciences and Humanities*, vol. 1 (1965), pp. 1-12.
Ayalon "Population"	D. Ayalon, "Regarding Population Estimates in the Countries of Medieval Islam," *Journal of the Economic and Social History of the Orient*, vol. 28 (1985), pp. 1-19.
Baladhuri	Aḥmad b. Yaḥyā al-Balādhurī, *Kitāb Futūḥ al-Buldān*, ed. M.J. de Goeje, Leiden, 1866.
Bar Hebraeus *Chron.*	Gregory Abū al-Faraj Bar Hebraeus, *The Chronography*, 2 vols., ed. and tr. E.A.W. Budge, London, 1932.

---

81 Salibi "Maronites".

82 I am grateful to my colleagues Professor Moshe Gil, Professor Joshua Prawer, Dr. Menachem Ben-Sasson and Dr. Ami Elad for reading a draft of this article and for their thoughtful comments.

Battutah	Ibn Baṭṭūṭah, *Tuḥfat al-Nuẓẓār fī Gharā'ib al-Amṣār wa ʿAjā'ib al-Asfār*, 4 vols., ed. C. Defrémery and B.R. Sanguinetti, Paris, 1877-93.
Brock	S.P. Brock, "Syriac Views of Emergent Islam," in *Studies on the First Century of Islamic Society*, ed. G.H.A. Juynboll, Carbondale-Edwardsville, 1982, pp. 9-21.
Broshi	M. Broshi, "The Population of Eretz-Israel during the Roman-Byzantine Period," in *Eretz-Israel from the Destruction of the Second Temple to the Muslim Conquest*, ed. Baras, Safrai, Tsafrir and Stern, Jerusalem, 1982 (in Hebrew), pp. 442-55.
Browne	Laurence E. Browne, *The Eclipse of Christianity in Asia from the Time of Muhammad till the Fourteenth Century*, Cambridge, 1933 (rpt. New York, 1967).
Cahen "Accueil"	C. Cahen, "Notes sur l'accueil des chrétiens d'Orient à l'Islam," *Revue de l'histoire des religions*, vol. 166 (1964), pp. 51-58.
Cahen "Adaptation"	C. Cahen, "Histoire économico-sociale et islamologie: La question préjudicielle de l'adaptation entre les indigènes et l'Islam," in *Colloque sur la sociologie musulmane*, Correspondence d'Orient, vol. 5, Centre pour l'étude des problèmes du monde musulman contemporain, Brussels, 1962, pp. 197-215.
Cahen "Crusade"	C. Cahen, "An Introduction to the First Crusade," *Past and Present*, vol. 6 (1959), pp. 6-29.
Cahen *Syrie*	C. Cahen, *La Syrie du nord à l'époque des croisades*, Paris, 1940.
Constantelos	D.J. Constantelos, "The Moslem Conquests of the Near East as Revealed in the Greek Sources of the Seventh and the Eighth Centuries," *Byzantion*, vol. 42 (1972), pp. 325-57.
Crone & Cook	P. Crone and M. Cook, *Hagarism: The Making of the Islamic World*, Cambridge, 1977.
Dan	Y. Dan, "Eretz-Israel under Byzantine Rule," in *The History of Eretz-Israel*, ed. Y. Shavit, vol. 5, ed. M.D. Herr, Jerusalem, 1985 (in Hebrew), pp. 231-374.

Donner	F.M. Donner, *The Early Islamic Conquests*, Princeton, 1981.
Drori	J. Drori, "Eretz-Israel under the Mamluks (1260-1516)," in *The History of Eretz-Israel*, ed. Y. Shavit, vol. 7, ed. A. Cohen, Jerusalem, 1981 (in Hebrew), pp. 11-58.
El'ad	A. El^c^ad, "The Coastal Cities of Eretz-Israel in the Arab Period (640-1059)," *Cathedra*, vol. 8 (1978), pp. 156-78 (in Hebrew).
Fraenkel "Bedouins"	J. Fraenkel, "The Penetration of Bedouins into Eretz-Israel in the Fatimid Period (969-1069)," *Cathedra*, vol. 11 (1979), pp. 86-108 (in Hebrew).
Fraenkel "Seljuks"	J. Fraenkel, "The Seljuks in Eretz-Israel (1071-1093)," *Cathedra*, vol. 21 (1981), pp. 49-72 (in Hebrew).
Gil "Jerusalem"	M. Gil, "Political History of Jerusalem in the Early Islamic Period," in *The History of Jerusalem*, ed. J. Prawer, Jerusalem, 1987, pp. 1-31 (in Hebrew).
Gil *Palestine*	M. Gil, *Palestine during the First Muslim Period: 634-1099*, 3 vols., Tel Aviv, 1983 (in Hebrew).
Goitein *Society*	S.D. Goitein, *A Mediterranean Society: The Jewish Communities of the Arab World as Portrayed in the Documents of the Cairo Geniza*, 4 vols., Berkeley, 1967-83.
Haddad *Syrian*	Robert M. Haddad, *Syrian Christians in Muslim Society: An Interpretation*, Princeton, 1970.
Hasson	I. Hasson, "The Penetration of Arab Tribes in Eretz-Israel during the First Century of the *hijra*," *Cathedra*, vol. 32 (1984), pp. 54-65 (in Hebrew).
Hitti "Crusades"	Ph.K. Hitti, "The Impact of the Crusades on Moslem Lands," in Zacour & Hazard, 1985, pp. 33-58.
Hitti *Syria*	Ph.K. Hitti, *History of Syria*, London, 1951.
Kaegi	Walter Emil Kaegi, Jr., "Initial Byzantine Reactions to the Arab Conquest," *Church History*, vol. 38 (1969), pp. 139-49.
Kedar "Agriculture"	B.J. Kedar, "The Arab Conquests and Agriculture," *Asian and African Studies*, vol. 19 (1985), pp. 1-15.
Levtzion "Conver."	N. Levtzion, "Conversion under Muslim Domination: A Comparative Study," in *Religious Change and Cultural Domination*, ed. D. Lorenzen, Mexico City, 1981, pp. 19-38.

Levtzion "Islamiz."	N. Levtzion, "Towards a Comparative Study of Islamization," in *Conversion to Islam*, ed. N. Levtzion, New York, 1979, pp. 1-23.
Levtzion "Migration"	N. Levtzion, "Migration and Settlement of Muslim Nomads and Conquerors: Their Contribution to Islamization," in *Emigration and Settlement in Jewish and General History*, ed. A. Shinan, Jerusalem, 1982, pp. 95-107 (in Hebrew).
Levtzion "Patterns"	N. Levtzion, "Patterns of Islamization: The Encounter of Islam with 'Axial Age' Religions," in *The Historical Experience of Change and Patterns of Reconstruction of Axial Age Civilizations*, ed. S.N. Eisenstadt (in press).
Lewis *Archives*	B. Lewis, *Notes and Documents from the Turkish Archives*, Tel Aviv, 1952.
Linder	A. Linder, "The Christian Communities in Jerusalem," in *The History of Jerusalem*, ed. J. Prawer, Jerusalem, 1987, pp. 97-132 (in Hebrew).
Little "Coptic"	Donald P. Little, "Coptic Conversion to Islam under the Baḥrī Mamlūks, 692-755/1293-1354," *Bulletin of the School of Oriental and African Studies*, vol. 39 (1976), pp. 552-69.
Michael the Syrian	Michel le Syrien, *Chronique de Michel le Syrien, patriarch jacobite d'Antioch*, 4 vols., tr. J.-B. Chabot, Paris, 1899-1910 (rpt. Brussels, 1963).
Planhol	X. de Planhol, *Les fondements géographiques de l'histoire de l'Islam*, Paris, 1968.
Poliak	A.N. Poliak, "L'arabisation de l'orient sémitique," *Revue des Etudes Islamiques*, vol. 12 (1938), pp. 35-63.
Prawer *Institutions*	J. Prawer, *Crusader Institutions*, Oxford, 1980.
Prawer "Intro."	J. Prawer, "Introduction," in *The History of Eretz-Israel*, vol. 6, ed. J. Prawer, Jerusalem, 1981 (in Hebrew), pp. 7-14.
Prawer *Kingdom*	J. Prawer, *The Latin Kingdom of Jerusalem*, London, 1972.
Prawer "Minorities"	J. Prawer, "Social Classes in the Crusader States: The Minorities," in Zacour & Hazard, 1985, pp. 58-115.

Richards	D. Richards, "The Coptic Bureaucracy under the Mamlūks," in *Colloque international sur l'histoire du Caire*, ed. A. Raymond, M. Rogers and M. Wahba, Cairo, 1969, pp. 373-81.
Salibi "Maronites"	K.S. Salibi, "The Maronites of Lebanon under Frankish and Mamluk Rule, 1099-1516," *Arabica*, vol. 4 (1957), pp. 287-303.
Sharon	M. Sharon, *Notes and Studies on the History of the Holy Land under Islamic Rule*, Jerusalem, 1976 (in Hebrew).
Shavit	Y. Shavit, ed., *The History of Eretz-Israel*, 10 vols., Jerusalem, 1981-85 (in Hebrew).
Strauss	Eli [Strauss] Ashtor, *History of the Jews in Egypt and Syria under the Mamluks*, 2 vols., Jerusalem, 1944-51 (in Hebrew).
Tsafrir	Y. Tsafrir, "The Arab Conquest and the Gradual Decline of the Population in Eretz-Israel," *Cathedra*, vol. 32 (1984), pp. 69-74.
Zacour & Hazard	N.P. Zacour and H.W. Hazard, eds., *The Impact of the Crusades on the Near East*, vol. 5 of *The History of the Crusades*, ed. K.M. Setton, Madison, 1985.

IV

Aspects of Islamization: Weber's Observations on Islam Reconsidered

Max Weber did not write a full monograph on Islam, but he often refers to Islam in his comparative studies of world religions. Much of what Weber wrote about Islam is unacceptable to contemporary scholarship on Islam, but some of his observations offer insights into the dynamics of Islam. The purpose of this paper is to examine some of Weber's statements concerning Islam, mainly by reviewing several aspects of Islamization.

On Islamic Universalism

Weber asserted that Islam was "obviously not a universalistic salvation religion."[1] He presented the case for that statement elsewhere:

> In Islam, religion makes obligatory the violent propagation of the true Prophecy, which consciously eschews universal conversion and enjoins the subjugation of unbelievers...without recognizing the [need for] salvation of the subjugated.... The religious commandments of the holy war were not directed in the first instance to the purpose of conversion.[2]

Weber was wrong in considering holy war as antithetical to universalism. Indeed, the notion of the *jihad* "stems from the fundamental principle of the universality of Islam. This religion, along with the temporal power which it implies, ought to embrace the whole universe."[3] But, Weber was right that the holy war was not directed for the purpose of conversion. The aim of the jihad was to extend Dar al-Islam through military conquest and the imposition of Muslim rule. A country under Muslim rule is considered Dar al-Islam even if its population remains predominantly non-Muslim. In other words, the purpose of the *jihad* was a political rather than missionary, territorial expansion rather than conversion.

Islamic law recognized the existence of non-Muslim people within the Muslim state. These were the *dhimmis*, Jews and Christians, adherents of the other revealed religions. They could practice their religion if they submitted to Muslim rule, observed a number of restrictions, and paid the poll-tax (*jizya*). During the early Umayyad period the Arab conquerors discouraged conversion of the local population in the newly conquered territories, among other reasons, because they wanted to keep them as taxpaying subjects. This is why Weber says that the survival of non-Muslims in the Muslim state "was considered desirable because of the financial contribution they could make."[4]

This practice, however, was the reason for one of the most serious crises in early Islam, because it contradicted the concept of Islamic universalism, as the pious caliph 'Umar ibn 'Abd al-'Aziz (717–720) wrote to one of his governors: "I have sent you as a missionary not as tax-collector." The resentment of the local converts, known as *mawali*, who were forced to continue the payment of taxes, and were deprived of their rights as equal members of the Muslim community, fueled the 'Abbasid revolution. The rise of the 'Abbasids therefore marked the triumph of Islamic universalism over Arab particularism.

Fixed as he was on events and developments that took place in the first century of Islam, Weber believed that the Arab warriors brought about a decline in "the Islamic missionary ardor" and a recession of "those religious elements of ancient Islam which had the character of an ethical religion of salvation."[5] In fact, Arab warriors could not have made a lasting impact on the development of Islam, because by the third century of Islam they had been replaced in the Muslim armies by the Turks. More important still was the direction of the religious dynamics of Islam. Rather than a regression from an earlier, more advanced stage of an ethical universalistic religion, as implied by Weber, Islamic universalism was on the ascent. This paved the way for the acceleration of the process of Islamization, first under Muslim rule, and then far beyond the frontiers of the military expansion of the Muslims.

On Conversion Under Muslim Rule

Military conquest did not in itself bring about conversion to Islam. Conversion among the local population of the lands that came under

Muslim rule was a long process, and the number of Muslims equaled that of non-Muslims only about the middle of the tenth century, that is, a full three centuries after the conquest.

We have already referred to the policy of the Arab rulers during the first century that did not encourage conversion. Indeed, in view of the numerical superiority of the non-Muslim population, a liberal religious policy also aided the consolidation of Muslim rule and helped maintain preexisting administrative structures, where non-Muslims performed important functions.

The pace of conversion was accelerated when, following the 'Abbasid revolution, the distinction between Arabs and non-Arabs became blurred, whereas that between Muslims and non-Muslims became more pronounced. From that time one could have changed his status by converting to Islam. Since the middle of the tenth century, the discriminatory regulations, that emphasized the inferiority of non-Muslims, were more strictly applied.

Non-Muslims participated in the Intellectual, scientific and scholarly activities of the "classical age" of Islam, in the ninth and tenth centuries, which thrived in an urban society and benefited from an expanding mercantile economy. Everything changed in the transitory period to the late medieval period.

In the eleventh century the government in Muslim countries was taken over by a Turkish military elite. Weber rightly connected the creation of "the Islamic warriors' fief," and "the feudalization of the economy" through "the assignment of the tax yield of lands and subjects," to the decline and stagnation of the "oriental market economy."[6] For Weber, the Mamluk regime in Egypt, the epitome of a government by a closed military elite, represented a model of the patrimonial state.

The religion of Islam was the only bond between the Turkish military elite and the Arabic- and Persian-speaking civilian population, with the Islamic religious establishment, the *'ulama'* as mediators. The military rulers considered religious conformity essential for social and political stability, and they collaborated with the *'ulama'* in stifling creative intellectual movements, which had stirred much religious, social and political unrest of the ninth and tenth centuries. The consolidation of Sunni orthodoxy left its stamp on late medieval Islam until the eighteenth century.

Because the military elite had appropriated all the economic resources of the land, they alone were able to support religious institutions, which they did generously. They built *madaris* as colleges of learning, *khanaqhs* as hostels for Sufis, as well as mosques. Graduates of the *madaris* were appointed not only to remunerative religious posts, but also to bureaucratic offices, where they met Christian functionaries. Competition over employment added to religious bigotry. The *'ulama'* who had limited influence in all matters of state, were able to exert pressure, with popular support, for strict enforcement of the discriminatory regulations against non-Muslims, and particularly for their removal from administrative offices. Popular pogroms and official persecutions, mainly in thirteenth and fourteenth century Mamluk Egypt, resulted in waves of conversions of Christians to Islam. It was therefore under what Weber considered a feudal and patrimonial state that religious intolerance peaked, conditions of non-Muslims became harsher, and the process of conversion accelerated.

Islamization Beyond the Frontiers: On the Role of Sufism and Magic

Until the tenth-century conversion to Islam occurred only within the boundaries of the Muslim states. Even there Islam did not penetrate deep into the lower strata of society, and to peripheral groups. Only heterodox sects—Kharijis, Shi'a, Isma'ilis—developed missionary networks that operated independently of the state, which was often hostile to them, and beyond its boundaries. In this respect, the heterodox sects preceded the Sufis, who after the tenth century carried Islam into the steppes of Central Asia, to India and other remote lands. Sufis also played an important role in the Islamization, that is, in deepening the religious experience, of local societies in lands that had been conquered by the Turks after the tenth century, particularly in Anatolia and India.

Weber, who was acquainted only with the most popular unorthodox forms of Sufism, had a poor view of what he referred to as "the dervish religion, with its orgiastic and mystical elements, with its essentially irrational and extraordinary character."[7] But he does emphasize that Sufism "became influential in Islam's missionary enterprise because of its great simplicity." Weber was more specific about the success of Islam in Africa: "the propaganda of Islam in Africa rested primarily on a massive foundation of magic, by means of which it has continued to outbid other competing faiths."[8]

Muslim clerics in general, and Sufis in particular, presented Islam in terms which were familiar to the local people, playing roles similar to those of the traditional religious experts. In rural Anatolia, the dervishes, known as Babas, were in fact the old Turkish shamans of Central Asia, who had acquired a veneer of Islam. "The credal gap between the ill-instructed Christians and the ill-instructed Muslims became progressively narrower and easier to cross" through the mediation of the Babas.[9]

For West Africa, there are numerous accounts about Muslim clerics who succeeded in winning over an African ruler, by demonstrating the omnipotence of Allah. Praying to Allah saved the country from drought, or brought victory in war, after the local priest had failed. In other words, Islam's first appeal was in competition with the traditional religion and its practitioners. The latter, however, were not eliminated, and rulers who turned to Muslim divines, also continued to seek the aid of their traditional priests. Though Muslim clerics introduced what seem to have been more sophisticated techniques, particularly through the use of the written word, they operated within a spiritual and cultural realm, which they shared with the local people, in recruiting supernatural aid.[10]

Weber pointed to "the essentially ritualistic character of religious obligations" in Islam and to "the great simplicity of religious requirements."[11]

Both statements may be related to early stages in the process of Islamization in places like Africa, where the ritual rather than the legal aspects of Islam were more important. The Quoran had first been accepted as a sacred object rather than as a source for legislation. Hence, the written word was important for its magical qualities more than for the message that it carried.

Similarly, the argument for the simplicity of Islam's religious requirements was valid only during the first encounter with new societies. At that stage Islam was not presented in all its vigor, and initial demands were minimal. But, once Islam had a foothold in a society, it began to assert itself, articulating its legal, ethical, social and political essence. Latitudinarian attitudes and tolerance of symbiotic relations with other religions gave way to the rigorous exclusiveness of a prophetic religion. This was the stage of reform that sometime took the form of a revolution or of a *jihad*.

On Clerics and Warriors

Weber seems to have been haunted by the martial character of Islam, and by the image of the Arab warriors as carrying the religion of

Islam by the sword. Hence his assertion that the ideal personality type in the religion of Islam was not scholarly scribe, but the warrior.[12] We have already mentioned that the Arab warriors ceased to play any significant role as early as the third century of Islam. Islam as we know it is a religion developed by scholars, jurists, theologians and mystics, without virtually any input of those in political authority or those who held military power.

Weber's suggestion that the warrior was "the ideal personality type" of Islam suggests that he must have had little respect for the religion of Islam, especially in view of what he himself had to say about the warriors' attitude to religion:

> The life pattern of a warrior has very little affinity with the notion of beneficent providence, or with the systematic ethical demands of a transcendental god. Concepts like sin, salvation, a religious humility have not only seemed remote from all ruling strata, particularly the warrior nobles, but have indeed appeared reprehensible to its sense of honor.... The chances and adventures of mundane existence fill [the warrior's] life to such an extent that he does not require of his religion anything beyond protection against evil magic or ceremonial rites congruent with his sense of status, such as priestly prayers for victory.[13]

These traits of the warriors in their attitude to religion may in fact be clearly demonstrated for West Africa, where there is a clear dichotomy between clerics and warriors. Clerics are thought of a peacemakers, and their houses and mosques as sanctuaries. Clerics did not carry arms, and were completely outside the arena of political competition. Clerics were therefore at the opposite end from the warriors, who held political authority, shed blood, and drank alcohol.

But, African warrior chiefs also needed the services of the Muslim clerics to produce amulets, to pray for victory, and to secure the flow of blessing. These warrior chiefs, who came under Islamic influence, began to pray and to perform other Islamic rituals. But because the term for a Muslim was synonymous to that of a cleric, and considering the dichotomy referred to above between warriors and clerics, warriors chiefs did not become Muslims. There are cases on record of princes who had become Muslims and succeeded to the throne, but facing the dilemma, they had to choose between Islam and the chieftaincy. In most cases they either resigned or were deposed.[14] Among the Wolof, in present-day Senegal, Islam had been almost fully integrated into the court. But when Muslim militants demanded that the Wolof kings convert to Islam, the kings reacted passionately, because their perception was that a converted warrior chief became a cleric, emasculating his political and warlike nature.[15] In Weber's words, quoted above, "it appeared reprehensible to his sense of honor."

The Role of Warriors in Reform Movements

In addition to what Weber has said about the warriors' attitude to religion he was aware that in certain circumstances warriors played a role in Islamic militant movements:

> As a rule the warrior nobles have not readily become the carriers of a rational religious ethic.... [But,] periods of strong prophetic or reformist religious agitation have frequently pulled the nobility in particular into the path of prophetic ethical religion.... Prophetic religion is naturally compatible with the status feeling of the nobility when it directs its promises to the warrior in the cause of religion.[16]

It is significant that another sociologist, the fourteenth century Ibn Khaldun, made similar statements concerning the role of charismatic leadership in mobilizing warriors:

> Because of their savagery, the Arabs are the least willing of nations to subordinate themselves to each other.... But when there is religion (among them) through prophecy or sainthood, then they have some restraining influence in themselves.... It is, then, easy for them to subordinate themselves and to unite.... When there is a prophet or a saint among them, who calls upon them to fulfill the commands of God and rids them of blameworthy qualities and cause them to adopt praiseworthy ones, and who has them concentrate all their strength in order to make the truth prevail, they become fully united and obtain superiority and royal authority.[17]

Warriors were not the carriers of ideas but there are historical cases that nomad warriors provided the military strength to support a charismatic leadership. The most obvious case was that of the Prophet Muhammad, who mobilized the Arab tribes to the cause of Islam. Other examples were the Almoravid movement in the eleventh century, where Ibn Yasin recruited the nomad Sanhaja of the Sahara; the Wahhabiyya of the eighteenth century, where the reformer Ibn 'Abd al-Wahhab allied himself with the Bedouin chief Ibn Sa'ud; and the Sokoto *jihad*, at the beginning of the nineteenth century, when 'Uthman dan Fodio led the Fulbe pastoralists.

Under the charismatic leadership of a prophet, a saint or a scholar the nomad warriors became united. In all these cases, the leader shared language and cultural values with the warriors, but invariably he himself was of an urban background. The military exploits of these joint ventures resulted in the creation of states that were committed to the realization of the ideals articulated by the charismatic leader. The warriors themselves, in most cases, after completing their task, returned to their old tribal ways of life on the periphery of the state, with little or no interest in the religious and political dynamics of the state.

Conclusions

Our discussion of Weber's observations on Islam began with asserting the universalism of Islam. We have argued that rather than a regression from what had first been a missionary religion, as implied by Weber's writings, there was a progression from Arab particularism to Islamic universalism. One may add in support of the universalistic character of Islam that Islam maintained a measure of uniformity in spite of its geographical expansion and its adaptation to diverse cultural environments.

We have also criticized Weber's emphasis of the martial character of Islam and the predominant role he assigned to the Arab warriors in shaping the religion of Islam. We have argued that the religion of Islam was molded through the work of jurists, scholars and mystics, without any significant intervention of the political authorities.

On the other hand, we were able to elaborate on Weber's observations concerning the feudalization of the economy of the Muslim countries. We have suggested that those remarks by Weber were relevant to the period that followed the transition from "classical" to late medieval Islam. It was during that period, in the thirteenth and fourteenth centuries, that conversion to Islam under Muslim rule peaked.

Beyond the political frontiers of Islam Sufis played an important role in the expansion of Islam. We have corrected some of Weber's remarks concerning "the religion of the dervishes," whereas his statements concerning the importance of magic in the spread of Islam are fully endorsed.

Weber viewed only part of the process of Islamization, and was not aware of the reform movements as the final stage of this process. But Weber identified the role of the warriors when they responded to the call of charismatic leaders and were recruited to provide the military power for the reform movements. It is significant that Weber's observations in this context echoed some of the pronouncements of the fourteenth century Ibn Khaldun.

Notes

1. Max Weber, *Economy and Society* (Berkeley: University of California Press, 1978), 594.

2. Max Weber, *Economy and Society,* 624.
3. Tyan, "Djihad," *The Encyclopaedia of Islam,* 2nd edition, ii: 238.
4. Weber, *Economy and Society,* 474.
5. Ibid., 344, 474.
6. Ibid., 1016, 1076.
7. Ibid., 626.
8. Ibid., 467.
9. V. L. Menage, "The Islamization of Anatolia," in *Conversion to Islam,* edited by N. Levtzion (New York: Holmes and Meier, 1979), 66.
10. Levtzion, *Conversion to Islam.*
11. Weber, *Economy and Society,* 626.
12. Ibid.
13. Ibid., 472.
14. See, for example, a case in Kano: Palmer, *Sudanese Memoirs* (Lagos: Government Publishing House,1928), iii: 108–9.
15. Colvin, "Islam and the State of Kajoor: a case of successful resistance to *jihad,*" *Journal of African History* 15 (1974): 596.
16. Weber, *Economy and Society,* 472–73.
17. Ibn Khaldun, *The Muqaddima of Ibn Khaldun,* trans. F. Rosenthal (Princeton: Princeton University Press, 1958), I: 305–6.

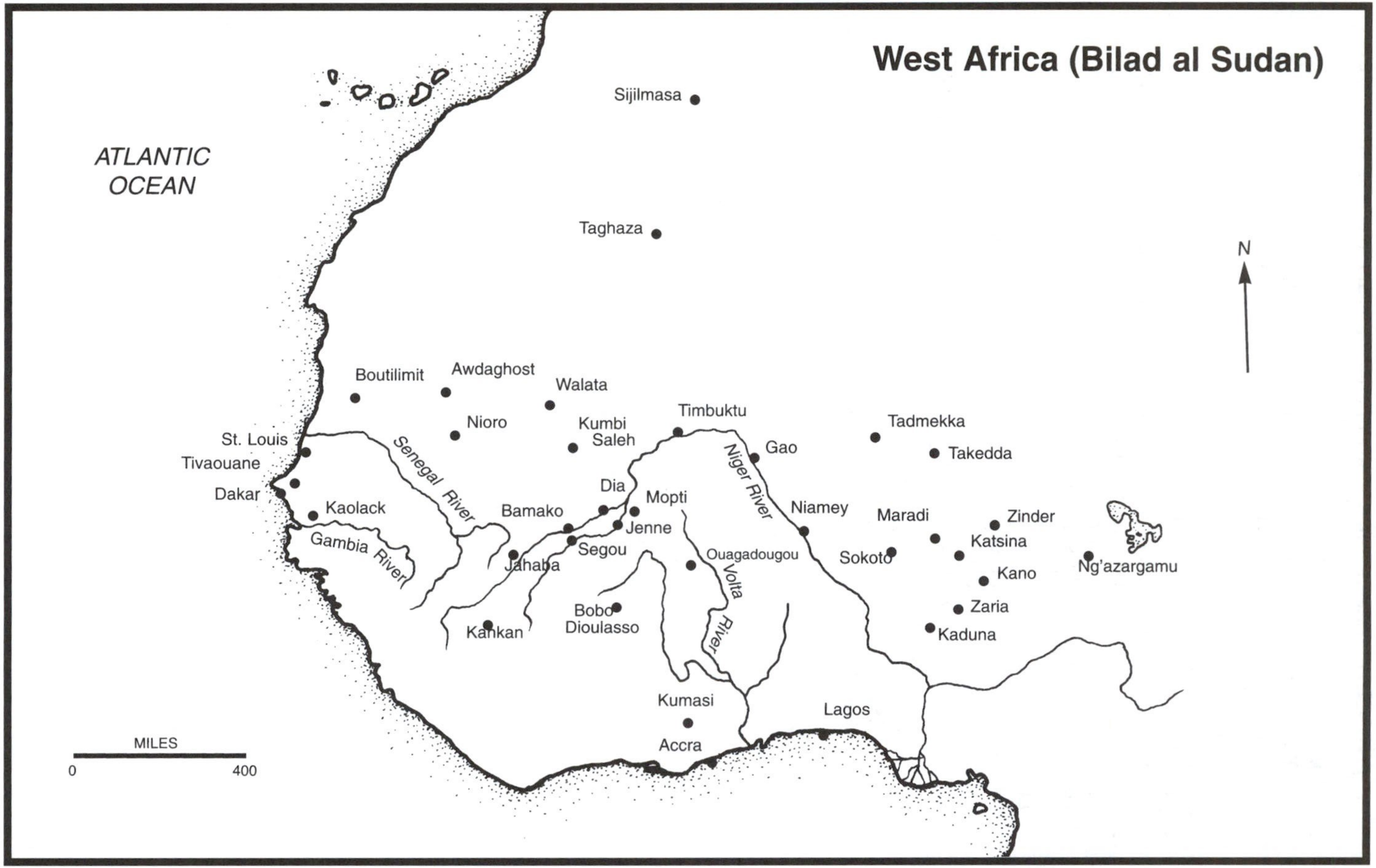
West Africa (Bilad al Sudan)
ATLANTIC OCEAN
N
Sijilmasa
Taghaza
Boutilimit
Awdaghost
Walata
Nioro
Kumbi Saleh
Timbuktu
Gao
Tadmekka
Takedda
St. Louis
Tivaouane
Dakar
Kaolack
Senegal River
Gambia River
Dia
Mopti
Bamako
Jenne
Segou
Jahaba
Kankan
Bobo Dioulasso
Ouagadougou
Volta River
Niger River
Niamey
Maradi
Zinder
Katsina
Sokoto
Kano
Zaria
Kaduna
Ng'azargamu
Kumasi
Accra
Lagos
MILES
0
400

V

Islam in the Bilad al-Sudan to 1800

The earliest Arab expeditions in North Africa in the seventh and eighth centuries penetrated into the Sahara in two directions, the one from Tripoli toward Fezzan and the other from the Sus in southern Morocco. The Arab expeditions must have made their way on beaten routes along which trade had been moving for some time. Trade across the Sahara was carried by nomad Berbers, who occupied both ends of the Sahara. By the tenth century, Muslim traders from North Africa had their base in the commercial centers of Awdaghust and Tadmekka in the southern Sahara. From these towns, they traded with the capitals of the Sudanic kingdoms of Ghana and Gao.

It appears that the North African traders preferred to have their southern entrepôt in the domains of the Berbers, which they considered as being within *Dar al-Islam*. These traders might have observed the injunction by Ibn Abi Zayd (d. 996), the authoritative jurist of Qayrawan: "Trade to the territory of the enemy and to the Land of the Sudan is reprehensible."[1] In the following centuries, with the progress of Islam, the boundary between the Berber domains of the Sahara and *Bilad al-Sudan* (the Land of the Black People) became blurred, and the southern termini of the Saharan trade—Walata and later Timbuktu—had a Muslim population of Berbers and Sudanese.

In the eleventh century, the two capital cities of Ghana and Gao were composed in part of a Muslim town, which was separated from the royal town. Both parties seem to have been rather cautious to expose themselves to the full impact and consequences of unrestricted commercial and social relations between the Muslims and those local people who adhered to their ancestral traditions. This residential separation allowed each group to maintain and practice religious rites that may have been offensive to the other group.

Writing in 1068, the Andalusian geographer al-Bakri was able to gather precious information about Islam in three contemporary African kingdoms—Gao,

Takrur, and Ghana. The king of Gao was Muslim and the royal emblems Islamic, but "the common people worshipped idols as did the [other] Sudanese." Also, pre-Islamic customs persisted. The only-partial acceptance of Islam in Gao is contrasted with the zealous adherence to Islam of the king of Takrur on the Lower Senegal, who compelled his subjects to observe the Islamic law, and carried jihad against his infidel neighbors.[2] The Islamic militancy of Takrur was exceptional, whereas Gao represented symbiotic relations between Islam and the traditional religion that were typical of Islam in West Africa.

In Ghana, the Muslims lived under the auspices of a non-Muslim king who invited Muslim traders to the capital and employed literate Muslims in his court. According to the geographer al-Zuhri, writing in 1137, the people of Ghana converted in 1076.[3] This must have happened under the influence of the Almoravids, a militant Islamic movement in the southwestern Sahara. In 1154, according to al-Idrisi, Ghana was a Muslim state and was still among the most powerful in the Western Sudan.[4] But by the middle of the thirteenth century, the power of Ghana had declined and the political center of gravity shifted southward, where Mali, on the upper reaches of the Niger, emerged as the dominant power. Al-Bakri's distinction between Muslims and "followers of the king's religion" *(ahl din al-malik),* and not between Muslims and local people, suggests that not all the Muslims in Ghana were foreigners. Al-Bakri referred to the Banu Naghmarata, "merchants who export gold to other countries." These were traders who were part of a commercial network that extended from the towns of the Sahel to the sources of the gold in the south. They opened routes among friendly non-Muslim people. When the traders "enter their country the inhabitants treat them with respect and step out of their way."[5]

☾ ☾ ☾

Muslims established new trading centers, which by the end of the fifteenth century reached the fringes of the forest. They created a "commercial diaspora," with a common religion, a lingua franca, and a common legal system, the Shariʿa, a personal, extraterritorial divinely ordained law, that added to the mutual trust among merchants. Conversion to Islam became necessary for those who wished to join the commercial network. The first stage in the spread of Islam in West Africa was therefore the dispersion of Muslims. The next phase began when Muslim clerics began to communicate with the host kings. Another text of al-Bakri presents an account of such an encounter that brought about the Islamization of a West African king:

> The king of Malal is known as al-Musulmani. He is thus called because his country became afflicted with drought one year following another; the inhabitants prayed for rain, sacrificing cattle till they had exterminated almost all of them, but the drought and the misery only increased. The king had as his guest a Muslim who used to read the Quran and was acquainted with the Sunna. To this man the king complained of the calamities that assailed

> him and his people. The man said: "O king, if you believed in God (who is exalted) and testified that He is One, and testified as to the prophetic mission of Muhammad (God bless him and give him peace), and if you accepted all the religious laws of Islam, I would pray for your deliverance from your plight and that God's mercy would envelop all the people of your country, and that your enemies and adversaries would envy you on that account." Thus he continued to press the king until the latter accepted Islam and became a sincere Muslim. The man made him recite from the Quran some easy passages and taught him religious obligations and practices which no one may be excused from knowing. Then the Muslim made him wait till the eve of the following Friday, when he ordered him to purify himself by a complete ablution, and clothed him in a cotton garment which he had. The two of them came out toward a mound of earth, and there the Muslim stood praying while the king, standing at his right side, imitated him. Thus they prayed for a part of the night, the Muslim reciting invocations and the king saying "Amen." The dawn had just started to break when God caused abundant rain to descend upon them. So the king ordered the idols to be broken and expelled the sorcerers from his country. He and his descendants after him as well as his nobles were sincerely attached to Islam, while the common people of his kingdom remained polytheists. Since then their rulers have been given the title of al-Musulmani.[6]

The Muslim divine succeeded in winning over the king by demonstrating the omnipotence of the great Allah. Praying to Allah saved the kingdom in a situation where all sacrifices performed by the local priests had failed.

Al-Bakri's account, like other traditions, emphasizes the role of the rulers as early recipients of Islamic influence, and therefore also the importance of kingdoms in the process of Islamization. Indeed, Islam did not penetrate into segmentary societies even when and where Muslim traders and clerics were present. Kings sought supernatural aid from external religious experts, because in the process of state-building they experienced situations of uncertainties and strain, like competition over the chieftaincy, fear of plots, wars with other states, and the responsibility for the welfare of the whole community. By contrast, the common people, even when integrated into the new states, did not undergo radical social and economic changes that called for a readjustment of religious life. Their way of life remained harmonized with the rhythm of the traditional religion: its fertility rites, ancestor worship, and the supplication of the deities.

This argument may be related to Robin Horton's theory of conversion, according to which the peasant who lives in his own community is likely to be taken up by the cult of the lesser spirits, whereas his ritual approach to the Supreme Being is intermittent and of marginal importance. On the other hand, kings and other office-holders, by being directly involved in long-distance trade or by interaction with merchants and interstate diplomacy, were opened to the wider world, beyond their own microcosms. They were cultivating and simultaneously performing the cults of communal and dynastic guardian spirits and the cult of the Supreme Being. For the latter, they drew selectively from Islam. Thus, the religious life of the rulers was the product of the adaptation of a unified cosmology and ritual organization, and imams that directed the rituals for the chiefs were part of the court, like the priests of the other cults.[7] In al-Bakri's account, the Muslim cleric taught the king of Mali only those religious obligations and practices that no one may be excused from knowing. Hence, the king was instructed only with the rudiments of Islam and was not heavily burdened from the beginning with the obligations of prescriptive Islam.

In Malal and, as noted above, Gao, only the king, his family, and entourage accepted Islam, whereas the commoners remained loyal to their ancestral religions. Situated between the majority of their pagan subjects and an influential Muslim minority, kings adopted a middle position between Islam and the traditional religion. They behaved as Muslims in some situations but followed traditional customs on other occasions. They patronized Muslim religious experts but referred also to traditional priests and shrines. From this middle position, dynasties and individual kings, in given historical circumstances, could develop greater commitment to Islam or fall back upon ancestral religion. This may be demonstrated by following the development of Islam in Mali from the eleventh to the fourteenth centuries.

☾ ☾ ☾

Malinke chiefs had come under Islamic influence before the time of Sunjata, founder of the empire of Mali.[8] Sunjata, a great hunter and magician, fought against Sumanguru, the king of Soso, another powerful magician. Though a nominal Muslim, he turned to the traditional religion for support, to the particularistic spirit of the nation, rather than to the universalistic appeal of Islam. Two centuries later, Sonni Ali, who made the small kingdom of Songhay into a large empire, behaved in a similar way. Kings like Sunjata and Sonni ʿAli, founders of empires, are the heroes of the national traditions, whereas the exploits of their Muslim successors—Mansa Musa of Mali and Askiya Muhammad of Songhay—were recorded by the Arabic sources.

From its center on the upper Niger, Mali expanded into the Sahel. Muslim towns became part of the empire, and Muslim traders traveled over the routes that traversed the empire. Through the control of the Saharan trade and when they performed the pilgrimage to Mecca, the kings of Mali came closer to the wider Muslim world. As the small Malinke kingdom turned into a vast, multiethnic empire, with influential Muslim elements inside and extensive Islamic relations with the outside, its kings moved along an imagined continuum, from attachment to the traditional heritage toward greater commitment to Islam. Mansa Musa (1312–37) was "a pious and righteous man, and made his empire part of the land of Islam." He built Friday mosques with minarets and instituted the public prayer. He attracted Maliki scholars and was devoted to Islamic studies.[9]

In 1352–53, during the reign of Mansa Musa's brother Mansa Sulayman, the Moroccan traveler Ibn Battuta visited the king's court and described the celebration of the two great Islamic festivals. The presence of the king made the public prayer an official occasion to which non-Muslims were drawn; in return, the prestige of the new religion was mobilized to exhort loyalty to the ruler. The alliance between kingship and Islam made the latter into an imperial cult. As the Islamic festivals became national feasts, they also accommodated traditional ceremonies. On the two festivals following the afternoon prayer, the sultan sat on the dais, surrounded by army officers, the *qadi* (the Muslim judge), and the preacher. Dugha the linguist, accompanied by slave girls, played an instrument made of reed with gourds underneath, and recited songs of praise to the king. He was followed by the bards *(dyali),* dressed as birds in red-beaked masks of feathers. They recited the history of the kingdom and called for the sultan to be remembered by posterity for his good deeds.[10]

Ibn Battuta regarded this "ridiculous reciting of the poets" among "the vile practices" of the people of Mali. He criticized other practices, too, such as the custom of sprinkling dust and ashes on the head as a sign of respect before the king.[11] In eleventh-century Ghana, under a non-Muslim king, only those who followed the king's religion kneeled down and sprinkled themselves with dust; the Muslims were exempted from this practice and greeted the king by clapping hands.[12] In the Islamized empire of Mali, all subjects, Muslims and non-Muslims, had to follow the custom.[13] In other words, under non-Muslim rulers, Muslims were not obliged to perform some traditional ceremonial acts, but under Islamized kings, who themselves combined Islamic and traditional elements, pre-Islamic customs had to be accommodated. But Ibn Battuta was also impressed by the way Malian Muslims observed the public prayer on Friday, dressed in white clothes. He also commended their concern for the study of the Quran.[14]

Mansa Musa visited Cairo on his way to Mecca in 1324, where he was described by an Egyptian official as a pious man, who "strictly observed the prayer, the recitation of the Koran, and the mention of Allah's name." But, the same informant added that beautiful daughters of his subjects were brought to Mansa Musa's bed without marriage, as if these freewomen were slave concubines. When Mansa Musa was told that this was not permitted to Muslims, he asked: "'Not even to kings?' 'Not even to kings,' was my reply, 'ask the learned scholars.' 'By Allah,' he said, 'I did not know that. Now I will renounce it completely.'"[15] Shortcomings in the application of the Muslim law were most apparent in marriage customs and sexual behavior.

In the fifteenth century, Mali lost its control over Timbuktu, Jenne, and the other centers of the Sahel, thereby being cut off from direct contact with the trans-Saharan routes and the wider Muslim world. The capital declined and was deserted by the foreign Muslim community. As more ethnic groups escaped the domination of Mali, the kingdom gradually contracted back to its Malinke nucleus and the traditional particularistic spirit of the Malinke nation triumphed over the universal, supratribal appeal of Islam. Muslim divines remained attached to the courts of the successor states of Mali and continued to render religious service to those minor kings, but the latter lost the Islamic zeal and appearance of the fourteenth-century kings of Mali. The Malinke chiefs returned to the middle position between Islam and the traditional religion, with a greater inclination toward the latter. Muslims in the capital of the empire and provincial centers of government rendered religious service to Islamized kings and became integrated into the social and political system of the state. They were pious and observant believers themselves, but had to tolerate the more diluted forms of Islam as practiced by their kings, and even to take part in ceremonies in which pre-Islamic rites were performed. The situation of these Muslims was different from that of Muslims in commercial towns, which were often autonomous. The king of Mali did not enter Diaba, a town of the *fuqaha`* (jurists), where the qadi was the sole authority. Anyone who entered this town was safe from the king's oppression and his outrage, and it was called "the town of Allah."[16]

☾ ☾ ☾

Merchants were the carriers of Islam rather than agents of Islamization. Merchants opened routes and exposed isolated societies to external influences, but they were not themselves engaged in the propagation of Islam, which was the work of religious divines. The latter joined the commercial caravans and it was through them that Islam actually left traces along the trade routes. Clerics often abandoned the caravan when a local chief requested their religious services. Clerics followed the merchants to the commercial towns, where they served the Muslim community as imams and teachers. The clerics became integrated into African societies by playing religious, social, and political roles similar to those of traditional priests. Like traditional priests, Muslim clerics were peacemakers, who pleaded for the wrongdoers, and mosques, like the traditional shrines, were considered sanctuaries. Clerics were expected not to interfere in the political competition within African societies, and immunity of life and property was extended to Muslims only as long as they posed no threat to the existing sociopolitical order. Muslims had limited political objectives; they sought to win the favor of the rulers toward the Muslims. A non-Muslim ruler, the eleventh-century king of Ghana, was highly praised "on account of his love of justice and friendship for Muslims."[17]

Songhay and Timbuktu

In the middle of the fourteenth century when Ibn Battuta visited Timbuktu, it was still a small town inhabited mainly by the Massufa Berbers.[18] There was, however, a community of foreign Muslims in Timbuktu, because Ibn Battuta noted the tombs of two foreigners, the Egyptian Saraj al-Din ibn al-Kuwayk and the Andalusian Abu Ishaq al-Sahili. The former, a merchant from Alexandria, died in Timbuktu in January 1334,[19] on his way to Mali to claim a debt of loan from Mansa Musa. In Timbuktu, he was a guest of Abu Ishaq al-Sahili, a poet and architect from

Andalusia, who had accompanied Mansa Musa back from the pilgrimage. Abu Ishaq built a magnificent palace for Mansa Musa in the capital and then settled in Timbuktu, where he died in October 1346.[20] He must be credited also with the building of the great Friday mosque of Timbuktu, which according to Leo Africanus was built by an Andalusian architect.[21] The two chronicles of Timbuktu confirm that this mosque was built by the order of Mansa Musa.[22] But, during Ibn Battuta's visit, Walata was still more important than Timbuktu, and the descendants of Abu Ishaq al-Sahili preferred to live there and not in Timbuktu.[23]

Mansa Musa encouraged intellectual life in Timbuktu, and sent Malian scholars to study in Fez.[24] By the first half of the fifteenth century, the level of scholarship in Timbuktu was such that Sidi Abd al-Rahman al-Tamimi, who came from the Hijaz, realized that the scholars of Timbuktu surpassed him in the knowledge of Islamic jurisprudence *(fiqh)*. Sidi Abd al-Rahman himself therefore traveled to Fez to study fiqh before he settled in Timbuktu.[25] He became integrated into the scholarly community of Timbuktu, and his descendant Habib served as qadi of Timbuktu from 1468 to 1498.[26]

The senior scholar in Timbuktu under the rule of Mali was Mobido Muhammad, a native of Kabora, which had been mentioned together with Zagha (Dia) by Ibn Battuta, as two old Muslim towns on the Niger. Kabora was perhaps the most important center of Islamic learning on the Middle Niger, where famous scholars *(ʿulamaʾ)* who later held positions in Jenne and Timbuktu studied until the sixteenth century. Around the tomb of Mobido Muhammad al-Kabori in Timbuktu "were buried some thirty men of Kabora, all scholars and men of piety." Two prominent white scholars of Timbuktu, ʿUmar ibn Muhammad Aqit and Sidi Yahya, also studied with Modibo Muhammad al-Kabori.[27] Under the rule of Mali, the imams of the Friday mosque were Sudanese. After the Tuareg conquest of Timbuktu in 1433, scholars from the oases of the northern Sahara replaced Sudanese scholars as imams of the Friday mosque. It was about the same time that the Sankore scholars, members of three Sanhaja families, who had migrated from Walata, became prominent in Timbuktu.[28]

Even a source as hostile to Sonni Ali as *Taʾrikh al-Sudan* admits that, notwithstanding Sonni Ali's persecution of the scholars of Timbuktu, "he acknowledged their eminence, saying: 'without the *ʿulamaʾ* the world would be no good.' He did favors to other *ʿulamaʾ*, and respected them."[29] The ʿulamaʾ favored by Sonni Ali were the descendants of scholars who had come from the northern Sahara and beyond, who unlike the Sanhaja of the southern Sahara, had no relations with the Tuareg, Sonni ʿAli's enemies. Except for his violent encounter with the Sankore scholars, Sonni ʿAli was a typical Islamized king of the western Sudan. Sonni ʿAli combined elements of Islam with beliefs and practices of the Songhay traditional religion, and was greatly respected as the magician-king. He observed the fast of Ramadan and gave abundant gifts to mosques, but he also worshipped idols, sacrificed animals to trees and stones, and sought the advice and help of traditional diviners and sorcerers.

He pronounced the *shahada* (the Islamic confession of faith), without understanding its meaning. He prayed but was careless in observing the correct time of the prayers.

Sonni ʿAli therefore was not different from most West African kings, who maintained a middle position between Islam and the traditional religion, but he encountered different historical circumstances. His successful military exploits brought him to rule over regions that had been under stronger Islamic influence. It was the political confrontation with the representatives of Islam, and not the deficiency in the practice of Islam, that brought about *takfir,* the declaration of Sonni ʿAli as an infidel. Since the early days of Islam, it was the consensus *(ijmaʿ)* of the scholars of Islam to avoid such declarations, so that those who proclaimed themselves Muslims by making the profession of the faith could not be anathematized. It was on the basis of this consensus that West African kings were not challenged as infidels. The legal and doctrinal justification to the declaration against Sonni ʿAli, against the general consensus, was provided by Muhammad b. ʿAbd al-Karim al-Maghili.

☾ ☾ ☾

Shortly after Sonni ʿAli's mysterious death, his son was overthrown by Askiya Muhammad, a senior commander in Sonni ʿAli's army. He entered into an alliance with the ʿulamaʾ of Timbuktu and with chiefs and governors of the more Islamized western provinces. A new balance was achieved between those provinces west of the Niger bend and Songhay proper, down the river, which remained strongly traditional and had hardly been affected by Islam. Askiya Muhammad made Islam one of the central pillars of the state and cultivated close relations with the scholars of Timbuktu. Shortly after his accession, he went to Mecca on pilgrimage. On the way he visited Egypt, where he met Jalal al-Din al-Suyuti. Al-Suyuti introduced Askiya Muhammad to the ʿAbbasid caliph in Egypt. The caliph invested Askiya Muhammad with the title of caliph. In Egypt, Askiya Muhammad "learned from him [al-Suyuti] what is lawful and what is forbidden, . . . and benefitted from his advice and admonitions."[30]

Our sources suggest that Askiya Muhammad sought the advice of al-Suyuti and al-Maghili in matters of state. But these remained theoretical exhortations, because from what we know about Songhay under Askiya Muhammad and his successor, little was done in practice to reform the empire in line with Islamic political theory. The scholars of Timbuktu were less demanding, and were satisfied with their privileged position. They praised the askiya for his love of scholars and for his humility before the scholars and his generosity to them. The court ceremonies and the protocol were adjusted to accommodate Muslim scholars. Sharifs were permitted to sit with the askiya on his dais, and only they and other scholars could eat with the askiya.

In 1498, Askiya Muhammad appointed Mahmud ibn ʿUmar Aqit as qadi. Mahmud ibn ʿUmar was succeeded by his three sons, who held office until the end of the sixteenth century. The transfer of the office of qadi to the Aqit family marked the growing influence of the Sankore Sanhaja scholars, led by members of the Aqit family. The qadi Mahmud b. ʿUmar asserted his independence in Timbuktu to the extent that he sent away Askiya Muhammad's messengers and prevented them from carrying out the askiya's orders.[31] The qadi Muhmad b. ʿUmar behaved as mentor of Askiya Muhammad who requested the qadi to save him the fire of hell, by guiding him in the right way.[32] There were also tensions in the next generation, between Askiya Dawud, son of Askiya Muhammad, and the qadi al-ʿAqib, son of the qadi Mahmud. Once, following an exchange of unworthy words, the qadi refused to see the askiya, who was made to wait before the qadi's home for a long time before being given permission to enter. The askiya humiliated himself before the qadi until the latter was reconciled. The character of the qadi al-ʿAqib and his attitude toward the askiya and his officials were described by his nephew Ahmad Baba: "He was of stout heart, bold in the mighty affairs that others shrink from, courageous in dealing with the sultan and those under him. He had many confrontations with them and they would be submissive and obedient to him in every matter. If he saw anything he disapproved of, he would suspend his activities as qadi and hold himself aloof. Then they would conciliate him until he returned."[33]

There were other ʿulamaʾ who fitted better to the traditional role of Muslim divines in a Sudanic state, as intimate advisers, whose relations with the rulers were devoid of the tensions between the askiyas and the qadis. These clerics prayed for the ruler and recruited supernatural powers to protect him and his kingdom.[34] These clerics received grants of land and charters of privilege. Such documents were known as *hurma* in Songhay, *mahram* in Bornu, both meaning "sanctity," "immunity," or "inviolability."

Askiya Muhammad was deposed by his son Musa in 1528. During the civil war that followed between Askiya Musa and his brothers, the qadi Mahmud b. ʿUmar sought to bring about a reconciliation, but Askiya Musa refused. A provincial governor who had taken arms against Askiya Musa sought sanctuary in the house of the qadi of Timbuktu. Askiya Musa ordered to seize him at the qadi's house.[35] Askiya Musa's defiance of the qadi's intercession was a departure from the accepted norms of political conduct, a sign of unmitigated rule of violence, seemingly unconcerned even for its own legitimacy. The period of illegitimate despotism came to an end with the accession of Askiya Ismaʿil in 1537. He set free his father Askiya Muhammad, who in return ceremonially invested Askiya Ismaʿil with the insignia he had received in Cairo from the ʿAbbasid caliph: green gown, green cape, white turban, and an Arabian sword.

Askiya Dawud, the last ruler in the line of Askiya Muhammad's sons, ruled for thirty-three years (1549–82). As a prince, he received a good Islamic education, and even as king he continued to study with a *shaykh,* who came to the palace every morning. He exceeded his father in his generosity to Muslim scholars. He gave his daughters in marriage to scholars and merchants.[36] Whenever Askiya Dawud passed near Timbuktu, the merchants of Timbuktu came out to greet him in his camp outside the city. But the askiya went in person to visit the qadi at his home, and then proceeded to pray at the great mosque.[37]

When one of the scholars of Timbuktu visited Askiya Dawud in his palace, he was shocked by the persistence of pre-Islamic practices at the court. "I was amazed," the scholar said, "when I came in, and I thought you were mad, despicable and a fool, when I saw the people carry dust on their heads." The askiya laughed and replied, "No, I was not mad myself, and I am reasonable, but I am the head of sinful and haughty madmen and I therefor made myself mad to frighten them so that they would not act unjustly toward the Muslims."[38] Even a devoted Muslim like Askiya Dawud was unable to relieve the monarchy of its pre-Islamic heritage.

After Askiya Dawud's death in 1582, scholars and merchants of Timbuktu became involved in succession disputes among the Songhay princes. When one of these princes gave up his right to the throne and wished to retire to Timbuktu to become a student of the Islamic sciences, his wish was rejected and he was detained because the commanders of the army thought that if the prince resided in Timbuktu, officials and princes on visits to Timbuktu would be suspected of intriguing with him. In 1588, when the governor of Timbuktu and the Tuareg chief supported a rebellious prince, the merchants of Timbuktu also supported the rebel; they donated gold to the prince, and the imams prayed for him. Following the defeat of the prince by the reigning askiya, the political supporters—namely, the governor of Timbuktu and the Tuareg chief—were executed; the scholars and merchants, however, were pardoned, because they were not considered a political threat. Referring to a certain merchant, the askiya said: "He is a poor trader of no importance and not to be worried about."[39]

In the middle of the sixteenth century there were 150 or 180 Quranic schools in Timbuktu.[40] They formed the broad basis for the higher levels of learning in all the branches of the Islamic sciences. Students studied a subject with the scholar best known for his authority in that field. By the end of the century, scholarship in Timbuktu was highly regarded, and during Ahmad Baba's exile in Marrakesh (1594–1607), leading scholars of the Maghrib, including the qadis of Fez and Meknes and the *mufti* of Marrakesh, came to hear his lessons.

At that time, intellectual life in Timbuktu was influenced by Egyptian scholars, with whom scholars from Timbuktu studied when they visited Cairo on their way to Mecca. It is significant that almost all these Egyptian scholars were Shafiʿis, with whom the Maliki scholars of Timbuktu must have studied subjects like *hadith* (Hadith), *tafsir* (Quran exegesis), and mysticism, rather than jurisprudence, which one learned with scholars of one's own school of law. Al-Suyuti boasted that scores of his books had been taken to the land of Takrur, as Egyptians called Bilad al-Sudan at that time.[41] Thus the scholars of Timbuktu had wider exposure than the parochial Maliki scholars of Morocco. Indeed, Ahmad Baba complained that Moroccan scholars were concerned only with the study of Maliki handbooks such as the *Risala* of Ibn Abi Zayd and the *Mukhtasar* of Khalil.[42]

On two issues that were central to West African Muslims—namely, the use of amulets and coexistence with non-Muslims—the scholars of Timbuktu accepted the advice of the more sophisticated Egyptian al-Suyuti than the admonitions of the zealous Maghribi reformer Muhammad b. ʿAbd al-Karim al-Maghili. Whereas al-Suyuti saw no harm in the manufacture of amulets, provided there was nothing reprehensible in them, al-Maghili was against any trade in amulets. Al-Suyuti gave license to some forms of association with non-Muslims, whereas al-Maghili insisted that between Muslims and infidels there was only jihad.[43]

Sufism was brought to Timbuktu from the Maghrib and the northern Sahara in the fifteenth century. In the sixteenth century, the leading scholars of Timbuktu, on their way to Mecca, sought the blessing and guidance of Muhammad al-Bakri (d. 1545), the Egyptian poet and mystic. It is significant that, like al-Bakri and other Egyptian sufis of the sixteenth century, those of Timbuktu were also not affiliated to any sufi brotherhood *(tariqa)*.[44]

It seems that much of the wealth of the scholars of Timbuktu came from gifts by the askiyas and by the city's merchants. Donations by the askiya were in gold or in the form of grants of land with slaves to cultivate them.[45] Members of scholars' families were sometimes important merchants.[46] An individual might spend the first part of his life as a merchant before retiring to scholarship.[47] Scholars of Timbuktu referred to as saints and ascetics were known to have been quite wealthy.[48] Commerce seems to have been problematic to mystics. Sidi Yahya al-Tadilsi, the patron-saint of Timbuktu, not wanting to depend on donations, became engaged in commerce; gradually, he was deprived of his nightly visionary encounters with the Prophet. "Look," says the author of *Taʾrikh al-Sudan,* "to the misfortune caused by business, even though the blessed *shaykh* had been extremely heedful of what is forbidden in transactions."[49]

Timbuktu was a city of commerce and scholarship. The scholars of Timbuktu were spokesmen of the trading community of the city, which benefited commercially from being part of the Songhay empire. Even legal opinions were influenced by commercial interests; there was, for instance, Ahmad Baba's ruling on the lawfulness of tobacco because Timbuktu was an important center for the tobacco trade.

The Seventeenth and Eighteenth Centuries

Following the Moroccan conquest in 1591, the people of Timbuktu, under the leadership of the qadi, first adopted a policy of passive submission and noncooperation with the conquering army. The ʿulamaʾ and the merchants were called on to provide slaves for the construction of the fort *(qasaba)*. The *shurafaʾ* (believed to be descendents of the prophet Muhammad) led popular discontent and two of them were publicly executed. Timbuktu, after having been autonomous, became the seat of a military government. The presence of the occupying force disturbed life in a city of commerce and scholarship and led to unrest and disobedience of the civilian population, led by merchants and fuqahaʾ. The pasha and his troops resorted to harsh disciplinary measures, when all conventions were broken. People deposited their valuables in the houses of the fuqahaʾ, which in the past had been considered immune and sanctuary, but the pasha ordered the arrest of the leading fuqaha and let his soldiers pillage their houses and to take away what had been deposited there. Seventy prominent fuqahaʾ were deported in chains to Marrakesh, among them the qadi ʿUmar and Ahmad Baba. The fuqahaʾ were under arrest in Marrakesh for two years, and the qadi ʿUmar died in prison. Even after their release in May 1596, the fuqahaʾ were not allowed to return to Timbuktu. Only Ahmad Baba returned, after almost twenty years in exile.

After the exile of the fuqahaʾ, according to the author of *Taʾrikh al-Sudan,* Timbuktu "became a body without a soul."[50] The line of qadis from the Aqit family that had held office for about a century was replaced by qadis from other families, but they did not enjoy the authority and prestige of their sixteenth-century predecessors.

During the seventeenth century, the elite of Timbuktu was made up of the *arma,* the descendants of the Moroccan conquerors, who held military and political power. The elite of the civilian population were the merchants and the ʿulamaʾ. Under the rule of Songhay, the ʿulamaʾ had served as spokesmen for the merchants and other sectors of the civil population; they acted as intermediaries with the political authorities. But under the rule of the arma, the political influence of the merchants increased, because the merchants contributed to defray the cost of military operations to secure the Niger waterway and other routes to Timbuktu. The merchants no longer needed the ʿulamaʾ as intermediaries.

By the end of the seventeenth century, the impoverished mercantile community of Timbuktu was no longer able to support a large, specialized, scholarly community. Scholars left Timbuktu and the city went into a period of intellectual decline. Lesser scholars, known as *alfas,* earned their living as traders and artisans, mainly weavers and tailors.

The suffering of the people of Timbuktu increased as the struggle for power among the Moroccan military commanders intensified. The supply of food from the inner delta was cut off as the routes were intercepted by Fulbe and Tuareg. By the middle of the eighteenth century, the pashalik of Timbuktu was in total eclipse. About 1770, the Tuareg took possession of Gao, and in 1787 they entered Timbuktu and abolished the office of the pasha. Not only was military and political ascendancy taken over by the nomads of the southern Sahara; spiritual leadership, too, passed to the clerics of the southern Sahara. The harshness of the nomads was mitigated by the clerics, whose religious prestige also carried political influence, reaching its peak with the revivalist movement led by Sidi al-Mukhtar al-Kunti (1729–1811).

☾ ☾ ☾

Linked by the Niger waterway to Timbuktu, Jenne developed as a distribution center for trade to the south. Merchants from the Sahara and North Africa extended their business from Timbuktu to Jenne. Their agents were Juula, who carried the trade to the sources of gold and kola in the Akan forest (chapter 4).

In Jenne, deep in the world of the Mandingue, Islam gained ground slowly. Pre-Islamic customs persisted there until the end of the fifteenth century, when a pious Juula came to Jenne from the south and destroyed the house of the idols that the people continued to worship.[51] Clerics and scholars in Jenne—all Soninke and Mandingue—were highly respected by the rulers of Jenne, who sought their blessings.[52]

Between Jenne and Timbuktu, the Fulbe pastoralists of Massina, though they remained attached to magical-religious rites and observances to secure the prosperity of their cattle, became exposed to Islamic influences. Clans of Muslim clerics rendered religious services to the Fulbe chiefs, who gradually adopted Muslim names and began to practice some Islamic rites. There had been no signs to suggest that under the leadership of these Fulbe clerics a theocratic state would be established through jihad in Massina.

The Bambara state of Segu was established in the first half of the eighteenth century by Biton Kulibali, who forced greater centralization to overcome older egalitarian patterns of Bambara communal life. He was supported by Muslim merchants and clerics, but was careful to maintain the balance between traditional and Islamic elements.

It was customary for chiefs to send their sons to study with a Muslim cleric as part of their princely education. Though they were not meant to become Muslims, some of them did, and even turned scholars. A qadi of Jenne in the second half of the sixteenth century was "from among the sons of the chiefs of Kala. He withdrew from authority and became a scholar."[53] In this way, Bakary, the son of Biton Kulibali, became a Muslim. When he succeeded his father (c. 1755), the prospects of a growing Islamic influence at the court was unacceptable to the *ton-dyon,* the core of Biton's supporters, and Bakary was deposed and killed.

Ngolo Diara, a former slave of Biton Kulibali, seized power and established a new dynasty in Segu. Ngolo had spent some years in Jenne with an important Muslim cleric and was influenced by Islam, but he was also steeped in the Bambara traditions. He had been appointed by Biton Kulibali to the office of the "guardian of the four cults of Segu," one of the principal posts of the Segu state, and Ngolo retained this position after Biton's death. It was in the central shrine that he gathered the warriors in his move to seize power.[54] Ngolo skillfully maintained the balance between traditionalism and Islam. Muslim clerics extended their religious services at his court and the Muslim trading communities enjoyed the protection of the Bambara state. Though Ngolo followed Islamic customs, he also remained the great priest of the protecting idols.[55]

As subjects of the Islamized empires of Mali and Songhay, the Bambara had hardly been influenced by Islam, and might have even exhibited a tendency to resist Islam. But when Bambara clans became themselves involved in the process of state-building, their chiefs became exposed to Islamic influence. As ruling dynasties, the

Kulibali and the Diara became culturally differentiated from the peasants, though they shared with them most practices and beliefs. Through chiefly courts, where Islamic rituals were held, Islamic elements penetrated also the culture of the common Bambara, including the celebration of Islamic festivals as national feasts.[56] The Bambara worship Ngalla (Allah), but because they have a sense of impurity, they call on the help of Muslim clerics to approach him.[57]

Mungo Park, who visited Segu in 1796 during the reign of Mansong Ngolo's, was impressed by the influence of Muslims at the court of Segu. Mansong, he said, "would willingly have admitted me into his presence at Sego; but was apprehensive he might not be able to protect me against the blind and inveterate malice of the Moorish inhabitants."[58] In the rival Bambara state of Kaarta, Mungo Park observed that "the disciples of Mahomet composed nearly one half of the army," and therefore "the mosques were very crowded" when the whole army gathered into the capital. Mungo Park, however, recognized the persistence of pre-Islamic beliefs and practices, saying: "Those Negroes, together with the ceremonial part of the Mahomedan religion, retain all their ancient superstitions and even drink strong liquors."[59]

The Maraka were Soninke that came to live among the Malinke and the Bambara, whose language they adopted. Bambara or Bobo that converted to Islam became identified as Maraka.[60] Whereas, during the age of the great empires, Islam had been mainly an urban phenomenon, restricted to merchants and scholars, in the seventeenth and eighteenth centuries Muslims made inroads into the countryside and won adherents among peasants and fishermen, who until then had hardly been influenced by Islam.

In the midst of the general sense of insecurity, caused by the violence generated by the demand for slaves, Muslims traveled as traders or pilgrims, and in pursuit of learning. Though there were cases of Muslims who were captured and sold as slaves, Muslims were generally immune and safe. They were protected by the reverence for their supernatural powers and found hospitality among fellow Muslims in the commercial communities that developed along the trade routes.

Muslims among the Bambara are known as Maraka, and they consist of two groups: one is made up of those early Soninke Muslims who claim to have migrated from Wagadugu (i.e., old Ghana); the other group were Bambara who had converted to Islam and assumed the identity of Maraka.

In the eighteenth century, when there was an abundant supply of slaves, the Maraka owned more slaves for farming than did the Bambara. Whereas Bambara peasants owned a few slaves who worked in the field together with members of the household, the Maraka owned many slaves who worked in the fields under the supervision of a foreman, himself a slave. The Maraka master was then able to follow his commercial or clerical pursuits. Slave farming became the economic basis for Islamic scholarship. The most elaborated tradition of rural scholarship was developed by the Jakhanke, about whom more will be said in the next chapter.

Islam in the Senegambia during the Eighteenth Century

Islam in the area of present-day Senegal was always somewhat different from other parts of Bilad al-Sudan; it resembled more the Sahara and the Maghrib, particularly in the role of holymen (marabouts). This might be explained by the continuous habitation in the western parts of the Sahara, from Morocco to the Senegal River, where the ocean's influence moderates the harsh desert conditions. In the central parts of the Sahara, on the other hand, the nomads lived only in oases, separated by stretches of inhabitable desert. It was therefore on the lower Senegal River that contacts between the Saharan nomads and black sedentaries were more intensive.

Indeed, in the eleventh century the recently converted Juddala nomads reached the land of the black sedentaries of the Senegal valley, and this might explain the Islamic militancy in Takrur, as described by al-Bakri. Its king, War-Jabi, who pursued an Islamic militant policy, died in 1040, about the time ʿAbdallah ibn Yasin first arrived in the southern Sahara. "When ʿAbdallah ibn Yasin saw that the Juddala turned away from him, and followed their own passions, he wanted to leave them, and to go to live among the Sudanese, who had already adopted Islam." By that time, therefore, the teaching of Islam had found a fertile ground in Takrur. Labi, son of War Jabi, was an ally of the Almoravids.[61]

Writing in 1286, Ibn Saʿid first noted the distinction between the sedentary Tokolor and the nomad Fulbe, saying that the people of Takrur "are divided into two sections; a section who have become sedentary and live in towns, and a section who are nomads in the open country."[62] Beyond that, there is no information about Takrur, or Futa Toro, as the area is known, except for oral traditions that are difficult to interpret. But toward the end of the fifteenth century, Portuguese sources and the chronicles of Timbuktu converge to throw light on a process of state-building led by a Fulbe warrior by the name of Tengella. He first created a Fulbe state in the Futa Jallon and then moved farther north to Futa Toro. In 1512, after Tengella had been defeated and killed by a Songhay army, the conquest of the Futa Toro was accomplished by his son Koli Tengella, who created the Deniankobe dynasty of Futa Toro.[63]

According to the author of *Tarikh al-Sudan,* a seventeenth-century scholar from Timbuktu, the descendants of Koli Tengella were considered to be good Muslims as the rulers of Mali. Of Koli's second son he says that he was "equal in justice of Mansa Musa of Mali," and of his contemporary Samba Lam, Koli's grandson, who ruled in the first half of the seventeenth century, al-Saʿdi says that he "pursued justice and prohibited iniquity."[64] But the Torodbe, the clerics of Futa Toro, viewed the Deniankobe as warrior chiefs. At the interface of the Sahara and the Senegal valley, warriors were in confrontation with Muslim clerics.

The term Torodbe, as the clerics of Futa Toro were known, covered persons of diverse social status and ethnic origin. They spoke Fulfulde and embraced customs of the pastoral Fulbe, but they were sedentaries, and not necessarily of Fulbe origin. The maxim "Torodbe is a beggar" associated them with the mendicant activities of Muslim clerics and students, who lived on charity. The openness of the Torodbe society is expressed in another maxim: if a fisherman pursues learning he becomes a Torodo. In Futa Toro, learning among the Torodbe was at a lower level compared with the scholarship of their Toronkawa brethren, whom we meet later in this chapter in Hausaland. The Torodbe of Futa Toro were an integral part of the peasant society, unlike the Toronkawa of Hausaland, who separated themselves from both the Fulbe pastoralists and the Hausa-speaking peasants. Though the Toronkawa lived in rural enclaves, they cultivated an urban tradition of learning.

The symbiotic relations between the Deniankobe and the Torodbe had first been disturbed in 1673, when the Torodbe joined the militant movement of Nasir al-Din that spilled over from the southern Sahara to the Futa Toro. This jihad was defeated by a coalition of the Deniankobe and the Arab warrior tribes of the Sahara. The nomads of the Sahara, north of the Senegal river, continued during the eighteenth century to disturb life in the Futa Toro. The Torodbe rose again in the 1770s against the Deniankobe that had failed to stop the nomads' raids. This uprising developed into a jihad movement that overthrew the Deniankobe and created an Islamic imamate in the Futa Toro.

Oral traditions connected the history of the Wolof to the Almoravids through the founding king of Jolof, who is said to have been a descendant of Abu Bakr b. ʿUmar.[65] The Grand Jolof was one of the great Muslim states in medieval West Africa. It was for some time a tributary of Mali, but because its marginal position and its own direct commercial relations with the Sahara, Jolof was autonomous culturally and economically. The kingdom of Jolof disintegrated in the sixteenth century under the impact of the Atlantic trade. Kayor, which had been part of Jolof, emerged as the most powerful state of the Wolof, due to its favorable position on the coast and the benefits it derived from the trade with the Europeans. Intensive commercial activities and a process of political centralization enhanced the position of Muslims in Kayor. Early in its history, the son and successor of the first independent king *(damel)* of Kayor, became known as "the clerical *Damel.*" He refrained from drinking alcohol and preferred the companionship of clerics. But Islam remained marginal in Kayor, and the growing influence of the Muslims in the court was counterbalanced by the *tyeddo,* the core of the damel's military power, and by the *griots,* the custodians of the traditional heritage.

European visitors since the middle of the fifteenth century were impressed by the role of Muslims in the courts of the Wolof chiefs as secretaries, counselors, and divines. They described the Wolof chiefs as Muslims who observed the prayers, but added that "they render it almost unrecognizable with a multitude of omissions and additions."[66] It is significant, however, that neither in the European sources nor in the oral traditions is there any account of a viable traditional African religion among the Wolof. Oral traditions know no other religion than Islam from the dawn of Wolof history. It seems that most vestiges of organized traditional religion were eliminated under the influence of Islam. Minor cults survived only among women and castes. Muslim clerics took over functions of the traditional priests, and even magic became the prerogative of Muslim clerics.[67]

Most of the clerics In the Wolof courts were of foreign origin—Znaga or Arabs from the Sahara, Tokolor from Futa Toro, and Mandingue-speaking from Mali. The Wolof rulers kept the clerics as an isolated community, not permitted to marry into families of the nobility. Sons of the nobility who took too seriously their Quranic studies and became disciples of a cleric or married his daughter lost whatever rights they might have had to political office. The political and military elite were a warrior class for whom drinking alcohol became a symbol of belonging. We have already referred to the tensions and confrontation between clerics and warriors. The growing influence of the Muslims in the court was counterbalanced by the tyeddo. For the military and political elite, conversion to Islam implied joining the clerical community and change of vocation and lifestyle. The Wolof chiefs therefore rejected demands by Muslim militants to convert.

In the eighteenth century, in the aftermath of the failure of the first jihad, in an attempt at reconciliation, clerics were given, for the first time, territorial chieftaincies. The royal family also sought to cement its relations with the clergy through political marriages. It was expected that by involving the clergy in the political life, the danger of another religious insurgency would be avoided. But in the 1770s, following a successful jihad in the Futa Toro, Wolof cleric collaborated with the militants. They were severely punished, and even sold into slavery, which was a violation of the clerical immunity.

Confrontation with the militant Islamic movements changed political perceptions toward Islam. Whereas earlier European accounts referred to the Wolof as Muslims, later European travelers, from the end of the eighteenth century and throughout the nineteenth century, say that the Wolof were Muslims but their rulers were "pagans." It has been only since the end of the nineteenth century that the whole Wolof society converted to Islam.

☾ ☾ ☾

Further south from Futa Toro and the Wolof, the Portuguese, followed by other Europeans, sailed up the Gambia River, where they were impressed by the number of Muslims on the Gambia. Their numbers increased with the intensification of the Atlantic trade. In 1621, Jobson described Muslim traders on the Gambia who had "free recourse through all places," even in times of war.[68] These were the Jakhanke, who represented the western extension of the Mandingue-speaking trade system. In 1698, Andre Brue found the Jakhanke "confederated in a way that they formed a republic, . . . [with] a considerable town called Conjour, built of stone, where the greatest merchants live, serves as the capital of the marabouts' republic."[69] The near-contemporary author of *Tarikh al-Fattash* confirmed that Conjour was autonomous "under the authority of the qadi and the ʿulamaʾ. No warrior may enter the town, and no tyrant has ever lived there."[70]

The founders of the Mandingue states on the Gambia migrated from the territories of the empire of Mali. They were accompanied by clerics, who played roles similar to those in other states. The Muslim traders on the Gambia carried the slave trade in response to a growing demand by the Europeans on the coast. They controlled also the supply of firearms, bought from the Europeans, which made them an asset but also a potential threat to the rulers.

Islam in Kanem and Bornu

An early trans-Saharan route connected Tripoli on the Mediterranean with Lake Chad in Bilad al-Sudan. Kanem emerged as one of the earliest African kingdoms on the northeastern corner of Lake Chad. Its founders were the Zaghawa nomads of the central Sahara. In the middle of the tenth century, the Egyptian al-Muhallabi described the religion of the Zaghawa in Kanem as divine kingship: "They exalt their king and worship him instead of Allah. They imagine that he does not eat any food. He has unlimited authority over his subjects. Their religion is the worship of kings, for they believe that they bring life and death, sickness and health."[71]

Traits of divine kingship survived at the court of the *mai* (the title of the kings of Kanem and Bornu) long after their conversion to Islam. In the middle of the fourteenth century, Ibn Battuta reports that the king of Bornu "does not appear to the people and does not address them except from behind a curtain."[72]

Kanem became Muslim at the beginning of the twelfth century. Its Saifawa dynasty claimed descent from the legendary Arab hero Sayf b. Dhi Yazan.[73] By the thirteenth century, Islam gained almost universal adherence in Kanem. Its king was "well known for his religious warfare and charitable acts, . . . [with] scholars around him."[74] In the first half of the thirteenth century, the king of Kanem went on pilgrimage; he also built a *madrasa* in Cairo for students from Kanem.[75] About the same time, a devout Muslim king broke with tradition, as recounted in a sixteenth-century chronicle in Arabic: "In the possession of the Saifawa there was a certain thing wrapped up and hidden away, whereon depended their victory in war. It was called Mune and no one dared to open it. Then the sultan Dunama son of Dabale wished to break it open. His people warned him, but he refused to listen to them. He opened it, and whatever was inside flew away."[76] Traditions suggest that this breach of tradition alienated the Bulala clan, of more traditionalist disposition, and in the hostilities that followed, the Saifawa were forced to abandon Kanem on the northeastern corner of Lake Chad. They resettled in Bornu, on the southwestern corner of Lake Chad, in the middle of the fourteenth century. But the Saifawa consolidated their hold over the new country only toward the end of the fifteenth century, with the establishment of the capital at N'Gazargamu.

This was during the reign of ʿAli Ghaji b. Dunama (1476–1503), who is remembered as an exemplary Muslim, a contemporary of other reformist rulers in Bilad al-Sudan, like Rumfa of Kano and Askiya Muhammad of Songhay. He was also the first ruler of Bornu who assumed the title of caliph. The claim to the caliphate might have been in response to a similar claim by Askiya Muhammad. ʿAli Ghaji visited Cairo on his way to Mecca in 1484 and met Jalal al-Din al-Suyuti. It is likely that it was al-Suyuti who obtained the title of caliph from the ʿAbbasid caliph in Cairo.

The Bornu caliphate reached its peak under Mai Idris Alawma (1570–1603), when all the state dignitaries were Muslims and the capital N'Gazargamu was an important center for Islamic learning. Qadis, imams, and teachers were granted privileges and were exempted from taxation. The Shariʿa was considered the law of the state, which is said to have been imposed on the whole population.[77]

Until the sixteenth century, Kanem and Bornu expanded only northward, along the Saharan routes. Bornu did not expand to the lands south of Lake Chad, which were reserved as a hunting ground for slaves. But following the Ottoman annexation of Fezzan in 1577, Bornu turned south because northward expansion was blocked.

About the same time, late in the sixteenth century, the state of Bagirmi emerged in a region that had formerly been raided for slaves. The rulers of Bagirmi became Islamized, but, as late as the middle of the nineteenth century, Barth commented on Bagirmi: "Their adoption of Islam is very recent, and the greater part of them may, even at the present day, with more justice be called pagans than Mohammedans."[78]

The mai of Bornu generously supported scholars and attracted students from far and wide. Scholars from Bornu went to study at Al-Azhar in Cairo, where the madrasa that had been established in the thirteenth century was still in existence in the eighteenth century. The mai issued mahram to encourage the integration of Muslims of different ethnic origins: Fulbe from Hausaland, Tubu from the central Sahara, and North Africans. These privileges gave these foreigners the sense of belonging to Bornu society and a stake in the political economy of Bornu. By the end of the eighteenth century, Islam was deeply rooted in everyday life of the ordinary man, affecting him from the naming ceremony to his funeral.[79] This was admitted even by Muhammad Bello: "Islam was widespread not only among the rulers and ministers, but also among the local people. Indeed there are not to be found in these countries ordinary people more scrupulous than they in reciting the Quran and reading it and memorizing it and writing it out."[80]

But even in Bornu, perhaps the most Islamized of all African states, pre-Islamic elements persisted. The most damaging criticism of the contemporary scene was by a Kanuri scholar Muhammad b. al-Hajj Abd al-Rahman al-Barnawi (d. 1755), known as Hajirmai. He accused the rulers of Bornu of being tyrants and corrupt, and of imposing illegal taxation; the rich, he said, hoarded food at times of famine in the hope of profit; and judges and governors he charged with accepting gifts.

There also were allegations of human sacrifices at the time of the annual flood in the River Komadugu Yobe, and of libations of milk from a black cow before the annual repairs to the city wall.[81] These accusations were echoed by Muhammad Bello as a pretext for the jihad against Bornu: "Their rulers and chiefs have places to which they ride, and where they offer sacrifices and then pour the blood on the gates of their towns. . . . They also perform rites to the river."[82] ʿUlamaʾ who collaborated with the rulers of Bornu were criticized by radical scholars, who withdrew from the centers of political power to establish autonomous religious communities. But even they received mahrams to encourage and sustain the development of Islamic learning in these enclaves of rural scholarship, known as *mallamati.* These communities jealously guarded their autonomy and maintained minimal communications with the state. The mallamati were in fact sufi communities in rural enclaves that performed mystical exercises, including retreats in the bush. Like their contemporary sufis in Timbuktu, they claimed no tariqa affiliation.[83]

Islam in Hausaland before the Jihad

In the whole corpus of Arabic sources for West African history, there is but one reference to the Hausa states; this lone exception is that of Ibn Battuta, who mentioned Gobir (Kubar) as one of the destinations for the export of the copper of Takedda.[84] Because Arab geographers were acquainted only with those regions of Bilad al-Sudan that had commercial relations with North Africa, it follows that Hausaland was not directly connected to the Saharan trade. This is confirmed by the Kano Chronicle, our principal source for the development of Islam in Hausaland.[85] According to the chronicle, it was only in the middle of the fifteenth century that salt caravans came from Air (Asben) in the north and kola caravans came from Gonja in the southwest.

Islam had first been introduced less than a century earlier, at the time of Yaji, king of Kano (1349–1385), when Wangara traders and clerics came from Mali in the west. "When they came they ordered the Sarki to observe the times of prayer, and he complied. . . . The Sarki ordered every town in the country of Kano to observe the times of prayer. . . . A mosque was built beneath the sacred tree facing east, and prayers were made at the five appointed times in it." The chief priest was opposed to the prayer, "and when the Muslims after praying had gone home, he would come with his men and defile the whole mosque and cover it with filth. The Muslim prayed and the Chief of the Pagans was struck blind together with all the pagans who were present at the defilement." The custodians of the traditional religion were defeated on their own ground by a superior magical power. The efficacy of the new religion was tested when the Muslims brought victory to Yeji, the king of Kano, over his most forceful enemy. But when Yeji's son Kanajeji (1390–1410) failed to win a war, he turned back to the traditional priest, who promised his help if the king restored the rites that his father had abandoned. Kanajeji complied, and the traditional priest secured victory over the enemies. Islam temporarily lost ground.

The second generation reverted to the traditional religion, but the third generation turned over completely to Islam. In Kano, as in other African states, kings' sons received elementary Quranic instruction. A few of them went beyond what was expected from princes and became sincere Muslims. ʿUmaru, son of Kanajeji (1410–21), was a pupil of the son of one of the Wangarawa who had come in the time of Yaji. When he became king of Kano, his friend Abu Bakr left Kano for Bornu, where he remained eleven years. On his return to Kano, finding ʿUmaru still king of Kano, he said to him: "O ʿUmaru, you still like the fickle dame who has played you false." He preached to him about the next world, its pains and punishments, and reviled this world and everything in it. ʿUmaru said: "I accept your admonition." He called together all the people of Kano and said to them: "This high estate is a trap for the erring: I wash my hands of it." Then he resigned and went away with his friend. He spent the rest of his life in regret for his actions while he had been king. This tradition, once again, demonstrates the built-in contradiction between being a warrior chief and being a Muslim.

The coming of Islam to Kano coincided with the shift of the Saifawa dynasty from Kanem to Bornu, where they became close neighbors of the Hausa states. Though the first Muslim clerics came from Mali in the west, it seems that Islamic influence from Bornu was at least as important.

Islamic learning in Hausaland became upgraded with the coming of the Fulani in the middle of the fifteenth century. They were the so-called "settled Fulani," Torodbe or Toronkawa. They lived in rural enclaves, where they cultivated their tradition of learning. Unlike the urban scholars of Timbuktu, they were not strangers to horsemanship and warfare. They did not render religious services to local rulers and were therefore not involved in non-Islamic ceremonies. They communicated with the rulers, but did not become integrated into the political system. The tensions generated by that mental and physical distance later led to the confrontation and to the jihad.

Islam became integrated into the religious, social, and cultural life of the Hausa without a break with the past. Those who called for a reform were, according to the Kano Chronicle, shurafaʾ, and their leader was ʿAbdur-Rahman. He is later identified in the text with Abdu-Karimi, undoubtedly Abd al-Karim al-Maghili, the North African militant scholar, who left his impact both in Kano and in Songhay. He ordered Rumfa, the king of Kano, to cut the sacred tree under which the original mosque had been built which symbolized the symbiosis of Islam and the remnants of the traditional religion. Muhammad Rumfa was the contemporary of the reformist kings of Songhay, Askiya Muhammad, and Bornu, ʿAli Ghaji.

In Kano, as in Bornu, piety and scholarship among the kings peaked in the second half of the sixteenth century. Ramfa's son Abu Bakr Kado (1565–73) did nothing but religious offices. He disdained the duties of king. He and all his chiefs spent their time in prayer. He was the king who made the princes learn the Quran. But then the traditional religion surfaced again at the time of Mohammad Zaki (1582–1618), with the appearance of syncretistic practices, such as the veneration of the Dirki, a Quran covered with layers of goatskin. Facing the recurring attacks by the Kworarafa and Katsina in the seventeenth and eighteenth centuries, the kings of Kano sought relief in rituals and magic from both "non-Muslim" priests and local Muslim clerics. Kano chiefs vacillated between traditional and Islamic rituals, depending on which promised to produce the best results. The cult of *bori* spirits was the most common pre-Islamic survival in Hausaland, mainly among women. Bori spirits were given Muslim names, and Muslim *jinns* (demons) became identified with the bori spirits. Indeed, the fact that the bori spirits became Islamized made it more difficult to eradicate them.

Until the nineteenth century, Katsina, north of Kano, was the most important commercial town in Hausaland. Indeed, the Wangara in Katsina maintained their identity over a period of four hundred years; as late as the middle of the nineteenth century, Barth observed that most of the merchants of Katsina were Wangara.[86] Toward the end of the fifteenth century, the leaders of the Wangara community of Muslim clerics and traders in Katsina felt strong enough to take over political power, and Muhammad Korau, a cleric, became the king of Katsina. Ibrahim Sura (1493–98), the second Muslim ruler of Katsina after Korau, is referred to by al-Suyuti in a treatise addressed to the kings and sultans of Takrur.[87] The general thrust of this treatise indicates that Islam was still relatively a new element in the social and political structure. The Muslim rulers of Katsina were not completely successful in their efforts to turn Katsina into an Islamic state. In the face of strong resistance, they were forced to reach an agreement with the *durbi,* the priest-chief. The outcome was a sort of dual paramountcy, in which the durbi was responsible for choosing the king. Kingship in Katsina took on the characteristics of a sacred traditional kingship.

The reformer of Islam in Katsina was Ibrahim Maje (1549–66). He ordered implementation of the Shariʿa laws of marriage and threatened to arrest those who transgressed the religious prescriptions. The number of scholars in his time increased considerably. Scholars from Timbuktu, who visited Kano and Katsina on their way to Mecca, taught there for some time and contributed to the growth of local Hausa scholarship. During the seventeenth century, scholarship in Katsina was associated with Muhammad b. al-Sabbagh (fl. 1650), known in Hausaland as Dan Marina. He gathered around him a scholarly community that was well versed in all the branches of Islamic learning. Some members of a self-conscious Muslim intelligentsia were employed at the court, but the leading roles in the administration were held by slaves and eunuchs.

One of the last kings of Katsina before the jihad, Gozo (c. 1795–1801), was closer to Islam than many of his predecessors. He built mosques and supported the Shariʿa, but even he was involved in the worship of traditional deities, because the legitimacy of the dynasty continued to be embedded in the traditional belief system. His actions were those of a ruler who was genuinely torn by a dilemma between two systems of religious beliefs. The slaves of the palace opposed the attempts of Gozo to impose the Shariʿa, and they made his successor Bawa dan Gima a tool in their hands.

Scholars who were alienated from the rulers preferred to live on the periphery of Katsina, in towns within a radius of fifteen kilometers from the capital; there, they enjoyed greater autonomy, and the mosques of these towns attracted more people to pray than those of the larger city. It was from these small towns that the supporters of the jihad of dan Fodio came. The rulers ignored them because of their small numbers and their peripheral location, away from the major centers of the population and political power.

The old town of Yandoto, founded by Wangara traders and clerics, prospered with the growth of trade in kola nuts from the Volta basin in the second half of the eighteenth century. This prosperous Muslim community preferred the status quo and opposed the jihad of ʿUthman dan Fodio.[88]

Background to the Jihads

The rise of Islamic militancy in the eighteenth and nineteenth centuries was a radical departure from earlier patterns of relationship between Muslim clerics and scholars, who had been outside the field of political competition, and chiefs, who though not practicing Muslims were not considered unbelievers. This change came about as a result of several factors.

All the jihad movements were carried by Fulfulde-speaking groups, Fulbe pastoralists under the leadership of Torodbe or Toronkawa scholars. Their role should be viewed in the wider context of the expansion of Islam from town to countryside. It is significant that all leaders of the jihad movements in West Africa came from the countryside and not from commercial or capital towns. The challenge to the marginal role of Islam in African societies could not have come from those who benefited from the existing political order—neither from traders who were protected by the rulers nor from clerics who rendered religious services in the chiefly courts.

The new Muslim leaders articulated the grievances of the peasants. In Hausaland, ʿUthman dan Fodio criticized the rulers for killing people, violating their honor, and devouring their wealth. He declared that "to make war upon the oppressor is obligatory by assent."[89] ʿUthman's son, the sultan Muhammad Bello, evoked the wrath of Allah over "the *amir* (ruler) who draws his sustenance from the people but does not bother to treat them justly."[90]

The expansion of Islam to the countryside widened the popular basis for religious teaching and preaching. The dissemination of the knowledge of Islam to the illiterate peasants and herdsmen could have been only in the vernacular languages. Parallel to the transformation of Islam as a popular religion and as a political force, Muslim societies gradually developed a pious literature. The oldest known written texts in Fulfulde date from the second part of the eighteenth century. These poems were written by reformers who sought to reach people of all walks of life. Poems, easily committed to memory and therefore an excellent pedagogical device, became a major vehicle for teaching and preaching (chapters 19 and 23). Vernacular poems were disseminated in handwritten copies among groups of Muslim literati and were then recited in public.[91]

ʿAbdallah dan Fodio described the role of the vernacular verse: "Then we rose up with the Shaykh, helping him in his mission work for religion. He traveled for that purpose to the east and west, calling people to the religion of God by his preaching and his *qasidas* [poems] in *ʿajami* [the vernacular], and destroying customs contrary to Muslim law."[92] When the shaykh saw that his community was ready for the jihad, "he began to incite them to arms . . . and he set this in verse in his non-Arabic Qadiri poem *(qasida ʿajamiyya qadiriyya).*" This mystical verse had a hypnotic effect upon devotees on the eve of the jihad.[93]

Muhammad Tukur (d. 1817), a companion of Dan Fodio, composed poems in Fulfulde and in Hausa. One of his poems, "Bringers of Good Tidings," is said to have had such an impact that on the day it was composed, possibly in 1789, "forty persons repented and entered the Sunna of the Prophet."[94] Islamic vernacular literature appeared also—about the same time, in the seventeenth and eighteenth centuries—in East Africa, the Indian subcontinent, and Southeast Asia. Everywhere mystical verse was the earliest and most widespread literary genre. This, one may argue, is because all over the Muslim world there were renewal movements in the eighteenth century, which developed out of restructured and reformed sufi brotherhoods. As already mentioned, there were sufi ideas and practices in Timbuktu and Hausaland in the fifteenth and sixteenth centuries, but there is no evidence of sufi brotherhoods in West Africa before the eighteenth century.

The Qadiriyya brotherhood had first been introduced into the Sahara probably at the end of the fifteenth century. But the Qadiriyya had been loosely organized and rather ineffective until its resurgence, in the second half of the eighteenth century, under the leadership of Sidi al-Mukhtar al-Kunti. He skillfully used his religious prestige to acquire wealth and political influence, as individuals and tribal factions sought his patronage. He reinforced the dependency of these clients by fostering the spiritual chains of the Qadiriyya. His emissaries spread the new branch, known as Qadiriyya-Mukhtariyya, in the Sahara, the Sahel, and as far as Futa Jallon. Sidi al-Mukhtar did not advocate militant jihad, and his son and grandson opposed the jihad of Shaykh Ahmad of Massina and that of Al-Hajj ʿUmar. But Sidi al-Mukhtar, the nonmilitant sufi, supported the jihad of ʿUthman dan Fodio: "It was he, according to what we hear, who roused the people to follow what Shaykh ʿUthman said."[95]

In ʿUthman's own career, mystical experiences were of great significance. In 1794, he had a mystical encounter with ʿAbd al-Qadir al-Jilani, who girded him with the "Sword of Truth" to draw against the enemies of Allah. Ten years later, in another visionary encounter, ʿAbd al-Qadir al-Jilani instructed ʿUthman dan Fodio to perform the pilgrimage to Degel, which was the last stage before the jihad.[96]

Notes

1. Ibn Abi Zayd al-Qayrawani, in Levtzion and Hopkins 1981, *Corpus of Early Arabic Sources for West African History* (hereafter, *Corpus*), 55.
2. al-Bakri, in *Corpus,* 77.
3. al-Zuhri, in *Corpus,* 98.
4. al-Idrisi, in *Corpus,* 109.
5. al-Bakri, in *Corpus,* 81–82.
6. Ibid., 82–83.
7. Horton 1975, 374–75.
8. Ibn Khaldun, in *Corpus,* 322–23.
9. al-Umari, in *Corpus,* 261; *Ta'rikh al-Sudan* (hereafter TS) text 7/translation 13.
10. Ibn Battuta, in *Corpus,* 292–93.
11. Ibn Battuta, in *Corpus,* 296–97.
12. al-Bakri, in *Corpus,* 80.
13. Ibn Battuta, in *Corpus,* 292. Ibn Juzayy, to whom Ibn Battuta dictated his story, added at that point that an ambassador from Mansa Sulayman followed the custom back home and sprinkled dust on his head before the Moroccan sultan. Ibn Khaldun (ibid., 342) also describes the sprinkling of dust by a Malian mission before the Moroccan sultan.
14. Ibn Battuta, ibid., 296.
15. al-Umari, ibid., 268.
16. *Ta'rikh al-Fattash* (hereafter, TF), text 179/translation 314.
17. al-Bakri, in *Corpus,* 79.
18. Ibn Battuta, in *Corpus,* 299.
19. For this date, see Ibn Hajar al-Asklani, in *Corpus,* 358.
20. For this date, see al-Maqqari, in *Corpus,* 321.
21. Leo Africanus 1956, ii, 467.
22. TS 66/91; see also TF 32/56.
23. Ibn Khaldun, in *Corpus,* 334.
24. TS 67/92.
25. TF 51/83–84.
26. Ibid.
27. Ibid., 47–48/78; TS text 16, 28, 61/translation 29, 78, 99–100; Ibn Battuta, in *Corpus,* 287.
28. TS 21/36–37.
29. Ibid., 67/109.
30. al-Ifrani, 75–76.
31. Ibid., 60/116
32. TF 61/117.
33. Baba 1931–32, 218; Hunwick 1996, 186.
34. Hunwick 1996, 181n.
35. TS 83–84/139–40; cf. Hunwick 1996, 190–91.
36. Hunwick 1996, 182; TS 83/138, 109/178; TF 118/216–17.
37. TF 110/202–3.
38. TF 114/209–10.
39. TS 122–30/196–208; the quotation is 129/205.
40. TF 180/315–16.
41. Sartain 1971, 194.
42. Baba 1931–32, 114.

43. Hunwick 1970, 29–30.
44. Levtzion 1997, 153–54.
45. TS 34/55; TF 107, 109/198, 201.
46. *Tadhkirat al-Nisyan* (hereafter TN) 87/141; TS 254/389.
47. Baba 1931–32, 344; TS 39/64.
48. TS 34/56; TF 212–13/222–24.
49. TS, 50–51/82–83.
50. TF 175/308.
51. TS 17–18/31.
52. Ibid., 18/31–32; Hunwick 1996, 187–88.
53. TS 19/34.
54. Roberts 1975, 43.
55. Ibid.
56. Tauxier 1927, 186–92.
57. Ibid., 186–92.
58. Park 1928, 200.
59. Ibid., 195.
60. Gallais 1967, 109–14.
61. al-Bakri, in *Corpus,* 73, 77; Ibn Abi Zarʿ, in *Corpus,* 239.
62. Ibn Saʿid, in *Corpus,* 184.
63. Boulegue 1987, 155–60.
64. TS 77/128.
65. Boulegue 1987, 33–35.
66. Colvin 1974, 593, quoting Durand in 1802, whose report she found at the archives of AOF, Dakar. See also Boulegue 1987, 98.
67. This is convincingly argued by Colvin 1974.
68. Jobson 1932, 17–18, 84, 106.
69. Labat 1728, iii, 335, 371, 338.
70. TF 179–80/314–15.
71. Quoted by Yaqut in *Corpus,* 171.
72. Ibn Battuta, in *Corpus,* 302.
73. *K. al-Istibsar,* in *Corpus,* 138; Ibn Saʿid, ibid., 188.
74. Ibn Saʿid, in *Corpus,* 188.
75. al-Maqrizi, in *Corpus,* 353.
76. Palmer 1936, 184.
77. Ibn Fartuwa 1926, 12–13, 20, 33.
78. Barth 1857, ii, 561.
79. Lavers 1971, 39.
80. Bello 1951.
81. Lavers 1971, 39–42; Bivar and Hiskett, 1/12.
83. Lavers 1971, 32–34.
84. Ibn Battuta, in *Corpus,* 302.
85. The Kano Chronicle, in Palmer 1928, iii, 104–15.
86. Barth 1857, ii, 82.
87. See text in *Tanbih al-Ikhwan,* in Palmer 1914, 407–14.
88. See Bello 1951, 104, on the *mallams* of Yandoto.
89. ʿUthman dan Fodio 1961, 241.
90. Muhammad Bello 1921, 80.
91. Sow 1966, 12–16; Seydou 1973, 184; Hiskett 1957, passim; Brenner and Last 1985, 434.

92. Abdallah dan Fodio 1963, 85.
93. Ibid., 105.
94. Haafkens 1983, 412; Hiskett 1975, 32.
95. Abdallah dan Fodio 1963, 104.
96. Martin 1976, 20; Hiskett 1973, 66.

Bibliography

'Abdallah dan Fodio. 1963. *Tazyin al-waraqat.* Ed. and trans. M. Hiskett. Ibadan: Ibadan University Press.

Abitbol, M. 1979. *Tombouctou et les Arma.* Paris: G. P. Maisonneuve.

Ahmad Baba. 1931–32. *Nayl al-ibtihaj bi-tabriz al-dibaj.* Cairo.

Barth, H. 1857. *Travels and Discoveries in North and Central Africa.* London (reprinted by Frank Cass, 1968).

Bello, Muhammad. 1951. *Infaq al-Maysur.* Ed. C. E. J. Whitting. London.

———. 1971. *Usul al-Siyasa.* Ed. and trans. B. G. Martin. In *Aspects of West African Islam,* ed. D. F. McCall and N. R. Bennet. Boston: African Studies Program.

Bivar, A. D. H. and M. Hiskett. 1962. "The Arabic Literature of Nigeria to 1804," *Bulletin of the School of Oriental and African Studies* 25:104–48.

Bobboyi, Hamidu. 1992. "The 'Ulama' of Borno: A Study of the Relations between Scholars and the State under the Sayfawa (1407–1808)," Ph.D. thesis, Northwestern University.

———. 1993. "Relations of the Borno *'ulama'* with the Sayfawa Rulers: The Role of the *Mahrams,*" *Sudanic Africa* 4:175–204.

Boulegue, J. 1987. *Le Grand Jolof.* Blois: Editions Facades.

Brenner, L., and M. Last. 1985. "The Role of Language in West African Islam," *Africa* 55:432–46.

Colvin, L. G. 1974. "Islam and the State of Kajoor: A Case of Successful Resistance to Jihad," *Journal of African History* 15:587–606.

———. 1987. "The Shaykh's Men: Religion and Power in Senegambian Islam." In *Rural and Urban Islam,* ed. N. Levtzion and H. J. Fisher, 55–65. Boulder, Colo: Lynne Riener.

Ibn Fartuwa, Ahmad. 1926. *History of the First Twelve Years of the Reign of Mai Idris Aloma of Bornu (1571–1583),* trans. H. R. Palmer. Lagos: The Government Printer.

Fisher, H. J. 1973. "Conversion Reconsidered: Some Historical Aspects of Religious Conversion in Black Africa," *Africa* 43:27–40.

Gallais, J. 1967. *Le delta intérieur du Niger.* Dakar: IFAN.

Haafkens, J. 1983. *Chants musulmans en peul: textes de l'héritage musulmane de la communaute mususlmane de Maroua, Cameroun.* Leiden: E. J. Brill.

al-Hajj, M. A. 1968. "A Seventeenth Century Chronicle on the Origins and Missionary Activities of the Wangarawa," *Kano Studies* 1:7–42.

Hiskett, M. 1957. "Material Relating to the State of Learning among the Fulani before Their Jihad," *BSAOAS* 19:550–78.

———. 1973. *The Sword of Truth.* New York: Oxford University Press.

———. 1979. *A History of Hausa Islamic Verse.* London: The School of Oriental and African Studies.

Horton, R. 1975. "On the Rationality of Conversation," *Africa* 45, 3–4:219–35; 373–99.

Hunwick, J. O. 1970. "Notes on a Late Fifteenth-Century Document Concerning 'al-Takrur'." In *African Perspectives,* ed. C. Allen and R.W. Johnson. Cambridge: Cambridge University Press.

———. 1985. *Shari'a in Songhay.* Oxford: Oxford University Press.

———. 1996. "Secular Power and Religious Authority in Muslim Society: The Case of Songhay." *Journal of African History* 37:175–94.

al-Ifrani, n.d. *Nuzhat al-hadi fi akhbar muluk al-qarn al-hadi,* lithographed in Fez.

Jobson, R. 1932. *The Golden Trade.* London. (Reprinted in 1968 by Dawson and Pall Mall).

Kaba, Lansine. 1984. "The Pen, the Sword, and the Crown: Islam and Revolution in Songhay Reconsidered, 1464–1493," *Journal of African History* 25:241–56.

Labat, J. B. 1728. *Nouvelle relation de l'Afrique occidentale.* Paris: G. Cavalier.

Lange, D. 1978. "Progrès de l'Islam et changement politique au Kanem du 11e au 13e siècle: Un essai d'interprétation," *Journal of African History* 19:495–513.

Last, M. 1993. "The Traditional Muslim Intellectuals in Hausaland: The Background." In *African Historiography: Essays in Honor of J. Ade Ajayi,* ed. T. Falola, 116–31. Harlow: Longman.

Lavers, J. E. 1971. "Islam in the Bornu Caliphate," *Odu* 5:27–53.

———. 1987. "Two Sufi Communities in Seventeenth and Nineteenth Century Bornu," paper presented to a workshop at SOAS, September 1987, on Sufism in Africa in the seventeenth and eighteenth centuries.

Leo Africanus. 1956. *Description de l'Afrique,* trans. A. Epaulard. Paris: Adrien-Maisonneuve.

Levitson, N. 1968. *Muslims and Chiefs in West Africa.* Oxford: Clarendon Press.

———. 1986. "Mamluk Egypt and Takrur." In *Studies in Islamic History and Civilization in Honour of David Ayalon,* ed. M. Sharon, 183–207. Leiden: E. J. Brill (reprinted in Levtzion 1994).

———. 1994. *Islam in West Africa: Religion, Society and Politics to 1800.* Aldershot, Hamps.: Variorum.

———. 1997. "Eighteenth Century Sufi Brotherhoods: Structural, Organizational and Ritual Changes." In *Essays on Scripture, Thought and Society,* A Festschrift in Honor of A. H. Johns, ed. P. G. Riddel and Tony Street, 147–60. Leiden: E. J. Brill.

Levtzion, Nehemia, and J. F. P. Hopkins, eds. 1981. *Corpus of Early Arabic Sources for West African History.* Trans. J. F. P. Hopkins. Cambridge: Cambridge University Press.

Martin, B. G. 1976. *Muslim Brotherhoods in Nineteenth-Century Africa.* Cambridge: Cambridge University Press.

Palmer, H. R. 1914. "An early Fulani Conception of Islam," *Journal of the African Society* 13:407–14.

———. 1928. *Sudanese Memoirs.* Lagos: The Government Printer.

———. 1936. *Bornu, Sahara and Sudan.* Rpt. New York: Negro Universities Press, 1970.

Park, Mungo. 1928. *Travels in the Interior Districts of Africa.* London: Bulmer.

Roberts, R. 1975. *Warriors, Merchants and Slaves: The State and the Economy in the Middle Niger Valley, 1700–1914.* Stanford: Stanford University Press.

Robinson, D. 1975. "The Islamic Revolution of Futa Toro," *International Journal of African Historical Studies* 8:185–221.

Sartain, E. M. 1971. "Jalal al-Din al-Suyuti's Relations with the People of Takrur," *Journal of Semitic Studies* 16:193–98.

Seydou, C. 1973. "Panorama de la Literature Peule," *Bulletin de l'IFAN* 35:176–212.

Sow, A. I. 1966. *La femme, la vache, la foi: Ecrivains et pouvoir du Fouta Djalon.* Paris: Julliard.

Tadhkirat al-Nisyan. 1966. Ed. and trans. O. Houdas. Paris: Adrien-Maisonneuve (reprint of the 1913–14 edition).

Ta'rikh al-Fattash. 1964. Ed. and trans. O. Houdas and M. Delafosse. Paris: Adrien-Maisonneuve (reprint of 1912 edition).

Ta'rikh al-Sudan. ʿAbd al-Rahman al-Sadi. 1964. Ed. and trans. O. Houdas. Paris: Adrien-Maisonneuve (reprint of 1911 edition).

Tauxier, L. 1927. *La Religion Bambara.* Paris: Paul Geuthner.

ʿUthman dan Fodio. 1961. "Wathiqat ahl al-Sudan," *Journal of African History* 2:235–44.

VI

Arab Geographers, the Nile, and the History of Bilad al-Sudan

Dedicated to the memory of the late J. F. P. Hopkins of Cambridge University, with whom I edited Corpus of Early Arabic Sources for West African History, *in which the Nile features so prominently*

The sources of the Nile were a riddle for humanity until the middle of the nineteenth century. This chapter investigates what the Arab geographers knew or theorized concerning the Nile, its sources, and its course. We meet information about the Nile in texts that deal with sub-Saharan Africa, known in the sources as *Bilad al-Sudan*. This part of Africa was better known to the Arabs than the lands south of Egypt.

The Arab geographers adopted Ptolemy's theory of astronomical geography about the sources of the Nile in the *Jabal al-Qamar* (Mountains of the Moon). *Surat al-Ard* of al-Khuwarizmi (died sometime after 846) is an adaptation to Arabic of Ptolemy's *Geography.* But al-Khuwarizmi was able to add names of places (like 'Alwa, Zaghawa, Fezzan, and Dunqula) that represent the new geographical knowledge of the Arabs:

> There are two round lakes. Into the first pour five rivers from the Mountain of the Moon. Five rivers also issue from the Mountain of the Moon into the second lake. [All these rivers finally unite in a single lake called the Little Lake.] From the Little Lake issues a great river which is the Nil of Egypt. It passes through the land of the Sudan, and 'Alwa and Zaghawa and Fezzan and the Nuba, and passes through Dunqula, the city of Nuba.[1]

In the tenth and eleventh centuries the knowledge of the Arabs about the countries south of the Sahara expanded, based on the direct observation of military commanders, travelers, and traders.

Ibn al-Faqih, writing shortly after 903, begins with Ptolemy's theory: "Some people say that the Nil issues beyond the equator from two lakes. . . . It flows around the land of the Habasha, and then it passes between Bahr al-Qulzum and the desert, to flow on and to pour itself at Dimyat into the Mediterranean." But he soon adds information based on direct observation: "Abu'l-Khattab [d. 761] related that al-Mushtari b. al-Aswad said: 'I have raided the land of Anbiya twenty times from al-Sus al-Aqsa, and I have seen there the Nil. Between the river and the salty sea is a dune of sand and the Nil emerges from beneath it.'"[2]

The raids of Abu'l-Khattab were from Morocco to the Sahara, and the evidence suggests that as early as the middle of the eighth century, the Arabs had some idea about a system of rivers south of the Sahara, which they identified as the Nile.

Writing in 1067, a work of descriptive geography, based on information gathered from travelers and traders, al-Bakri refers to the major river of West Africa as the Nile. The town of Takrur, which was located in Futa Toro, in present-day Senegal, was "situated on the Nil."[3] In Sila, close to Takrur, "in the Nil, where it adjoins their country, an animal is found living in the water, which resembles the elephant in the size of its body as well as its snout and tusks." This was undoubtedly a hippopotamus, which as al-Bakri described, "goes to pasture on land, but then seeks its abode in the Nil."[4] The Nile described in those two references was undoubtedly the Senegal River as it approached the Atlantic Ocean.

Al-Bakri's informants were acquainted with the routes from Ghana to the sources of the gold in the south. From the town of Yarisna, on the Nile, African merchants exported gold to other countries. On the opposite side of the Nile were the two kingdoms of Do and Malal.[5] These were undoubtedly Malinke principalities, predecessors of Mali, and the Nile in question was undoubtedly the upper reaches of the Niger River, where the Bure goldfields seem to have been opened about that time. It should be noted, however, that the Upper Senegal and the Upper Niger Rivers are not very far apart, close enough to confuse them as being one river. When al-Bakri referred again to the Nile, it was in his description of the bend of the Niger River, at Tiraqqa, which must have been not far from where Timbuktu developed later:

> At a place called Ra's al-Ma' you meet the Nil coming out of the land of the Sudan. One of its banks is inhabited by tribes of Muslim Berbers, called Madasa, and opposite them, on the other bank, live pagan Sudan. Then you go from there six stages along the Nil to the town of Tiraqqa.

> . . . From Tiraqqa the Nil turns towards the south into the land of the Sudan.[6]

Al-Bakri seems to have had quite an accurate idea of the course of the Niger at that point, in its flow to the northeast to the farthest point of penetration into the Sahara, the land of the nomad Berbers, where it turned to the southeast back into the land of the Sudan.

Al-Idrisi, writing in 1145, goes back to Ptolemy's theory, first presented by al-Khuwarizmi. Arguments concerning the reliability of the information provided al-Bakri and al-Idrisi touched on one of the more important issues in the history of *Bilad al-Sudan,* namely the location of the capital of Ghana. According to al-Bakri, the capital was in the Sahel, far away from any river. Its people obtained water from wells.[7] Al-Idrisi, on the other hand, located Ghana astride the Nile.[8] Historians suggested that the capital of Ghana was relocated, perhaps as a result of the Almoravids intervention during the period in between the writing of al-Bakri and al-Idrisi.

But our argument is that al-Idrisi's location of Ghana on the Nile was simply a geographical aberration, a result of his adherence to the theory of Ptolemy. Al-Idrisi followed Ptolemy in assuming that all of the southern lands are in an arid torrid zone, where life depended completely on the river. Here is al-Idrisi's description of the town of Bilaq in the land of the Nuba: "There is no rain at all in the town of Bilaq, nor in all the other regions of the Sudan. . . . They have no rain or mercy from God nor succor other than the inundation of the Nil, on which they rely for agriculture."[9]

No town could have therefore existed away from the river, and al-Idrisi placed all the towns of *Bilad al-Sudan,* including the capital of Ghana, on the Nile. The Nile of al-Idrisi was indeed a very strange river that meandered in order to pass through all the towns of the region. Al-Idrisi imagined Ghana as situated on a river surrounded by a terrible desert. He described the route from Ghana to Mali as "being over dunes and deep sands where there is no water."[10] As we know well, this route was in plain savannah country, which a traveler like Ibn Battuta found safe and easy.

Al-Idrisi followed al-Khuwarizmi in the account of the sources of the Nile in Jabal al-Qamar, from where a number of springs come in and out of a series of lakes. Al-Idrisi had new information concerning the last lake:

> This lake is just beyond the equator, and touching it. In the lowest part of this lake in which the rivers collect, a mountain protrudes, splitting the main part of the lake into two, and extending from the lake to the northeast. One of the branches of the Nil flows along this mountain on the western side. This is the Nil of *Bilad al-Sudan,* on which most of the towns are situated. The second branch of the Nil comes out of the lake on

> the eastern rift of the mountain, and flows to the north, through the country of the Nuba and the country of Egypt.[11]

Al-Idrisi produced an answer to the existence of two "Niles," which split in the lake, one—"the Nil of Egypt"—that flows to the north, and the other—"the Nil of *Bilad al-Sudan,* on which most of their towns are situated." Ibn Sa'id, writing sometime after 1269, added that the Nile flows past Ghana and Takrur into the Atlantic Ocean.[12]

Ibn Sa'id named the great lake where the Nile splits as Lake Kuri. An elaborated Ptolemy's theory is being collated with concrete evidence from an informant, a certain Ibn Fatima who traveled extensively in Africa. In connection with Lake Kuri, Ibn Sa'id quoted Ibn Fatima as saying: "I have never met anyone who has seen its southern side. It is navigated only by the people of Kanim and their neighbors, such as we encountered on the northern side."[13] Ibn Sa'id's Lake Kuri was therefore Lake Chad, on the northeastern corner of which was Kanim.

Ibn Sa'id fitted another piece of concrete evidence into the elaborated theory when he described not two but three "Niles" coming out of his Lake Kuri. In addition to the Nile of Egypt and the Nile of Ghana he also recorded the "Nil of Maqdishu."[14] Writing half a century after Ibn Sa'id and relying on him, though without acknowledgment, al-Dimashqi (d. 1327) was more specific concerning a river that "flows towards the east then bends towards the south and is the river of Maqdishu of the Zanj," which pours itself into "the Southern Sea."[15] *Zanj* is the term used by the Arabs for the black people of East Africa, and the "Southern Sea" is the designation of the Indian Ocean. Hence, the third river was undoubtedly the Juba River of Somalia.

Al-Dimashqi departed from earlier geographers by reserving the name Nile for the true Nile only, saying, "the river of the Nuba, otherwise called the Nil."[16] He referred to the two other "Niles" as "rivers" only. But the Nile that cuts across *Bilad al-Sudan* "resembles the Nil in its rise and fall and the manner of the tilling of its lands."[17]

The Nile of *Bilad al-Sudan* was in fact a creation of the Arab geographers, who gathered pieces of information from traders and travelers and put them together. They made one long river out of several rivers that flow in the region immediately south of the Sahara, between the Atlantic Ocean and the Nile itself. These rivers are the Senegal, the Niger, the Shari, Bahr al-Arab, and Bahr al-Ghazal. Some of these rivers flow from west to east and others from east to west. Al-Idrisi, and all those who followed him, made the long river flow from east to west, perhaps because they were aware that a river poured itself into the Atlantic Ocean.

But Ibn Battuta made the river flow in the other direction, from west to east. The reason was that Ibn Battuta, who visited *Bilad al-Sudan* in

1352 and 1353, sailed on the Niger River from Timbuktu to Gao and was able to ascertain its direction. From Gao he believed that the Nile continues to flow to the same direction, until it descends to "the Country of the Nuba, who are Christians, then to Dunqula. . . . Then it descends to the cataracts, which are the last district of the Sudan (meaning of the blacks) and the beginning of the district of Aswan of Upper Egypt."[18]

Ibn Battuta still considered the major river of *Bilad al-Sudan* to be part of the Nile system. Those who made this river flow from east to west had to make the two or three Niles split in a lake. But, for Ibn Battuta, who believed that the river continued in the direction that he saw, namely from west to east, the two Niles became one. The origin of the Egyptian Nile, according to Ibn Battuta, was therefore somewhere south of ancient Mali.

No more information on the Nile came from West Africa after the fourteenth century. Thus, our exploration of the Nile came to an end, together with the examination of a fascinating venture in following the Arabs' discovery of *Bilad al-Sudan*, a collation of theory, myth, and eyewitness evidence.

NOTES

1. Abu Ja'far Muhammad b. Musa al-Khuwarizmi, *Surat al-ard,* edited by Hans von Mzik, Vienna, 1926, pp. 106–107, also in N. Levtzion and J. F. P. Hopkins, *Corpus of Early Arabic Sources for West African History,* Cambridge, 1981, p. 9 (referred to in the following notes as *Corpus*).

2. Abu Bakr Ahmad b. Muhammad al-Hamadhani Ibn al-Faqih, *Mukhtasar kitab al-buldan,* edited by M. J. de Goeje, Leiden, 1885, p. 64, also in *Corpus,* p. 27.

3. Abu 'Ubayd 'Abd Allah b. 'Abd al-'Aziz al-Bakri, *Kitab al-masalik wa'l-mamalik,* edited by Baron MacGuckin de Slane, Leiden, 1911, p. 172, also in *Corpus,* p. 77.

4. Ibid., p. 173, also in *Corpus,* p. 78.

5. Ibid., pp. 177–178, also in *Corpus,* p. 82.

6. Ibid., pp. 180–181, also in *Corpus,* pp. 84–85.

7. Ibid., p. 175, also in *Corpus,* p. 80.

8. Abu 'Abd Allah Muhammad b. Muhammad al-Sharif al-Idrisi, *Nuzhat al-mushtaq fi ikhtiraq al-afaq,* edited by R. Dozy and M. J. de Goeje, Leiden, 1866, p. 6, also in *Corpus,* p. 109.

9. Ibid., p. 20, also in *Corpus,* p. 115.

10. Ibid., p. 6, also in *Corpus,* p. 109.

11. Ibid., p. 15, also in *Corpus,* p. 115.

12. Ali b. Musa Ibn Sa'id al-Maghribi, *Kitab bast al-ard fi'l-tul wa'l-'ard,* edited by J. Vernet Gines, Tetuan, 1958, p. 23, also in *Corpus,* 184.

13. Ibid., p. 27, also in *Corpus,* p. 187.

14. Ibid., pp. 27–28, also in *Corpus,* pp. 187–188.

15. Shams al-Din Abu 'Abd Allah Muhammad b. 'Ali Talib al-Ansari al-Dimashqi, *Nukhbat al-dahr fi 'aja'ib al-barr wa'l-bahr,* edited by M. A. F. Mehren, St. Petersburg, 1866, p. 89, also in *Corpus,* p. 206.

16. Ibid., p. 89, also in *Corpus,* p. 206.

17. Ibid., p. 110, also in *Corpus,* p. 207.

18. Shams al-Din Abu ‘Abd Allah Muhammad Ibn Battuta, *Tuhfat al-nuzzar fi ghara’ib al-amsar wa-‘ja’ib al-asfar,* edited by Defremery and Sanguinetti, Paris, 1858, pp. 395–396, also in *Corpus,* pp. 287–288.

VII

Islam in African and Global Contexts: Adventures in Comparative Studies of Islam[1]

For the past 30 years I have combined intensive studies of Islam in Africa with comparative studies of the same aspects across the Muslim world. Most general studies on Islam begin with the Central Lands of Islam, before taking account of the Further Lands of Islam (as suggested by the titles of the two volumes of the *Cambridge History of Islam*). Our own work, however, began with the experience of African Islam, because sometimes the view from the periphery offers new insights into the central world of Islam. This is the case with conversion to Islam, because patterns of Islamization may be more easily traced where the process took place closer to our own time.

In Africa, I chose to study the process of Islamization farther south on the fringes of the forest, in the Middle Volta Basin, where conversion to Islam has occurred mostly since the eighteenth century and is still going on. My early work was evaluated by Jan Vansina as follows: "Less dismissive views than Trimingham's [on African Islam] became dominant only after 1968, when Nehemia Levtzion published his *Muslims and Chiefs in West Africa.*"[2]

Field research on the frontiers of Islam provided a key to a better understanding of the process of Islamization farther north and earlier in time, in ancient Ghana and Mali. An article, "Patterns of Islamization in West Africa", first published in 1971, was my earliest attempt at a comparative study of Islamization.[3]

---

[1] This chapter was originally presented as a paper to the Conference on "Islam in Africa: A Global, Cultural and Historical Perspective", Binghamton University, 19–22 April, 2001.

[2] J. Vansina, *Living with Africa.* Madison: University of Wisconsin, 1994, p. 132.

[3] N. Levtzion, "Patterns of Islamization in West Africa", in *Aspects of West African Islam*, edited by D.F. McCall and N.R. Bennet. Boston: Boston University Press, 1971, pp. 31–39; reprinted in N. Levtzion, *Islam in West Africa: Religion, Society and Politics to 1800.* Aldershot: Variorum, 1994.

In eleventh-century Ghana, Muslims lived in a separate quarter, like the *zongo* in Kumasi, the Asante capital. They enjoyed the patronage of a non-Muslim king, who according to al-Bakrī, "was praised for his love of justice and generosity towards the Muslims."[4] A parallel situation was described by two British visitors to Kumasi, Bowdich and Dupuis, in 1817 and 1820 respectively. A Muslim community enjoyed a privileged position at the court of the Asantehene, where the Muslim headman, Baba, was a member of the king's council.[5]

As long as Islam was confined to the trading communities, there was a dispersion of Muslims rather than the spread of Islam. The process of Islamization took place when Muslims succeeded in winning over kings by demonstrating the omnipotence of Allāh. This is related by al-Bakrī for the eleventh-century chiefdom of Malal,[6] by the Kano Chronicle for fourteenth-century Kano,[7] and by the Gonja Chronicle for the sixteenth-century king of Gonja.[8] Kings were therefore the early recipients of Islamic influence, and centralized states were important in the process of Islamization.

In Malal, as in Gonja, only the king converted, while the common people remained loyal to the traditional religion. A similar situation existed in Gao, where according to the tenth-century al-Muḥallabī, "the king pretends to be a Muslim".[9] A century later, al-Bakrī said about Gao: "they entrust the kingship only to Muslims".[10] One may suggest that Islam of the royalty was a fiction. I arrived at that conclusion in my study of Islam in Dagomba, in northern Ghana. According to tradition, Islam was introduced to Dagomba during the reign of the eighteenth-century Na Zangina. In response to my question, "was Na Zangina a Muslim?", my Muslim informants responded reluctantly: "he was praying".[11]

---

[4] N. Levtzion and J.F.P. Hopkins, *Corpus of Early Arabic Sources for West African History.*, Princeton, NJ: Markus Wiener, 2nd edition, 2000, p. 79.

[5] T.E. Bowdich, *A Mission from Cape Coast Castle to Ashantee.* London, 1819, pp. 271–2, 393; J. Dupuis, *Journal of a Residence in Ashantee.* London, 1814, pp. 97, 161, 180, 243, 247.

[6] *Corpus* 2000, pp. 82–3.

[7] "The Kano Chronicle", in H.R. Palmer, *Sudanese Memoirs.* Lagos, 1928, iii, pp. 104–15.

[8] I.G. Wilks, N. Levtzion and B.M. Haight, *Chronicles from Gonja: A Tradition of West African Muslim Historiography.* Cambridge: Cambridge University Press, 1986.

[9] *Corpus* 2000, p. 174.

[10] Ibid., p. 87.

[11] N. Levtzion, *Muslims and Chiefs in West Africa.* Oxford: Clarendon Press, 1968, pp. 108–109.

Chiefs indeed prayed occasionally, but they were not fully committed Muslims. They maintained a middle position between Islam and the traditional religion, between an influential Muslim minority and the majority of their subjects. From their middle position, some rulers and dynasties moved towards greater commitment to Islam, as was the case with the kings of Mali and the Askiya dynasty of Songhay. The sixteenth-century Askiya Dāwūd of Songhay was visited in his court by a scholar from Timbuktu. The latter was shocked by the persistence of pre-Islamic practices at the court. He said to the Askiya: "I thought you were mad when I saw you doing all these." "No," the Askiya replied, "I am not mad myself, but I am the king of the mad."[12]

The experience of West African kingdoms like Songhay, Kano and Bornu suggests that even after internal attempts at reform, the dynasties remained tied to tradition. A more radical change was needed for an African kingdom to become fully commited to Islam. The Islamic revolutions of the eighteenth and nineteenth centuries brought Muslim scholars into positions of political power. For the first time, Islam moved into the centre of the socio-political system, as the only source of legitimacy for the state and its rulers. Under these circumstances, the commoners gradually moved towards Islam in order to become the privileged subjects of a Muslim state. Those who continued to follow the traditional religion were relegated to the lowest status and to the fringes of society.

My training was in Arabic language and literature and in the history of the Muslim peoples. My first encounter with conversion to Islam was in a class of the late Professor David Ayalon, who impressed us with his analysis of the conversion of the Turks on the fringes of *dār al-Islam* from the tenth century onwards. As a result of my African experience, I became convinced that conversion to Islam was a topic that lent itself to comparative study. An ambitious project, like a worldwide comparative study of conversion to Islam, called for a collaborative effort. The School of Oriental and African Studies (SOAS), where I did my doctoral studies, is unique in having specialists on Islam from all parts of the Muslim world. My proposal to colleagues at SOAS to hold a seminar on conversion to Islam met with great enthusiasm. The outcome of this seminar, held in 1973, was the book I edited on *Conversion to Islam* (1979). This, I believe, was the first general book on Islam edited by a scholar whose work focused on Islam in Africa. Indeed, the Introduction to this volume,

---

[12] *Ta'rīkh al-Fattāsh*, edited and translated by O. Houdas and M. Delafosse. Paris, 1913, p. 114, trans. pp. 208–10.

entitled "Toward a Comparative Study of Conversion to Islam", was inspired by my African experience.[13]

Contemporary evidence on conversion to Islam must come from external sources. Thus Ibn Faḍlān reported in the tenth century on the conversion of the Bulgars on the Volga, and Ibn Baṭṭūṭa provided eye-witness evidence on the state of Islam in fourteenth-century Mali. The Portuguese reported on the spread of Islam in Indonesia in the sixteenth century. Only gradually did Islamized societies articulate their own perception of the process of Islamization in narrative accounts. In West Africa, traditions on conversion are incorporated into local chronicles written in Arabic, such as the Gonja Chronicle and the Kano Chronicle. Interpretation of these traditions yield evidence on agents of Islamization, modes of conversion and the reaction of different sections of the society to this process.

Until the tenth century, conversion to Islam took place under Muslim political rule established by conquest. The militant expansion of Islam in the Fertile Crescent, Egypt and the Maghrib had been carried out by Arabs, the nomads of the desert. Later, the conquest of Asia Minor and India was carried out by the Turks, nomads of the steppes. Even the relatively few cases in Africa of Islamic militancy were linked to nomads. The Almoravid movement emerged among the nomad Sanhaja of the south-western Sahara in the eleventh century. The Fulbe pastoralists were the warriors of the *jihād* movements of the eighteenth and nineteenth centuries in West Africa.

In a paper presented to the seminar on conversion to Islam at SOAS, the late Mervyn Hiskett wrote about the process of Islamization that followed the successful *jihād* in Northern Nigeria: "Military conquest cannot, of itself, force men to abandon their beliefs and ideas. But the Muslim political authorities set up the institutions which, given time, will persuade them or pressure them into doing so." Hiskett's statement could apply to other cases of conversion under Muslim rule imposed by military conquest.

In Africa, as in Indonesia, Islam challenged syncretistic and latitudinarian religions and infiltrated into the religion of the politically dominant groups, in a process that eventually led to the Islamization of the state and the society. Where Islam had been adopted first by the upper classes and only later permeated other levels of the society, as in Africa and Indonesia, the revolutionary impact of Islamization was mitigated and pre-Islamic structures, customs and beliefs survived.

---

[13] N. Levtzion (ed.), *Conversion to Islam*. New York: Holmes & Meier, 1979, pp. 1–23.

Africa provides an excellent example for the contribution of a "trading diaspora" to the spread of Islam. Traders carried Islam to new lands, but were not themselves engaged in religious teaching. This was the role of the Muslim clerics, who rendered religious services to rulers.[14] We know more about the work of those rustic divines in Africa than elsewhere in the Muslim world. Non-Muslims sought the services of Muslim clerics, and were drawn into the orbit of Islam.[15]

In Africa, Islam was adopted by groups into their own social and cultural milieus, without breaking with past traditions. These were cases of communal conversion, when Islam won more adherents and gained larger territories, but its hold was superficial. Communal conversion is distinguished from individual conversion, when converts broke with their former social groups and moved to live within a Muslim community. Fewer people converted in this way, but because of the break with the past the impact of Islam was stronger and converts became fully committed to Islam. In a comparative study of Islamization, regions like Africa, Anatolia, Bengal and Java fall into the category of communal conversion, whereas the process in Egypt, Syria and Palestine was that of individual conversion.

The two patterns of communal and individual conversion can already be discerned at the time of the Prophet. When a man from the tribe of Juhayna came to pay allegiance to the Prophet he was asked what kind of a pledge he had in mind; whether *bay'a 'arabiyya* (the Bedouin's pledge) or *bay'at al-hijra* (the migrant's pledge).[16] The Bedouin's pledge was made on behalf a group that continued to follow their former way of life. In this pattern, whole tribes accepted Islam collectively without an act of conversion. On the other hand, the migrant's pledge was taken by those who had left their tribes to join the Muslim community in Medina. Their individual conversion implied a break with the past and an unqualified commitment to Islam.

In communal conversion, the agents of Islam emphasized what was common to Islam and to local religions. This process, where the initial demands made on the new Muslim were minimal, is called by Nock "adhesion", as distinguished

---

[14] N. Levtzion, "Merchants versus scholars and clerics in West Africa: Differential and complementary roles" in *Rural and Urban Islam in West Africa*, edited by N. Levtzion and H.J. Fisher. Boulder: Lynne Rienner, 1987, pp. 21–37; reprinted in N. Levtzion, *Islam in West Africa*, 1994.

[15] D. Owusu-Ansah, "Prayer, Amulets and Healing" in *The History of Islam in Africa*, edited by N. Levtzion and R.L. Pouwels. Athens: Ohio University Press, 2000, pp. 477–88.

[16] Ibn Sa'd, *Kitāb al-ṭabaqāt al-kabīr*, edited by J. Lippert. Leiden, 1908, iv, part 2, p. 66.

from "conversion".[17] With "adhesion", the completion of the initial commitment to Islam was achieved through reform movements. The full extent of the process can be observed in West Africa, from nominal acceptance, through revolutionary *jihād* movements, to conformity and commitment.

The rise of Islamic militancy in the eighteenth century was a radical departure from earlier patterns in West Africa. For centuries, Muslim clerics remained outside the arena of political competition. They never challenged the existing social and political order, and it was unthinkable that Muslims would take up arms. My next research question therefore was: under what circumstances did Muslim *'ulamā'* departed from the mode of accommodation to become revolutionaries?[18]

Several developments in the seventeenth and eighteenth centuries seem to have contributed to this change: the expansion of Islam from the towns to the countryside; the role of the Fulbe pastoralists; the destabilizing effects of the growth of slavery in West African societies; the contribution of Sufi brotherhoods; and the influence of the southern Sahara on militant movements on the desert edge. Whereas the first three factors are internal, the last two could be further investigated only in the wider context of the Muslim world. Once again, as in the case of the comparative study of Islamization, I needed the collaboration of scholars specializing in different parts of the Muslim world.

In 1985 I convened an international conference in Jerusalem, which resulted in the publication of a book, *Eighteenth-Century Renewal and Reform in Islam* (1987), edited by John Voll and myself. Viewed within a global context, the Islamic revolutions of the eighteenth and nineteenth centuries in West Africa were part of a worldwide wave of renewal and reform. Currents of renewal and reform could be identified in Egypt, North Africa, the Ottoman Empire and India, but militant movements erupted mostly in the periphery of the Muslim world; in China, Indonesia, Bengal, India, the Caucasus and West Africa.

Some historians suggested that these movements were ramifications of the Wahhābiyya, the best known and the most radical of these movements. This hypothesis, however, must be rejected, because unlike the anti-Sufi Wahhābiyya, all the other movements developed within reformed Sufi *ṭuruq*. Still, the leaders of these movements, including Muḥammad Ibn 'Abd al-

---

[17] A.D. Nock, *Conversion: The Old and New in Religion from Alexander the Great to Augustine of Hippo*. Oxford, 1933, p. 7.

[18] N. Levtzion, "Sociopolitical roles of Muslim clerics and scholars in West Africa" in *Comparative Social Dynamics: Essays in Honour of S. N. Eisenstadt*, edited by E. Cohen, M. Lissak and U. Almagor. Boulder: Westview Press, 1985, pp. 95–107; reprinted in Levtzion, *Islam in West Africa*, 1994.

Wahhāb, were linked together through networks made up of numerous scholastic and Sufi chains (*silsila*s) of masters and disciples. Mecca and Medina were the hub of this dynamic network, that brought together centre and periphery to create a global Muslim intellectual community.[19]

There were several West African connections to these networks. Ṣāliḥ al-Fūlanī (1752–1803) was the only West African scholar known to have earned a place of honour among the teaching scholars of the Ḥaramayn. He studied with Murtaḍā al-Zabīdī (1732–90), who was universally recognized as the greatest scholar of the age.[20] Jibrīl b. ʻUmar, ʻUthmān dan Fodio's mentor, visited Cairo in 1784 on his way to Mecca, where he also received an *ijāza* from Murtaḍā al-Zabīdī.

The West African reformists were inspired by the Khalwatiyya that dominated religious life in Egypt in the eighteenth century. Jibrīl b. ʻUmar was initiated into the Khalwatiyya by Aḥmad al-Dardīr (1715–80). ʻAbdallāh dan Fodio recorded his own Khalwatiyya *sanad* from his brother ʻUthmān, who obtained it from Jibrīl b. ʻUmar, who received it from Aḥmad al-Dardīr.[21] Muḥammad al-Ghālī, who reinitiated *al-ḥajj* ʻUmar into the Tijāniyya in the Hijāz, had himself been initiated into the Khalwatiyya by Maḥmud al-Kurdī (1715–80), who also initiated Aḥmad al-Tijānī, the founder of the Tijāniyya.[22]

ʻUthmān dan Fodio and his brother ʻAbdallah studied *Ḥadīth* with their paternal uncle, Muḥammad Raj. The latter studied in Medina in 1786 with Abu'l-Ḥasan al-Ṣaghīr, who had been the student of Muḥammad Ḥayya al-Sindī

---

[19] N. Levtzion and J.O. Voll, "Eighteenth-century renewal and reform movements in Islam: An Introductory Essay" in *Eighteenth-Century Renewal and Reform in Islam*, edited by N. Levtzion and J.O. Voll. Syracuse: Syracuse University Press, 1987, pp. 13–20; N. Levtzion and G. Weigert, "The Muslim holy cities as foci of Islamic revivalism in the eighteenth century" in *Sacred Space: Shrine, City, Land*, edited by B.Z. Kedar and R.J. Zwi Werblowsky. London: Macmillan, 1998, pp. 259–77.

[20] J.O. Hunwick, "Sāliḥ al-Fūlanī of Futa Jallon; an eighteenth-century scholar and *mujaddid*", *Bulletin of the School of Oriental and African Studies (BSOAS)*, 40 (1978), pp. 879–85; J.O. Hunwick, "Sāliḥ al-Fūlanī: the career and teachings of a West African *ʻālim* in Madina", in *In Quest of an Islamic Humanism: Arabic and Islamic Studies in Memory of Mohamed al-Nowaihi*, edited by A.H. Green. Cairo: American University in Cairo Press, 1984, pp. 139–54.

[21] J.O. Hunwick, "Accessions to microfilm collection: analytical list", *Research Bulletin: Centre of Arabic Documentation*. University of Ibadan, 1, 3 (1965), p. 48.

[22] ʻUmar b. Saʻīd al-Fūtī, *Rimāḥ ḥizb al-raḥīm*, in the margins of *Jawāhir al-Maʻānī*. Cairo, 1977, I, p. 190.

(d. 1750). The latter was among the teachers of Muḥammad Ibn ʻAbd al-Wahhāb, the founder of the Wahhābiyya.[23]

But networks by themselves could not explain the rise of social and political movements. My argument is that Sufi brotherhoods, which had themselves experienced radical structural changes, were the driving force behind the renewal and reform movements. Before the seventeenth century Sufi brotherhoods had been rather diffused, without a central organization. The direction of change in the eighteenth century was from old patterns of diffusive affiliations to larger-scale organizations, more coherent and centralized. The Nilotic Sudan provides some of the best examples of this process. Even in Morocco, a country of Sufism *par excellence*, there had been no structured hierarchical brotherhoods, but independent *zawāyā*, seats of holy men or *marabouts*. Only from the late seventeenth century did new brotherhoods evolve out of the local *zawāyā*, on a wider geographical and societal scale.[24]

In 1977 I was somewhat surprised to realise that there was no evidence in the chronicles of Timbuktu about Sufi brotherhoods, at least until the middle of the seventeenth century, but there were clear references in the chronicles to "mysticism and asceticism".[25] Turning to the study of Sufism in other parts of the Muslim world, I found that Sufism without brotherhoods was a more general phenomenon. Before the eighteenth century there had been Sufi shaykhs who belonged to no brotherhood at all, as was the case with the Bakrī shaykhs of Cairo in the sixteenth century.[26] It is significant that these Bakrī shaykhs were the spiritual mentors of the scholars of Timbuktu.[27]

Also, before the eighteenth century Sufi *shaykh*s were able to obtain initiation into several *ṭuruq*. Because medieval Sufi brotherhoods were only

---

[23] ʻAbdallāh b. Fūdī, *Tazyīn al-Waraqāt*, edited and translated by M. Hiskett. Ibadan, 1963, p. 36, trans. p. 95; J.O. Voll, "Muhammad Ḥayya al-Sindī and Muhammad ibn ʻAbd al-Wahhāb: An analysis of an intellectual group in eighteenth-century Medina", BSOAS, 38 (1975), pp. 32–39.

[24] N. Levtzion, "Eighteenth-Century Ṣūfī Brotherhoods: Structural, Organizational and Ritual Changes", in *Essays on Scripture, Thought and Society: A Festschrift in Honour of Anthony H. Johns*, edited by P.G. Riddell and T. Street. Leiden: Brill, 1997, pp. 147–60.

[25] N. Levtzion, "North Africa and the Western Sudan from 1050 to 1590", *Cambridge History of Africa*. Cambridge, UK, 1977, iii, p. 419.

[26] G. Weigert, "Three Bakri *ʻUlamā'* in Egypt at the End of the Mamluk and the Beginning of the Ottoman Periods", M.A. dissertation, Hebrew University of Jerusalem, 1985.

[27] ʻAbd al-Raḥman al-Saʻdī, *Taʻrīkh al-Sūdān*, edited and translated by O. Houdas. Paris, 1900, pp. 16–19, 29-34; trans. pp. 30–33, 48–57.

mystical chains (*salāsil*), that represented alternative devotional mystical ways (*ṭuruq*) to approach Allāh, Sufis even saw an advantage in experiencing more than one way to Allāh. Hence, meaningful distinctions between brotherhoods were blurred. Belonging to a brotherhood signified little more than an additional title to one's name.

Muṣṭafā al-Bakrī, under whose influence the Khalwatiyya in Egypt experienced a period of renewal, insisted that his own disciples should be affiliated exclusively to the Khalwatiyya, and ordered them to break their former allegiances to other *ṭuruq* and shaykhs.[28] Aḥmad al-Tijānī, founder of the Tijānīyya, had been a Khalwatī before he proclaimed his own *ṭarīqa*, and it was from the Khalwatiyya that he adopted the concept of exclusive affiliation.[29] Exclusivity gave greater cohesion to a *ṭarīqa*, and added to the commitment of its members. The Tijāniyya introduced exclusive affiliation as well as greater militancy to West Africa, an example of a brotherhood functioning as the organizational framework for a militant movement.[30]

Another feature of the new reformed brotherhoods was a positive attitude to this world, departing from the other-worldly orientation of most pre-eighteenth century Sufi brotherhoods. In Fez, Aḥmad al-Tijānī lived in comfort without any manifestation of asceticism. He opposed withdrawal from this world, and promised his followers access to paradise without forsaking their possessions. This positive attitude to worldly affairs attracted rich merchants and senior officials who joined the brotherhood.[31] In the Sahara, Sīdī al-Mukhtār al-Kuntī advocated a positive attitude towards the accumulation of wealth, and emphasized the direct link between religious piety and economic prosperity. For him, wealth was a clear sign of dignity and status.[32] This change in attitude towards this world prepared the reformed Sufi brotherhoods to be more actively involved in social and political affairs.

---

[28] G. Weigert, "The Khalwatiyya in Egypt in the Eighteenth Century", Ph.D. dissertation, Hebrew University of Jerusalem, 1989.

[29] B.G. Martin, "Notes sur l'origine de la tariqa des Tijaniyya et sur les débuts d'al-hajj 'Umar", *Revue des Etudes Islamiques*, 37 (1969), pp. 267–90.

[30] N. Levtzion, "Eighteenth-Century Renewal and Reform in Islam: The role of Sufi Turuq in West Africa", in Levtzion, *Islam in West Africa*, 1994. Louis Brenner, "Concepts of *tariqa* in West Africa", in *Charisma and Authority in African Islam*, edited by C. Cruise O'Brien and C. Coulon. Oxford, 1988, p. 49.

[31] N. Levtzion and G. Weigert, "Religious Reform in Eighteenth-century Morocco", in *North African, Arabic and Islamic Studies in Honor of Pessah Shinar*, published as *Jerusalem Studies in Arabic and Islam* 19 (1995), pp. 192–4.

[32] L. Brenner, "Concepts of *Tarīqa*", p. 39.

From the seventeenth century, Islam developed in rural areas in different parts of the Muslim world and particularly in the further lands of Islam, such as the Caucasus and Africa. In West Africa, the growth of Islam in the countryside after the seventeenth century made it possible to support a body of itinerant scholars and preachers. The new Muslim leaders began to articulate the grievances of the peasants, challenging the rulers and contributing to the radicalization of Islam. In Hausaland, 'Uthmān dan Fodio criticized the rulers for killing people, violating their honour and devouring their wealth. He declared that "to make war upon the oppressor is obligatory by assent".[33] 'Uthmān's son, the Sulṭān Muḥammad Bello, evoked the wrath of Allāh over "the *amir* who draws his sustenance from the people but does not bother to treat them justly".[34]

The expansion of Islam into the countryside widened the popular basis for religious teaching and preaching, and prepared the ground for the recruitment of common people to the brotherhoods. The dissemination of the knowledge of Islam to the peasants and herdsmen could only have been done in the vernacular languages. This might explain why written literatures in the Islamic vernacular languages reached maturity almost simultaneously all over the Muslim world in the seventeenth and eighteenth centuries – in India, Malaysia, East and West Africa. It is significant that mystical verse was the predominant genre in most vernacular literatures, because it served the charismatic shaykhs of Sufi brotherhoods as a means of communicating with the common people.

The earliest written poems in Fulfulde were by the leaders of the reformist movements, who had been active teachers and preachers, and who sought to reach people of all walks of life. Poetry became a major vehicle for teaching and preaching. Parallel to the transformation of Islam as a popular religion and a political force, Muslim societies developed a pious literature.[35] 'Abdallah dan Fodio described the preaching of his brother, the Shaykh 'Uthmān dan Fodio, in vernacular verse, and how this verse was used to mobilize people:

> Then we rose up with the Shaykh, helping him in his mission work for religion. He travelled for that purpose to the east and west, calling people

---

[33] 'Uthmān b. Fūdī, "*Wathīqāt ahl al-sūdān*", edited and translated by A.D.H. Bivar. *Journal of African* History, 2 (1961), pp. 235–44.

[34] Muhammad Bello, "*Uṣūl al-siyāsa*", edited and translated by B.G. Martin, in *Aspects of West African Islam*, edited by D.F. McCall and N.R. Bennet. Boston: African Studies Program, p. 80.

[35] A.I. Sow, *La femme, la vache, la foi: écrivains et pouvoir du Fouta Djalon*. Paris, 1966, pp. 12–13, 15; M. Hiskett, *A History of Hausa Islamic Verse*. London, 1975, p. 18.

> to the religion of God by his preaching and his *qaṣīda*s in *'ajamī*.[36] When the Shaykh saw that his community was ready for the *jihād*, he began to incite them to arms . . . and he set this in verse in his non-Arabic Qādirī poem (*qaṣīda 'ajamiyya qādiriyya*).[37]

This mystical verse had a hypnotic effect on devotees on the eve of the *jihād*.

Before the eighteenth century, knowledge of Islam had been the concern of an elitist minority, all of whom were literate in Arabic or Persian. After the eighteenth century, the discourse of the elite continued in the classical languages of Islam, while the vernacular literature was important in building bridges to the common people.[38]

In India, Muslim Sufis well as Hindu mystics turned to regional idioms for their preaching, because the sacred liturgical languages – Sanskrit, Arabic and Persian – were inaccessible to the masses. Mystical poetry in the regional idioms had been recited in *samā'* assemblies since the thirteenth century, but it was not committed to writing before the seventeenth century.[39] There is hardly any text in the north-western regional languages of India dated before the end of the sixteenth century. Sufis, especially those of the Chishti order, who sought to reach people who had no access to Arabic and Persian, led the way in breaking the literary taboo against the use of the Indian vernaculars.[40]

In sixteenth- and seventeenth-century Egypt, a period of literary decline, when works of theology and law were written in bombastic style Sufis wrote in precise, down-to-earth language.[41] Also, the preaching of Imām Manṣūr in the Caucasus in 1785 is said to have been simple and directed at the peasants.[42]

---

[36] 'Abdallah b. Fūdī, *Tazyīn al-Waraqāt*, p. 85.

[37] *Ibid.*, p. 51.

[38] A. Schimmel, *Islamic Literatures of India*. Wiesbaden, 1973, pp. 48–50; A. Schimmel, *Pain and Grace: A Study of Two Mystical Writers in Eighteenth-century Muslim India*. Leiden, 1976, pp. xi, 11.

[39] Schimmel, *Pain and Grace*, 1976, p. 12; A. Schimmel, *As Through a Veil: Mystical Poetry in Islam*, New York, 1982, pp. 138, 141–2, 148–50.

[40] C. Shackle, "Early vernacular poetry in the Indus valley: Its contexts and its character" in *Islam and Indian Regions*, edited by A.L. Dallapicola and S. Zingel-Ave Lallemant. Stuttgart, 1993, pp. 265, 285; A. Roy, *The Islamic Syncretistic Tradition in Bengal*. Princeton, 1984, p. 58.

[41] M. Winter, *Society and Religion in Early Ottoman Egypt: Studies in the Writings of 'Abd al-Wahhāb al-Sha'rānī*. New Brunswick, 1982, p. 27.

[42] A. Bennigsen, "Un mouvement populaire au Caucase au 18e siècle: la guerre sainte du sheikh Mansur, 1785-1791", *Cahiers du Monde Russe et Soviétique* 2 (1964), p. 195.

Presented in a global context, through comparative studies of different aspects of Islam, African Islam has been shaking off its marginality. The history of Islam in Africa becomes more meaningful when viewed in a worldwide context, and not in isolation.

Bibliography

Bello, M. "*Uṣūl al-siyāsa*", edited and translated by B.G. Martin, in *Aspects of West African Islam*, edited by D.F. McCall and N.R. Bennet. Boston: African Studies Program.

Bennigsen, A. "Un mouvement populaire au Caucase au 18e siècle: la guerre sainte du sheikh Mansur, 1785-1791", *Cahiers du Monde Russe et Soviétique* 2 (1964).

Bowdich, T.E. *A Mission from Cape Coast Castle to Ashantee*. London, 1819.

Brenner, L. "Concepts of *tariqa* in West Africa", in *Charisma and Authority in African Islam*, edited by C. Cruise O'Brien and C. Coulon. Oxford, 1988.

Dupuis, J. *Journal of a Residence in Ashantee*. London, 1814.

b. Fūdī, 'Abdallāh. *Tazyīn al-Waraqāt*, edited and translated by M. Hiskett. Ibadan, 1963, p. 36, trans. p. 95.

b. Fūdī, 'Uthmān. "*Wathīqāt ahl al-sūdān*", edited and translated by A.D.H. Bivar. *Journal of African* History, 2 (1961), pp. 235–44.

al-Fūtī, 'Umar b. Sa'īd. *Rimāḥ ḥizb al-raḥīm*, in the margins of *Jawāhir al-Ma'ānī*. Cairo, 1977, I, p. 190.

Hiskett, M. *A History of Hausa Islamic Verse*. London, 1975.

Houdas, O. and M. Delafosse (eds. and trans.) *Ta'rīkh al-Fattāsh*, Paris, 1913.

Hunwick, J.O. "Accessions to microfilm collection: analytical list", *Research Bulletin: Centre of Arabic Documentation*. University of Ibadan, 1, 3 (1965).

Hunwick, J.O. "Sāliḥ al-Fūlanī of Futa Jallon; an eighteenth-century scholar and *mujaddid*", *Bulletin of the School of Oriental and African Studies (BSOAS)*, 40 (1978), pp. 879–85.

Hunwick, J.O. "Sāliḥ al-Fūlanī: the career and teachings of a West African *'ālim* in Madina", in *In Quest of an Islamic Humanism: Arabic and Islamic Studies in Memory of Mohamed al-Nowaihi*, edited by A.H. Green. Cairo: American University in Cairo Press, 1984, pp. 139–54.

Ibn Sa'd, *Kitāb al-ṭabaqāt al-kabīr*, edited by J. Lippert. Leiden, 1908.

Levtzion, N. (ed.), *Conversion to Islam*. New York: Holmes & Meier, 1979.

Levtzion, N. "Eighteenth-Century Renewal and Reform in Islam: The role of Sufi Turuq in West Africa", in Levtzion, *Islam in West Africa*, 1994.

Levtzion, N. "Eighteenth-Century Ṣūfī Brotherhoods: Structural, Organizational and Ritual Changes", in *Essays on Scripture, Thought and Society: A Festschrift in Honour of Anthony H. Johns*, edited by P.G. Riddell and T. Street. Leiden: Brill, 1997, pp. 147–60.

Levtzion, N. "Merchants versus scholars and clerics in West Africa: Differential and complementary roles" in *Rural and Urban Islam in West Africa*, edited by N. Levtzion and H.J. Fisher. Boulder: Lynne Rienner, 1987, pp. 21–37; reprinted in N. Levtzion, *Islam in West Africa*, 1994.

Levtzion, N. *Muslims and Chiefs in West Africa*. Oxford: Clarendon Press, 1968.

Levtzion, N. "North Africa and the Western Sudan from 1050 to 1590", *Cambridge History of Africa*, vol. 3, edited by R. Oliver. Cambridge, 1977, pp. 331–462.

Levtzion, N. "Patterns of Islamization in West Africa", in *Aspects of West African Islam*, edited by D.F. McCall and N.R. Bennet. Boston: Boston University Press, 1971, pp. 31–39; reprinted in N. Levtzion, *Islam in West Africa*: Religion, Society and Politics to 1800. Aldershot: Variorum, 1994.

Levtzion, N. "Sociopolitical roles of Muslim clerics and scholars in West Africa" in *Comparative Social Dynamics: Essays in Honour of S.N. Eisenstadt*, edited by E. Cohen, M. Lissak and U. Almagor. Boulder: Westview Press, 1985, pp. 95–107; reprinted in Levtzion, *Islam in West Africa*, 1994.

Levtzion, N. and J.F.P. Hopkins, *Corpus of Early Arabic Sources for West African History*, Princeton, NJ: Markus Wiener, 2nd edition, 2000.

Levtzion, N. and J.O. Voll, "Eighteenth-century renewal and reform movements in Islam: An Introductory Essay" in *Eighteenth-Century Renewal and Reform in Islam*, edited by N. Levtzion and J.O. Voll. Syracuse: Syracuse University Press, 1987, pp. 13–20.

Levtzion, N. and G. Weigert, "Religious Reform in Eighteenth-century Morocco", in *North African, Arabic and Islamic Studies in Honor of Pessah Shinar*, published as Jerusalem Studies in Arabic and Islam 19 (1995), pp. 192–4.

Levtzion, N. and G. Weigert, "The Muslim holy cities as foci of Islamic revivalism in the eighteenth century" in *Sacred Space: Shrine, City, Land*, edited by B.Z. Kedar and R.J. Zwi Werblowsky. London: Macmillan, 1998, pp. 259–77.

Martin, B.G. "Notes sur l'origine de la tariqa des Tijaniyya et sur les débuts d'al-hajj 'Umar", *Revue des Etudes Islamiques*, 37 (1969), pp. 267–90.

Nock, A.D. *Conversion: The Old and New in Religion from Alexander the Great to Augustine of Hippo*. Oxford, 1933.

Owusu-Ansah D. "Prayer, Amulets and Healing" in *The History of Islam in Africa*, edited by N. Levtzion and R.L. Pouwels. Athens: Ohio University Press, 2000, pp. 477–88.

Palmer, H.R. *Sudanese Memoirs*. Lagos, 1928.

Roy, A. *The Islamic Syncretistic Tradition in Bengal*. Princeton, 1984.

al-Saʻdī, ʻAbd al-Raḥman. *Taʻrīkh al-Sūdān*, edited and translated by O. Houdas. Paris, 1900.

Schimmel, A. *As Through a Veil: Mystical Poetry in Islam*. New York, 1982.

Schimmel, A. *Islamic Literatures of India*. Wiesbaden, 1973.

Schimmel, A. *Pain and Grace: A Study of Two Mystical Writers in Eighteenth-century Muslim India*. Leiden, 1976.

Shackle, C. "Early vernacular poetry in the Indus valley: Its contexts and its character", in *Islam and Indian Regions*, edited by A.L. Dallapicola and S. Zingel-Ave Lallemant. Stuttgart, 1993.

Sow, A.I. *La femme, la vache, la foi: écrivains et pouvoir du Fouta Djalon*. Paris, 1966.

Vansina, J. *Living with Africa*. Madison: University of Wisconsin, 1994.

Voll, J.O. "Muhammad Ḥayya al-Sindī and Muhammad ibn ʻAbd al-Wahhāb: An analysis of an intellectual group in eighteenth-century Medina", *BSOAS*, 38 (1975), pp. 32–39.

Weigert, G. "The Khalwatiyya in Egypt in the Eighteenth Century", Ph.D. dissertation, Hebrew University of Jerusalem, 1989.

Weigert, G. "Three Bakri *'Ulamā'* in Egypt at the End of the Mamluk and the Beginning of the Ottoman Periods", M.A. dissertation, Hebrew University of Jerusalem, 1985.

Wilks, I.G., N. Levtzion and B.M. Haight, *Chronicles from Gonja: A Tradition of West African Muslim Historiography*. Cambridge: Cambridge University Press, 1986.

Winter, M. *Society and Religion in Early Ottoman Egypt: Studies in the Writings of ʻAbd al-Wahhāb al-Shaʻrānī*. New Brunswick, 1982.

VIII

THE ALMORAVIDS IN THE SAHARA AND *BILĀD AL-SŪDĀN*: A STUDY IN ARAB HISTORIOGRAPHY

The Sources

From Cordova in Andalusia, Abū ʿUbaydallah al-Bakrī observed and recorded the rise of the Almoravid movement in the south-western Sahara and in southern Morocco over a period of twenty years, from 440/-1048 to 460/1068. An analysis of al-Bakrī's detailed descriptions and dynamic accounts of Morocco, the Sahara and *Bilād al-Sūdān*[1] reveals that he had an inquisitive mind; he skillfully combined written and oral narratives, as well as historical and contemporary sources. Al-Bakrī thus provided a solid and reliable basis for exploring the historiography of the Almoravids.

Our next valuable source is Abū ʿAbdallah Muḥammad al-Zuhrī. All that is known about him, from references in his own work, is that he visited some towns in al-Andalus between 532/1137 and 549/1154. His informants about Ghāna and its neighbours could have been "some of their chief leaders [who] have come to al-Andalus." Al-Zuhrī offers some intriguing pieces of information on *Bilād al-Sūdān* in the aftermath of the Almoravids. The material found in his work is subjected to conflicting interpretations by modern historians.

Abū 'l-Faḍl ʿIyāḍ al-Sabtī, known as *al-qāḍī* ʿIyāḍ (476/1083–544/-1149), lived under the Almoravids, and was their ardent supporter. Though his biography of ʿAbdallah b. Yāsīn was written less than a century after the death of Ibn Yāsīn, his narrative is totally different from that of al-Bakrī. ʿIyāḍ's narrative was followed by Ibn al-Athīr (555/1160–630/1233), and through the latter by Ibn Khallikān (608/1211–681/1282). Ibn Khallikān [129/165][2] refers to Ibn al-Athīr as "our *shaykh*."

[1] The term *sūdān* refers to the black people of West Africa, just as the black people of East Africa are referred to in the Arabic sources as *zanj* or *zunūj*.

[2] The Arabic sources are referred to in square brackets in the text as follows: [page number of the edition of the Arabic text/page number to the English translation in the Corpus]. The present reference, for example, is to the Arabic text of Ibn Khallikān, p. 129, and to the English translation in the Corpus, p. 165. The Corpus refers to *Corpus of Early Arabic Sources for West African History* by N. Levtzion and J.F.P. Hopkins (Cambridge University Press, 1981, second edition, Princeton, 2000). A list of the Arabic sources appears at the end of the article in chronological

Other than al-Qāḍī ʿIyāḍ, Ibn al-Athīr and Ibn Khallikān, the other chronicles of the Almoravids from the fourteenth century follow al-Bakrī's account before starting their own narratives.

Ibn ʿIdhārī, who wrote around 712/1312 is by far the most informative and reliable of all the fourteenth century historians. He enriched al-Bakrī's account by drawing on other sources, which are not otherwise available. One of them was a work by Yaḥyā b. al-Sayrafī, who died in 557/1162, a scribe in the service of the Almoravids. From his history of the Almoravids, Ibn ʿIdhārī derived genealogical information about the leaders of the Almoravids [77/232]. The anonymous author of *al-Ḥulal al-mawshiyya*, written in 783/1381, also consulted the work of al-Sayrafī.

The last group of sources consists of Aḥmad b. Abī Zarʿ, who died around 715/1315 and Ibn Khaldūn (732/1332–806/1406). The text of Ibn Abī Zarʿ is in fact a manipulation of al-Bakrī's text, enriched by the historian's creative mind. Ibn Abī Zarʿ, however, has a series of quite reliable dates, which he borrowed from an unknown source.

Ibn Khaldūn follows the text of Ibn Abī Zarʿ rather uncritically. Ibn Khaldūn's account becomes more valuable as he embarks on a fascinating exploration of oral traditions that he had recorded from informants from *Bilād al-Sūdān* whom he met in Cairo.

Berbers and *sūdān* before the eleventh century

Between the fourth and the eighth centuries C. E. the southern Sahara was infiltrated by Berber-speaking pastoralists, who gradually replaced the sedentary black population that had inhabited parts of the southern Sahara. But as late as the eleventh century, remnants of those *sūdān* waylaid caravans six days north of Awdaghust [al-Bakrī 157/67].

The earliest reference to Awdaghust, the major town of the southern Sahara, is in al-Yaʿqūbī's *Kitāb al-buldān,* written in 276/889–90:

> He who travels from Sijilmāsa towards the south, making for *Bilād al-Sūdān*, ... goes in a desert a distance of 50 stages. Then he will meet a people called Anbiya, of the Ṣanhāja, who have no permanent dwellings. It is their custom to veil their faces with their turbans. ... Then the traveller will reach a town called Ghust, which is an inhabited valley with dwellings. It is the residence of their king, who has no religion or law. He raids the land of the *sūdān*, who have many kingdoms [360/22].

In his *Taʾrīkh* [219–220/21] written in 259/872–3, al-Yaʿqūbī enumerated many kingdoms of the *sūdān*. The so-called "king of the Ṣanhāja"

---

order; the editions are cited in the references.

was not a Muslim and raided the land of the *sūdān*. He was a tribal chief, who had accumulated wealth and power from his position as the guardian of Awdaghust, the terminus of the Saharan trade. But as a nomad he must have lived outside Awdaghust, just as the Tuareg chief, who was in control of Timbuktu in the fifteenth century, lived outside that city.[3]

We learn more about Awdaghust and the Ṣanhāja from Ibn Ḥawqal. He travelled in the Maghrib and Spain in the years 336/947–340/951, and visited Sijilmāsa in 340/951. He saw there a promissory note of 42,000 *dīnār*s in the possession of Abū Isḥāq Ibrāhīm. The debtor, Muḥammad b. Saʿdūn, a trader from Sijilmāsa, lived at that time in Awdaghust. The creditor, Abū Isḥāq Ibrāhīm, used to travel between Sijilmāsa and Awdaghust. He was the informant of Ibn Ḥawqal [99–100/47–48] about Awdaghust and its "king," who by the tenth century had converted to Islam.

Ibn Ḥawqal's information is complemented by that of his contemporary Muḥammad b. Yūsuf al-Warrāq (292/904–363/973). His geographical work, now lost, was consulted by al-Bakrī [158–159/68–69]. According to al-Warrāq, most of the inhabitants of Awdaghust in the tenth century were natives of Ifrīqiya and its Saharan oases. They were Ibāḍī merchants, who controlled the Saharan trade.

The Ṣanhāja "king" of Awdaghust (Tinbarutan according to Ibn Ḥawqal or Tinyarutan according to al-Warrāq) brought weaker nomadic tribes under his protection. His authority extended farther south, and was recognised by more than twenty kings of the *sūdān*. He invaded one of those kingdoms (Awgham) at the request of another king of the *sūdān* (Masin). Ibn Ḥawqal highlighted another aspect of the relations between the *sūdān* and Berbers on the desert-edge:

> The king of Awdaghust maintains relations with the ruler of Ghāna. Ghāna is the wealthiest king on the face of the earth because of his treasures and stocks of gold extracted in olden times for his predecessors and himself. They [the kings of Ghāna and Kugha] stand in pressing need of [the goodwill of] the kings of Awdaghust because of the salt which comes to them from the lands of Islam. They cannot do without this salt [101/49].

Gold, which lubricated the economy of the Maghrib, was exchanged for salt, a basic element in the diet of the *sūdān*. This exchange is the key for understanding the economy and politics of the desert-edge.

[3] *Ta'rīkh al-Fattāsh*, ed. O. Houdas and M. Delafosse (Paris, 1913–14), text 22, trans. 38.

Almost a century after Ibn Ḥawqal and al-Warrāq, when the Almoravids conquered Awdaghust in 446/1054, they "persecuted the people of Awdaghust only because they recognized the authority of the king of Ghāna" [al-Bakrī 167–168/74]. There had not necessarily been a military conquest of Awdaghust by Ghāna. It is likely that Ghāna was then at the peak of its power, and the merchants of Awdaghust might have thought that their commercial interests would be better served if they recognized the authority of the king of Ghāna.

By the eleventh century Islam became established among the Ṣanhāja of the southern Sahara, whose leaders exhibited their piety by performing the pilgrimage [al-Bakrī 164/70]. The raids of the Ṣanhāja king of the ninth century, as described by al-Yaʿqūbī [360/22], turned into a *jihād* in the eleventh century. Muḥammad, known as Tarashni, "king of the Ṣanhāja" was killed in the land of the *sūdān* [al-Bakrī 164/70].

Takrūr, on the Senegal River, became Muslim under the influence of their nomad neighbours, the Gudāla, "whose territory touches the land of the *sūdān*" [al-Bakrī 172/77]. The king of Takrūr War-Dyabe, who forced his people to accept Islam, died in 432/10401, or about the time ʾAbdallah b. Yāsīn first came to the desert. As a Muslim state, Takrūr became an ally of the Almoravids. Labi, son of War Dyabe, fought with the Lamtūna Almoravids against the Gudāla in 448/1056–7 [al-Bakrī 167/73].

The Almoravids in the Tradition of Mālikī Militancy

According to the master narrative of the Almoravids' history [al-Bakrī, 165/71], Yaḥyā b. Ibrāhīm, the chief of the Gudāla, went on pilgrimage. During his return journey he met the jurist Abū ʿImrān al-Fāsī in Qayrawān. When the Gudāla chief realized that Islam in the Sahara was deficient, he asked Abū ʿImrān to send one of his disciples with him to the desert. None of Abū ʿImrān's students in Qayrawān wished to undertake this trip, and Abū ʿImrān sent Yaḥyā to his former student Wajjāj b. Zalwī in southern Morocco. Wajjāj chose among his disciples ʿAbdallah b. Yāsīn, whom he considered most suitable, because his mother was of the Jazūla, from the edge of the desert enjoining Ghāna.

According to the chronology of Ibn Abī Zarʿ [77, 78/237, 239], Yaḥyā b. Ibrāhīm left for the pilgrimage in 427/1036, and met Wajjāj in Rajab 430/March-April 1039. It follows that Yaḥyā, the Gudāla chief, met Abū ʿImrān al-Fāsī in Qayrawān shortly before Abū ʿImrān died in Ramaḍān 430/June 1039.

According to the fourteenth century anonymous *Mafākhir al-Barbar* [69/232], "Wajjāj and Ibn Yāsīn were responsible for the emergence of the *mulaththamūn*, known as *murābiṭūn*, from the desert by the order of

Abū ʿImrān al-Fāsī." This text implies that the Almoravid movement was masterminded by three *fuqahāʾ*, who represented three generations of masters and disciples, and formed the link between Qayrawān, southern Morocco and the Sahara.

These three *fuqahāʾ* represented a militancy of the Mālikī school in Ifrīqiya that was the result of a long struggle for survival of persecution by successive religious rivals; Ḥanafī scholars and Muʿtazilī theologians, supported by the Aghlabid rulers, and Ismāʿīlī missionaries supported by the Fāṭimids. Piety and self- sacrifice won popular support for the Mālikī *fuqahāʾ* among the common people. Abū ʿImrān al-Fāsī was among the Mālikī *fuqahāʾ* who encouraged the Zīrīd governors of Ifrīqiya to break away from their Fāṭimid overlords.[4]

Many Mālikī *fuqahāʾ* combined the study of *fiqh* with the practice of *zuhd* (asceticism). They were trained in the *ribāṭs*, which in the ninth and tenth centuries ceased to function as military outposts against the Byzantine fleet, and became centres of devotion and propagation of Sunnī Islam. The *murābiṭūn* (*ribāṭ* dwellers) were thus imbued with a mission to carry out a perpetual *jihād*. The Mālikī tradition of militancy became diffused over the Maghrib through disciples who returned to their homeland, as in the case of Wajjāj, a disciple of Abū ʿImrān, who returned to his homeland in southern Morocco. There he built *Dār al-murābiṭīn* "for students of religious learning and reciters of the Qur'ān" [al-Tādilī 66/155, also *al-qāḍī* ʿIyāḍ, 781–2/101–2].

Dār al-murābiṭīn of Wajjāj was a stronghold of Sunnī Islam in the mountains of Southern Morocco. These mountains had become a refuge for various heretical groups, like the Barghawāṭa, an ethnic group that apostatized, and recognized their own prophet who revealed to them a Berber Qur'ān, and for extreme Shīʿī sects. *Jihād* against these heretics was considered a religious obligation. *Dār al-murābiṭīn* of Wajjāj, which carried on the militant spirit of Qayarwān, bequeathed it in its turn to the Almoravids.

It is likely that the name of the movement is derived from the name of Wajjāj's *Dār al-murābiṭīn.* The term *ribāṭ* carried the meaning of *jihād.*[5] Al-Bakrī [164, 169/70, 75] says that Ibn Yāsīn "called the people to the *ribāṭ*" (in the sense of *jihād*), and that the Almoravids compelled those whom they vanquished "to join their *ribāṭ*." Other sources [Ibn ʿIdhārī 49/220–21, Ibn al-Athīr 426/160, and Ibn Khaldūn 238/329], each in their own way, explain the name *al-murābiṭūn* given to them by Ibn

[4] N. Levtzion, "ʿAbdallah b. Yāsīn and the Almoravids," in J.R. Willis, ed., *Studies in West African Islamic History*, (London, 1979), pp. 78–80. Reprinted in N. Levtzion, *Islam in West Africa* (Aldershot, 1994).

[5] P.F. Moraes Farias, "The Almoravids: Some Questions Concerning the Character of the Movement During its Periods of Closest Contact with the Sūdān." *Bulletin de l'IFAN* (Dakar) 29B (1967): 802–4.

Yāsīn as a reward for their successful *jihād.*

Going back to the suggestion that the Almoravid movement was masterminded at *Dār al-murābiṭīn* of Wajjāj, some texts might even imply that Wajjāj sent ʿAbdallah b. Yāsīn to recruit the nomads of the desert to eradicate heresy from southern Morocco. Ibn Yāsīn continued to communicate with Wajjāj, and when he encountered the hostility of the Gudāla, "he left the tribes of the Ṣanhāja secretly and travelled to Wajjāj." Wajjāj seems to have had some moral authority in the desert, for "he reproached them ... and informed them that whoever disobeyed [Ibn Yāsīn] would be regarded as severing himself from the community...He then ordered Ibn Yāsīn to return to them" [al-Bakrī 166/72].

According to Ibn Abī Zarʿ [80–81/241–42], Ibn Yāsīn "sent much of the wealth collected from the legal alms, the tithe and the fifth, to the scholars and *qāḍīs* of the land of the Masamida." Undoubtedly he sent the alms to his master Wajjāj and his disciples. Ibn Abī Zarʿ even says that the Almoravids moved north to conquer Morocco in response to the invitation of "the pious men of Siljilmāsa and Dārʿa." The latter "wrote to the *faqīh* ʿAbdallah b. Yāsīn, to the *amīr* Yaḥyā b. ʿUmar and the Almoravid *shaykhs*, urging them to come to their country to purify it of the evil practices, the injustice, and tyranny which were rife there." Following Ibn Abī Zarʿ, Ibn Khaldūn [238/330] is even more explicit, saying that it was Wajjāj himself who invited the Almoravids to the Maghrib. Ibn Abī Zarʿ may represent a fourteenth century Maghribī perception of the role of the Almoravids, rather than a concrete reconstruction of a series of events.

Ibn Yāsīn had visited the land of the heretic al-Barghawāṭa before his departure to the desert [Ibn ʿIdhārī 48/219]. Committed to the eradication of all heretics in southern Morocco, Ibn Yāsīn, at the head of the Almoravids, led the fighting against the Barghawāṭa, where he was killed [al-Bakrī 168/74, Ibn ʿIdhārī 52/223–4]. Abū Bakr b. ʿUmar, the military head of the Almoravids, accomplished Ibn Yāsīn's mission. "He routed the Barghawāṭa. ... They submitted to him and accepted Islam anew" [Ibn Abī Zarʿ 85/246]. The Almoravids continued their warfare against heretics and destroyed a Shīʿī stronghold in Tarudant [Ibn Abī Zarʿ 82/243, 84/244]. The Almoravids also contributed to reduce the presence of the Ibāḍiyya to several isolated oases in the northern Sahara.

There are different versions which describe the way Ibn Yāsīn reacted to the hostility of the Gudāla. Once again the narrative of Ibn Abī Zarʿ [79/240] is the most creative, but probably also the furthest from reality. He describes Ibn Yāsīn's *hijra* from the hostile Gudāla to an island where he built a *rābiṭa* or *ribāṭ*. It was, according to Ibn Abī Zarʿ, after this *ribāṭ* that Ibn Yāsīn called his followers *murābiṭūn*. Ibn

Khaldūn [238/329], who followed Ibn Abī Zarʿ in proposing a *hijra* to an island, did not assume the construction of a physical *ribāṭ*. Rather, Ibn Yāsīn and his followers "entered the thickets of this island, withdrawing to worship God."

Al-qāḍī ʿIyāḍ of Ceuta (476–544/1083–1149), writing about half a century or more after al-Bakrī, offers the only alternative narrative to that of al-Bakrī. According to *al-qāḍī* ʿIyāḍ [781/102], Ibn Yāsīn was brought to the Sahara not by a Gudāla chief, as in the main narrative, but by al-Jawhar "a man of the Jazūla (sic), one of those who love virtue." Jazūla is probably a mistake for Gudāla. The two narratives, however, agree that al-Jawhar, described by al-Bakrī [165/71] as "a man learned in law," disputed Ibn Yāsīn's legal pronouncements and led the Gudāla's revolt against Ibn Yāsīn.

Ibn Yāsīn's Mālikīsm is presented by al-Bakrī [165, 169–170/71,74–75] as an inferior religious form, a sort of religion made simple for rude Saharan camel-breeders. Ibn Yāsīn himself is described as ignorant. But it was this new doctrine that inspired the Saharan nomads and helped harness their energies. These nomads, in the words of one of the *shaykh*s of the Maṣmūda, are not "willing to submit to the judgement of anyone not from their own tribe" [Ibn ʿIdhārī 48/219]. A religious leader and a religious mission united the nomads, as in the days of the Prophet, as well as in other cases of Islamic religious movements that emerged among pastoralists. Still, the leaders of the Almoravids had to meet the challenge of tribal dissension more than once.

The Tribal Factor in the Almoravid Movement

In the tenth and eleventh centuries there were internal conflicts among different tribes and factions of the Ṣanhāja. Ibn Ḥawqal [100–01/48] described a battle in which the Ṣanhāja "king," with the help of reinforcements from his wealthy sister, defeated another Berber tribe. Conflicts between the Lamtūna and the Gudāla erupted at crucial moments in the early history of the Almoravids.

Soon after Ibn Yāsīn came with Yaḥyā b. Ibrāhīm, the Gudāla chief, his people "raided the Banu Lamtūna, whom they besieged on one of their mountains. They defeated them, and regarded what they had taken of their possessions as booty" [al-Bakrī 165/71]. In the desert economy, raiding for booty was a legitimate way to generate resources needed to achieve military superiority. The rule stipulated by Ibn Yāsīn that a third of the property of defeated tribes must be confiscated, as a means of "purifying" the remaining two thirds, effectively augmented the Almoravids' resources [al-Bakrī 166/72].

According to Ibn Abī Zarʿ [79–80/241] and Ibn Khaldūn [i238/329], when the Almoravids came out of their retreat, they "sallied forth and fought those among the tribes of Lamtūna, Gudāla (Jazūla in Ibn Khaldūn), and Masūfa, who resisted them until they returned to the truth." This was in Ṣafar 434/September-October 1042.

After he had been rejected by the Gudāla, Ibn Yāsīn accepted the allegiance of two Lamtūna chiefs, Yaḥyā and ʿUmar, sons of Abū Bakr. The Lamtūna then turned against the Lamta, another Ṣanhāja tribe [al-Bakrī 166/72]. When Ibn Yāsīn became settled among the Lamtūna, he employed "trickery against those of the Gudāla who had rebelled against him. He ordered that all of those who merited death among them should be killed" [Ibn ʿIdhārī 47/218]. In 446/1054–5, when the Almoravids were consolidating their rule over Siljilmāsa, the Gudāla broke away, and went to the coast. Yaḥyā b. ʿUmar was ordered by Ibn Yāsīn to go back to the desert. He was killed in the battle against the Gudāla in 448/1056–7 [al-Bakrī 167–8/73; also Ibn ʿIdhārī 50–51/222].

Ibn Yāsīn sent the senior commander of the Almoravids back to the desert to deal with the Gudāla revolt, and appointed his brother, Abū Bakr b. ʿUmar, as commander of the troops in the Maghrib. Fifteen years later, in the year 463/1070–1, once again, the senior commander, Abū Bakr b. ʿUmar went back to the desert and left a deputy, Yūsuf b. Tāshfīn, to command the Maghrib. This is an indication of the importance of the desert for the Almoravids.

In 463/1070–1 Abū Bakr b. ʿUmar was supervising the building of the walls of Marrakech, when a man came to him, riding on a horse, with his hair in disarray. He said, "the Gudāla have made raids on your brothers and have killed men and seized property and routed them." Abū Bakr replied: "I am going to travel there, if God wills, to seek revenge." He appointed Yūsuf b. Tāshfīn as his deputy, and left a third of the Lamtūna with him. He waged war against the Gudāla until he took revenge on them [Ibn ʿIdhārī 55–56/227–8]. The same sense of urgency and commitment to the desert is presented by Ibn Khaldūn [239/330]:

> When Abū Bakr received news of discord which had broken out between Lamtūna and Masūfa (sic) in the desert, where the stock of their leaders, the tap-roots of their family tree, and the source of their military strength lay, he feared the collapse of their cohesion, and the severance of the bonds of their unity, so he proceeded to rectify this state of affairs by returning to his base.

Abū Bakr b. ʿUmar was a man of the desert; "a simple good-natured man, having no inclination for a luxurious life, preferring his own country to the land of the Maghrib." This is a description of Abū Bakr by the biographer Ibn Khallikān [113/164], who wrote between 654/1274 and 672/1274, but relied on an earlier history of the kings from the Maghrib which is now lost. According to the same source, Abū Bakr b. ʿUmar was an emotional person. "He heard that an old woman in his homeland, who had lost a she-camel in a raid, wept saying: ʿAbū Bakr b. ʿUmar has ruined us by entering the Maghrib." He then decided to go back to the desert. Abū Bakr's emotional attachment to the desert is used by our sources to explain how graciously he conceded authority in the Maghrib to Ibn Tāshfīn, and returned to the desert.

The Almoravids Divided: Abū Bakr b. ʿUmar and Ibn Tāshfīn

We have no idea from what source Ibn Abī Zarʿ got his dates for the history of the Almoravids. These dates seem reliable for the period between 427/1036 and 452/1060. But the date provided by Ibn Abī Zarʿ [86/246–47] for the departure of Abū Bakr b. ʿUmar to the desert in Dhū 'l-Qaʿda 453/Nov-Dec 1061 is too early by ten years, if we follow the chronology of Ibn ʿIdhari, which is undoubtedly more reliable here.

According to Ibn ʿIdhārī [55/227], Abū Bakr had begun the building of Marrakech in Rajab 462/May 1070, before he left for the desert in Shaʿbān 463/May 1071.[6] This chronology, however, seriously conflicts with the contemporary account of al-Bakrī [170/75]:

> The commander of the Almoravids until this day, namely the year 460/1067–8, is Abū Bakr b. ʿUmar. But their power is divided, not unified, and they stay in the desert.

By 460/1067–8, according to al-Bakrī, Abū Bakr was already in the desert, and the Almoravid movement was divided. Aware of this contradiction, Ibn ʿIdhārī [53/225] rewrote al-Bakrī's text:

> In the year 460/1067–8 the *amīr* Abū Bakr b. ʿUmar became firmly established in his rule. All the countries obeyed him and he sent governors to them. His residence was the town of Aghmāt.

By interfering with al-Bakrī's contemporary evidence, Ibn ʿIdhārī cleared up ambiguities in his own account and chronology; in 460/1067–8 the Almoravids were still united under the command of Abū Bakr b. ʿUmar, who resided in Aghmāt, before the building of Marrakech.

According to Ibn ʿIdhārī [56–7/228–9], Abū Bakr b. ʿUmar remained the supreme leader of the Almoravids after his departure for the desert, because Ibn Tāshfīn "used to write to the *amīr* Abū Bakr about everything that he was doing and the latter would thank him." Also, when

[6] Levi-Provencal, "La fondation de Marrakech (462/1070)," *Mélanges d'histoire et d'archéologie de l'occident musulman: hommage à Georges Marçais* (Alger, 1957), vol. 2, pp. 117–120.

Ibn Tāshfīn established the mint at Marrakech in 464/1071–2, he struck gold *dīnārs* in the name of the *amīr* Abū Bakr b. ʿUmar.

This information of Ibn ʿIdhārī is corroborated by numismatic findings. Numismatic collections include examples of *dīnārs* between 450/1058 and 480/1087, in the name of the *amīr* Abū Bakr b. ʿUmar. The name of Yūsuf b. Tāshfīn appears only on later coins.[7] This numismatic evidence further confirms the date given by Ibn Abī Zarʿ [87/248] for the death of Abū Bakr b. ʿUmar in Shaʿbān 480/November 1087.

Ibn Tāshfīn carefully observed all the formalities, but at the same time he was busy consolidating his power. He wrote to some of his relatives in Abū Bakr's camp urging them to join him, and promised them great benefits. A great number of them joined him [Ibn ʿIdhārī 57/229].

After he had pacified the desert, Abū Bakr b. ʿUmar made his way back to the Maghrib in Rabiʿ II 465/November 1072. He soon realized that Ibn Tāshfīn had already consolidated his power in the Maghrib, and Abū Bakr returned to the desert. Once again Ibn Tāshfīn promised: "I will not decree anything without your authority." He agreed to pay tribute to Abū Bakr in the form of gifts.[8]

According to the numismatic collections, Ibrāhīm b. Abī Bakr issued *dīnārs* between 462/1070–1 and 467/1074–5 in Sijilmāsa.[9] He seems to have been appointed governor of Sijilmāsa by his father, and continued to hold this office with a measure of autonomy when Ibn Tāshfīn ruled the Maghrib. He returned to the desert, because according to Ibn ʿIdhārī [61–62],[10] Ibrāhīm b. Abī Bakr came from the desert in 469/1076–7 to reclaim his father's kingdom from Ibn Tāshfīn. He camped at the outskirts of Aghmāt with many of his Lamtūna brothers, but Yūsuf b. Tāshfīn dismissed him with generous gifts as he had done to his father Abū Bakr before.

These events become more meaningful if one closely follows the chronology of Ibn ʿIdhārī. According to Ibn ʿIdhārī [59/232], Abū Bakr b. ʿUmar was killed while fighting the *sūdān* in 468/1075–6. Ibrāhīm might have come to the Maghrib in 469 to assert himself as heir to his father.

This chronology and the sequence of events might be linked to the information from al-Zuhrī [98/125] that the conversion of Ghāna to Islam in 469/1076–7 coincided with the appearance of Yaḥyā b. Abī Bakr.

---

[7] H.W. Hazard, *The Numismatic History of Late Medieval North Africa* (New York, 1952), 61–62.

[8] Ibn ʿIdhārī 58–59/230–1; *al-Ḥulal al-mawshiyya* 16–17/315–6.

[9] Hazard 1952, 99–10; Hanna E. Kassis, "Observations on the First Three Decades of the Almoravid Dynasty (A.H. 450–480): a numismatic study," *Der Islam* 62 (1985): 315.

[10] This reference, which is not in the Corpus, provided by Farias 1967, p. 849.

Hence, in 469/1076–7, a year after the death of Abū Bakr b. ʿUmar (according to Ibn ʿIdhārī's chronology), one of his sons — Ibrāhīm — went to Morocco to confront Ibn Tāshfīn, while the other son — Yaḥyā — was at the head of the Almoravids from the south when Ghāna converted to Islam.

A year later, in 470/1077–8, *al-Ḥulal al-mawshiyya* [46] reported that many Lamtūna, Masūfa and Gudāla left the desert, responding to the call of Ibn Tāshfīn to join him. This migration from the desert might also be associated with the death of Abū Bakr b. ʿUmar.[11]

This reconstruction of the events between the years 468/1075–469/1076 is quite plausible, and should have been accepted. But it runs against the most important date recorded by Ibn Abī Zarʿ [87/248] for the death of Abū Bakr b. ʾUmar, 480/1087, a date that, as we have already shown, is supported by numismatic evidence.

The Almoravids in *Bilād al-Sūdān*

Among the fallacies committed by Ibn Abī Zarʿ, one may count his obsession with holy war against the *sūdān*. At the point where al-Bakrī's text [168/73] refers to the conquest of Awdaghust, Ibn Abī Zarʿ [81/243] says that the *amīr* Yaḥyā "made raids on the land of the *sūdān*, conquering much of it." Whereas according to al-Bakrī [167–68/73], Yaḥyā b. ʿUmar was killed in battle against the Gudāla, Ibn Abī Zarʿ [81/243] says that he "died on one of his *jihād*s to the land of the Sūdān." According to Ibn ʿIdhārī [56/228], Abū Bakr went back to the desert and "made war on the Gudāla until he took vengeance on them." Ibn Abī Zarʿ [86/247] referred again to *jihād* against the *sūdān*, which resulted in the conquest of "an area of their country which would take three months' travelling to cross." Ibn Abī Zarʿ [87–88] repeated that claim, when saying that following Abū Bakr's death, authority passed exclusively to Yūsuf b. Tāshfīn, his dominions extended as far as "the mountains of gold" in *Bilād al-Sūdān.*

Leaving aside Ibn Abī Zarʿ's text, there are a few pieces of evidence regarding the relations between the Almoravids and *Bilād al-Sūdān*:

a. Al-Bakrī's account [167/73] that the son of the king of Takrūr fought together with the Lamtūna Almoravids against the Gudāla suggests an alliance of Takrūr and the Almoravids.

b. Al-Bakrī's report [167–8/74] that the Almoravids persecuted the people of Awdaghust because they recognized the authority of Ghāna, suggests enmity towards Ghāna.

---

[11] Farias (1967, 849) who provides this reference, which is also missing in the Corpus, suggests that following the conversion of Ghāna some Almoravids felt free to travel north to the Maghrib.

c. Ibn ʿIdhārī [59/232] and Ibn Abī Zarʿ [87/248] provide different dates for the death of Abū Bakr b. ʿUmar, but both agree that he was killed when fighting in the land of the *sūdān.*

d. In 587/1191, an adherent of the Almohads said that the authority of the Almohads extended "from Tripoli to the towns of Ghāna and Kawkaw" [*Kitāb al-Istibṣār* [111/138]. This pratically contemporaneous evidence suggests that the Almohads, as successors of the Almoravids, enjoyed an influence of some kind over the lands of the *sūdān.*[12]

But the most significant impact of the Almoravid movement on *Bilād al-Sūdān* was, in all probability, its association with the conversion of Ghāna to Islam. By the time al-Idrīsī [6–7/109–10] wrote in 548/1154, the king of Ghāna and his people had become Muslim. Al-Zuhrī [125/98], writing at about the same time, even provides an exact date for the conversion of the people of Ghāna:

> The people of this country [Ghāna] professed paganism (*kufr),* until the year 469/1076–7, when Yaḥyā b. Abī Bakr the *amīr* of Masūfa made his appearance. They turned Muslims in the days of Lamtūna and became good Muslims.

The text of al-Zuhrī is often ambiguous, and it is even more difficult because no two manuscripts are in agreement. Fortunately, there is a version of the text, copied as early as 783/1381 by the anonymous author of *al-Ḥulal al-mawshiyya* [7/31]:

> Abū ʿAbdallah al-Zuhrī says that the people of the lands of the *sūdān*, whose capital is the city of Ghāna, formerly professed Christianity until the year 469/1076–7 when they turned Muslim and became good Muslims. That was when the *amīr* Abū Yaḥyā son of the *amīr* Abū Bakr b. ʿUmar al-Lamtūnī made his appearance.

We prefer the date 469, which appears in most manuscripts, as well as in the text of *al-Ḥulal al-mawshiyya*, to the date 496.[13] The latter appears in the printed text, edited by Muḥammad Hadj-Sadock, who followed the manuscript from Paris. This manuscript is the oldest, but it is also the most corrupt.

Al-Zuhrī's text refers to Yaḥyā b. Abī Bakr as "the *amīr* of Masūfa." This was corrected by *al-Ḥulal,* who clearly identified him with Yaḥyā (whom he mistakenly called Abū Yaḥyā), son of the *amīr* Abū Bakr

[12] On the "Reviser," the last editor of *Kitāb al-Istibṣār* see N. Levtzion, "The Twelfth Century Anonymous *Kitāb al-Istibṣār*: a History of a Text," *Journal of Semitic Studies* 24 (1979): 201–217. Reprinted in *Islam in West Africa: Religion, Society and Politics to 1800* (Aldershot, 1994).

[13] Humphrey Fisher prefers the later date of 496, but his arguments are not convincing. See H. J. Fisher, "Early Arabic Sources and the Almoravid Conquest of Ghāna," *Journal of African History* 23 (1982): 552.

b. ʿUmar al-Lamtūnī. Yaḥyā, we have already seen, was one of the two sons of Abū Bakr [Ibn ʿIdhārī 53/225].

That the conversion of Ghāna was linked to the activities of the Almoravids may be deduced also from other events recorded by al-Zuhrī [126/99]:

> The people of Tadmakka became Muslims seven years after the people of Ghāna. There had been much warfare between them. The people of Ghāna sought the help of the Almoravids. ... The Almoravids live between the two towns of Warqlan and Sijilmāsa. These people accepted Islam when the people of Warqlan did so at the time of Hishām b. ʿAbd al-Malik (the Umayyad *amīr* of Andalusia, 105/724–125/743). But [then] they adopted a school that took them outside the Holy Law. They returned to orthodox Islam when the people of Ghāna, Tadmakka and Zafun adopted Islam.

Sijilmāsa, Wargala, Tadmekka, as well as Awdaghust, were the major commercial centres in the Sahara, which in the ninth and tenth century were inhabited by the Ibāḍīs. Ibāḍī chronicles [in the *Corpus* 24–25, 89–91] provide evidence of the Ibāḍīs' commercial activities in the Sahara and in the major towns of *Bilād al-Sūdān* from the ninth to the twelfth centuries. In the wake of the upheavals created by the Almoravids, which caused tremors throughout the Sahara and the Maghrib, the Ibāḍīs lost their prominent role in the trade of the Sahara. The Sahara's major commercial centres then became Sunnī.

The Barbara, according to al-Zuhrī [125–6/98–9], were pagans and their country was a hunting ground for slaves raided by their neighbours. Yet, in spite of their miserable conditions, "the Barbara, in their own opinion, are the most noble and aristocratic of men. This is because the *amīr* of Ghāna is related to them and used to be one of them. Every *amīr* of the land of Janawa (Guinea) acknowledges their nobility except the Muslims." In a brilliant article, to which we shall return later, Sheryl Burkhalter pointed out that the phrase "used to be" refers to the past, and that the Muslims who did not acknowledge the nobility of the Barbara included the people of Ghāna, who had converted to Islam.[14] Perhaps there was even a change of dynasty in Ghāna, and the rulers who had traced their origin to the Barbara were replaced by a Muslim dynasty, which according to al-Idrīsī [6/109] "belongs to the progeny of Ṣāliḥ b. ʾAbdallah b. al-Ḥasan b. al-Ḥasan b. ʿAlī b. Abī Ṭālib."

---

[14] S. Burkhalter, "Listening for Silences in Almoravid History: Another Reading of "The Conquest that Never Was," *History in Africa* 19 (1992): 114.

The fourteenth century historian Ibn Khaldūn [i, 263/ 333] described the conversion of Ghāna in the wider context of political developments at the Sahara-Sahel interface:

> When Ifrīqiya and the Maghrib were conquered [by the Arabs] merchants penetrated the western part of *Bilād al-Sūdān* and found among them no king greater than the king of Ghāna. ... Later the authority of the People of Ghāna waned and their prestige declined whereas the power of the veiled people, their neighbours from the north, next to the land of the Berbers, grew. They extended their dominion over the Sūdān and pillaged, imposed tribute and poll tax, and converted many of them to Islam. Then the authority of the rulers of Ghāna dwindled away and they were overcome by the Susu, a neighbouring people of the *sūdān*, who subjugated and absorbed them.

Ibn Khaldūn recorded this information from the "*shaykh* ʿUthmān, *faqīh ahl Ghāna*, [who was] the most learned, pious, and celebrated among the people of Ghāna." Ibn Khaldūn met him in Egypt in 796/ 1394. The text quoted above is only the first part of a longer account that covers the history of *Bilād al-Sūdān* from the tenth to the fourteenth centuries.

In the eleventh century Ghāna extended its authority over Awdaghust, which marked the peak of Ghāna's power. Ibn Khaldūn's account describes the change in the balance of power at the desert edge with the rise of the Almoravids. The power of Ghāna declined and the desert nomads invaded *Bilād al-Sūdān*, imposed tribute and converted many of the *sūdān* to Islam.

In 595/1199 al-Sarakhsī [quoted by al-Maqqarī ii 72/372] saw an exchange of letters between the Almohad governor of Sijilmāsa and "the king of the Sūdān in Ghāna," complaining of the detention of traders from the Maghrib. The governor of Sijilmāsa opened the letter, saying: "We are neighbours in benevolence even if we differ in religion." This text suggests that at the very end of the twelfth century "the king of the *sūdān* in Ghāna" was not a Muslim. The reason for that setback to Islam was the result of the conquest of Ghāna, a Muslim state, by the non-Muslim Susu. Tradition says that the Susu rulers harassed the Muslim traders, who left Ghāna to establish a new commercial centre at Walata.[15]

Among the towns or countries that became Muslim at the same time as Ghāna, al-Zuhrī [126/99] mentioned the town of Zafunu. According to the seventeenth century *Ta'rīkh al-Fattāsh,* Diafunu was one of the

[15] M. Delafosse, Haut-Senegal-Niger, 1912, ii, 165–6.

Soninke states that emerged in the twelfth century, with the disintegration of Ghāna.[16]

Yāqūt [ii 908/170–71], writing in 1124, presented the most detailed account of Zafunu and its relations with the Almoravids:

> Zafunu is a vast province in the land of the Sūdān, near the Maghrib, and adjoining the land of the *mulaththamūn*.... Their king leads a nomadic life, seeking [pasture] in places where the rains have fallen. ... The king of Zafunu is stronger than the *mulaththamūn* and more versed in the art of kingship. The *mulaththamūn* acknowledge his superiority over them, obey him and resort to him in all-important matters of government. ... One year this king, on his way to the Pilgrimage, came to the Maghrib to pay a visit to the *amīr al-muslimīn*, the veiled king of the Maghrib, of the Lamtūna tribe. *Amīr al-muslimīn* met him on foot, whereas the king of Zafunu did not dismount for him. ... He entered the palace of *amīr al-muslimīn* mounted, while the latter walked in front of him.

The event, described by Yāqūt, could have occurred in the 1130s and 1140s, when the Almohads harassed the Almoravids. Yāqūt recorded this precious piece of information through a chain of informants, going back to an eyewitness to the events in Marrakech. The latter described the king of Zafunu as "tall, of deep black complexion and veiled." Yāqūt described the king of Zafunu as a nomad and veiled on the one hand and of deep black complexion on the other. Ethnicity at the desert edge is complex, where *sūdān* were culturally influenced by the nomads of the desert. The confusion goes back to the twelfth century anonymous author of *Kitāb al-istibṣār* [218/145], who, in updating al-Bakrī's text, changed the identity of Zafunu in [137/78] (spelled Zafqu] from being "a nation of the *sūdān*" to Berbers.

The relationship between the Ṣanhāja *mulaththamūn* and Diafunu, as described by Yāqūt, suggests yet another phase in the cycle of changes in the balance of power between the states of the *sūdān* and the Berbers of the Sahara, between the twelfth and the fourteenth centuries. The power of the Ṣanhāja, the descendants of the Almoravids, is described by Ibn Khaldūn [260/331] in the fourteenth century:

> "Those of them who stayed in the desert remained in their primitive state of dissension and divergence and are now subject to the kings of the Sūdān, pay him tribute, and are recruited to his armies."

[16] *Ta'rīkh al-Fattāsh*, text 39/trans. 70–71; see also T. Lewicki, "Un état soudanais médiéval inconnu: le royaume de Zafun(u)," *Cahiers d'Études Africaines* 9 (1971): 501–25.

This is confirmed by Ibn Faḍl Allah al-ʿUmarī [46/262], another fourteenth century source, who reported that Berber tribes were under the suzerainty of the king of Mali.

With Ibn Khaldūn we are in the realm of oral traditions. Abū Bakr b. ʿUmar is prominent in the traditions of Mauritania as well as on the Senegal River. Until the present time there are tribes that proudly claim to have been part of the armies of Abū Bakr b. ʿUmar.[17] In Mauritania traditions attribute to Abū Bakr b. ʿUmar the expulsion of the *sūdān* from the Sahara. Thus, the long process of the uprooting of the *sūdān* from the Sahara is attributed to the leader of the Almoravids. Traditions also agree with the fourteenth century sources that a black archer killed Abū Bakr b. ʿUmar.[18]

The Wolof royals of Walo claim descent from Abū Bakr b. ʿUmar. It is said that he married a Torodo wife, who gave birth to Amadu Bubakar b. ʿUmar, the first Brak of Walo, whose royal name was Ndyadyan Ndyay. His successor, the second Brak, as befitted the matrilineal Wolof, was the son of the daughter of Abū Bakr b. ʿUmar.[19]

Following the death of Abū Bakr, those who had participated in the Almoravid movement remained warriors until the successive invasions from the north by the Id ou Ali, the Kunta, and the Arab Banū Ḥassān. The successors of the Almoravids lost their military prowess but retained their religious ardour and became men of religion, *marabouts* or *zawāyā*.[20] Traditions in Mauritania, Senegal and the Western Sahara remember the Imām al-Haḍramī, the spiritual mentor of Abū Bakr b. ʿUmar. Abū Bakr Muḥammad b. al-Hasan al-Haḍramī al-Murādī, a venerated saint in the Sahara, was an eminent scholar in Aghmāt Urika. According to his twelfth century biographers, he accompanied Abū Bakr b. ʿUmar when the latter returned to the Sahara in 465/1072. Abū Bakr entrusted him with the administration of the justice. Al-Haḍramī settled at Azukki, the capital of the Almoravids, where he died in 489/1096, nine years after Abū Bakr b. ʿUmar.[21]

The Almoravids and *Bilād al-Sūdān* in Modern Historiography

Our perception of history is influenced by the nature of the evidence. Because the writings of Arab geographers and historians are our ear-

---

[17] P. Amilhat, "Petite chronique des Id ou Aich, héritiers guerriers des Almoravides sahariens," *Revue des Études Islamique* 11 (1937): 44.

[18] P. Marty, Tableau historique des Cheikh Sidia, *Bulletin d'études historiques et scientifiques de l'Afrique occidentale francaise* 4 (1921): 78–83; see also Farias 1967, 850.

[19] Farias 1967, 850–51.

[20] Amilhat 1937, 45–46.

[21] Farias, 1967, 855–56.

lier sources, the history of the Sahara and the *Bilād al-Sūdān* unfolds from north to south. The view from the north led modern historians to emphasize the dominant role of the nomads of the desert and their confrontation with the sedentaries of the Sahel. The conquest of Ghāna by the Almoravids was considered the climax of an on-going southwards advance of the Berber-speaking nomads at the expense of the *sūdān*. John Hunwick suggested that the influence of the Almoravids in *Bilād al-Sūdān* extended beyond Ghāna to Gao, where the twelfth century royal tombstones are of Andalusian style, which might point to links between Gao and the Almoravids of Spain. Hunwick's hypothesis is that the rulers whose names are inscribed on the tombstones were Masūfa Ṣanhāja influenced by the Almoravid ideology. They seized power in Gao between c. 1080 and 1120.[22]

According to Dierek Lange, the Almoravid movement generated religious fervor among the Muslim residents in the capitals of the major kingdoms of the *sūdān*, which might explain the fact that Ghāna and Kanem on Lake Chad converted at about the same time.[23]

In 1967 Paulo Moraes Farias published a pioneering study of the Almoravid movement in the Sahara and *Bilād al-Sūdān*, in which he critically examined the Arabic sources. His reference to "the supposed triumph over Ghāna" was perhaps the earliest word of caution concerning the outcome of the confrontation between Ghāna and the Almoravids.[24]

But it was Humphrey Fisher who ardently argued that the conquest of Ghāna never occurred.[25] He maintained that if there had been an Almoravid conquest of Ghāna, we could expect a clear statement in the external sources. Instead, the incident escapes mention for more than a quarter of a millenium. But, given that there is not even a single direct reference to any such destructive conquest, the logical conclusion is that no such event occurred.[26]

Fisher agrees that there was fighting between the Almoravids and the *sūdān*, but he assumes that "these operations were small beer, and did not overwhelm the central power of Ghāna." Fisher's scenario of the events is that a long process of the gradual strengthening of Islam in the western Sūdān was highlighted by the peaceful conversion of Ghāna, probably early in the twelfth century. The conversion of Ghāna facili-

[22] Hunwick, J.O., "Gao and the Almoravis: a Hypothesis," in B. Swartz & R. Dumett (eds.), *West African Cultural Dynamics: Archaeological and Historical Perspectives*. (The Hague, 1979), 413, 417–8.

[23] D. Lange, "Les rois de Gao-Sane et des Almoravides," *Journal of African History* 32 (1991): 275.

[24] Farias 1967, 850.

[25] D. Conrad and H.J. Fisher, "The Conquest that Never Was: Ghāna and the Almoravids, 1076," *History in Africa* 9 (1982): 21–59 and 10 (1983): 53–78.

[26] Conrad and Fisher 1983, 62.

tated co-operation with the Almoravids.[27]

Fisher succeeded in forcing historians to qualify statements concerning a military conquest of Ghāna, speaking instead of some kind of Almoravid influence on Ghāna. Fisher, however, has hardened his own position. Almost fifteen years after he had first come out with the battle cry of "the conquest that never was," Humphrey Fisher rejected the "influence hypothesis" that replaced the "conquest hypothesis." "There seems to us," he says, "little reason to believe that the Almoravids exercised any kind of determining political influence over Ghāna, be it by force or by insinuation."[28]

Humphrey Fisher's reading of the texts remained unchallenged for a decade until 1992 when Sheryl Burkhalter criticized Fisher's handling of the Arabic texts.[29] She further questioned Fisher's argument based on the silence of the texts. There are at least two examples, even in connection with the Almoravids, where the texts are silent about events that are highlighted by other evidence. The sources are silent about developments in Gao that can be reconstructed by analyzing the royal tomb inscriptions. Similarly, we know that Ibrāhīm b. Abī Bakr was governor of Sijilmāsa from numismatic and not from textual evidence.[30]

Humphrey Fisher refers to a text written by Aḥmad Bābā in 1024/1615, where this eminent scholar from Timbuktu denied any conquest of the *sūdān* by Muslims.[31] Fisher thinks that Aḥmad Bābā's emphatic rejection of any form of the "conquest hypothesis" carried particular weight "since he was writing relatively early, more or less on the spot geographically." In the same article, however, Fisher refers to "Ibn Khaldūn's notoriously brief and vague mention of these events, *written centuries afterwards*."[32] Strangely, in relation to an event in the eleventh century, 1621 is considered by Fisher "relatively early," whereas 1393–4 is "centuries afterwards."

In handling the text by Aḥmad Bābā, Fisher seems unaware of the

---

[27] Conrad and Fisher 1982, 40; H.J. Fisher, "Early Arabic Sources and the Almoravid Conquest of Ghāna," *Journal of African History* 23 (1982): 559.

[28] P. Masonen and H.J. Fisher, "Not Quite Venus from the Waves: The Almoravids Conquest of Ghāna in the Modern Historiography of Western Africa," *History in Africa* 23 (1996): 218. The two articles on the conquest of Ghāna, published at an interval of fifteen years, were co-authored by Fisher with former students, namely David Conrad in 1982, and Pekka Masonen in 1996.

[29] S. Burkhalter, "Listening for Silences in Almoravid History: Another Reading of "The Conquest That Never Was," *History in Africa* 19 (1992): 103–31.

[30] Burkhalter (1992, 17–18).

[31] Aḥmad Bābā, *al-Kashf wa'l-bayān li-aṣnāf majlūb al-sūdān* ("Enslavable categories among the blacks revealed and explained") in B. Barbour, Bernard and Michelle Jacobs, "The Mi'rāj: A Legal Treatise on Slavery by Aḥmad Bābā," in J.R. Willis, ed., *Slaves and Slavery in Muslim Africa* (London, 1985), vol. 1, text 143–4, trans. 129.

[32] Masonen and Fisher (1996, 201, 205).

problematic nature of legal treatises as historical sources. Legal treatises often reconstruct historical accounts in order to create precedents for a legal argument.[33] Aḥmad Bābā's treatise was in fact a *fatwā* against the enslavement of the *sūdān*. From a legal point of view, the *sūdān* could be enslaved only if they had been pagans when conquered by the Muslims. Hence, Aḥmad Bābā had to provide evidence that the *sūdān* had been Muslims before they were conquered in order to make them legally immune to slavery.

An interpretation of the external Arabic sources between the ninth and fourteenth centuries, and of the internal Arabic sources of the seventeenth century, suggests a cyclical pattern of relationships between the states of the *sūdān* and the Berber-speaking nomads of the southern Sahara. The states of the *sūdān*, Ghāna in the eleventh century and Mali in the fourteenth century, extended their influence into the Sahara not by conquest, but as a result of the nomads' own choice to be incorporated into the hegemonic state of the day. On the contrary, when the power of the *sūdān*'s state declined, the nomads pressed south into the Sahel.

Neither side could have penetrated deeply into the other's ecological milieu. The troops of the *sūdān* were no match for the camel-riding Berbers in the desert, whereas the camels of the nomads became ineffective as they advanced to the more humid climate in the south. Even so the question of the conquest of Ghāna is left open, because the eleventh century capital of Ghāna was located at the desert-Sahel interface, and could have been militarily controlled by either nomads or *sūdān*.[34]

Arabic Texts (in chronological order):

Al-Yaʿqūbī. *Ta'rīkh*. Ed. M. Th. Houtsma. Leiden, 1883.

Al-Yaʿqūbī. *Kitāb al-buldān*. Ed. M.J. de Goeje. Leiden, 1892.

Ibn Ḥawqal. *Kitāb ṣūrat al-arḍ*. Ed. J.H. Kramers. Leiden, 1938–9.

Al-Bakrī. *Kitāb al-masālik wa-'l-mamalik*. Ed. M.G. de Slane. Algiers 1911.

Ibāḍī texts edited by T. Lewicki in *Folia Orientalia* 2 (1960): 1–27.

Al-Zuhrī. *Kitāb al-Jaʿrafiyya* [sic]. Ed. M. Hadj-Sadok, in *Bulletin d'Études Orientales* 21 (1968): 1–194.

ʿIyāḍ b. Mūsā al-Sabtī. *Tartīb al-madārik wa-taqrīb al-masālik li-maʿrifat aʿlām madhhab Mālik*. Ed. Aḥmad Bakīr Maḥmūd. Beirut, 1967.

[33] Cf. R. Brunschvig, "Ibn ʿAbd al-Ḥakam et la conquête de l'Afrique du nord par les Arabes: étude critique," *Annales de l'Institut Oriental* 6 (1942–7): 121–2.

[34] N. Levtzion, "Berber Nomads and Sudanese States: The Historiography of the Desert-Sahel Interface" in N. Levtzion, *Islam in West Africa: Religion, Society and Politics to 1800* (Aldershot, 1994).

al-Idrīsī. *Nuzhat al-mushtāq fī ikhtirāq al-āfāq*. Ed. R. Dozy and M.J. De Goeje. Leiden, 1866.

Anon. *Kitāb al-Istibṣār*. Ed. Saʿd Zaghlūl ʿAbd al-Ḥamīd. Alexandria, 1958.

Al-Tādilī. *Kitāb al-tashawwuf ilā rijāl al-taṣawwuf*. Ed. A. Faure. Rabat, 1958.

Ibn al-Athīr. *al-Kāmil fī 'l-ta'rīkh*. Ed. C.J. Tornberg. Leiden and Uppsala, 1851–76, vol. iii.

Ibn Khallikān. *Wafayāt al-aʿyān wa-anbā' al-zamān*. Ed. Iḥsān ʿAbbās. Beirut, 1968, vol. vii.

Yāqūt, *Muʿjam al-buldān*. Ed. F. Wüstenfeld. Lepzig, 1866–73, vol. ii.

Ibn ʿIdhārī. *al-Bayān al-mughrib fī akhbār al-andalus wa'l-maghrib*. Ed. Ambrosio Huici Miranda in *Hesperis-Tamuda* ii (1961), pp. 43–111.

Anon. *Mafākhir al-Barbar*. Ed. E. Levi-Provencal. Rabat, 1964.

Ibn Abī Zarʿ. *Kitāb al-anīs al-muṭrib bi-rawḍ al-qirṭās fī akhbār mulūk al-maghrib wa-ta'rīkh madīnat Fās*. Ed. C.J. Tornberg. Uppsala, 1843.

Al-ʿUmarī. *Masālik al-abṣār fī mamālik al-amṣār* in *Mamlakat Mālī ʿinda al-jughrāfiyyīn al-muslimīn*. Ed. Ṣalāḥ al-Dīn al-Munajjid. Beirut, 1963.

Anon. *Al-Ḥulal al-mawshiyya*. Ed. I.S. Allouche. Rabat, 1936.

Ibn Khaldūn. *Kitāb ta'rīkh al-duwal al-islāmiyya bi 'l-maghrib min Kitāb al-ʿibar*. Ed. M.G. de Slane. Algiers, 1847–51, vol. 1.

Al-Maqqari. *Nafḥ al-ṭīb min ghuṣn al-andalus al-raṭīb*. Ed. R. Dozy et al. Paris, 1855–61.

IX

Slavery and the Slave Trade in the Early States of Bilād al-Sūdān[1]

Early Trans-Saharan Trade Systems: Slaves and Gold

In 666 'Uqba b. Nāfi', one of the first commanders of the Arab conquest of North Africa, led an expedition south of Tripoli to Waddan, Jarma (the capital of the Garamantes) and on as far as Kawar, halfway between Fezzan and Lake Chad. He exacted 360 slaves from each of these three locations.[2]

The ninth-century Egyptian historian, Ibn 'Abd al-Ḥakam, who recorded these events from early sources, also reported that in 734 Ḥabīb b. Abī-'Ubayda b. 'Uqba, a grandson of 'Uqba b. Nāfi', was sent on an expedition to the Sūs and to the country of the Sudan. "He achieved a success the like of which had never been seen and got as much gold as he wanted. Among the booty was a slave girl or two of the women of that region."[3] Both these expeditions followed two ancient trans-Saharan routes: an eastern route, over which an early slave trade between Lake Chad and Libya had taken place, and a western route, by which some gold had reached North Africa.

There are no references to slavery and the slave trade in the Western Sudan in Arabic sources before the eleventh century. Even then, we have only two references in al-Bakrī, who wrote in 1068. He reported that "the people of Sila, as well as the inhabitants of the other regions of the land of the Sudan … observe the law that a person who falls victim to a thief may either sell or kill

---

[1] This chapter was originally presented as a paper to the Conference on "Islam, Slavery and Diaspora", York University, Great Britain, 24–26 April 2003.

[2] Ibn 'Abd al-Ḥakam, in *Corpus of Early Arabic Sources for West African History*, edited by N. Levtzion and J.F.P. Hopkins, Cambridge: Cambridge University Press, 1981, pp. 12–13. [hereafter: *Corpus*]

[3] Ibid., p. 13; see also al-Balādhurī (d. 892), *Corpus*, p. 18.

him, as he chooses."[4] The other reference in al-Bakrī illustrated the wealth of the people of Awdaghust, in that "they owned great riches and slaves so numerous that one person among them might possess a thousand servants or more."[5]

On the other hand, along the eastern trans-Saharan route there is constant reference to slaves from the ninth century onward. Al-Ya'qūbī wrote in 890:

> Beyond Waddān to the south is the town of Zawīla. Its people are Muslims, all of them Ibāḍīs, and they go on pilgrimage to Mecca. They export black slaves from among the peoples of the Sudan, because these live close to Zawīla, whose people capture them. Fifteen days' journey beyond Zawīla is a town called Kawar, inhabited by Muslims from various tribes, most of them Berbers. It is they who bring in the Sudan [as slaves].[6]

Al-Iṣṭakhrī (d. after 951) followed al-Ya'qūbī's information: "Zawīla is on the frontier of the Maghrib bordering on the land of the Sudan. The black slaves who are sold in the Islamic countries are taken from among them [the Sudan] … Most of those black slaves converge on Zawīla."[7] Al-Bakrī also focused on Zawīla: "From there slaves are exported to Ifrīqiya [Tunisia] and other neighbouring regions. They are bought for short pieces of red cloth." But al-Bakrī referred to the emerging state of Kānim as well: "The Kānimīs live beyond the desert of Zawīla and scarcely anybody reaches them. They are pagan Sudan."[8]

Kanīm became Muslim only at the beginning of the twelfth century. It was established by the Zaghāwa, whose king, according to the tenth-century al-Muhallabī, "has unlimited authority over his subjects and enslaves from among them anyone he wants."[9] A century earlier al-Ya'qūbī wrote: "I have been informed that the kings of the Sudan sell their [own] people without any pretext or war."[10] Both statements about the enslavement by rulers of their own subjects might be considered views from across the Sahara, and it is more likely that even at that early period the rulers of Kanīm raided their neighbors for slaves.

---

[4] Ibid., p. 78.
[5] Ibid., p. 74.
[6] Ibid., p. 22.
[7] Ibid., pp. 41–2.
[8] Ibid., p. 64.
[9] Ibid., p. 171.
[10] Ibid., p. 22.

Ibn Sa'īd described such raids in 1286: "To the east is the territory of the Kanīm with their Berber followers who were converted to Islam by Ibn Ḥabal the sulṭān of Kanīm. They are his slaves. He uses them on his raids and takes advantage of their camels, which have filled these regions."[11] More than two centuries later, horses would be used for slave raids.

The two trade systems, one dominated by the slave trade, because Kanīm had no gold to offer, and the other by the gold trade, had far-reaching historical consequences. For the gold trade, it was vital that peace and security prevail over all the country between the sources of the precious metal and the market towns of the Sahel. This commercial activity encouraged the formation of states and their integration into large-scale empires, and also the spread of Islam far inland to the south. An intensive slave trade, on the other hand, was based on continual raids, which created a boundary of terror and hostility, and slowed down the process of state building and the expansion of Islam south of Lake Chad. Indeed, during its periods of strength, Kanīm expanded northwards to the Sahara, and as far as Fezzan.

Gold and slaves as the alternative commodities in the Saharan trade appear in the following account from the middle of the eleventh century, related in *Kitāb al-Siyar* ("The Book of Biographies") by al-Wisyānī, one of the most famous Ibāḍī historians, who died in the second half of the twelfth century:

> Abū Muḥammad travelled to the south to trade for gold and bought a camel to ride on. He had with him a townsman (*ḥaḍarī)*, who came to Abū Muḥammad asking: "What shall I trade for?" He replied: "I don't know." So the *ḥaḍarī* traded for slaves. Then they set off to return to their people. Abū Muḥammad never suffered from fatigue. When the caravan set off he would ride his camel and when it encamped he would pitch his tent and rest. But the *ḥaḍarī* was exhausted with his slave women and men – this woman had grown thin, this one was hungry, this one was sick, this one had run away, this one was afflicted by the guinea-worm – and when they encamped they had much to occupy them. Meanwhile the *ḥaḍarī*, tired and anxious, would see Abū Muḥammad sitting in the shade with his wealth bag upon bag, not at all tired. The *ḥaḍarī* would say: "Glory be to God who has spared Abū Muḥammad these trials.[12]

---

[11] Ibid., p. 188.
[12] Ibid., p. 90.

The Slave Trade to the Maghrib, the East and Europe

The supply of slaves to Morocco seems to have grown in the second half of the eleventh century, probably as a result of the military operations of the Almoravids in the southern Sahara, where, as already mentioned, the people of Awdaghust owned a great number of slaves. By 1071 the power and prestige of Yūsuf b. Tāshfīn, whom Abū Bakr b. 'Umar had appointed as his deputy in Morocco when he left for the southern Sahara, increased. He bought a group of black slaves and sent them to al-Andalus, probably as part of his army. When a year later Abū Bakr b. 'Umar returned from the desert most of his companions deserted him, as they were lured by Ibn Tāshfīn's generosity and gifts of slaves.[13]

Writing in 988, Ibn Ḥawqal described comely slave girls (*muwalladāt*) and male slaves (*khadam*) from the land of the Sudan among what was exported from the Maghrib to the East, together with "those imported from the land of the Slavs by way of al-Andalus."[14] As early as the eleventh century, Sudanese slaves were also sent in the other direction, from Morocco across the straits to Andalusia. In the eleventh and twelfth centuries, Sudanese slaves were recorded in Cordova and Algeciras. In the fourteenth century, they appeared in the Christian states of Catalan Valencia and Majorca, and in Marseille and Montpellier.[15]

As slaves were sent in great numbers every year to Morocco,[16] two mid-twelfth-century authors – al-Zuhrī (*fl.* 1137–54) and al-Idrīsī (wrote in 1154) – sought to to explain the source of these slaves and the way they were procured. The best they could do was to elaborate on the theme of slave raiding by the organized states, led by Ghana, on peoples to the south, who were described as primitive, pagan, and fighting with clubs of ebony that were no match for the iron swords and spears of the people of Ghana. They walked naked or wore sheepskins. They are called Barbara and Amīna by al-Zuhrī[17] and Lamlam by al-Idrīsī.[18] This stereotypic account was not repeated in following centuries, except by Ibn Khaldūn,[19] who was mimicking al-Idrīsī.

---

[13] Ibn 'Idhārī (*fl.* 1312), *Corpus*, pp. 229–30; Al-Ḥulal al-Mawshiyya, completed 783/1381, *Corpus*, pp. 314–15

[14] Ibid., pp. 47.

[15] Ch. Verlinden, "Esclavage noir en France méridoniale et courants de traite en Afrique", *Annales du Midi* 73 (1966), pp. 335–43.

[16] Al-Idrīsī, in *Corpus*, p. 109.

[17] Ibid., p. 98.

[18] Ibid., pp. 108, 109, 112.

[19] Ibid., p. 320.

According to the Spanish al-Sharīshī (d. 1222), many merchants from the Maghrib were found in Ghana, where they bought slaves for concubinage. Al-Sharīshī added praise for the slave girls: "God has endowed the slave girls there with laudable characteristics, both physical and moral, more than can be desired: their bodies are smooth, their black skins are lustrous, their eyes are beautiful, their noses well shaped, their teeth white, and they smell fragrant."[20]

Slave girls from the Sudan were in great demand in Morocco. In 1353 Ibn Baṭṭūṭa returned to Morocco from Takedda, in a convoy that brought about 600 slave girls to Morocco.[21] These girls came from Borno, from where, Ibn Baṭṭūṭa reported earlier, handsome slave girls and young men were brought to Takedda.[22] Ibn Baṭṭūta's caravan from Takedda passed through Tuwāt. In 1447 Antoine Malfante, writing from Tuwāt, emphasized the importance of this oasis in the trans-Saharan trade. He pointed out the cheapness of slaves there, "which the blacks take in their internecine wars."[23]

The people of Takedda, according to Ibn Baṭṭūṭa, sold educated slave girls only rarely, and at a high price. When he came to Takedda, he wished to buy an educated slave girl but could not find one, and those who eventually sold him one soon changed their minds and wished to retract the bargain.[24]

Just as slaves were sent from east to west, from Borno via Takedda to Morocco, so too there was a traffic in slaves from the Western Sudan to Ifrīqiya and Tripoli, probably via Wargala, as reported by Ibn Sa'īd in 1286: "Warglan is a place of palm trees and slaves. From here the slaves enter the central Maghrib and Ifrīqiya. There is much traffic across the desert from here to the land of the Sudan."[25] Leo Africanus recorded that the merchants of Mesrata (east of Tripoli) traded Sudanese slaves for European goods, which they had bought from the Venetians.[26] A trader from Mesrata, 'Abd al-Wāsi' al-Masrātī,

---

[20] Ibid., p. 153.

[21] Ibid., p. 303–4.

[22] Ibid., p. 302.

[23] Malfante's letter from Tuwāt in C. de La Roncière, *La Découverte de l'Afrique au moyen âge, cartographes et explorateurs*, Cairo, 1925, i, pp. 143–57.

[24] *Corpus*, p. 302

[25] Ibid., p. 194

[26] Leo Africanus, *Description de l'Afrique.* New edition translated by A. Epaulard and annotated by A. Epaulard, Th. Monod, H. Lhote, and R. Mauny. 2 vols. Paris, 1956, ii, pp. 414

was present at the court of Askiya Dāwūd (1549–82) in Gao, where he proposed to buy 500 slaves.[27]

In 1446 Joao Fernandes reported that the Arabs and the Sanhaja of the Western Sahara captured black slaves and sold them to the Moroccans, or themselves took them as far as Barca in the kingdom of Tunisia.[28] A decade later, Ca da Mosto observed that slave caravans conducted by the Arabs were divided at Waddān; one part was taken to Barca and thence to Sicily, one part to Tunisia, another to the coast of Barbary, and a fourth to the Portuguese in Arguin.[29]

Towards the end of the fourteenth and during the fifteenth centuries, Sudanese slaves were exported to Italian cities from "the Mountains of Barca", or Cyrenaica. They amounted to 83 per cent of the slave population in Naples. In Sicily they were employed in agriculture. Genoa and Venice also had black slaves at that period.[30] At the beginning of the sixteenth century, Leo Africanus noted a great number of black people and mulattos born of Sudanese slave women in southern Morocco and the oases of the northern Sahara. Most of the servants of the royal household in Fez were Sudanese slaves, and Sudanese eunuchs guarded the royal harem. Slaves were probably rather inexpensive in sixteenth-century Morocco because commoners could also own Sudanese slaves, and in Fez it was a custom to add a slave girl to the gift given to a fiancée.[31]

Slaves in Mali

The number of slaves further increased from the thirteenth century, which George Brooks associates with the climatic dry period, *c.*1000–*c.*1500, when Mandekan-speaking horse warriors conquered vast territories in the savanna and savanna woodland zones. Many members of conquered societies were sold into

---

[27] *Ta'rīkh al-Fattāsh* [TF] edited and translated by O. Houdas and M. Delafosse, Paris: de l'Ecole des Langues Orientales Vivantes, V^{e} serie, vol. X, 1913–14, reprinted 1964, 104/ tr. 193–4.

[28] Zurara (wrote 1453), *Chronique de Guinée.* French translation by L. Bourdon. Dakar, 1960, pp. 216–17.

[29] Alvise Ca da Mosto (1455–7), *Relations des voyages à la côte occidentale d'Afriqe.* French translation by C. Schefer. Paris, 1895, p. 48.

[30] Verlinden 1966; M. Malowist, "Les fondaments de l'expansion européene en Afrique au 15e siècle: Europe, Maghreb et Soudan occidentale," *Acta Poloniae Historica*, 18 (1968), pp. 174–6.

[31] Leo Africanus, 1956, i, pp. 94, 209, 238; ii, pp. 424, 429.

trans-Saharan slavery via Mande trade networks, and others were held as domestic slaves.[32]

Slaves were particularly numerous in the trading centres in the southern Sahara close to Bilād al-Sūdān, like Awdaghust in the eleventh century and Takedda and Walata in the fourteenth century. Wealthy people lived comfortably and were proud of the number of male and female slaves that they had.[33]

Mansā Mūsā's visit to Cairo and Ibn Baṭṭūṭa's visit to Mali opened up a significant window to view the importance of slaves in all walks of life in the Mali Empire. Ibn Baṭṭūṭa counted about 300 slaves in the audience of the king of Mali.[34] The Queen Qasa ostensibly began to ride every day with her slave girls and men with dust on their heads.[35] About 100 slave girls accompanied Dugha the interpreter ("a griot") when he performed before the king. They were dressed in fine clothes and wore on their heads bands of gold and silver adorned with gold and silver balls. With them were about 30 of his slave boys wearing red tunics of cloth and with white *shāshiyyas* on their heads.[36]

During Ramaḍān, Ibn Baṭṭūṭa was present when the officers of the court broke the fast in the house of the sulṭān, and each one brought his food carried by 20 or more of his slave girls, all naked. On the night of 25th Ramaḍān he saw about 200 naked slave girls bringing out food from the king's palace.[37]

Slaves accompanied dignitaries when they came into the presence of the king.[38] When one of them went on a journey, his male and female slaves carried his furnishings, and the vessels made of gourds from which he ate and drank followed him.[39] Among the slaves in the audience of the king were about 30 Turkish slaves, who had been bought for him in Egypt.[40] Members of the entourage of Mansā Mūsā bought in Cairo Turkish and Ethiopian slave girls.[41] A pilgrim emir, the governor of a village, who served as host to Ibn Baṭṭūṭa, had an Arab slave girl from Damascus who spoke Arabic.[42]

---

[32] G. Brooks, *Landlords and Strangers: Ecology, Society, and Trade in Western Africa, 1000–1630*, Boulder: Westview Press, 1993, p. 106.

[33] Ibn Baṭṭūṭa, *Corpus*, pp. 301–2.

[34] Ibid., p. 290.

[35] Ibid., p. 295.

[36] Ibid., pp. 292–3.

[37] Ibid., pp. 296–7.

[38] Al-'Umarī, wrote c. 1336, *Corpus*, p. 266.

[39] Ibn Baṭṭūṭa, *Corpus*, p. 287.

[40] Al-'Umarī, 1301–49, *Corpus*, p. 265.

[41] Al-Maqrīzī (1364–1442) *Corpus*, pp. 351, 355.

[42] Ibn Baṭṭūṭa, *Corpus*, 299–300.

A great number of slaves accompanied Mansā Mūsā on his pilgrimage, though different sources give different figures.[43] Many slaves also arrived with other pilgrims from the Western Sudan in the course of the fifteenth century.[44] It is likely that most of these were sold in the East, though the sources give no indication about their fate, and though Mansā Mūsā paid in gold for what he purchased in Egypt.

Eunuchs

Egyptian chroniclers recorded the career of a eunuch from Bīlād al-Sūdān by the name of Khāliṣ al-Takrūrī. He began his career in Egypt as a eunuch of an emir. Later, he was promoted to the service of the Sulṭān al-Ẓāhir Jaqmaq (1438–53), until the Sulṭān al-Ashraf Īnāl (1453–61) made him head of a corps and he became one of the eunuchs in charge of the barracks. In 1465 the Sulṭān al-Ẓāhir Khushqadam (1461–67) appointed him Deputy Chief Eunuch of the Royal Mamluks. In 1480, during the reign of Qāyit Bāy (1468–96) he was elevated to Chief Eunuch of the Royal Mamluks. He died in 1497. Khāliṣ is described as tender, kind and humble.[45] There is another record of a Takrūrī eunuch, ʻAnbar al-Takrūrī, the Chief Eunuch of the Mamluks, who died in 1509. He was pious, benevolent and mild. He had originally been one of the eunuchs of the Emir Jānī Bik *al-murtadd*.[46] These two records of eunuchs suggest that there were quite a few eunuchs in Egypt from Takrūr, which in this case covered the whole of Bilād al-Sūdān.

---

[43] According to *Ta'rīkh al-Fattāsh* [TF 34-5/ tr. 58–60] 9,000 slaves accompanied Mansā Mūsā and 500 slave girls accompanied his wife. According to *Ta'rīkh al-Sūdān* [TS 7/ translation in John O. Hunwick, *Timbuktu and the Songhay Empire: al-Sa'dī's Ta'rīkh al-Sūdān down to 1613 and other Contemporary Documents*, Leiden: Brill, 1999, p. 9] 500 slaves ran in front of Mansā Mūsā as he rode on his pilgrimage. Al-Muʻammar Abū ʻAbd Allāh b. Khadīja al-Kūmī, who met Mansā Mūsā on his return journey, told Ibn Khaldūn that "his equipment and furnishings were carried by 12,000 private slave women (*waṣā'if*) wearing gowns of brocade and Yemeni silk." [*Corpus*, p. 335] According to al-Maqrīzī, Mansā Mūsā brought with him to Egypt 14,000 slave girls for his personal service. [*Corpus*, p. 351.]

[44] Al-Maqrīzī, *Corpus*, p. 356.

[45] Ibn Taghrī Birdī (1410–70), *Corpus*, p. 360; Al-Sakhāwī (1427–97), *Corpus*, p. 362; Ibn Iyās (1448–1524), *Corpus*, p. 364–5.

[46] Ibn Iyās (1448–1524), *Corpus*, p. 365.

By that time there must have been eunuchs in their place of origin in Bilād al-Sūdān. The source of eunuchs was in all probability Nupe.[47] In the fifteenth century, the ruler of Nupe sent twelve eunuchs to Kano in exchange for ten horses. Queen Amīna of Zaria, in the fifteenth or sixteenth century, received eunuchs from Nupe. Muḥammad Rumfa, in the late fifteenth century, was the first to appoint eunuchs as important state officials.[48]

In the sixteenth century, eunuchs became important in the service of the *askiya*s of Songhay. At the beginning of the century Leo Africanus spoke of a private palace of the *askiya*, containing a great number of concubines and slaves, guarded by eunuchs.[49] The chronicles of Timbuktu reported great numbers of eunuchs, perhaps even exaggerated. At the court of Askiya Dāwūd there were 700 eunuch slaves. In 1591, after his defeat, Askiya Isḥāq took with him 40 slaves from among the eunuchs.[50] In 1584, Askiya al-Hājj responded to an embassy from the Moroccan sulṭān with valuable gifts, including 80 eunuchs. For 1588, there is a record of 4,000–strong cavalry force of eunuchs in Songhay.[51]

Legal Aspects of Concubinage

Ibn Amīr Ḥājib, a companion of Mansā Mūsā in Cairo, was told by him about a custom that if one of of his people reared a beautiful daughter he offered her to the king as a concubine, and the king possessed her without a marriage ceremony, as slaves are possessed. This in spite of the fact that Islam had triumphed among them and that they followed the Malikite school, and that this Sulṭān Mūsā was pious and assiduous in prayer, Koran reading, and mentioning God. "I said to him [says Ibn Amīr Ḥājib] that this was not permissible for a Muslim, whether in law or reason, and he said: 'Not even for kings?' and I replied: 'No! Not even for kings! Ask the scholars!' He said: 'By God, I did not know that. I hereby leave it and abandon it utterly!'"

---

[47] G.B. Allan and H.J. Fisher, *Slavery and Muslim Society in Africa: The Institution in Saharan and Sudanic Africa and the Trans-Saharan Trade*, New York: Hurst & Co., 2nd edition, 1972, p. 172.

[48] The Kano Chronicle in H.R. Palmer, *Sudanese Memoirs*, Lagos, 1928, iii, pp. 109–12.

[49] Leo Africanus 1956, ii, p. 471.

[50] TF 114, 153/ tr. 208, 273.

[51] TS 120, 124/ translation in Hunwick 1999, pp. 166, 171.

It was only in Egypt that the legal issue concerning concubinage was raised in the case of Mali. Less than two centuries later, such legal issues were current in Songhay among the *askiyas*. They used to take the daughters of their soldiers as concubines, which the author of *Ta'rīkh al-Fattāsh* referred to as "a misfortune that preceded the reign of Askiya Dāwūd."[52] In the same context, *Ta'rīkh al-Fattāsh* described Askiya Dāwūd's initiative that the *askiya* should inherit the soldiers because they were his slaves. Previously, the *askiya* had inherited only the horse, the shield and the javelins of the soldiers. It is likely that this move by the pious Askiya Dāwūd was taken in order to legitimize, according to the Muslim law, the custom of taking the soldiers' daughters as concubines, in order to continue it.

John Hunwick suggests that these slave soldiers belonged to the Sorko and the Arbi.[53] Askiya Muḥammad declared members of these two ethnic groups to be his property (*mamlūks*). If a freeman married a woman of these two tribes, her child would be free, but she would again become the *askiya*'s property when her husband died or if she was divorced.[54]

When Sunnī 'Alī raided a Fulani tribe he sent many of their women as gifts to the elders of Timbuktu and to some of the scholars and holy men, telling them to take them as concubines. Those who were not scrupulous about the practice of their religion did so, while the punctilious married them.[55] In a note to the translation, Hunwick suggests that these Fulani women were Muslims.

Liberation as an Act of Piety and Enslavement of Free Muslims

Emancipating slaves was considered an act of piety. According to *Ta'rīkh al-Fattāsh*, Mansā Mūsā emancipated one slave every day.[56] On his accession, Askiya Muḥammad liberated from slavery all those who claimed freedom and returned to them their property that Sunnī 'Alī had seized unlawfully.[57] The *faqīh* 'Uryān al-Ra's purchased many slaves and set them free for the sake of God and for the hereafter.[58]

---

[52] TF 116/ tr. 211.
[53] Hunwick, 1999, pp. xlvi-xlvii.
[54] TF 73-4/ tr. 140–1.
[55] TS 67/ translation in Hunwick 1999, pp. 95–6.
[56] TF 32/ tr. 55.
[57] TF 59/tr. 115.
[58] TS 52/ translation in Hunwick 1999, p. 74.

The enslavement of free Muslims was of great concern in sixteenth century Timbuktu. An enquiry came to Aḥmad Bābā from Tuat, about the propriety of enslaving black Muslims. His response: "the reason for enslavement is unbelief. In this respect there is no difference between the races." In *Mi'rāj al-ṣu'ūd*, written in 1615, Aḥmad bābā advised that any slave who claimed that his origin was from Borno, Kano, Katsina or Songhay should be freed, because these were the lands of Islam. Quoting Ibn Khaldūn, Aḥmad Bābā said that the people of Mali were longstanding Muslims, and he also declared that most of the Fulani were Muslims. At the end of the *Mi'rāj* Aḥmad bābā gave a list of non-Muslim groups that could be retained in slavery, including the Dogon, Bobo, and Mossi and as far as Dagomba, Borgu and Yorubaland.[59]

Slavery in Songhay

If the number of slaves in thirteenth and fourteenth century Mali increased compared to earlier periods, there was another upward leap in number under Songhay. The cumulative evidence of the two chronicles shows that very large numbers of slaves were amassed in the area of the Middle Niger in the sixteenth century.[60] The campaigns of the *askiya*s against Mossi, Futa Kingui, and Borgu brought in so many slaves that at a certain point the price of a slave in the Gao market dropped considerably.[61] Leo Africanus described busy slave markets in Gao and Timbuktu, where captives were sold.[62] Royals gave slaves as gifts to *'ulamā'*, as did Mansā Mūsā,[63] Askiya Muḥammad[64] and Askiya Dāwūd.[65]

It was in Songhay, with its great number of slaves, and perhaps only from the time of Askiya Dāwūd, that the *askiya*s had their own estates where rice was cultivated, along the Niger River from Dendi to Lake Debo. These lands at the heart of the Songhay Empire had been marginal to Mali, where no such estates seem to have existed. The estates were worked by slaves and supervised by slave officials, some of whom grew quite rich and powerful.[66]

---

[59] J.O. Hunwick, "Notes on slavery in the Songhay Empire", in *Slaves and Slavery in Muslim Africa*, edited by J.R. Willis, London: International Specialized Book Services, 1985, ii, p. 21.

[60] Hunwick 1985, p. 20.

[61] TS 95/ translation in Hunwick 1999, p. 136.

[62] Leo Africanus in Hunwick 1999, pp. 281, 283.

[63] Ibn Baṭṭūṭa, *Corpus* 295–6.

[64] TF 59/ tr. 115.

[65] TF 71-2, 106–8, 109, 113/tr. 137-8, 196–9, 201, 207.

[66] TF 94-95/178–80.

Economic Activities of Slaves in Bilād al-Sūdān

Slaves were used to excavate salt in the mine of Taghaza,[67] and copper in the mine of Takedda.[68] As the trade routes for the gold mines extended to the south, where pack animals could not go, slaves were used as porters. At the end of the fifteenth century Dyula traders bought slaves in Elmina, whom the Portuguese had shipped from Benin. These slaves were needed as porters to carry gold and other commodities.[69] At the beginning of the sixteenth century, Leo Africanus described how the merchants of Guangara (west of Bornu and southeast of Zamfara), on their way to the land of the gold, had their merchandise and necessities carried by slaves on their heads in wide deep calabashes. Armed slaves accompanied these caravans.[70] Also, the merchants of Agades on the road to Kano or Borno had a great number of armed slaves to serve as escort to guard against tribes that roamed the desert, and continually attacked and killed the merchants.[71]

George Brooks, following Charles Bird's linguistic evidence, suggests that because slaves were extensively used as caravan porters and soldiers, they contributed significantly to the spread of standardized and simplified Mandekan dialects. Together with traders, these porters were probably the principal diffusers of Mandekan languages outside the Mande heartland.[72]

The Exchange of Horses for Slaves

Horses became important in a military strike force only in thirteenth- and fourteenth-century Mali.[73] Al-'Umarī reported that the king of Mali imported Arab horses and paid high prices for them. His army numbered about 100,000, of whom about 10,000 were cavalry mounted on horses, the remainder being infantry without horses or other mounts.[74] Ibn Baṭṭūṭa found that horses in Mali

---

[67] Al-Qazwīnī, wrote 674/1275, *Corpus*, p. 178; Ibn Baṭṭūṭa, *Corpus*, p. 282.

[68] Ibn Baṭṭūṭa, *Corpus* 301–2.

[69] A. Teixeira da Mota, "The Mande trade in Costa de Mina according to Portuguese documents until the mid-sixteenth century". Paper presented at the Conference on Mandingue Studies, SOAS, 1972.

[70] Leo Africanus in Hunwick 1999, p. 289.

[71] Leo Africanus in Hunwick 1999, pp. 285–6.

[72] Brooks 1993, pp. 98–9.

[73] Ibid., pp. 99, 102.

[74] *Corpus*, p. 266.

were very expensive, and one of them was worth 100 *mithqals*.[75] At the beginning of the sixteenth century, the native horses in Timbuktu consisted only of some small hacks. The better quality horses came from North Africa with caravans, and were first brought to the king of Songhay, who took as many as he liked and paid accordingly. A horse worth ten ducats in Europe was sold in Gao for 40 or 50.[76] The artisans of Beni Goumi in the northern Sahara used to invest their earnings in horses they bought in Fez, and later sold them to merchants going down to the Sudan.[77]

From the late fifteenth century the Portuguese paid for slaves mainly in horses, which were in great demand among the African chiefs.[78] Like firearms, horses were paid for in slaves, and both forms of barter contributed to the intensity of slave raiding. During this century, according to the Kano Chronicle, the king of Kano received slave tribute from the Kwararafa in exchange for horses. The *galadima* of Kano raided southwards, sending slaves back to his ruler, who in return supplied him with horses.[79] Leo Africanus provides a detailed account of the exchange of horses for slaves in Borno:

> The king of Borno has no revenue other than what he obtains from raiding and killing his neighbours, who are his enemies. These live beyond the desert of Seu and are of an infinite number. Formerly they used to cross this desert and ravage the whole kingdom of Bornu. But the present king of the land got Barbary merchants to come and bring horses, which they exchanged for slaves at the rate of one horse for fifteen or twenty slaves. With these horses he mounted expeditions against the enemy, and made the merchants wait until his return. They sometimes spent two or three months waiting for him, and during this time lived at his expense. When he returned from the expedition he sometimes brought back enough slaves to pay the merchants, but at other times they

[75] Ibid., 297.

[76] Leo Africanus in Hunwick 1999, pp. 281, 283–4.

[77] Leo Africanus 1956, ii, p. 433.

[78] Zurara (1960), pp. 123–4, 132, 190, 217, 248–50, 256; Ca da Mosto 1895, pp. 39, 48, 88, 116–17; V. Fernandes (1506–07), *Description de la côte d'Afrique de Ceuta au Sénégal*. French translation annotated by P. de Cenival and Th. Monod, Paris 1938, pp. 47, 63, 71; V. Fernandes, (1506–10), *Description de la côte occidentale d'Afrique (Sénégal au Cap de Monte, Archipels)*. French translation annotated by Th. Monod, A. Teixeira da Mota and R. Mauny, Bissau 1951, pp. 7, 19–21, 27, 37, 43, 69, 77; Pacheco Pereira (c. 1506–08), *Esmeraldo du Situ orbis (Côte occidentale d 'Afrique du Sud Marocain au Gabon)*. Translation by R. Mauny, Bissau, 1956, pp. 47, 53, 59, 61, 73.

[79] Kano Chronicle, in Palmer 1928, iii, pp. 109–10.

> had to wait until the following year because the king did not have enough slaves to pay them, and they could not make such an expedition more than once a year without danger.[80]

The close connection between slaves and horses is shown by the fact that in Ifrīqiya the *nakhkhās* traded in both; he transported horses on the way south and slaves on the way back north.[81]

Conclusion

The evidence presented in this chapter suggests a growth in the size of the slave trade from the Western Sudan as well as in the number of slaves employed in Bilād al-Sūdān. This growth was in three large steps: the eleventh and twelfth centuries (Ghana and the Almoravids), the thirteenth and fourteenth centuries (Mali), and the fifteenth and sixteenth centuries (Songhay). Beyond the period discussed here, and mainly in the eighteenth and nineteenth centuries, slave farming gained in importance, mostly among Muslims. Jakhanke, Toronkawa and Marka usually had more slaves than their non-Muslim neighbours. Slave farming became the economic basis for rural Islamic scholarship.[82]

---

80 Leo Africanus in Hunwick 1999, pp. 290–91.

81 H.R. Idris, *La berberie orientale sous les Zirides, 10e–12e siècles*, Paris, 1962, ii, p. 684.

82 N. Levtzion, "Rural and urban Islam in West Africa: an introductory essay," in *Rural and Urban Islam in West Africa*, edited by N. Levtzion and J.H. Fisher, Boulder: Lynne Rienner Publishers, 1987, pp. 9–14; reprinted in N. Levtzion, *Islam in West Africa: Religion, Society and Politics before 1800*, London: Variorum, 1994.

Bibliography

Africanus, Leo. *Description de l'Afrique.* New edition translated by A. Epaulard and annotated by A. Epaulard, T. Monod, H. Lhote, and R. Mauny. 2 vols. Paris, 1956.

Allan, G.B. and H.J. Fisher, *Slavery and Muslim Society in Africa: The Institution in Saharan and Sudanic Africa and the Trans-Saharan Trade*, New York: Hurst & Co., 2nd edition, 1972.

Brooks, G. *Landlords and Strangers: Ecology, Society, and Trade in Western Africa, 1000–1630*, Boulder: Westview Press, 1993.

Ca da Mosto, A. *Relations des voyages à la côte occidentale d'Afrique.* French translation by C. Schefer. Paris, originally written around 1455–7, 1895.

Fernandes, V. *Description de la côte d'Afrique de Ceuta au Sénégal.* French translation annotated by P. de Cenival and T. Monod, Paris, originally written around 1506–07, 1938.

Fernandes, V. *Description de la côte occidentale d'Afrique (Sénégal au Cap de Monte, Archipels).* French translation annotated by Th. Monod, A. Teixeira da Mota and R. Mauny, Bissau, originally written around 1506–10, 1951.

Houdas, O. and M. Delafosse (eds.), *Ta'rīkh al-Fattāsh*, Paris: de l'Ecole des Langues Orientales Vivantes, Ve série, vol. X, 1913–14, reprinted 1964.

Hunwick, J.O. "Notes on slavery in the Songhay Empire", in *Slaves and Slavery in Muslim Africa*, edited by John R. Willis, London: International Specialized Book Services, 1985, pp. 16–32.

Hunwick, J.O. *Timbuktu and the Songhay Empire: al-Sa'dī's Ta'rīkh al-Sūdān down to 1613 and other Contemporary Documents*, Leiden: Brill, 1999.

Idris, H. R. *La berberie orientale sous les Zirides, 10e–12e siècles*, Paris, 1962.

La Roncière, Charles de. *La Découverte de l'Afrique au moyen âge, cartographes et explorateurs*, Cairo, 1925.

Levtzion, N. "Rural and urban Islam in West Africa: an introductory essay," in *Rural and Urban Islam in West Africa*, edited by N. Levtzion and J.H. Fisher, Boulder: Lynne Rienner Publishers, 1987, pp. 9–14; reprinted in N. Levtzion, *Islam in West Africa: Religion, Society and Politics before 1800*, London: Variorum, 1994.

Levtzion, N. and Hopkins, J.F.P. (eds.), *Corpus of Early Arabic Sources for West African History*, Cambridge: Cambridge University Press, 1981.

Malowist, M. "Les fondaments de l'expansion européenne en Afrique au 15e siècle: Europe, Maghreb et Soudan occidentale", *Acta Poloniae Historica*, 18 (1968).

Palmer, H.R. *Sudanese Memoirs*, Lagos, 1928.

Pereira, P. *Esmeraldo du Situ orbis (Côte occidentale d 'Afrique du Sud Marocain au Gabon).* Translation by R. Mauny, Bissau, originally written around 1506–08, 1956.

Teixeira da Mota, A. "The Mande trade in Costa de Mina according to Portuguese documents until the mid-sixteenth century". Paper presented at the Conference on Mandingue Studies, SOAS, 1972.

Verlinden, C. "Esclavage noir en France méridoniale et courants de traite en Afrique", *Annales du Midi* 73 (1966), pp. 335–43.

Zurara, G.E. de. *Chronique de Guinée.* French translation by L. Bourdon, Dakar, originally written in 1453, 1960.

X

RELIGIOUS REFORM IN EIGHTEENTH-CENTURY MOROCCO

Nehemia Levtzion and Gideon Weigert

1. The Reformist Sultans

During the second half of the eighteenth century and the first two decades of the nineteenth, Morocco was ruled by two reformist sultans, Sīdī Muḥammad ibn ʿAbdallāh (1171–1205/1757–1790) and his son Mawlāy Sulaymān (1207–1238/1792–1822). Scholarly interest in this period has been clearly manifested in three recent doctoral dissertations. Two of the authors of these studies, Mohamed El-Mansour and Fatima Harrak, concentrate on internal dynamics in Morocco to explain the religious policies of the two sultans.[1] The third author, Rachid Abdalla El-Nasser, though he pays due attention to the Moroccan historical context, argues for a strong Wahhābī influence on religious developments in Morocco, calling Mawlāy Sulaymān the "Wahhābī."[2]

Mawlāy Sulaymān was indeed one of the very few Muslim rulers who expressed a certain sympathy towards the Wahhābīs. But, as a *sharīf* and a practicing *ṣūfī*, he rejected the basic Wahhābī tenets. In fact, the assumption that all reform movements of the eighteenth century were ramifications of the Wahhābiyya has been disproved by the argument that only the Wahhābiyya was anti-*ṣūfī*, whereas all the other movements developed within reform *ṣūfī* orders.

Reformed *ṣūfī* orders appeared also in Morocco in the seventeenth and eighteenth centuries, and were patronized by the two reformist sultans, who sought to eradicate popular sufism and its religious and political manifestations. The two sultans did not, of course, operate in a vacuum but were influenced by a renewed spirit of orthodoxy among the *ʿulamāʾ* of Fez, who were in contact during that period with Muslim scholars in the eastern parts of the Muslim world. We therefore suggest

---

[1] Mohamed El-Mansour, "Political and social developments in Morocco during the reign of Mawlāy Sulaymān, 1792–1812," Ph.D. dissertation, SOAS, University of London, 1982; now published as *Morocco in the Reign of Mawlāy Sulaymān*. Wisbach: Menas Press, 1990. Fatima Harrak, "State and religion in eighteenth-century Morocco: the religious policy of Sidi Muḥammad ibn ʿAbdallāh, 1757–1790," Ph.D. dissertation, SOAS, University of London, 1989.

[2] Rachid Abdalla El-Nasser, "Morocco from Kharijism to Wahhabism: the quest for religious purism," Ph.D. dissertation, University of Michigan, 1985; see title of ch. 5, p. 478.

that religious developments in Fez ought to be studied within the wider context of Islamic renewal and reform in the eighteenth century.[3]

2. Influence of the Egyptian Khalwatiyya

A world-wide view of eighteenth-century renewal and reform in Islam is only now beginning to develop, and a more coordinated research is needed in order to understand the particular characteristics of individual movements. The growth in scale of the pilgrimage was undoubtedly one of the reasons for the simultanuous appearance of such movements in different parts of the Muslim world. It may also explain the role of the *ḥaramayn*, Mecca and Medina, as foci of Islamic revivalism.[4]

There are no figures to prove that the number of pilgrims from the Maghrib increased significantly in the eighteenth century. But accounts of Moroccan pilgrims, in the genre of the "*Riḥla* literature," which had declined since the fourteenth century, were resurrected in the seventeenth century, and flourished in the eighteenth, a period during which the number of Maghribi *raḥḥāla* increased considerably.[5]

Many of the leading *ʿulamāʾ* of Fez in the eighteenth century made the pilgrimage, and stopped in Cairo on their way to Mecca. Religious and scholarly life in Cairo was then dominated by the Khalwatiyya order. For one hundred and twenty years, from 1137/1724 to 1254/1838, all but one of those who held the office of *shaykh al-Azhar* were Khalwatīs. Before the eighteenth century, however, the Khalwatiyya in Egypt had been marginal and of little significance, since most of its adherents were Turks, apart from some members of the upper classes.

It was Muḥammad Sālim al-Ḥifnī (1100–1181/1689–1768) who made the Khalwatiyya a truly Egyptian order which spread among all walks of life. Al-Ḥifnī was inspired by the mystical teachings of Muṣṭafā ibn Kamāl al-Dīn al-Bakrī (1099–1161/1688–1749).[6] Four elements in the

---

[3] See the Introductory Essay to N. Levtzion and J.O. Voll (eds.), *Eighteenth Century Renewal and Reform in Islam*, Syracuse 1987.

[4] N. Levtzion and G. Weigert, "The Muslim holy cities (*al-ḥaramayn*), Mecca and Medina, as foci of Islamic revivalism in the eighteenth century," paper presented to the International Conference on "Sacred Space: shrine, city, land," in memory of Professor Joshua Prawer, Jerusalem, June 8–13, 1992.

[5] El-Nasser, 186–87, 194–95; On the "*Riḥla* literature," see also A. El-Moudden, "The ambivalence of *riḥla*: community integration and self-definition in Moroccan travel accounts, 1300–1800," in D.E. Eickelman and J. Piscatori (eds.), *Muslim Travellers: Pilgrimage, Migration and the Religious Imagination*, Berkeley 1990.

[6] G. Weigert, "The Khalwatiyya in Egypt in the Eighteenth Century: a nucleus for Islamic revival," Ph.D. Dissertation, Hebrew University of Jerusalem, 1989 (in Hebrew with a summary in English); see a detailed analysis of the *ṣūfī* affiliation of *shuyūkh al-Azhar* in app. B, pp. 239–44. On the revival of the Khalwatiyya in Egypt, see earlier studies by: E.L. Bannerth, *Le Khalwatiyya en Egypte*, *M.I.D.E.O.* (Cairo), 1964–66; B.G. Martin, "A Short history of the Khalwati order of dervishes," in

teaching of al-Bakrī could have contributed to the revivalism of the Khalwatiyya in Egypt. First, greater discipline in the performance of the litanies of the *ṭarīqa*. Second, exclusive affiliation to the *ṭarīqa*. Third, a greater scope for the participation of common people in the ceremonies of the *ṭarīqa*. Fourth, strict adherence to the *sharī'a*. Hence, the revived Khalwatiyya that gained ascendancy in Egypt under the leadership of al-Ḥifnī, was a cohesive, *sharīʿa* oriented *ṭarīqa* that could accommodate the leading scholars, but it was also a popular and activist *ṭarīqa* that reached out to the common people.[7]

We have dealt at some length with the Khalwatiyya because many of the *ʿulamā'* of Fez, on their way to Mecca, met the leading Khalwatī *shaykhs* in Cairo. Aḥmad ibn ʿAbd al-ʿAzīz al-Hilālī al-Sijilmāsī (d. 1175/1761) went to Mecca twice. In Cairo he received a certificate of study (*ijāza*) for *Dalā'il al-khayrāt* from Muṣṭafā ibn Kamāl al-Dīn al-Bakrī and from al-Ḥifnī. He was proud of the numerous *ḥadīths* with their *asānīd* that he had learned from al-Ḥifnī, and often quoted them to his students in his *majlis* in Fez. Al-Hilālī also composed a poem in praise of al-Ḥifnī (or al-Ḥifnawī, as he called him).[8]

Aḥmad ibn Muḥammad al-Ṣaqalī (d. 1177/1763–4), the leading Ṣūfī personality in Morocco in the middle of the eighteenth century, went to Mecca three times. During the third pilgrimage he met al-Ḥifnī in Cairo, and was initiated by him to the Khalwatiyya. Al-Ḥifnī also gave him licence to propagate the *wird* (*wa-akhadha ʿanhu wa-adhina lahu fī qabūl al-khalq wa-jamʿihim ʿalā Allāh*). On his return to Fez, al-Ṣaqalī taught his disciples the mystical litanies he had learned from al-Ḥifnī (*laqqanahum al-aḥzāb wa-'l-awrād*). As long as al-Ṣaqalī lived, they used to gather to perform these litanies.[9]

We may speculate about Aḥmad al-Ṣaqalī's *ṣūfī* affiliation after his encounter with al-Ḥifnī on the basis of a *silsila* of Aḥmad Ibn Idrīs: *akhadha ṭarīq al-sāda al-shādhiliyya ʿan al-ustādh al-shaykh ʿAbd al-Wahhāb al-Tāzī ʿan al-shaykh Abī 'l-ʿAbbās Aḥmad al-Ṣaqalī ʿan al-shaykh Muṣṭafā al-Bakrī wahātahu (sic) al-ṭarīqa shādhiliyya khalwatiyya*.[10] At that stage, it seems, the Khalwatiyya could not have

N.R. Keddie (ed.), *Scholars, Saints and Sufis*, Berkeley 1972, pp. 276–305; F. de Jong, "Muṣṭafā Kamāl al-Dīn al-Bakrī (1688–1749): revival and reform of the Khalwatiyya tradition?," in Levtzion and Voll 1987, pp. 117–32.

[7] Weigert Ph.D. 1989, pp. 104–24; Weigert and Levtzion, "Renewal and reform of the Khalwatiyya in Egypt in the eighteenth century," paper presented at the 24th Annual Meeting of MESA, San Antonio, November 1990.

[8] Al-Qādirī, *Nashr al-mathānī*, ed. by Muḥammad Hajwī and Aḥmad al-Tawfīq, Rabat 1986, vol. 4, pp. 144–49. Al-Qādirī himself attended al-Hilālī's *majlis*.

[9] Al-Qādirī, vol. 4, pp. 156–57; ʿAbd al-Ḥayy al-Kattānī, *Fihris al-fahāris wa-'l-ithbāt*, Beirut, 1982, vol. 1, p. 262.

[10] Makhlūf (Muḥammad), *Shajarat al-nūr al-zakiyya fī ṭabaqāt al-Mālikiyya*, Beirut, reprinted 1930–1, p. 396; the same *silsila* is repeated in the entry for

replaced the rooted Shādhiliyya in Morocco. Aḥmad al-Ṣaqalī, who was deeply influenced by what he had learned in Egypt, may have introduced Khalwatī litanies into the already variagated Shādhiliyya.[11]

Muḥammad b. al-Ṭayyib al-Qādirī (1123–1187/1711–1773), the author of *Nashr al-mathānī*, also received an *ijāza* from al-Ḥifnī.[12] He dedicated a long biography to al-Ḥifnī, an honour accorded to only few scholars of the East. It was an acknowledgement of al-Ḥifnī's contribution to the Maghrib in the two fields of *ḥadīth* and Ṣūfism (*al-muḥaddith al-ṣūfī . . . kathura atbāʿuhu wa-talāmidhatuhu fi'l-ʿilm wa-'l-ṭarīqa*).[13]

The *ṣūfī* and *sharīf* Abū Muḥammad ʿAbd al-Majīd b. ʿAlī al-Manālī (d. 1163/1750), who accompanied Aḥmad al-Ṣaqalī to Cairo and Mecca, met both al-Ḥifnī and his student Maḥmūd al-Kurdī.[14] Sīdī ʿUmar al-Fāsī (d. 1188/1774–5), a prominent teacher in the scholastic network of Fez, also received an *ijāza* from al-Ḥifnī, *shaykh al-ṭarīqa al-khalwatiyya*.[15]

The *qāḍī* al-Tawūdī Ibn Sūda (d. 1210/1795), the senior scholar in Fez during the reign of Sīdī Muḥammad, was initiated to Ṣufism by Aḥmad al-Ṣaqalī.[16] Ibn Sūda therefore might have been acquainted with the Khalwatiyya through al-Ṣaqalī. During his visits to Cairo, on his way to the *ḥajj* and back, in 1181 and 1182/1767–8, he met Maḥmūd al-Kurdī (1127–1195/1715–1780) and other Khalwati *shaykhs*, like ʿAlī al-Bayūmī, Ḥasan al-Jabartī and ʿAbd al-Raḥmān al-ʿAydarūsī. Ibn Sūda gave an outstanding lecture on Mālik's *al-Muwaṭṭa'* at *riwāq* al-Maghāriba of al-Azhar, before a large audience, attended by the most prominent scholars, and was acclaimed *Hilāl al-Maghrib*. Murtaḍā al-Zabīdī praised Ibn Sūda's erudition and acknowledged his indebtedness to him for everything that he had learned from him. Al-Jabartī dedicated a long biography to Ibn Sūda, in appreciation of his scholarly status, an honour accorded to few scholars from the Maghrib.[17]

It was probably on the advice of Maḥmūd al-Kurdī that both al-Tawūdī Ibn Sūda in 1191/1777 and Aḥmad al-Tijānī three years earlier,

---

Muḥammad b. ʿAli al-Sanūsī, ibid., p. 400.

[11] This *silsila* omits al-Ḥifnī, who initiated Aḥmad al-Ṣaqalī. Also, ʿAbd al-Wahhāb al-Tāzī (1099–1206/1688–1792), the teacher of Aḥmad ibn Idrīs and of Muḥammad b. ʿAli al-Sanūsī, was indeed a devoted disciple of Aḥmad al-Ṣaqalī. But according to Makhlūf (pp. 371–72), he was initiated to the Khalwatiyya directly by al-Ḥifnī himself, and he studied also with Maḥmūd al-Kurdī.

[12] Makhlūf, pp. 352–53

[13] Al-Qādirī, vol. 4, pp. 182–88.

[14] Makhlūf, p. 353

[15] Ibid., p. 356; see also p. 357: the *ṣūfī* al-Ḥusayn b. Muḥammad al-Saʿīd al-Sharīf al-Wartilātī studied with al-Ḥifnī.

[16] M. Lakhdar, *La vie litteraire au Maroc sous la dynastie ʿAlawide (1075–1311/1664–1894)*, Rabat 1971, pp. 258.

[17] Al-Jabartī, *ʿAjā'ib al-athār fi'l-tarājim wa'l-akhbār*, Cairo 1297, vol. 2, pp. 242–44.

were anxious to meet Muḥammad b. ʿAbd al-Karīm al-Sammān in Medina. Al-Sammān had been initiated to the Khalwatiyya by Muṣṭafā al-Bakrī himself, and was famous among the ṣūfī *shaykhs* of the *ḥaramayn*. His disciples established Sammāniyya orders in Indonesia and in the Sudan, which were in essence offshoots of the Khalwatiyya.[18]

3. Sīdī Muḥammad's Orientation to the Mashriq

All these Khalwatī *shaykhs* became known in Morocco, and were honoured by Sīdī Muḥammad. In 1198/1783 he sent a generous gift (*ṣila*) to the Khalwatī *shaykh* Aḥmad al-Dardīr (1127–1201/1715–1786), who was also the chief Mālikī *muftī* in Cairo. A certain incident took place in Cairo involving the son of the Moroccan sultan, which al-Dardīr resolved to the satisfaction and admiration of Sīdī Muḥammad. The latter rewarded al-Dardīr, sending him tenfold the original sum. Al-Dardīr used this generous gift to go on the pilgrimage and to build a *zāwiya*, in which he was buried less than two years later.[19]

The most prominent scholar in Cairo at that time was Murtaḍā al-Zabīdī (1145–1205/1732–1790), author of the dictionary *Tāj al-ʿarūs*. His interest in the Arabic language was motivated by the study of *ḥadīth*, which was his major concern. He came to Cairo in 1167/1753 and was closely associated with the leading Khalwatī *shaykhs*. He studied with al-Ḥifnī, and wrote commentaries on works by Muṣṭafā al-Bakrī and al-Ḥifnī. There is, however, no positive evidence that al-Zabīdī was formally initiated into the Khalwatiyya.[20] Al-Jabartī was so impressed with the Moroccans' veneration of al-Zabīdī that, in a way of exaggeration he said that "if one of them arrived in Cairo on his pilgrimage and he did not visit al-Zabīdī, and did not give him a gift, his pilgrimage was not complete."[21]

The Moroccan sultan used to send gifts to al-Zabīdī, which he accepted with gratitude. But towards the end of his life, after the death of his first wife, al-Zabīdī shut himself up in his home, refused to see visitors and to accept gifts, and even stopped teaching. It was under these circumstances that al-Zabīdī refused to accept the gift of Sīdī Muḥammad in 1201/1786.[22]

---

[18] On Ibn Sūda's meeting with al-Sammān, al-Jabartī, vol. 2, 243; on al-Sammān and the Sammāniyya, see Weigert, pp. 206–209.

[19] al-Jabartī, vol. 2, p. 148.

[20] Following Weigert's study of al-Zabīdī, Ph.D. dissertaion, appendix A, pp. 224–38.

[21] Al-Jabartī, vol. 2, p. 200.

[22] Ibid., pp. 202–203; see also al-Duʿayyif (Muḥammad al-Ribāṭī), *Ta'rīkh al-dawla al-saʿīda*, Rabat 1986, vol. 1, p. 347, who mistakenly dates this incident to 1197/1778.

Sīdī Muḥammad again showed his respect for the Egyptian scholars when in 1203/1788 he sent a copy of his controversial royal decree (*manshūr*) to the *ʿulamāʾ* of Cairo, seeking their comments, whether favourable or critical. Indeed, he solicited their opinion in an attempt to overcome the opposition of local *ʿulamāʾ* to his religious reforms. The positive reply from Egypt was written by Muḥammad al-Amīr al-Mālikī al-Maghribī (1154–1232/1817–1742), and was endorsed by two other Egyptian scholars; Muḥammad al-Ḥarīrī al-Ḥanafī and al-Fayūmī al-Mālikī.[23]

After the death of Aḥmad al-Dardīr (in 1201/1786) Muḥammad al-Amīr became the leading Mālikī scholar in Egypt. He came to Egypt at the age of nine, but maintained extensive Maghribī connections. He studied with al-Tāwūdī Ibn Sūda, during the latter's visit to Cairo in 1181/1767–8, and with Muḥammad b. ʿAbd al-Salām al-Nāṣirī during his *ḥajj* in 1196/1781. Muḥammad al-Amīr received annual gifts from the Moroccan sultan, who also sent students from Morocco to study with him.[24] When Sīdī Muḥammad completed the writing of *al-Futūḥāt al-Ilāhiyya* in 1198/1783, he sent copies to the East. Muḥammad al-Amīr and Muḥammad al-Ḥarīrī praised it as a "ray of the *sunna*."[25]

The sultan Sīdī Muḥammad, more than his predecessors, sought closer political relations with the *mashriq*. He exchanged missions and gifts with two Ottoman sultans, Muṣṭafā III (1757–1774) and ʿAbd al-Ḥamīd I (1774–1789). He also cultivated relations with the *sharīf* of Mecca Surūr b. Musāʿid (died 1202/1788), to whom he gave his daughter in marriage in 1182/1768–9.[26] On several occasions he sent gifts to the *shurafāʾ*, scholars and ṣūfīs of the *ḥaramayn*, and established hostels in Mecca for the Maghribīs.[27]

Abuʾl-Qāsim al-Zayyānī, an official historian of the ʿAlawī sultans, built up the image of Sīdī Muḥammad, saying that he was famous in the Mashriq as a saint (*quṭb* or *walī*). On his travels in Egypt and Syria between 1206/1792 and 1210/1795 (i.e., after the death of Sīdī Muḥammad), people sought the blessing of al-Zayyānī, because of his association with Sīdī Muḥammad.[28]

---

[23] Ibn Zaydān (ʿAbd al-Raḥmān b. Muḥammad), *Itḥāf aʿlām al-nās bi jamāl akhbār ḥāḍirat Miknās*, Rabat 1347–1352 /1928–1933, vol. 3, p. 214; the two scholars were identified by Harrak, p. 324.

[24] For al-Amīr's biography, see al-Jabartī, vol. 4, pp. 284–86; Makhlūf, pp. 362–63. On his reply to Sīdī Muḥammad, see al-Ḥujjī, *al-Fikr al-sāmī fi al-fiqh al-islāmī*, Rabat, vol. 4, p. 130), quoted by Harrak pp. 323–25.

[25] El-Nasser, p. 324 (quoting Malin's introduction to *al-Futūḥāt* rather than a contemporary source); see note 32 below.

[26] Al-Zayyānī (Abū ʾl-Qāsim), *al-Turjumān al-muʿrib ʿan duwal al-Mashriq waʾl-Maghrib*. French translation by O. Houdas, *Le Maroc de 1631 a 1812*. Paris 1886, pp. 78, 84–85.

[27] Ibn Zaydan, pp. 227–28

[28] Al-Zayyānī (Abuʾl-Qāsim), *al-Turjumāna al-kubrā fi akhbār al-maʿmūr barran*

4. The Primacy of *Ḥadīth* Studies

Emphasis on the study of *ḥadīth* was one of the characteristics of eighteenth-century revivalism in the *ḥaramayn* and in Egypt.[29] Moroccan scholars were indeed exposed to the teaching of *ḥadīth* in the East. Aḥmad al-Hilālī al-Sijilmāsī, we have seen, studied *ḥadīth* with al-Ḥifnī. Al-Zabīdī, who was visited by almost all the Moroccan *ʿulamāʾ*, taught mainly *ḥadīth*. Muḥammad b. ʿAbd al-Salām al-Darʿī al-Nāṣirī studied *ḥadīth* in the *ḥaramayn*.[30]

In Morocco the most celebrated *ḥadīth* scholar of an earlier generation had been Idrīs b. Muḥammad al-ʿIrāqī (d. 1183/1769), who became known as "al-Suyūṭī al-Maghribī."[31] But Sīdī Muḥammad was not satisfied with the study of *ḥadīth* in Morocco, because the scope of the collections were limited to the *Muwaṭṭaʾ* of Mālik and the *Ṣaḥīḥān* of al-Bukhārī and Muslim. Moroccan scholars and students, as well as official delegates, who travelled to the East were encouraged by Sīdī Muḥammad to acquire books, in particular *ḥadīth*. He took pride in the fact that it was he who first introduced the *musnads* of Abū Ḥanīfa, al-Shāfiʿī and Ibn Ḥanbal to the Maghrib.[32]

Sīdī Muḥammad thus broadened the horizons of the scholars of Fez. He himself took part in a circle of *ʿulamāʾ* that held regular sessions on *ḥadīth*, and compiled works on *ḥadīth* with the help of the *ʿulamāʾ* of his *majlis*.[33] Moreover, he advised his son to abandon all branches of learning and to concentrate on the study of *ḥadīth*, expressing regret for the time he himself had wasted in his youth on the study of history and poetry.[34]

5. *Mālikī* by School of Law and *Ḥanbalī* by Doctrine

The emphasis on the study of *ḥadīth*, which is, by its nature, above *madhhab* partisanship, may be linked to Sīdī Muḥammad's attempt to ease somewhat the bonds of the Mālikī school. He expressed firm belief

wa baḥran, Rabat 1967, pp. 214, 278.

29 J.O. Voll, "*Ḥadīth* scholars and *ṭarīqas*: an *ʿulamāʾ* group in the eighteenth century *ḥaramayn* and their impact in the Islamic world," *Journal of Asian and African Studies* (Leiden), 15 (1980), pp. 264–73.

30 Lakhdar, pp. 293–94

31 Gannūn (ʿAbdallāh), *al-Nubūgh al-Maghribī fiʾl-adab al-ʿarabī*, Tetouan 1934, pp. 222–23; Lahkdar, pp. 232–33; Makhlūf, p. 356.

32 Sīdī Muḥammad ibn ʿAbdallāh, *al-Futūḥāt al-ilāhiyya fi aḥādīth khayr al-bariyya*, ed. Mulin, Rabat 1980, p. 1; al-Zayyānī, *al-Turjumāna al-kubrā*, pp. 126, 184.

33 Al-Nāṣirī (Aḥmad b. Khālid), *Kitāb al-istiqṣāʾ li-akhbār duwal al-Maghrib al-Aqṣā*, Casablanca 1954–56, vol. 8, p. 66

34 Al-Zayyānī, *al-Turjumāna al-kubrā*, pp. 63–64.

in the four *imāms*, founders of the four schools of law, asserting that they are all equal.[35] His departure from conventional Islamic thought was further demonstrated in his saying: "I am Mālikī by *madhhab* and Ḥanbalī by doctrine [*i'tiqād*]."[36]

Being aware of the controversial nature of this saying, Sīdī Muḥammad felt obliged to offer an explanation. He did this in the conclusion of *al-Futūḥāt al-Ilāhiyya*, which he completed in 1198/1784. He claimed to be "Ḥanbalī by doctrine" because Ibn Ḥanbal opposed the study of *'ilm al-kalām*. None of the *salaf*, the four *imāms* and *ahl al-ḥadīth* had been concerned with *kalām*, until al-Ash'arī became engaged in refuting the false ideas of the Mu'tazila. The Mālikīs followed al-Ash'arī and called him *nāṣir al-sunna* (defender of the *sunna*). But the Ḥanbalīs refused to have anything to do with *kalām*, and considered it a *bid'a*. Therefore the Ḥanbalīs' doctrine is simple, free of delusions and fantastic notions, in line with the doctrine of the *salaf*.[37]

Two years later, in 1200/1786, in a letter to al-Tāwūdī Ibn Sūda, Sīdī Muḥammad reiterated his opposition to the study of *'ilm al-kalām* and *'ilm al-manṭiq* (logics), because all the principles of the unity of Allāh were in the Qur'ān.[38] Sīdī Muḥammad goes back to *ahl al-ḥadīth* of the ninth and tenth centuries, the orthodox adversaries of the Mu'tazila. They represented scripturalism and opposed theological speculation. The Ḥanbalīs were in the forefront of *ahl al-ḥadīth*.

Sīdī Muḥammad's Ḥanbalism was, therefore, limited to the rejection of speculative theology, and was not connected in any way with the rise of the Wahhābiyya in Arabia. Though Muḥammad b. 'Abd al-Wahhāb had initiated his *da'wa* shortly before the accession of Sīdī Muḥammad, the influence of the Wahhābiyya was then restricted to Najd and other peripheral parts of Arabia. The Wahhābīs had an impact on the world of Islam only after they had conquered Mecca in 1803. That Sīdī Muḥammad was not allied with the Wahhābīs is confirmed also by his close relations with the *sharīf* of Mecca, a rival of the Wahhābīs.

But Sīdī Muḥammad also confirmed his commitment to the Mālikī school of law, though he advocated reforms in the study of *fiqh* as well as in legal procedures. He sought to limit the study of the *Mukhtaṣar* of Khalīl (died 1374), the most popular Mālikī legal manual. He did not, however, forbid it altogether because of the *'ulamā'*'s attachment to Khalīl (*naḥnu khalīliyyūn in ḍalla ḍalalnā wa-in ihtadā ihtadaynā*).

---

35 *Al-Futūḥāt*, p. 459.

36 Ibid., p. 457.

37 Ibid., pp. 457–58.

38 The correspondence between Sīdī Muḥammad and al-Tāwūdī Ibn Sūda is quoted in Dāwūd, pp. 31–34. Significantly, Ibn Abī Zayd himself was influenced by al-Ash'arī (H.R. Idris in *EI*², vol. 3, p. 695).

He conceded that the study of the *Mukhtaṣar* be permitted, but only with five approved commentaries, not with others like that of al-Zurqānī, which he considered a waste of time.[39]

Sīdī Muḥammad's edicts often went against the mood, views and conduct of the *ʿulamāʾ*, even those whom he admired. Aḥmad al-Dardīr, the Egyptian Khalwatī *shaykh* and a Mālikī *muftī*, wrote a commentary on Khalīl's *Mukhtaṣar*, in which he relied on al-Zurqānī, while al-Tāwūdī Ibn Sūda wrote a commentary on al-Zurqānī's commentary of Khalīl.[40]

Sīdī Muḥammad, in fact, sought to revise much of the curriculum which most scholars followed. A detailed autobiographical account of what might be taken as a typical education, is given by the historian al-Zayyānī, who worked with the most prominent scholars of his time. He studied Khalīl's *Mukhtaṣar* several times with different teachers. He also studied the commentary of al-Zurqānī with Muḥammad Banānī, and then attended Muḥammad b. Ibrāhīm's sessions on Khalīl, and became disgusted with his teaching (*fa-kuntu ashmaʾizzu min abḥāthihi*). Was he reflecting on the repetitive regurgitation of this legal manual and its commentaries?[41]

Sīdī Muḥammad was even more determined in a decree (*manshūr*) to the *qāḍīs* in 1203/1789. He criticised the conduct of the *qāḍīs* and the *muftīs*, who treated the poor and the orphans unjustly and wronged them. Sīdī Muḥammad had no doubt that this was the result of abandoning the teaching of the more ancient (*aqdamūn*) authorities, of Mālik and the first generations of his followers, and of confining themselves to Khalīl's *Mukhtaṣar* and its commentaries. He warned *qāḍīs* against continuing such aberrations.[42] He actually discharged about twenty *qāḍīs* of towns, tribes and villages.[43]

In view of Sīdī Muḥammad's concern with *ḥadīth* and his reliance on earlier authorities, it is significant that he rejected *ijtihād* and considered *ʿilm al-uṣūl* an exhausted subject, because "the books of *fiqh* had already been written down."[44]

In an edict to the teachers in the mosques of Fez concerning curricula and syllabi, Sīdī Muḥammad forbade the teaching of the following sci-

---

[39] Ibn Zaydān, *Itḥāf*, vol. 3, p. 212. (On al-Zurqānī, d. 1099/1688, author of *Sharkh Mukhtaṣar Khalīl*, see Brockelmann GAL, S II, p. 438). According to Sulaymān al-Hawwāt, in a biography of his master al-Tāwūdī Ibn Sūda, leading scholars, like Ibn Sūda, discontinued the teaching of Khalīl during the last two or three years of Sīdī Muḥammad's reign (Harrak, pp. 351–52, 360). See also *Kitāb al-istiqṣāʾ* (vol. 8, p. 67), saying that Sīdī Muḥammad forbade the teaching of Khalīl altogether, and that no one read *Mukhtaṣar Khalīl*.

[40] Al-Jabartī, vol. 2, p. 147 on al-Dardīr and p. 244 on Ibn Sūda.

[41] Al-Zayyānī, *al-Turjumāna al-kubrā*, p. 57.

[42] Ibn Zaydān, *Itḥāf*, vol. 3, pp. 188–207, 211.

[43] Ibid., pp. 215–16.

[44] Ibid., p. 213.

ences: *kalām* (theology), *mantiq* (logics), *ʿulūm al-falāsifa* (philosophy), and the study of the books of *ghulāt al-ṣūfiyya* (the extremist Ṣūfis). Those who wished to pursue these studies, he instructed, ought to do it in the privacy of their homes with their friends. This was not therefore a categorical prohibition. Its purpose, as Sīdī Muḥammad said explicitly, was to avoid misguiding students who came to Fez from the countryside to study *fiqh* and *ḥadīth*. When they were taught the sciences which had been forbidden, they might believe that they derived benefits from those sciences and would abandon the sessions of *fiqh*. Subsequently, when they would be asked for a legal opinion they would not be in a position to give a proper answer.[45]

The educational approach is evident also in Sīdī Muḥammad's reply to al-Tāwūdī ibn Sūda, in which he explained that his disapproval of Khalīl was based on what was known about leading *fuqahāʾ*, who refrained from reading Khalīl's chapters on the *jizya* and on the *ridda*, which were detestable. Similarly he censured *Kitāb al-shifā* of ʿIyāḍ following the agreement of the *ʿulamāʾ* that the last quarter of *al-Shifā* should not be read because of its abominable content.[46]

6. Sufism and the Speculative Sciences

Sīdī Muḥammad's objections to the teachings of Sufism, and in particular the *Kitāb al-Iḥyāʾ* of al-Ghazālī, were again educational and disciplinary. In his letter to al-Tāwūdī ibn Sūda he explained that in forbidding the teaching of al-Ghazālī in the mosques he followed *ʿulamāʾ* from all countries, who had warned against teaching it to all the Muslims.[47] He also censured Murtaḍā al-Zabīdī for writing a commentary on *Kitāb al-Iḥyāʾ*, saying that he should have used his time for something more beneficial.[48]

It appears, therefore, that Sīdī Muḥammad sought to avoid the dissemination of the speculative sciences among the wider public and to prevent people wasting their time on anything other than the basic Islamic sciences, and in particular *ḥadīth*. Indeed, time and again Sīdī Muḥammad said that he did all this out of love for the Prophet.[49]

As in the case of the *Mukhtaṣar* of Khalīl, some of the *ʿulamāʾ* accepted the sultan's censorship. According to the contemporary evidence

---

[45] Ibid., p. 213

[46] Dāwūd (Muḥammad), *Taʾrīkh Titwān*, Tetouan 1962, p. 32.

[47] Ibid.; El-Mansour (p. 133) suggests that Sīdī Muḥammad's objection to the speculative sciences reflected his own educational background and lack of sophistication.

[48] Al-Jabartī vol. 2, p. 203.

[49] Sīdī Muḥammad was not altogether opposed to al-Ghazālī. In 1200/1785 the historian al-Zayyānī was commissioned by the sultan to purchase books in Istanbul and Cairo according to a given list, which included an abbreviated version of al-Ghazālī's *Iḥyāʾ ʿulūm al-dīn*, known as *al-Ṭarīqa al-Muḥammadiyya* (al-Zayyānī, *al-Turjumāna al-kubrā*, pp. 126–27).

of al-Ḍuʿayyif, Muḥammad b. Abī al-Qāsim al-Sijilmāsī discontinued the teaching of the *Iḥyā*ʾ.[50] Subsequently, Sulaymān al-Hawwāt complained that the study of Sufism had declined.[51]

Al-Tāwūdī Ibn Sūda was the dominant scholar in Fez for about fifty years, and as *shaykh al-jamāʿa* he was the spokesman of the scholarly community. He felt obliged to defend such orthodox authorities as Khalīl, ʿIyāḍ, al-Subkī and al-Ghazālī, arguing that to oppose them was to attack the *ʿulamā*ʾ of Islam, who were "Allāh's *awliyā*ʾ" and "heirs of the Prophet." Diminishing their status would loosen the bonds of Islam. Ibn Sūda also blamed the sultan for listening to "devilish students" (*shayāṭīn al-ṭalaba*), who said nothing good about the *ʿulamā*ʾ.[52]

We may only guess who these young aspiring *ʿulamā*ʾ were, called the "devilish students". The historian Abu'l-Qāsim al-Zayyānī says that his fellow students and contemporaries were recruited to the service of Sīdī Muḥammad soon after his accession in 1171/1757. Al-Zayyānī was born in 1147/1734, and therefore he and his fellow students were then in their mid-twenties.[53] Muḥammad al-Tāwūdī Ibn Sūda was of an older generation, and probably resented whatever influence those youngsters might have had on Sīdī Muḥammad.[54]

Muḥammad al-Tāwūdī Ibn Sūda must have been uneasy about Sīdī Muḥammad's attack on two senior scholars, Aḥmad Ibn Mubārak al-Filālī (d. 1155/1743) and his student Sīdī ʿUmar al-Fāsī, because they had taught the sciences. "If I were a *qāḍī*," the sultan said, "I would not have accepted their testimony."[55] Ibn Sūda studied logics (*manṭiq*) and theology (*kalām*) with Ibn Mubārak. Ibn Sūda was his favourite student, and was responsible for Ibn Mubārak's burial rites.[56] Other students of Ibn Mubārak were Muḥammad Banānī, Muḥammad b. al-Ṭayyib al-Qādirī, author of *Nashr al-mathānī*, Yūsuf b. Aḥmad b. Nāṣir al-Darʿī, the *khalīfa* of the Nāṣiriyya, and Sīdī ʿUmar al-Fāsī. That the latter was engaged in the study of science is confirmed by his reputation as "the bearer of the banner of the sciences, the logical and the transmitted [*maʿqūlihā wa-manqūlihā*]."[57] The historian al-Zayyānī, who studied

---

[50] Al-Ḍuʿayyif, p. 214.

[51] Quoted by Harrak, pp. 360–61.

[52] Dāwūd pp. 31–32.

[53] Al-Zayyānī, *al-Turjumāna al-kubrā*, pp. 58–61. But according to al-Nāṣirī, in *K. al-istiqṣā*ʾ (vol. 8, p. 67), Sīdī Muḥammad was influenced in his attitude against the *Mukhtaṣar* by Abū-Bakr b. al-ʿArabī, Abū Isḥāq al-Shatirī, Abū Zayd ʿAbd al-Raḥmān Ibn Khaldūn and others.

[54] According to al-Jabartī (vol. 2, p. 242) Muḥammad al-Tāwūdī Ibn Sūda was born in 1128, but Makhlūf (p. 373) says that he was born in 1111 and died in 1209 at a very advanced age.

[55] Ibn Zaydān, *Itḥāf*, vol. 3, p. 214. The reason given by Sīdī Muḥammad is that he heard from trustworthy people that the two scholars had distorted justice.

[56] Al-Jabartī, vol. 2, p. 242.

[57] Makhlūf p. 356; see also pp. 352–53, 358–59 on Ibn Mubārak and his students.

with ʿUmar al-Fāsī at the mosque of al-Qarawiyyīn, mentions that the latter taught only the more famous students in Fez.[58]

In a period during which scholarship flourished in Fez, Sīdī Muḥammad complained in an epistle called "Admonition to the People" (*naṣīḥa li-ʾl-umma*), that there were no students among the tribes and no *ʿālim* even in a large village. He blamed the provincial governors for neglecting their duty to support the scholars (*ʿulamāʾ*) and the saints (*awliyāʾ*) and to encourage the nobles of their tribes to seek knowledge (*ṭalab al-ʿilm*). As a result the common people were ignorant in matters of the unity of Allāh and the *sharīʿa*. He deplored the neglect of prayers, the *zakāt*, the fast of Ramaḍān and the *ḥajj*. But, because he could not ignore the fact that the number of pilgrims had increased, he claimed that the majority made the pilgrimage only to be named "*al-ḥājj*." In society at large he criticized corruption in trade and in marital life as well as fornication and leniency towards thieves.[59]

If one adds Sīdī Muḥammad's criticism of the legal professionals, *qāḍīs* and *muftīs*, one may understand his perception of a social malaise and a deplorable religious and moral situation which would justify his reformist efforts and the claim, endorsed by the court *ʿulamāʾ*, according to which he was "the *imām* given to this community at the turn of the century to renew its religion" — *al-imām al-mawhūb li-hādhihi ʾl-umma ʿalā raʾs al-miʾa mujaddidan lahā dīnahā*.[60]

Sīdī Muḥammad came to power after thirty years of disputes over the succession within the ruling dynasty. In order to restore the authority of the *makhzin*, he sought to curb the power of those *marabouts* who used their religious charisma to gain popular support, not hesitating to order the killing of such saints.[61]

Nevertheless, Sīdī Muḥammad maintained good relations with heads of *ṣūfī* orders, and used their services to mediate in tribal conflicts and even between himself and his own subjects. In spite of his reformist thrust and his Ḥanbalī inclination, Sīdī Muḥammad did not consider saint worship as *bidʿa*, and even defended popular Sufism against *ʿulamāʾ* who accused its followers of heresy. He admired al-Jazūlī and believed in the holiness of *awliyāʾ*. He paid frequent visits to the mausoleum of Idrīs, the founder of Fez, and to the tomb of the saint Ibn Mashīsh. He encouraged the building of *qubab* over the graves of *awliyāʾ*, and celebrated the *mawlid* ostentatiously. He himself was initiated to the Nāṣiriyya, the most orthodox *ṭarīqa* at the time.[62]

---

[58] Al-Zayyānī, *al-Turjumāna al-kubrā*, p. 57.

[59] Ibn Zaydān, *Itḥāf*, vol. 3, pp. 216–22.

[60] Ibid., p. 149.

[61] Al-Zayyānī, *al-Turjumān al-muʿrib*, pp. 71, 83; *K. al-istiqṣāʾ*, vol. 8, pp. 10, 17, 50–51; Ibn Zaydān, *Itḥāf*, vol. 3, pp. 157, 166.

[62] Harrak, pp. 354–55.

Sīdī Muḥammad's positive attitude towards popular Sufism on the one hand and his criticism of scholastic Sufism on the other hand, seem out of place in the context of renewal and reform. Fatima Harrak suggests that Sīdī Muḥammad's religious policy was aiming at reducing the influence of the urban *ʿulamāʾ*. The latter failed to approve the levy of non-Qurʾānic taxes (*mukūs*), as well as the appropriation of land in Rabat for military purposes. Some of the *ʿulamāʾ* were also critical of his policy of encouraging trade with the Christians.[63] He sought to reduce the independence of the *ʿulamāʾ* by transferring their source of payment from the *habūs* to *bayt al-māl*, i.e., from property supervised by members of the religious establishment to the sultan's treasury.[64]

Some *ʿulamāʾ* avoided contact with the sultan, but most of them took a conventional and passive position, fearing a *fitna*. The *ʿulamāʾ* praised Sīdī Muḥammad for his dedication to the *ḥadīth*, and collaborated in the revitalization of *ḥadīth* studies. Ibn Sūda wrote a commentary on Sīdī Muḥammad's *al-Futūḥāt al-Ilāhiyya*.[65]

In defending the *ʿulamāʾ* of the past against Sīdī Muḥammad's disapproval of al-Ghazālī, Khalīl and ʿIyāḍ, Ibn Sūda was actually trying to strengthen the position of contemporary *ʿulamāʾ*. They were threatened by Sīdī Muḥammad's claim to religious authority, which he exercized by issuing directives on matters of religious substance, which since the ninth century had been the exclusive domain of the *ʿulamāʾ*.[66]

The *qāḍī* Muḥammad al-Tāwūdī Ibn Sūda was not only the most influential *ʿālim*, but was also typical of the urban *ʿulamāʾ* of the eighteenth century, those who were in contact with the Khalwatī *shaykh*s of Egypt, deeply concerned with the study of *ḥadīth* and devoted *ṣūfī*s. They were on the defensive facing Sīdī Muḥammad's reforms from above. But under his son Mawlāy Sulaymān religious authority and reformist initiatives were again in the hands of the *ʿulamāʾ*. The now very old Ibn Sūda was instrumental in the installation of Mawlāy Sulaymān.[67] It was left for his disciples to help formulate the new sultan's religious policy.

7. Mawlāy Sulaymān: Reform with the Guidance of the *ʿulamāʾ*

Muḥammad al-Tāwūdī Ibn Sūda connected the reigns of Sīdī Muḥammad and Mawlāy Sulaymān. He was also the link with an earlier generation of those *ʿulamāʾ*, like Aḥmad al-Hilālī al-Sijilmāsī, Aḥmad al-Ṣaqalī and ʿUmar al-Fāsī, who had brought to Morocco the teachings of the

[63] Ibid., p. 246.

[64] Ibid., p. 79.

[65] Ibid., pp. 280–81, 300, 314.

[66] See S.D. Goitein, "A Turning Point in the History of the Muslim State," *Islamic Culture*, 22 (1949), pp. 120–35.

[67] Al-Zayyānī, *al-Turjumān al-muʿrib*, p. 92; *K. al-istiqṣāʾ*, vol. 8, p. 172.

Khalwatī *shaykhs* on *ḥadīth* and Sufism. Ibn Sūda's encounter with the scholars of Cairo, as described by al-Jabartī, was a meeting between equals. During the last years of his life the old al-Tāwūdī Ibn Sūda was Mawlāy Sulaymān's spiritual mentor. He initiated Mawlāy Sulaymān into the Nāṣiriyya and his advice was sought in matters of state. Both Ibn Sūda's son, Aḥmad ibn al-Tāwūdī, and his grandson, al-ʿAbbās ibn Aḥmad, were *qāḍīs* of Fez under Mawlāy Sulaymān. Ibn Sūda's influence survived also through his students — al-Ṭayyib b. Kīrān, Sulaymān al-Hawwāt and Ḥamdūn b. al-Ḥājj — who were the senior *ʿulamāʾ* in Mawlāy Sulaymān's innermost circle.

Mawlāy Sulaymān reversed the religious policy of his father. Whereas Sīdī Muḥammad used his authority to formulate religious directives, Mawlāy Sulaymān followed the lead of the *ʿulamāʾ*. Sīdī Muḥammad, we have seen, put pressure on the *ʿulamāʾ* to issue *fatwas* to legitimate certain fiscal measures. Harrak suggests a certain tension in his relations with the urban *ʿulamāʾ*, whereas Mawlāy Sulaymān cultivated close relations with the former in preference to the *shurafāʾ*.

Mawlāy Sulaymān kept the promise he had made on his accession, to abide by the *sharīʿa*, even when it was against the interests of the state. Thus he abolished non-Qurʾānic taxes and forbade the planting of tobacco — two measures that adversely affected the treasury.[68] He was in fact an accomplished *ʿālim*, integrated into the scholarly network of Fez as a disciple of some of the leading *ʿulamāʾ*.[69]

In addition to Qurʾān, *tafsīr* and *ḥadīth* he also studied *taṣawwuf*. He became acquainted with *Iḥyāʾ ʿulūm al-dīn*, and encouraged the teaching of al-Ghazālī. He was involved in theological discussions and relegitimized the Ashʿarī doctrine. He permitted the teaching of Khalīl's *Mukhtaṣar*. Unlike his father, he followed what may be considered as conservative Mālikism and the tradition of al-Ashʿarī and al-Ghazālī. The spirit of reform, however, was in the air, and Mawlāy Sulaymān was disposed to come under the influence of the Wahhābīs.[70]

8. A Reformist Response to the Wahhābīyya

Little information about the Wahhābīs seems to have reached Morocco during the eighteenth century. Moroccan pilgrims do not mention the

[68] El-Mansour, pp. 18–19, 133–34

[69] Mawlāy Sulaymān's principal teachers were ʿAbd al-Qādir b. Shaqrūn (d. 1219/1804), Muḥammad al-Hawarī (1135–1220 /1722–1805), al-Ṭayyib b. Kīrān (1172–1227 /1758–9–1812), and Muḥammad al-Ruhūnī (1159–1230 /1746–1815); most of them had been students of al-Tāwūdī Ibn Sūda. (Makhlūf, pp. 374–76, 380–81; for a more detailed list of Mawlāy Sulaymān's teachers, see El-Nasser, pp. 395–402.)

[70] See El-Nasser, pp. 513–15.

Wahhābīs before the latter moved into the Ḥijāz, and eventually conquered Mecca in 1803. The French conquest of Egypt brought about the suspension of the pilgrimage from Morocco between 1798 and 1802. The first reports, therefore, were brought back by pilgrims in 1803, who had experienced the brutality of the Wahhābīs and the insecurity in the Ḥijāz. The prohibition of certain customs connected with the *ḥajj* and of visits to holy tombs, the general anti-ṣūfī attitude of the Wahhābīs, and in particular the proscription of *Dalā'il al-khayrāt*, the most popular prayer in praise of the Prophet, created an unfavourable popular reaction in Morocco towards the Wahhābīs.[71]

Though he does not explicitly connect it with Wahhābī influence, El-Mansour detects a change in the religious policy of Mawlāy Sulaymān immediately after 1803, when he became more hostile towards what he considered unorthodox practices. In 1805 he had the *qubba* removed from his father's tomb.[72] He declared the *mawāsim* illegal, because they were associated with reprehensible customs like music, dancing, the mingling of men and women and wasteful spending. But he permitted visits to tombs if these were conducted according to the provisions of the *sharīʿa*. His ban on the *mawāsim* damaged the interests of the *ṣūfī* orders and of the *shurafā'*.[73]

In 1811 the Wahhābī ruler Saʿūd b. ʿAbd al-ʿAzīz sent out letters to rulers and *ʿulamā'* in the provinces of the Ottoman empire. No letter seems to have been addressed to Morocco, which was not part of the empire, but a copy of the letter to the *ʿulamā'* of Tunis reached the court of the Moroccan sultan.[74] Unlike other Muslim rulers, Mawlāy Sulaymān felt compelled to respond to the Wahhābī message, and he commissioned three scholars — Ibn Kīrān, Ibn al-Ḥājj and Sulaymān al-Hawwāt — to draft the reply. They were all students of Ibn Sūda, and the first two were also among the teachers of Mawlāy Sulaymān. Nevertheless, they represented three different views concerning the Wahhābīs.

As a *ṣūfī* and *naqīb al-ashrāf* Sulaymān al-Hawwāt (c. 1160–1231/ c. 1747–1816) was a fierce opponent of the Wahhābīs, and considered them to be rebels. He also abstained from signing the *fatwā* that permitted the resumption of the *ḥajj*.[75]

Ḥamdūn b. al-Ḥājj (1174–1232/1760–1817), on the other hand, was sympathetic to the Wahhābīyya. He was known for his rigorous adher-

[71] El-Mansour, pp. 138–39.

[72] Ibid., 139–40; see also El-Nasser, pp. 514–15.

[73] El-Mansour, pp. 136–37. It is significant that Mawlāy Sulaymān renewed the celebration of the Prophet's birthday (*al-mawlid*), with long sessions of prayers and recitations. But he vigourously discouraged festivities which "overstepped the limits of religious decency" (El-Nasser, pp. 409–10).

[74] Al-Zayyānī, *al-Turjumāna al-kubrā*, pp. 394–96.

[75] Knut S. Vikor, *Sufi and Scholar on the Desert Edge: Muḥammad ibn ʿAlī al-Sanūsī, 1787–1859* University of Bergen, 1991, p. 68; El-Nasser, pp. 498–99.

ence to the *sharī'a*, which he demonstrated when he served as *muḥtasib*. He was known as *faqīh al-sulṭān*, and he later became a follower of Aḥmad al-Tijānī. His reply was in the form of a poem praising the Wahhābīs and their ruler, though he urged them to restrain their aggressiveness towards other Muslims, and not to replace one *bid'a* by another. He even implied some ideological affinity with the Wahhābīs, alluding probably to Sīdī Muḥammad's claim that he was Ḥanbalī by doctrine.[76]

Al-Zayyānī, an opponent of the Wahhābīs, who did not dare to criticize the sultan himself, denounced Ḥamdūn b. al-Ḥājj, claiming that if such a poem of praise for the Wahhābīs had actually been sent, the sultan would have punished him severely. Al-Zayyānī accused Ibn al-Ḥājj of being in fact a Wahhābī himself.[77]

The third draft was by Muḥammad al-Ṭayyib b. Kīrān (1172–1227/1758–1812), who succeeded Ibn Sūda as *shaykh al-jamā'a*, and was therefore the most prominent scholar of the time. Mawlāy Sulaymān continued to attend his classes even after he had become sultan. Ibn Kīrān was probably closest to Mawlāy Sulaymān in his views on the Wahhābīs, and his draft was sent out in the sultan's name.

The letter praised the asceticism of the Wahhābīs and their efforts to purify the religion of Islam from corrupting innovations. Ibn Kīrān accepted the ban on visits to the tombs of saints by commoners, because these led to reprehensible customs as well as to infringing the injunctions against the ornamentation of tombs, the building of *qubab*, the lighting of candles and the sacrifice of animals on the tombs. But he did not believe that such practices justified *takfīr*, and reiterated the view that the *shahāda* divided a Muslim from a *kāfir*. He pleaded that it was better to spare the life of one hundred infidels than to lose the life of one believer. He rejected the Wahhābī condemnation of the *shafā'a* of saints, and the ban on *Dalā'il al-khayrāt*.[78]

This response to the Wahhābīs reflected the spirit of reform in an Islamic milieu based on Sharifian legitimacy and imbued with *ṣūfī* mysticism. It was in line with eighteenth-century trends in other parts of the Muslim world of reformed Sufism.

Mawlāy Sulaymān's conciliatory approach towards the Wahhābīs was again manifested in a *fatwā* he obtained, signed by the leading *'ulamā'*, that permitted the renewal of the pilgrimage.[79] Subsequently the pilgrimage caravan set out with a delegation led by Mawlāy Ibrāhīm, the

---

[76] Vikor, pp. 39–40, 68; El-Nasser, pp. 432–33, 519–22.

[77] Al-Zayyānī, *al-Turjumāna al-kubrā*, pp. 388–89, 494. Al-Zayyānī, however, admired Ḥamdūn b. al-Ḥājj for his piety, erudition, and keeness. Al-Zayyānī therefore sought Ḥamdūn's opinion about a draft of his work (ibid., pp. 549–51).

[78] El-Nasser, pp. 516–18; El-Mansour, pp. 141–42.

[79] The text of the *fatwa* and the names of the signatories appear in a manuscript from the Bibliothèque Generale of Rabat, quoted in El-Mansour, Ph.D. dissertation, p. 273.

eldest son of the sultan, and in the company of distinguished *ʿulamāʾ*. The delegation was warmly received by the Wahhābīs, with whom they had open disputations on various issues, in particular on the anathemizing (*takfīr*) of Muslims, and the legitimacy of saint worship if performed moderately.[80]

The Wahhābī letter and the arguments surrounding it may have added a measure of militancy to Mawlāy Sulaymān's reformist policy. A *khuṭba* he wrote for preachers in the Friday mosques urged the eradication of all kinds of *bidʿas* and called for a stricter adherence to the *sharīʿa*.[81]

In his continuous efforts to curtail the activities of the *zawāyā* Mawlāy Sulaymān encountered the opposition of the leaders of the less orthodox *ṣūfī* orders in alliance with the *shurafāʾ*, who had also been adversely affected by his policy. Discontent escalated to a revolt which spread to many parts of the country in 1818–1820. By that time the *ʿulamāʾ* who had guided and supported his reformist policies were dead. Urban *ʿulamāʾ* of the new generation, perhaps in protest to the privileged position of members of the old families, such as the Ibn Sūda, also joined the anti-reform opposition and accelerated the abdication of Mawlāy Sulaymān in 1822.[82]

9. The Rise of New *Ṭuruq*: Ramifications of the Shādhiliyya

One important charcteristic of the pattern of renewal and reform in eighteenth-century Islam was the restructuring of the *ṣūfī* orders which became more cohesive, with a greater concern for unique doctrine, litanies and practices. They also became wider in scale, both geographically and socially. Though the reformed orders avoided extremist practices, they maintained enough ritual elements to attract the participation of common people in the ceremonies. At the same time the strong *sharīʿa* orientation accommodated the top *ʿulamāʾ*. All these features were, for example, important in the development of the Khalwatiyya in Egypt.[83]

Most, if not all, the *ṣūfī* orders that influenced religious and political life in Morocco developed in the seventeenth and eighteenth centuries. Except for the Tijāniyya they all came out of the Shādhiliyya-Jazūliyya, which connected different *ṣūfī* notions and practices, centered on the veneration of the Prophet and his descendants, the *shurafāʾ*. Before the

---

[80] El-Mansour, pp. 142–43.

[81] Al-Zayyānī, *al-Turjumāna al-kubrā*, pp. 466 ff. It is significant that al-Zayyānī, a fierce opponent of the Wahhābiyya, considered this *khuṭba* as the best he ever seen, and as a response to the rise of heretic marabouts.

[82] El-Mansour, pp. 153–54; El-Nasser, pp. 550–51, 560–61; Vikor, pp. 71–73.

[83] Levtzion and Voll, 1987, p. 10.

seventeenth century there had been no organized orders, only numerous independent *zawāyā*, seats of holy men or *marabouts*, whose political power was conditioned by the relative strength of and the distance from the government (*makhzin*). Compared to the loosely organized Shādhiliyya the new orders that developed in the eighteenth century were cohesive, centralized and authoritative.

New *ṣūfī* orders in Morocco evolved out of a local *zāwiya*, extending over a whole region until they became "nationwide" orders. In this way the Nāṣiriyya developed from the *zāwiya* of Tamegrout to become the most important *ṣūfī* order in eighteenth-century Morocco. Its origin goes back to ʿUmar b. Muḥammad al-Anṣarī (d. 1011/1602), the head of the *zāwiya* of Tamegourt. He lived during the transition from the Saʿdī to the ʿAlawī dynasties, a period of insecurity, which *marabouts* exploited in order to gain political inflence. Tamegourt was a meeting ground for the trans-Saharan caravans, and attracted both merchants and *ʿulamāʾ*. The development of scholarship in the rural south made far away *zawāyā* like Tamegourt alternative centres of learning to the urban centres in the north.

In 1056/1646 Muḥammad b. Nāṣir took over the leadership of the *zāwiya* of Tamegourt from the descendants of the founder, because of his erudition. As the *zāwiya* became also a *madrasa*, the combination of *taṣawwuf* and *ʿilm*, mysticism and learning, contributed to the rise of a new order which became known as Nāṣiriyya. Muḥammad b. Nāṣir reformed the Shādhilī way; he reduced the litanies of the Shādhiliyya to one, banned the use of musical instruments in the *dhikr*, discontinued sacrifices on tombs and forbade the use of tobacco. He advocated loyalty and submission to the *ṣūfī* master and called for a continuous struggle against human desires.[84]

Muḥammad b. Nāṣir (d. 1085/1674) and his son and successor Aḥmad al-Khalīfa (d. 1130/1717) maintained close relations with centres of Islamic studies in the East, mainly in Cairo. Muḥammad b. Nāṣir performed the pilgrimage to Mecca twice, and his son Aḥmad four times. An annual caravan of pilgrims was organized at Tamegourt. The challenge of Tamegourt to the *makhzin* was in creating a rival centre of Islam.[85]

As long as the new order was confined to the far south, its leaders behaved like other *marabouts* in guarding their political autonomy with minimal contact with the *makhzin*. But, as the *ṭarīqa* expanded and the new ʿAlawī dynasty consolidated its authority, the heads of the *ṭarīqa* sought to cultivate better relations with the sultans. Aḥmad

---

[84] ʿAbdallah Hammoudi, "Sainteté, pouvoir et société," *Annales: E.S.C.*, vol. 35, pp. 619–20, 629; Drague, *Esquisse l'historie religieuse du Maroc*, Paris 1951, pp. 188–89; Harrak p. 150

[85] Hammoudi, pp. 636–37.; Harrak, pp. 151–53.

al-Khalīfa gave the *bay'a* to Mawlāy Ismā'īl, and with the sultan's approval branches of the Nāṣiriyya were opened in the major towns. Following the death of Aḥmad al-Khalīfa in 1129/1717, succession disputes brought about the deterioration of Tamegourt. As a result, the centre of gravity of the Nāṣiriyya gradually moved from its rural cradle to the urban extensions, an important factor in the evolution from *zāwiya* to *ṭarīqa*.

As a *ṭarīqa* that emphasized adherence to the *sharī'a* and excluded ecstatic practices, the Nāṣiriyya became aligned with the reformist disposition of the sultans and the *'ulamā'*. Both Sīdī Muḥammad and Mawlāy Sulaymān were initiated to the Nāṣiriyya, as were also some of the leading scholars, such as Aḥmad al-Ṣaqalī and Muḥammad al-Tāwūdī Ibn Sūda. The latter's son Aḥmad (d. 1820) became the head of the *zāwiya* of the Nāṣiriyya in Fez.[86]

Another senior scholar and a prominent *shaykh* of the Nāṣiriyya was Muḥammad b. 'Abd al-Salām al-Nāṣirī al-Dar'ī (d. 1239/1824). He performed the *ḥajj* twice in the years 1196/1781 and 1211/1796, carrying presents from the sultan to the *ḥaramayn* and to the scholars of Cairo. He studied in Cairo with the Khalwatī *shaykh* Aḥmad al-Dardīr and with Murtaḍā al-Zabīdī. The Mālikī scholar of Maghribī origin, Muḥammad al-Amīr, who corresponded with Sīdī Muḥammad, was initiated by al-Nāṣirī to the Nāṣiriyya. Al-Nāṣirī was among the first who brought information about the Wahhābīs back to Morocco, and was among their opponents in the entourage of Mawlāy Sulaymān. As a staunch reformist he condemned the *bid'a* of *ṣūfī ṭuruq* both in the East and in Morocco. He partricularly criticized the deterioration of the *zāwiya* of Tamegourt.[87]

This is another indication that towards the end of the eighteenth century members of the order made a clear distinction between the mother *zāwiya* and the Nāṣiriyya. The increasing reformist orientation of the order might also be ascribed to the exposure of the Nāṣiriyya *shaykhs* to the influence of the Khalwatiyya in Egypt.

Two smaller orthodox orders, the Ṭayyibiyya and the Khaḍiriyya, also emerged from the Shādhiliyya and, like the Nāṣiriyya, developed from a maraboutic local *zāwiya* into a scholarly urban order. They too were considered respectable among the prominent scholars of Fez. The Khaḍiriyya was founded in Fez by 'Abd al-'Azīz b. Mas'ūd al-Dabbāgh (d. 1132/1720), who claimed that al-Khaḍir had revealed to him the ultimate meaning of Sufism. One of his successors was Aḥmad b. Mubārak al-Sijilmāsī al-Lamṭī, who in his turn was succeeded as head

---

[86] Drague, pp. 190–91; El-Mansour, p. 161–62; Vikor, p. 7. On Sīdī Muḥammad's affiliation to the Nāṣiriyya, see Ibn Zaydān, *Itḥāf*, vol. 2, p. 21, in the biography of Idrīs b. Mawlāy Sulaymān.

[87] Vikor, pp. 51–54; see also El-Nasser, pp. 202–205, 434.

of the Khaḍiriyya by ʿAbd al-Wahhāb al-Tāzī, a leading scholar and the *ṣūfī shaykh* who most deeply influenced Ibn Idrīs.[88]

Unlike the reformist Nāṣiriyya and Khaḍiriyya, another *ṭarīqa* that emerged at the same period, the Darqawiyya, represented a revitalization of popular Sufism. Its founder was Mawlāy al-ʿArabī (Larbi) al-Darqawī (d. 1239/1823), whose teacher, ʿAlī al-Jamāl al-Shādhilī (d. 1193/1779), instructed him in *tajrīd*, i.e., avoidance of this world. The *murīd* must strictly obey his *shaykh* and keep away from those in authority. He sought to infuse a new spirit in *ṣūfī* mysticism by rejecting materialism. When Muḥammad al-Ḥarrāk, *khaṭīb* of the great mosque of Tetwan, joined the Darqawiyya in 1818, he led it in a more orthodox direction to avoid antagonizing Mawlāy Sulaymān.[89]

The Wazzāniyya, an older sharifian order, also expanded in the eighteenth century. Both the Wazzāniyya and the Darqawiyya were on the defensive against Mawlāy Sulaymān's measures to curb the power of the *zawāyā*. The sultan was particularly opposed to the role of the *zawāyā* as places of sanctuary (*ḥurum*), which he claimed they had abused. The two orders joined the anti-reformist uprising against Mawlāy Sulaymān in the last two years of his reign. The orthodox orders, on the other hand, remained loyal to the sultan.[90]

10. Reformed Ṣūfī *Ṭuruq*

So far on new *ṣūfī ṭuruq*, both populist and orthodox, that were important in the context of Morocco only. But Fez at the time of Mawlāy Sulaymān also hosted three *ṣūfī* leaders — Aḥmad al-Tijānī, Aḥmad b. Idrīs and Muḥammad b. ʿAlī al-Sanūsī — whose names are associated with the rise of reformed *ṣūfī* movements that spread to other parts of the Muslim world.

Aḥmad al-Tijānī was born in 1150/1737 at ʿAyn Māḍī on the edge of the desert of southern Algeria. He turned to esoteric Sufism only after he had excelled in legal studies. In 1171/1757, at the beginning of Sīdī Muḥammad's reign, he visited Fez, where he successively experimented with the litanies of the major *ṣūfī* orders of Morocco — the Qādiriyya, Shādhiliyya, Nāṣiriyya and the Ṭayyibiyya — but soon forsook them, expressing disappointment with the established orders.[91]

---

[88] On al-Khaḍir, see A.J. Wensinck's article in EI^2, in particular p. 905 on his role in Sufism. On the Khaḍiriyya, B.G. Martin, *Muslim Brotherhoods in Nineteenth-Century Africa*, Cambridge 1976, p. 703; Voll, "Ḥadīth," p. 270; on the Ṭayyibiyya, Vikor, p. 56.

[89] Drague, pp. 264–65; El-Mansour, p. 168.

[90] El-Mansour, pp. 165–71.

[91] The main source for the biography and doctrines of al-Tijānī is ʿAlī Ḥarazm, *Jawāhir al-maʿānī wa-bulūgh al-amānī*, Cairo 1929. Two important studies of al-

In 1187/1773, on his way to Mecca, at Azwāwī near Algiers, he was initiated to the Khalwatiyya order by ʿAbd al-Raḥmān al-Azharī (d. 1208/1793), who had been a disciple of Muḥammad Sālim al-Ḥifnī. Al-Tijānī's attachment to the Khalwatiyya was very different from his earlier discontent with other *ṣūfī* orders. In Cairo he learnt the secrets of the Khalwatiyya from Maḥmūd al-Kurdī, whereas in Medina he was introduced to Muḥammad b. ʿAbd al-Karīm al-Sammān who had been initiated to the Khalwatiyya by Muṣṭafā al-Bakrī himself in Medina in 1145/1732. On his return to the Maghrib in 1188/1774, al-Tijānī initiated his first disciples to the Khalwatiyya.

In 1196/1782 al-Tijānī returned to the desert edge, where he had his greatest mystical experience. The Prophet Muḥammad appeared to him, and taught him a litany (*wird*), enunciating a new independent *ṭarīqa*. The Prophet instructed al-Tijānī to sever relations with other orders and *shaykhs*, asserting the exclusivity of the Tijāniyya.

Al-Tijānī's new independent order implied a break with the Khalwatiyya. However, elements of the revived Khalwatiyya remained embedded in the doctrines and rituals of the Tijāniyya, more than was admitted by its founder and adherents. Indeed, the most unique feature of the Tijāniyya, the exclusivity of the *ṭarīqa*, had been an elaboration of a principle advocated by Muṣṭafā al-Bakrī and applied, with qualified success, by the Khalwatiyya in Egypt.

Al-Tijānī's fame as a saint grew, and he was probably considered a threat to the old religious establishment and to the Ottoman authorities in Algeria. He left for Fez in 1213/1798 and lived there for seventeen years until his death in 1231/1815.

Al-Tijānī advocated a strict observance of the *sharīʿa*, and criticized unorthodox *ṣūfī* practices. He was therefore warmly received by the sultan Mawlāy Sulaymān. The sultan gave him a house and a salary, and protected him from the hostility of some senior scholars of Fez. The latter, led by Ibn Kīrān, resented and rejected al-Tijānī's claim that he had received his *wird* directly from the Prophet, and was therefore superior to all other *ṣūfī shaykhs*.[92] But there were also some prominent scholars, like Ḥamdūn b. al-Ḥājj, who joined al-Tijānī's order.

Al-Tijānī lived in Fez in comfort without any manifestations of asceticism. He opposed withdrawal from this world, and promised his

Tijānī are J. Abun-Nasr, *The Tijāniyya*, Oxford 1965, pp. 15–57; and B.G. Martin, "Notes sur l'origine de la *ṭarīqa* des Tijāniyya et sur ler debuts d'*al-ḥājj* ʿUmar," *Revue des Études Islamiques* 37 (1969), pp. 267–90.

[92] According to al-Zayyānī (*al-Turjumāna al-kubrā* pp. 460–63) the Tijānīs were *ahl al-bidʿa*, and Aḥmad al-Tijānī only made the appearance of being an *ʿālim* and a *ṣūfī*, having been a forger. He ridiculed al-Tijānī's claim to have encountered the Prophet. He admits that al-Tijānī succeeded in deceiving Mawlāy Sulaymān. Al-Zayyānī's lengthy treatment of al-Tijānī may reflect his image in the minds of some of his contemporaries.

adherents access to Paradise without requiring them to forsake their possessions, because they were on a higher spiritual level than even non-Tijānī saints. This positive attitude to worldly affairs attracted rich merchants and senior officials to the order.

The Tijāniyya, as an offshoot of the Khalwatiyya, represented a new concept of *ṭarīqa*, not only because of its exclusivity but also because it was a departure from the Shādhilī *ṣūfī* tradition to which most Maghribī orders belonged.

Sīdī Aḥmad Ibn Idrīs al-Fāsī (1163–1253 /1750–1837) himself did not establish his own *ṭarīqa*, but he bequeathed a tradition that gave rise to several reformist *ṣūfī* orders. Ibn Idrīs studied in Fez with some of the leading scholars of the time, including al-Tāwūdī Ibn Sūda, Ibn Shaqrūn and Ibn Kīrān. He himself became an eminent teacher in al-Qarāwiyyūn and organised his own *ḥalqa*. His students went out preaching, urging a strict adherence to the Qur'ān and the *sunna*, and agitated against the cult of saints. Hence, by the time of his departure to Mecca from Fez, in 1213/1798, Ibn Idrīs had already formulated his basic reformist concepts, undoubtedly influenced by the intellectual and religious trends of the time in Fez.[93]

In Sufism he was initiated into the Nāṣiriyya by Abu'l-Qāsim al-Wazīr and to the Khaḍiriyya by 'Abd al-Wahhāb al-Tāzī. All the sources in the Idrīsid tradition insist on the influence of al-Tāzī on the spiritual development of Ibn Idrīs. The *sanad* he received from al-Tāzī was particularly important because it took him immediately to the Prophet through al-Khaḍir and al-Dabbāgh. Later, while on one of his several visits to Egypt, Ibn Idrīs was initiated to the Khalwatiyya by a student of Maḥmūd al-Kurdī, Ḥusayn b. Ḥasan al-Qinā'ī. Indeed, Ibn Idrīs sought to accumulate as many *awrād* as he could, and objected to exclusivity and fanatical adherence (*taʿaṣṣub*) to one order, as advocated by al-Tijānī.[94]

Muḥammad b. ʿAlī al-Sanūsī, the best known of the disciples of Ibn Idrīs, also passed his formative years in Fez. The length of al-Sanūsī's stay in Fez is uncertain, and varies according to the different sources from seven to fifteen years, probably through most of the 1220s/1805–15.[95] He studied with more than twenty prominent scholars of Fez, among them the pro-Wahhābī Ḥamdūn b. al-Ḥājj and the anti-Wahhābī Muḥammad b. ʿAbd al-Salām al-Nāṣiri al-Darʿī. He also studied with Ibn Kīrān and Aḥmad b. Tāwūdī b. Sūda. These and most of his other

[93] R.S. O'Fahey and A.S. Karrar, "The enigmatic Imam: the influence of Aḥmad Ibn Idrīs," *International Journal of Middle Eastern Studies*, 19 (1987), pp. 205–20.

[94] R.S. O'Fahey, *Enigmatic Saint: Aḥmad Ibn Idrīs and the Idrīsi Tradition*, Evanston 1990, pp. 27–53. Significantly, al-Tāzī had been initiated to the Khalwatiyya by al-Ḥifnī and was also a *ṣūfī* disciple of al-Ṣaqalī (see above, note 11).

[95] Vikor, p. 24.

teachers were students of Muḥammad al-Tāwūdī Ibn Sūda and close associates of Mawlāy Sulaymān.

Al-Sanūsī also had *ṣūfī* mentors in Fez. He studied briefly with the eccentric ṣūfi Ibn ʿAjība (d. 1224/1809), who rather late in his life had joined the Darqawiyya. He was introduced to the Nāṣiriyya by Muḥammad b. ʿAbd al-Salām al-Nāṣirī as well as by the latter's son Muḥammad b. Muḥammad al-Madanī who died in 1238/1823, at the age of thirty-four. He also had *ijāzāt* from both the father and the son in *fiqh* and in the seven readings of the Qur'ān. Al-Sanūsī was praised for his memory of *ḥadīths*, in which he was second only to his teacher Muḥammad Ibn ʿAbd al-Salām al-Nāṣirī.[96]

Long after he had left Fez, al-Sanūsī recounted his experience as a student of Aḥmad al-Tijānī: "he had honoured me by letting me take the Qur'ān from him, by this noble *sanad*, after he had taken it from the Prophet."[97] Al-Sanūsī, it seems, accepted al-Tijānī's claim to direct contact with the Prophet, though he was also a student of Ibn Kīrān, al-Tijānī's fiercest critic.

Aḥmad Ibn Idrīs had left Fez in 1213/1798, before al-Sanūsī came there. It was in Mecca that al-Sanūsī became one of the closest disciples of Ibn Idrīs. According to the account of Aḥmad al-Sharīf, al-Sanūsī's grandson, Ibn Idrīs said to al-Sanūsī: "you are we and we are you [*anta naḥnu wa-naḥnu anta*]."[98] Surely, the intimate relationship between the two was based on their common experience, only one generation apart, in the intellectual and mystical milieu of Fez.

Conclusions

During the eighteenth century Morocco's relations with the Mashriq became more intensive. The sultan Sīdī Muḥammad pursued an eastern oriented policy and many of the leading *ʿulamāʾ* performed the pilgrimage. On their way to Mecca they visited Cairo, and came under the influence of the Khalwatī *shaykhs*. Though only some of them were formally initiated to the Khalwatiyya, others may have carried back something of a new *ṣūfī* spirit that had made the Khalwatiyya in Egypt a cohesive, activist, *sharīʿa* oriented *ṭarīqa* that accommodated scholars and also reached out to common people.[99]

---

[96] Ibid., pp. 40–44, 52–54

[97] Ibid., p. 63, quoting al-Sanūsī's grandson Aḥmad al-Sharīf, *al-Anwār al-qudsiyya*, Istanbul 1920–24, p. 13.

[98] Ibid., p. 103, quoting Aḥmad al-Sharīf, p. 68.

[99] In their comments on a draft of this article Mohamed El Mansour and Fatima Harrak wrote: "There is no doubt that the influence of the Mashriq in the domain of religious and *ṣūfī* ideas was more important than many of us realize. However, it should be pointed out that throughout Maghribī history Middle Eastern ideas

The Moroccan *ʿulamāʾ* acknowledged their debt to the *shaykhs* of Cairo not only in *taṣawwuf* but also in *ḥadīth* studies. The study of *ḥadīth* was also central to Sīdī Muḥammad's reformist thrust. He introduced *ḥadīth* collections that had been unknown in the Maghrib, and he sought to break away from narrow-minded Mālikism, exemplified by attachment to Khalīl's *Mukhtaṣar*, the popular legal manual. His reform could be traced back to *ahl al-ḥadīth* of the ninth and tenth centuries, which Sīdī Muḥammad expressed by asserting: "I am Ḥanbalī by doctrine."

In the spirit of *ahl al-ḥadīth* he opposed the teaching in the mosques of the speculative sciences of *kalām*, *manṭiq* and *taṣawwuf*. He articulated an educational approach designed to avoid misguiding students who came from the countryside to Fez and to ensure proper professional training for *qāḍīs* and *muftīs*. He issued directives for reforming the curriculum at the mosque of al-Qarwiyyūn.

Sīdī Muḥammad was motivated by his view of the deplorable religious and moral situation, pointing out the scarcity of *ʿulamāʾ* in the countryside and the corruption of *qāḍīs* and *muftīs*. He seems to have diagnosed and disapproved of a shift of learning from the countryside to the urban center of Fez, where scholarship flourished. There was probably a certain tension in Sīdī Muḥammad's relations with the urban *ʿulamāʾ*, who were reluctant to approve non-Qurʾānic taxation and who resented Sīdī Muḥammad's claim to religious authority and his interference in matters of religious substance.

On the other hand, Mawlāy Sulaymān, who belonged to the scholarly network of Fez as a disciple of some of the leading scholars, followed the guidance of the *ʿulamāʾ*. Under their influence he returned to the conservative tradition of Mālik, al-Ashʿarī and al-Ghazālī. In alliance with the urban *ʿulamāʾ*, and in confrontation with the *zawāyā* and the *shurafāʾ*, Mawlāy Sulaymān was more radical than his father in eradicating unorthodox popular Sufism.

In his response to the challenge of the Wahhābiyya, Mawlāy Sulaymān expressed greater sympathy towards them than any other Muslim ruler. He praised their asceticism and their efforts to purify Islam from corrupting innovations, but he criticized them for anathemizing Muslims. His reply to a letter of the Wahhābīs reflected the spirit of reform in a milieu informed by sharīfian legitimacy and imbued with *ṣūfī* mysticism.

In the late seventeenth and during the eighteenth centuries Sufism in Morocco experienced the evolution and restructuring of new *ṭuruq* out of

---

had to undergo a process of acclimatization before they could be assimilated. The religious and cultural particularism of the Maghrib militated against the simple and straightforward adoption of any doctrine that came from abroad."

local *zawāyā*, on a wider geographical and societal scale and with greater adherence to the *sharīʿa*. This was the case of the Nāṣiriyya, which by the middle of the eighteenth century had a popular following and also counted among its affiliates the two reformist sultans as well as senior scholars. One cannot dismiss some influence of the Khalwatiyya on the development of the Nāṣiriyya.

Like the Nāṣiriyya, other new *ṭuruq* also had their roots in the *ṣūfī* tradition of the Shādhiliyya. The Ṭayyibiyya and the Khaḍiriyya were similarly orthodox, but the Darqawiyya and the Wazzāniyya were sharīfian and populist orders that joined the anti-reformist rebellion against Mawlāy Sulaymān.

A new concept of a *ṭarīqa* was introduced by the Tijāniyya, which represented a departure from the Shādhilī tradition and demanded exclusivity. With Aḥmad al-Tijānī the influence of the Khalwatiyya was more direct. On his return from the pilgrimage and the visit to Cairo he initiated disciples to the Khalwatiyya until his visionary encounter with the Prophet, in the course of which he received a new *wird* directly from the Prophet. Because of this direct communication he claimed superiority over all other *shaykh*s and *ṭuruq*.

Religious reformism came to a halt in Morocco after Mawlāy Sulaymān, but its thrust was carried on in the teachings of Aḥmad Ibn Idrīs and Muḥammad b. ʿAlī al-Sanūsī, both of whom spent their formative years in the reformist milieu of Fez.

XI

EIGHTEENTH CENTURY SUFI BROTHERHOODS

Structural, Organisational and Ritual Changes

Papers presented at a conference held in Jerusalem on Eighteenth Century Renewal and Reform in Islam were published in 1987 in a volume that carries the same title. In the introduction to that volume the following points were emphasised:[1]

In the eighteenth century individuals and groups sought to bring a revived sense of adherence to Islam, and by the end of the century there were activist movements of renewal and reform in all parts of the Muslim world; in China, Indonesia, Bengal, India, the Caucasus, the Arabian Peninsula, Egypt, Algeria, Morocco and West Africa.

These movements could not have been ramifications of the anti-sufi Wahhābiyya, because they developed within reformed sufi *ṭuruq*.

Leaders of these movements, including Muḥammad ibn ʿAbd al-Wahhāb, were linked together through networks made up of numerous scholastic and Sufi chains (*salāsil*, sing. *silsila*) of masters and disciples.

Circulation of peoples and ideas within these networks was aided by the growing number of pilgrims to the Haramayn. Mecca and Medina were the hub of this dynamic network, that brought together centre and periphery to create a global Muslim intellectual community.[2]

Networks that cut across regions brought together scholars from different schools of law (*madhāhib*), who studied under the same teachers because of the emphasis on *ḥadīth* and *taṣawwuf* (mysticism), which are not confined to one *madhhab*.

At the Jerusalem conference the term "Neo-Sufism", coined by Fazlur Rahman for the eighteenth century reformed Sufi *ṭuruq*, has been adopted.[3] Shortly after the publication of our volume the term

---

[1] Levtzion and Voll 1987:3–20.
[2] See also Levtzion and Weigert: 1996.
[3] Fazlur Rahman 1960: chapter 12.

"Neo-Sufism" came under criticism. Thus, O'Fahey and Radtke concluded an article entitled "Neo-Sufism Reconsidered" as follows: "If the use of the term 'Neo-Sufism' is to be retained, it should be restricted to the organisational innovations of certain Sufi brotherhood in specific regions of the Muslim world."[4]

Because we believe that organisational innovations are at least as important, often even more important, than changes in ideology or teachings of religious institutions, O'Fahey and Radtke's concluding remark will be the starting point for the present essay. We seek to prove that changes in the structure and organisation of Sufi brotherhoods in the eighteenth century were far reaching, and that they occurred not in "certain Sufi brotherhoods", but in many of them, and not "in specific regions of the Muslim world", but all over the Muslim world.

1. *The Organisation of Sufi Brotherhoods Before the Eighteenth Century*

The organisation of the Sufi orders and their relations with the population at large raise important questions for which the sources fail to provide satisfactory answers.[5] But the accumulated evidence suggests that before the seventeenth century the great majority of the brotherhoods were rather diffused, without a central organisation, and without strong links among their members or among their dispersed branches.

The Shādhiliyya and the Qādiriyya had no central organisation, and there was no control over the nomination of *shaykh*s in individual *zawāyā*. Even the descendants of ʿAbd al-Qādir al-Jīlānī in Baghdad, guardians of his tomb, were not recognised as their superiors by other Qādiri *shaykh*s. The Shādhiliyya and the Qādiriyya brotherhoods did not encourage popular forms of devotion. Their members wore no common habit, and there were no regulations or practices through which affiliates to the brotherhoods could be recognised. They all shared only the respect for the founders of their respective *ṭuruq*.[6] Similarly, the Suhrawardiyya and the Kubrāwiyya

[4] O'Fahey and Radtke 1993:87.
[5] Lapidus 1967:105–106; Winter 1982:126.
[6] Trimingham 1971:50 and 179; Winter 1982:89 and 10; Clayer 1994:341; Zarcone 1993:76.

in India were not unified brotherhoods, but only lines of ascription. Their branches were localised independent convents.[7] The absence of a strong central authority in the Khalwatiyya, and the autonomy of its wide spreading *zawāyā*, are considered among the reasons for a perpetual process of fragmentation, so typical of this brotherhood.[8]

Only for two brotherhoods, both Ottoman, is there evidence of greater cohesiveness. The Mawlawiyya was a centralised organisation, and all its members acknowledged the authority of the supreme *shaykh* of Konya, who also maintained his right to confirm the accession of heads of local lodges. Similarly, the Bektāshiyya developed into a highly organised and centralised brotherhood. Its supreme *shaykh*, who resided in the chief *tekke* at Ḥajji Bektāsh, claimed the right to present candidates for the positions of heads of all the Bektāshi *tekke*s to the central Ottoman government.[9] It is likely that the power of the supreme *shaykh*s of these brotherhoods resulted from the policy of the Ottoman government. In order to control the dervishes of these brotherhoods, who exercised considerable influence over the common people, the government sought to integrate the brotherhoods into the centralised bureaucratic state.

It follows that before the eighteenth century most brotherhoods had not been self-supporting social organisations in their own right. In the absence of centralised structures, Sufi brotherhoods were socially allied with other organisations. In the countryside they became embedded in social (family and clans) and regional units, which *shaykh*s were able to manipulate through their charismatic power. In urban societies the brotherhoods were linked to the *futuwwa*, the *akhī*, and *aṣnāf* (trade guilds). Sufis also allied themselves with military formations, such as the *ghāzī*s and the Janissaries.

2. *From Diffusive Affiliations to Large-Scale Organisations*

The direction of the change that took place in the eighteenth century was from old patterns of decentralised diffusive affiliations to larger scale organisations, more coherent and centralised.

In the Nilotic Sudan the Qādiriyya and Shādhiliyya had been

---

[7] Trimingham 1971:55–56, 65 and 179.

[8] Trimingham 1971:74–75; Clayer 1994:34–35.

[9] Trimingham 1971:61–62 and 179; Faroqhi 1976:76.

assimilated into localised holy clans before the eighteenth century, each with its independent *shaykh*. The relationship between the *shaykh* and his followers was direct, face to face and personal, without any hierarchical organisation. But since the last quarter of the eighteenth century new Sufi brotherhoods entered the Sudan—the Sammāniyya, Khatmiyya and Rashīdiyya—that incorporated local holy families into large scale organisations.[10]

Even in Morocco, a country of Sufism *par excellence*, there had been no structured hierarchical brotherhoods before the seventeenth century, only independent *zawāyā*, seats of holy men or *marabout*s. They all followed the Shādhili Sufi tradition, which at that time lacked any meaningful organisation. Only since the late seventeenth century did new brotherhoods evolve out of the local *zawāyā*, on a wider geographical and societal scale.

Before the eighteenth century the Khalwatiyya in Egypt had been "marginal and of little significance".[11] It had adherents mostly among the Turks and members of the upper classes. But within a few years after 1737, the Khalwatiyya spread like a brush fire, winning adherents among the common people in Cairo, as well as in the provincial towns and in the villages of Egypt. For the first time the Khalwatiyya became a truly Egyptian order.[12] In terms of orthodoxy, al-Jabartī described the Khalwatiyya as "the best of the orders (*khayr al-ṭuruq*)".[13]

In 1769 Muḥammad b. ʿAbd al-Raḥmān al-Azharī returned to the Kabiliya from Cairo, where he had been initiated into the Khalwatiyya. In the Kabiliya he propagated the Khalwatiyya so successfully that by the time of his death in 1793 the Raḥmāniyya (as it became known after him) was the most popular *ṭarīqa* in Algeria. Its rapid expansion may be explained by al-Azharī's strategy of incorporating local saintly lineages into the expanding network that he created, making local *marabout*s, who had controlled the spiritual life of the Berbers of Kabiliya, *muqaddam*s or local representatives of the Raḥmāniyya.[14]

It is clear from the evidence that hierarchical centralisation of the *ṭarīqa* organisation was a novelty. The Kurdish Shaykh Khālid of the

---

[10] Karrar 1992:x, 20.
[11] de Jong 1987:123.
[12] Weigert 1989.
[13] Al-Jabartī 1390 AH: I, 295.
[14] Clancey-Smith 1986.

Naqshabandiyya, who died in Damascus in 1826, created a network of over one hundred *khalīfa*s, each with a delineated geographical area of responsibility.[15] In the Sudan, al-Mirghānī, founder of the Khatmiyya, appointed and deposed *khalīfa*s as mere administrative officials, who were completely dependent on the central leadership of the *ṭarīqa*. He also repeatedly reminded his representatives that they were not independent *shaykh*s, and that they owed their *baraka* to him.[16]

Before the eighteenth century, according to Kissling, brotherhoods had not created dynasties, and only rarely did a son succeed his father as *shaykh*.[17] Succession passed from the *shaykh* to a disciple, elected for his spiritual merits. The change to hereditary succession signified the shift from the transmission of spiritual mystical qualities through teaching to the transmission of the *baraka* through descent. This change occurred with the growing importance of the founder's tomb. In Sind it was in the middle of the seventeenth century, when the *daragh*, the tomb, became administered by the saint's descendants.[18] Hereditary succession was also related to the enhanced authority of the *shaykh* over his disciples, the growing numbers of lay affiliates, and the accumulation of material assets.

3. *Ritual Changes*

We shall now argue that these changes in the structure and organisation of brotherhoods might also explain changes in rituals. The *rābiṭa* was practised by the Naqshabandiyya and other *ṭuruq* to bind the heart of the *murīd* with the perfect *shaykh*. The *murīd* was instructed to keep the image of the *shaykh* in his imagination even when the latter was absent. Shaykh Khālid, who created his own branch of the Naqshabandiyya, instructed his deputies that their own *murīd*s should link directly with him, and concentrate on his image only. He did so against the general trend of the Naqshabandiyya that the *rābiṭa* was between the *murīd* and his immediate spiritual guide. Khālid introduced this innovation in order to enhance the Khālidī-Naqshabandiyya as a centralised disciplined organisation.[19]

---

15 Algar 1990:138; Abu Manneh 1990:295.
16 Hofheinz 1990:28–29; Grandin 1990:645; Karrar 1992:126 and 130–131.
17 Kissling 1954:29; see also Winter 1982:138; Eaton 1978:204.
18 Eaton 1978:207.
19 Abu Manneh 1990:302.

The *dhikr*, which is the central ritual in all the *ṭuruq*, is performed by the repetition of the name of Allah either in silence (*dhikr khafī*) or aloud (*dhikr jahrī* or *jalī*). The silent *dhikr* had the aura of orthodoxy, whereas the vocal *dhikr*, which may also be accompanied by music and dancing, was often criticised by the purists.

Joseph Fletcher suggested that the cause for the eighteenth century split within the Naqshabandiyya in China, between the so-called "Old Teaching" and "New Teaching", occurred when Ma Ming hsin introduced the vocal *dhikr*, and thus alienated the older Naqshabandis that insisted on the silent *dhikr*.[20]

The "New Teaching" of Ma Ming hsin was not the only case of an eighteenth century revivalist movement that changed from the silent to the vocal *dhikr*, namely from the more to the less orthodox. Muṣṭafā al-Bakrī, who inspired the revival of the Khalwatiyya in Egypt, also made that change. Al-Bakrī presided over *dhikr* ceremonies in Jerusalem, where participants fainted because of excitement and exhaustion. His disciple al-Ḥifnī adopted the vocal *dhikr* enthusiastically, and the ceremonies he conducted in Cairo became so popular that he had to repeat the *dhikr* days and nights to admit the many thousands who wanted to attend it.[21]

By changing to the vocal *dhikr* Muṣṭafā al-Bakrī offered a larger scope for the participation of common people in the rituals of the Khalwatiyya, which helped to make it more popular. At the same time al-Bakrī applied stricter discipline in the performance of the litanies by the *murīd*s of the *ṭarīqa*, and emphasised adherence to the *sharīʿa*. This would explain the success of the Khalwatiyya in Egypt, which as a cohesive, *sharīʿa*-oriented *ṭarīqa*, accommodated leading scholars, but also reached out the common people.

There are other examples to demonstrate that the change to a vocal *dhikr* was associated with a trend to popularise the *ṭarīqa* and to recruit adherents. According to the sixteenth century Naqshabandi *shaykh* Khwaja Makhdūm-i Aʿzam: "the Lords of the Naqshabandiyya preferred the silent *dhikr*, but some of them, if necessary, also performed the vocal *dhikr*. When Khwaja Aḥmad al-Yasawi set out to Turkestan he saw that the people did not take to the silent *dhikr*, and he immediately took up the way of the vocal *dhikr*".[22] At a much

---

[20] Fletcher 1986:19–21.

[21] al-Jabarti 1390 AH: 302; Weigert 1989:109–111.

[22] Fletcher 1977:116.

later date, in the nineteenth century, the most prominent of the disciples of Shaykh Khālid in the Volga region, the Bashkir *shaykh* Zaynullah Rasulev, went about recruiting *murīd*s with a speed that alarmed other *shaykh*s. Hostile rumours began to circulate that Zaynullah practised the vocal *dhikr*.[23]

Another innovation, also connected with more intensive recruitment, was introduced by Shaykh Khālid. In the Naqshabandi tradition the initiation of a *murīd* began through *ṣuḥba*, the association and companionship with a *shaykh*. This period extended from a few months to a few years. But Khālid felt a strong urge for a quick expansion, and he therefore replaced the longer *ṣuḥba* procedure with an intensive spiritual training of forty days only. His *murīd*s entered into seclusion in a *khalwa*, a sort of a cell, under the close supervision of Khālid or one of his deputies.[24]

4. *Ṭuruq Affiliation and Exclusivity*

Before the eighteenth century Sufi *shaykh*s obtained initiation into several *ṭuruq*. The sixteenth century Egyptian *shaykh* al-Shaʿrānī was initiated into twenty six *ṭuruq*.[25] A *shaykh* in Bijapur gave the *bayʿa* to eleven brotherhoods.[26] Because medieval Sufi brotherhoods were only chains of mystical saints (*salāsil*), that represented alternative devotional mystical ways (*ṭuruq*) to approach Allah, Sufis even saw an advantage in experiencing more than one way. Hence, meaningful distinctions between brotherhoods were blurred. Belonging to a brotherhood signified little more than an additional title to one's name. When the *shaykh* himself belonged to two brotherhoods simultaneously, his followers identified with neither one in particular, but rather with the person of the *shaykh*.[27]

It was not only that some Sufis belonged to two or more brotherhoods simultaneously, but in Bijapur there were Sufis who belonged to no brotherhood at all.[28] In Ottoman Egypt, the more orthodox and educated Sufis did not incline to pronounce their affiliation with

[23] Algar 1992:118–119.
[24] Abu Manneh 1990:292–293.
[25] Winter 1982:92 and 97.
[26] Eaton 1978:xxxi–xxxii, 207.
[27] Eaton 1978:207; Ansari 1992:23.
[28] Eaton 1978:xxxi–xxxii.

a brotherhood, but expressed their loyalty to the Islamic community at large, to the *sharīʿa*, and to Sufism generally (*ṭarīq al-qawm*). Al-Shaʿrānī sympathised with the Shādhili way, but did not adhere to this brotherhood.[29]

Al-Shaʿrānī continued a tradition of Egyptian Sufis who were not affiliated to Sufi brotherhoods. These Sufis—like al-Matbūlī, his disciples al-Dashtūtī and ʿAlī al-Khawwās, al-Shaʿrānī's mentor—were venerated because of their *baraka*. The Bakrī *shaykh*s of Cairo of the sixteenth century constituted a *bayt* (house) not a *ṭarīqa*.[30] These Bakrī *shaykh*s were spiritual mentors of the scholars of Timbuktu, who were themselves practising Sufis without an affiliation to a brotherhood.[31]

Like other Sufi *shaykh*s Muṣṭafā al-Bakrī was affiliated to several *ṭuruq*; to the Khalwatiyya, the Naqshabandiyya, the Qādiriyya and perhaps also to the Shādhiliyya. But later he insisted that his own disciples would be affiliated exclusively to the Khalwatiyya, and ordered them to break their former allegiance to other *ṭuruq* and *shaykh*s. This was not a minor innovation in the world of medieval Sufism, and it was not easily implemented. Al-Bakrī had long arguments over this issue with two of his senior disciples.[32]

Exclusivity gave greater cohesion to a *ṭarīqa*, and added to the commitment of its adherents. The concept of exclusive affiliation to a *ṭarīqa* was adopted from the Khalwatiyya, even with greater zeal, by Aḥmad al-Tijānī. The exclusivity of the Tijāniyya, in its turn, affected rival *ṭuruq* in the Maghrib and in West Africa, in particular the Qādiriyya, that also became more assertive and cohesive.[33]

5. *The Reformed Ṭuruq: Positive Attitude to This World*

Sufism oscillated between individualist renunciation of this world and community-oriented legalist world-affirmation.[34] Even the most pragmatic Sufi could not completely separate himself from the other-worldly aspects of mysticism. The *sharīʿa*-oriented brotherhoods were on the side of This World. This was the attitude of the Naqshabandiyya in Central Asia, the Suhrawardiyya in India, and the Shādhiliyya in

[29] Winter 1982:26 and 92–93.
[30] Weigert 1985.
[31] Levtzion 1977:419–420.
[32] al-Jabarti, 1390 AH: vol. 1, p. 295; vol. 2, pp. 61–62; Weigert 1989.
[33] Harazm 1929; Abun-Nasr 1965:15–57; Martin 1969; Brenner 1988.
[34] Karamustafa 1994:29–30, 96 and 98.

Egypt. The Shādhilis shunned mendicancy and renunciation of the world, and insisted that their adherents and sympathisers should lead socially active and economically productive life.[35] But many other Sufi brotherhoods had an otherworldly orientation, practised asceticism and adopted a negative attitude towards material possessions.

In China the older Qādiriyya, introduced in the late sixteenth century, had emphasised poverty and ascetic withdrawal from society, whereas the Naqshabandi *shaykhs*, who came in the late seventeenth and in the eighteenth centuries, had families and enjoyed material wealth accrued from the donations of their followers.[36]

In Sumatra, the old Sufi *ṭuruq* blended peacefully into the agrarian landscape, and issued no challenge to the wider society. Their teaching was concerned with esoteric knowledge and in pursuing the path to God. This other-worldly orientation was challenged by Sufi *shaykhs* who responded to the rapid growth of commercial agriculture late in the seventeenth century. Sufi *shaykhs* became involved in trade, and had a venerated *shaykh*, Tuanku Nan Tua, who became known as "patron of the traders".[37]

In Fez, Aḥmad al-Tijānī lived in comfort without any manifestations of asceticism. He opposed withdrawal from this world, and promised his adherents access to paradise without forsaking their possessions. This positive attitude to worldly affairs attracted rich merchants and senior officials who joined the brotherhood.[38]

In the Sahara, Sīdī al-Mukhtār al-Kuntī advocated a positive attitude towards the accumulation of wealth, and emphasised the direct link between religious piety and economic prosperity. For him wealth was a clear sign of dignity and status.[39]

This change in attitude towards this world prepared reformed Sufi brotherhoods to be more actively involved in social and political life.

6. *Mystical Verse in Vernacular Languages*

Our final argument is that the drive of the reformed Sufi brotherhoods to reach out to the common people and to recruit adherents

[35] Winter 1982:90.
[36] Gladney 1991:44–47.
[37] Dobbin 1983:125–127.
[38] Levtzion and Weigert 1995:193–194.
[39] Brenner 1988:39.

explains the simultaneous emergence of Islamic literatures in the vernacular languages, written in the Arabic or Persian script, all over the Muslim world in the seventeenth and eighteenth centuries. It is even more significant in this context that the predominant genre in all the vernacular literatures was the mystical verse.

Oral mystical poetry in folk idioms had been composed as early as the fourteenth century, mainly for *samāʿ* assemblies. In order to facilitate the spread of mystical teaching among the masses, poets resorted to imageries taken from daily life and from the landscape that surrounded them. It was meant to be recited or sung and was not written down until a much later period.[40]

It is likely that the writing down of folk mystical poetry was encouraged by the emergence of centralised brotherhoods, whose leaders sought to communicate with affiliates who lived not only in their immediate vicinity, but also in remote communities. Poems in the vernaculars, that had been sung and recited orally, were written down in Arabic script, and were disseminated in written copies among the literati, who gave them a wider circulation through public recitation.

The oldest known texts in the Muslim African languages—Fulfulde, Hausa and Swahili—date from the eighteenth century.[41] Before that Islam had been the concern of a literate minority, and all those who took part in the scholarly discourse were literate in Arabic. But with the progressive diffusion of Islam, when scholars sought to disseminate Islamic knowledge to the common people, poetry became a major vehicle for teaching and preaching. Poems were readily committed to memory and were therefore an excellent pedagogical device.[42]

The oldest documents from Northern Nigeria were poems written by the leaders of the reformist movement. The reformists were active preachers and composed poems in Fulfulde that could be recited in public. Written versions of the poems were made to help the memory of the singers, and to facilitate the diffusion of the texts.[43]

ʿAbdallāh dan Fodio described the preaching of his brother, the Shaykh ʿUthmān dan Fodio, in the vernacular verse:

---

[40] Schimmel 1982:135–136, 141–142, 148 and 150.

[41] Sow 1966:13 and 15; Hiskett 1975:18; Knappert 1979:102–103.

[42] Seydou 1973:184; Brenner & Last 1985:434.

[43] Sow 1966:12; Haafkens 1983:25.

> Then we rose up with the Shaykh, helping him in his mission work for religion. He travelled for that purpose to the east and west, calling people to the religion of God by his preaching and his *qaṣīdas* in *ʿajamī*.[44]

ʿAbdallāh dan Fodio also described how the vernacular mystical verse was used to mobilise support. When the Shaykh ʿUthmān dan Fodio saw that his community was ready for the *jihād*, "he began to incite them to arms . . . and he set this in verse in his non-Arabic Qādiri poem (*qaṣīda ʿajamiyya qādiriyya*)." This mystical verse had a hypnotic effect upon devotees on the eve of the *jihād*.[45]

It is significant that on the East African coast too, the oldest surviving Islamic text in Swahili, the *Ḥamziyya* by ʿAidarūsī, a poem in praise of the Prophet (*madīḥ*), was written in the second half of the seventeenth century.[46]

Malay was the *lingua franca* of the Muslims in Southeast Asia, and an essential vehicle for the spread of religious ideas throughout the region. The oldest Malay manuscripts in the Arabic script date from the end of the sixteenth and the beginning of the seventeenth centuries. Malay literature developed mainly through translations from Persian and Arabic.[47] A.H. Johns described these literary activities as "enriching the language of the tribe".[48]

Some of the most profound writings on metaphysics and *taṣawwuf* were by two Sufi poets, Ḥamza Fansuri (end of the sixteenth century) and Shams al-Dīn of Pasai (d. 1630). Ibn ʿArabī's doctrine of the *wujūdiyya* was widely articulated in their poetry, as well as in the writings of an anonymous author of the first half of the seventeenth century. The *wujūdiyya* was challenged by the Shaykh Nūr al-Dīn b. ʿAlī al-Rānīrī, a Gujarati who came from India to Acheh about 1637. During the seven years of his residence in Acheh, al-Rānīrī wrote strenuously, in Malay and in Arabic, against the pantheism of Ḥamza and Shams al-Dīn.[49]

The next important event in the literary history of Islam in South-East Asia was the translation of the Qur'ān to Malay by ʿAbd al-Ra'ūf of Singkel (c. 1620–1693). He returned in 1661 after a residence

---

[44] ʿAbdallāh ibn Fūdī 1963:85.

[45] ʿAbdallāh ibn Fūdī 1963:51.

[46] Knappert 1979:102–103.

[47] Andaya 1987:235; Ronkel 1987:240.

[48] Unpublished paper by A.H. Johns presented to the conference on Eighteenth century Renewal and Reform in Islam, Jerusalem 1985.

[49] Johns 1957:10, 33 and 35; al-Attas 1971:1220; Roolvink 1971:1233.

of nineteen years in Medina, where he had been initiated to the Shaṭṭāriyya brotherhood by al-Qushāshī (d. 1660) and Ibrāhīm al-Kurānī (d. 1690). ʿAbd al-Raʾūf propagated the Shaṭṭāriyya, which later played an important role in the Padri movement. He also composed a Malay textbook of practical mysticism giving detailed information about the methods of *dhikr* and containing litanies (*rawāṭib*). ʿAbd al-Raʾūf rejected the pantheist mysticism of Ḥamza and Shams al-Dīn, though he did not associate himself with the violent polemics of al-Rānīrī.[50]

Towards the end of the eighteenth century Malay scholars seem to have moved away from the teachings of Ibn ʿArabī towards the more sober mysticism of al-Ghazālī, as evidenced by the translation of some of al-Ghazālī's works to Malay. Between the years 1779 and 1788, a shortened version of al-Ghazālī's *Iḥyāʾ ʿulūm al-dīn*, was translated into Malay by ʿAbd al-Ṣamad of Palembang. ʿAbd al-Ṣamad had been resident in Medina for many years and was also responsible for the introduction of the Sammāniyya brotherhood to Indonesia.[51]

In India, not only Muslim Sufis but also Hindu mystics, turned to the regional idioms for their preaching, because the sacred liturgical languages—Sanskrit, Arabic and Persian—were inaccessible to the masses. Mystical poetry in the regional idioms had been recited for *samāʿ* assemblies since the thirteenth century, but it was not committed to writing before the seventeenth century.[52]

There is hardly any text in the north-western regional languages of India dated before the end of the sixteenth century. Sufis, especially those of the Chishti order, who sought to reach people that had no access to Arabic and Persian, led the way in breaking the literary taboo against the use of the Indian vernaculars.[53] The flowering of literature in the regional languages—Sindhi, Muslim Panjabi, and Urdu—early in the eighteenth century, followed the decline of Mughal authority and the emergence of local states. It seems that the breakdown of the Mughal empire, which had cultivated Persian culture, opened the way for new experiments with languages that had not been previously considered a medium fitting the expression of lofty ideas.[54]

---

[50] Johns 1957:10; Voorhoeve 1960:88; al-Attas 1971:1220; Roolvink 1971:1233.

[51] Voorhoeve 1960:92; Andaya 1987:235.

[52] Schimmel 1975:132–133 and 171; Schimmel 1976:12; Schimmel 1982:138, 141–142 and 148–150.

[53] Shackle 1993: 265 and 285; Roy 1985:58.

[54] Schimmel 1975:163; Shackle 1993:287–288.

Indeed, far from the centre of the Mughal court, where the influence of the Persian culture was weaker, literature in the regional languages had developed earlier. The consolidation of the independent principalities of Bijapur and Golkonda in the fifteenth century helped the growth of literature in Dakhni, the language of the Deccan, two centuries before the appearance of Urdu literature.[55]

In Delhi Sufi literature in Urdu developed only at the beginning of the eighteenth century. But even later, theologians and mystics continued to write also in Arabic and Persian, the classical Islamic languages. Even Mir Dard (1721–1785), who wrote the most perfect Urdu mystical verse, composed the largest part of his mystical poetry and prose in Persian. Hence, the discourse of the elite continued in the classical languages of Islam, whereas the vernacular literature was important in building bridges to the common people.[56]

Bengali Muslim literature is unique among the Indian regional vernaculars in that it was written mostly in the Bengali script, and not in the Arabic-Persian script. But, like the other vernacular literatures it was mainly the product of *pirs*, who in the sixteenth and seventeenth centuries developed mystical verse.[57]

Muslim literature in Chinese was also written mostly in Chinese characters. It developed since the middle of the seventeenth century, and as elsewhere mystical works were important. It was composed in an easy style, with tendency towards the spoken language, which suggests that it was addressed to the common people, with a limited literary culture, and not to the highly literate.[58]

There is additional evidence that Sufi texts were in a simple language addressed to the common people. In the sixteenth and seventeenth century, a period of literary decline in Egypt, when works of theology and law were written in bombastic style, Sufis wrote in precise, down-to-earth language.[59] Also, the preaching of Imam Mansur in 1785 in the Caucasus, is said to have been simple and directed to the peasants.[60]

---

[55] Schimmel 1975:131 and 135; Eaton 1978.
[56] Schimmel 1973:48–50; Schimmel 1976:xi, 11.
[57] Haq 1985:39–40; Roy 1985:58 and 71–73.
[58] Aubin 1990:496–497.
[59] Winter 1982:27.
[60] Bennigsen 1964:195.

7. *Conclusions*

Sufi brotherhoods played important roles in Muslim societies since the twelfth and thirteenth century. They provided moral guidance to voluntary associations, opened opportunities for release from the hardships of everyday existence, gave confidence to individuals, and helped sustain social stability. They also maintained lines of communications between the common people and the authorities. But pre-eighteenth Sufi brotherhoods had been localised and loosely organised.

The restructured brotherhoods of the eighteenth century mobilised popular following, a process that was closely associated with the expansion of Islam from towns to the countryside, and deeper into all strata of the population. The elitist discourse in the classical Islamic languages, Arabic and Persian, was supplemented by Islamic writings, mainly in mystical verse, in vernacular languages.

Structural, organisational and ritual changes prepared the reformed Sufi *ṭuruq* to play more active political and social roles. Under charismatic leadership some of these Sufi brotherhoods turned militant and developed into *jihād* movements. The Tijāniyya provided the framework for the *jihād* of *al-ḥājj* ʿUmar in West Africa. The Mahdī of the Sudan was a member of the Sammāniyya, which like the Tijāniyya was an offshoot of the Khalwatiyya. The Naqshabandiyya-Khālidiyya found expression in the *jihād* of Imam Shamīl in the Caucasus, where, according to Hamid Algar, the teaching of Shaykh Khālid survived in its purest and most integral form.[61]

When their countries were invaded by colonial powers, these three movements redirected their major efforts from internal reform to defending *Dār al-Islām*, but they were crushed by the military superiority of the Europeans. Thus the inroads of colonialism put an end to a process of revivalism of Muslim societies under the leadership of reformed restructured Sufi brotherhoods.

---

[61] Algar 1990:145.

BIBLIOGRAPHY
CHAPTER XI

Abu-Manneh, B. "Khalwa and Rābiṭa in the Khālidi Suborder," in *Naqshabandis*, edited by M. Gaborieau, A. Popovic and T. Zarcone. Istanbul: Institut Français d'Etudes Anatoliennes d'Istanbul, 1990, pp. 289–302.

Abun-Nasr, J. *The Tijaniyya*. Oxford: Oxford University Press, 1965.

Algar, H. "Political Aspects of Naqshabandi History," in *Naqshabandis*, edited by M. Gaborieau, A. Popovic and T. Zarcone. Istanbul: Institut Français d'Etudes Anatoliennes d'Istanbul, 1990, pp. 123–52.

Andaya, L.Y. "Malay Penisula," in *EI*[2], Vol. 6, pp. 232–9.

Ansari, S. *Sufi Saints and the State Power: the Pirs of Sind, 1843–1947*. Cambridge: Cambridge University Press, 1992.

al-Attas, S.M.N. "Indonesia," in *EI*[2], Vol. 3, pp. 1218–21.

Aubin, F. "En Islam Chinois? Quells Naqshabandis," in *Naqshabandis*, edited by M. Gaborieau, A. Popovic and T. Zarcone. Istanbul: Institut Français d'Etudes Anatoliennes d'Istanbul, 1990, pp. 491–572.

Bennigsen, A. "Un Movement Populaire au Caucase au 18e Siècle: la Guerre Sainte du Sheikh Mansur, 1785–1791," *Cahiers du Monde Russe et Soviétique*, Vol. 2, 1964, pp. 159–205.

Brenner, L. "Concepts of Tariqa in West Africa: the Case of the Qadiriyya," in *Charisma and Brotherhood in African Islam*, edited by D.C. O'Brien and C. Coulon. Oxford: Clarendon, 1988, pp. 32–52.

Clancey-Smith, J.A. "Saintly Lineages, Border Politics, and International Trade: Southeastern Algeria and the Tunisian Jarid, 1800–1881." PhD Dissertation, University of California, Los Angeles, 1986.

Clayer, N. *Mystiques, Etat et Société: les Halvetis dans l'Aire Balkanique de la Fin du 15e Siècle à nos Jours*. Leiden: Brill, 1994.

Dobbin, C. *Islamic Revivalism in a Changing Peasant Economy: Sumatra 1784–1847*. London: Curzon Press, 1983.

Eaton, R.M. *Sufis of Bijapur: Social Roles of Sufis in Medieval India*. Princeton: Princeton University Press, 1978.

Faroqhi, Suraiya N. "The Tekke of Haci Bektas, Social Position and Economic Activities," *International Journal of Middle East Studies*, Vol. 7, 1976, pp. 183–205.

Fletcher, J. "The Naqshabandiyya and the dhikr-I arra," *Journal of Turkish Studies*, Vol. 1, 1977, pp. 113–19.

Fletcher, J. "Les 'Voies' (*ṭuruq*) Soufies en Chine," in *Les Ordres Mystiques dans l'Islam: Cheminements et Situation Actuelle*, edited by A. Popovic and G. Veinstein. Paris: Editions de l'Ecole des Hautes Etudes en Sciences Sociales, 1986, pp. 13–26.

Ibn Fudi, *'Abdallah. Tazyin al-Waraqat*. edited and translated by M. Hiskett Ibadan: Ibadan University Press, 1963.

Gladney, D. *Muslim Chinese*. Cambridge: Harvard University Press, 1991.

Grandin, N. "A Propos des *asanid* de la Naqshabandiyya dans les Fondements de la Khatmiyya du Soudan Oriental: Stratégies de Pouvoir et Relation Maître/Disciple" in *Naqshabandis*, edited by M. Gaborieau, A. Popovic and T. Zarcone. Istanbul: Institut Français d'Etudes Anatoliennes d'Istanbul, 1990, pp. 621–55.

Haafkens, J. *Chants Muslumans en Peul: Texts de l'heritage religieux de la Communauté muslumane de Maroua, Cameroun*. Leiden: Brill, 1983.

Harazm, A. *Jawāhir al-Ma'ānī wa-bulūgh al-amānī*. Cairo, 1929.

Hiskett, M. *A History of Hausa Islamic Verse*. London: School of Oriental and African Studies, 1975.

Hofheinz, A. "Encounters with a Saint: al-Majdhub, al-Mirghani, and Ibn Idris as Seen through the Eyes of Ibrahim al-Rashid," *Sudanic Africa*, Vol. 1, 1990, pp. 19–59.

al-Jabarti, 'A. *'Ajā'ib al-'Āthār fi'l-Tarajim wa'l-Akhbār*. Cairo: Bulaq, 1879–1880.

Johns, A.H. "Malay Sufism, as Illustrated in an Anonymous Collection of Seventeenth-Century Tracts," *The Journal of Malaysian Branch of the Royal Asiatic Society*, Vol. 2, No. 178, 1957, pp. 5–111.

de Jong, F. "Muṣṭafā Kamāl al-Dīn al-Bakrī (1688–1749): Revival and Reform of the Khalwatiyya Tradition?," in J.O. Voll and N. Levtzion, eds. *Eighteenth Century Renewal and Reform in Islam*. Syracuse: Syracuse University Press, 1987, pp. 117–132.

Karamustafa, A.T. *God's Unruly Friends: Dervish Groups in the Islamic Later Middle Period 1200–1550*. Salt Lake City: University of Utah Press, 1994.

Karrar, A.S. *The Sufi Brotherhoods in the Sudan*. Evanston: Northwestern University Press, 1992.

Kissling, H.J. "The Sociological and Educational Role of the Dervish Orders in the Ottoman Empire," *Memoirs of the American Anthropological Association*, Vol. 76, 1954, pp. 23–35.

Knappert, J. *Four Centuries of Swahili Verse; a Literary History and Anthology*. London: Heinemann, 1979.

Lapidus, I.M. *Muslim Cities in the Later Middle Ages*. Cambridge: Harvard University Press, 1967.

Levtzion, N. "North Africa and the Western Sudan from 1050 to 1590," in *The Cambridge History of Africa*, edited by R. Oliver, Vol. 3, Cambridge: Cambridge University Press, 1977, pp. 331–462.

Levtzion, N. and Voll, J. O. *Eighteenth Century Renewal and Reform in Islam*. Syracuse: Syracuse University Press, 1987.

Levtzion, N. and Weigert, G. "Religious Reform in Eighteenth-Century Morocco," *Jerusalem Studies in Arabic and Islam*, Vol. 19, 1995, pp. 173–97.

Martin, B.G. "Notes sur l'origine de la ṭarīqa des Tijaniyya et sur les Débuts d'al-Hajj 'Umar," *Revue des Etudes Islamiques*, Vol. 37, 1969, pp. 267–90.

O'Fahey. S and Radtke, B. "Neo-Sufism Reconsidered," *Der Islam*, Vol. 70, 1993, pp. 52–87.

Rahman, F. *Islam*. Chicago: University of Chicago Press, 1960.

Roolvink, R. "Indonesia," in *EI*², Vol. 3, pp. 1230–35.

Roy, A. *The Islamic Syncretistic Tradition in Bengal*. Princeton: Princeton University Press, 1984.

Schackle, C. "Early Vernacular Poetry in the Indus Valley: Its Contexts and its Character," in *Islam and Indian Regions*, edited by A.L. Dallapicola and S. Zingel-Ave Lallemant. Stuttgart: Franz Steiner Verlag, 1993.

Schimmel, A. *Islamic Literatures of India*. Wiesbaden: Harrossowitz, 1973.

Schimmel, A. *Classical Urdu Literature from the Beginning to Iqbal*. Wiesbaden: Harrassowitz, 1975.

Schimmel, A. *Pain and Grace: a Study of Two Mystical Writers of Eighteenth-Century Muslim India*. Leiden: Brill, 1976.

Schimmel, A. *As Through a Veil: Mystical Poetry in Islam*. New York: Columbia University Press, 1982.

Sow, A.I. *La Femme, la Vache, la Foi: Ecrivains et Pouvoir du Fouta Djalon*. Paris, 1966.

Trimingham, J.S. *The Sufi Orders in Islam*. Oxford: Clarendon Press, 1971.

Voorhoeve, P. "'Abd al-Ṣamad," in *EI*², Vol. 1, p. 92.

Weigert. G. "Three Bakri 'Ulamā' in Egypt at the End of the Mamluk and the Beginning of the Ottoman Periods." M.A Dissertation, The Hebrew University of Jerusalem, 1985.

Weigert, G. "The Khalwatiyya in Egypt in the 18th Century." PhD Dissertation, The Hebrew University of Jerusalem, 1989.

Winter, M. *Society and Religion in Early Ottoman Egypt: Studies in the Writings of 'Abd al-Wahhab al-Sha'rani*. New Brunswick: Transaction Books, 1982.

Zarcone, T. *Mystiques, Philosophes, et Franc-Maçons en Islam: Riza Tevfik, Penseur Ottoman (1868–1949), du Soufisme à la Confrérie*. Istanbul: Librairie d'Amérique et d'Orient, 1993.

XII

The Muslim Holy Cities as Foci of Islamic Revivalism in the Eighteenth Century

Nehemia Levtzion and Gideon Weigert

The Wahhābiyya and Other Reform Movements

In 1744, a concordat between the *shaykh* Muḥammad Ibn ʻAbd al-Wahhāb and the *amīr* Muḥammad Ibn Saʻūd gave rise to the Wahhābiyya movement. Because of the centrality of Arabia and the militancy of the Wahhābiyya, some historians believed that other Islamic reform movements of the eighteenth century were ramifications of the Wahhābiyya. In this way they could also explain the simultaneous appearance of Islamic reform movements in places as distant from the centre as China, Indonesia and West Africa.

Recent research, however, has shown that the Wahhābiyya could not have influenced other movements directly, because only the Wahhābiyya rejected Sufism, whereas all the other movements developed within *ṣūfī ṭuruq*. Nevertheless, all these reform movements, including the Wahhābiyya, developed out of the internal dynamics of late medieval Islam. An awareness of the discrepancy between the ideals of Islam and the realities of Muslim life created a cyclical drive for renewal and reform (*tajdīd wa-iṣlaḥ*). However, while the phenomenon of reform in Islam may be explained in this way, the simultaneous rise of different reform movements in the eighteenth century may not.

The key may perhaps be found in the sprawling scholastic networks of masters and disciples through which the teaching of *ḥadīth* and *taṣawwuf* (mysticism) was transmitted. Almost all the leaders of the reform movements, including Muḥammad b. ʻAbd al-Wahhāb, were connected to these networks. Their hub was in the Ḥaramayn, the holy cities of Mecca and Medina, where scholars from all over the Muslim world converged to create a cosmopolitan intellectual community.[1]

The Pilgrim-Scholars

The pilgrimage to Mecca and Medina provided the Muslim world with a centre, which helped maintain a measure of unity and conformity within the diversity of regional forms of Islam. From biographies of *'ulamā'*, one gets the impression that the number of scholars and Sufis who performed the pilgrimage increased in the eighteenth century.[2]

Pilgrimage from India and Southeast Asia was always by sea. Until the end of the fifteenth century, shipping in the Indian Ocean was completely in the hands of Muslims. The aggressive intrusion of the Portuguese into the Indian Ocean and their hostile relations with the Muslim powers must have adversely influenced the movement of pilgrims. In the middle of the seventeenth century, the fleets of Oman and Muscat challenged the sea power of the Portuguese and drove them out of the Persian Gulf, and Arab ships again had a greater share in the trade between India and the Arabian Peninsula.[3]

In the eighteenth century, the Dutch controlled the trade of Southeast Asia, while the British gradually eliminated Muslim and European competitors in the trade along the shores of India. By then, both the British and the Dutch had larger ships with improved sails, which made navigation in the Indian Ocean faster and safer. In 1763, the Danish traveller Niebuhr reported that passengers on small Arab ships sailing between India and Arabia were exposed to pirates, and that it was much safer to take the larger European ships.[4] Surat in Gujarat was the major port for Indian trade, and contemporary documents mention pilgrims waiting there to embark on ships to Mokha and Muscat.[5] It was thus on board European ships that most pilgrim-scholars from Indonesia and India came to Mecca. In this way, quite paradoxically, the growing maritime power of Europe contributed to Islamic revivalism.

In the West, the Mediterranean was infested with Muslim and Christian pirates during the sixteenth and seventeenth centuries. By the eighteenth century, the superiority of European warships had put an end to the terror of the pirates, and it encouraged the growth of shipping, especially European, in the Mediterranean.[6] There are records of Muslim travellers who made the voyage from Tunisia to Egypt by sea in order to avoid the long, hard, dangerous overland routes, and in particular the treks across deserts.[7] Niebuhr even made the passage from Rosetta to Cairo by boat on the Nile, because it was safer than travelling by land. He then sailed from Suez to Jedda with pilgrims. Their number, however, was limited, because there were not enough Arab boats on the Red Sea, and European ships were not allowed to sail beyond Jedda.[8]

The majority of pilgrims from the Maghreb continued to travel to Egypt, and from there to Mecca, with the regular pilgrim caravans. The individuals who travelled by sea were mainly the pilgrim-scholars, whose pilgrimages were also journeys in search of knowledge (*fī ṭalb al-'ilm*). They travelled by themselves and stopped in the major towns on the way to associate and study with prominent scholars. Hence, whatever influence better shipping facilities may have had on the pilgrimage in general, they undoubtedly contributed to the growth in the number of pilgrim-scholars and to the development of the Ḥaramayn into important centres of learning.

Though we assume that the eighteenth century saw an increase in the number of pilgrims from most parts of the Muslim world, regional circumstances varied, and absolute figures and comparative data on trends over the course of centuries are not readily available. We shall probably have to be satisfied with circumstantial evidence, not only with regard to pilgrim-scholars, but also concerning the numbers of those who remained in the Ḥaramayn for the rest of their lives as *mujawirun*. Thus, if the number of *'ulamā' mujawirun* did increase in the eighteenth century, more resources must have been required to support scholarly activities in the Ḥaramayn. In order to substantiate this, we would have to investigate the flow of gifts to the Ḥaramayn in the eighteenth century compared to earlier centuries, and in particular the revenues from *awqāf* all over the Muslim world that were dedicated to the Ḥaramayn.

The Intellectual Milieu of the Ḥaramayn

Pilgrim-scholars from North and West Africa stopped in Cairo on their way to the Haramayn; Damascus was the base for the caravans of pilgrims from the Ottoman Empire; and pilgrims from India and Indonesia often landed in one of the ports of the Yemen, staying in Zabīd before proceeding to Mecca. In this way, Zabīd, Damascus and Cairo, as gateways to the Ḥaramayn, became important centres of learning in their own right for scholars and students on their way to Mecca. With Mecca and Medina, they formed the "inner circle."

In most Muslim centres of learning, the majority of teachers and students were of local origin, and they all belonged to the same *madhhab* (e.g., Mālikī in North Africa, Ḥanafī in Turkey and India, Shāfi'ī in Sumatra). But in the Ḥaramayn, teachers and students of different legal schools came together to participate in the thriving study of *ḥadīth*, which is common to all the *madhāhib*. To be sure, the level of scholarship in the Ḥaramayn did not reach that of Cairo, Damascus and Fez, and individual scholars from the Ḥijāz went to Cairo for advanced studies. The intellectual creativity that made the Ḥaramayn the foci for Islamic revivalism is therefore explainable only as an outcome of the convergence there of different traditions of *ḥadīth* studies and of different streams of Sufism, from North Africa, Egypt and India.[9]

There was no conformity in the ideational content of the scholastic networks. A student was influenced by several teachers, and students of the same teacher followed different tracks. Nevertheless, the fusion of *ḥadīth* and *taṣawwuf*, the exoteric and esoteric sciences, freed scholars from the fetters of a strict adherence to past legal precedents (*taqlīd*), and re-oriented Sufism towards a more rigorous observance of *sharī'a*.

The Scholarly Network

Our review of those who contributed to scholarly life in the Ḥaramayn begins with two contemporaneous *'ulamā'*: Muḥammad Ṣafī al-Dīn al-Qushāshī (1602–1660), a Mālikī native of Medina, and Muḥammad al-Bābilī (1591–1666), a Shāfi'ī Egyptian who spent ten years in Mecca.[10] A whole generation of scholars in the Ḥaramayn were students of al-Qushāshī and al-Bābilī. Five of their students, in particular, represented the core of the scholarly network. They reappear in the *asānīd* of prominent scholars in the Ḥaramayn and of others from places like Syria and Yemen who had studied *ḥadīth* in the Ḥaramayn. Three of them were natives of Mecca: Ḥasan b.

'Alī al-'Ujaymī (c. 1639–1702),[11] Aḥmad b. Muḥammad al-Nakhlī (c. 1634–1717),[12] and 'Abdallāh b. Sālim al-Baṣrī (1638–1722).[13] The other two were *mujāwirun*: Ibrāhīm b. Ḥasan al-Kūrānī (1616–1690) from Kurdistan and Muḥammad b. Muḥammad b. Sulaymān al-Maghribī (c. 1627–1683) from Fez in Morocco.[14]

Among those who studied with both al-Qushāshī and al-Bābilī, the most influential in our network was Ibrāhīm al-Kūrānī, a Shāfi'ī. He studied with al-Qushāshī in Medina and with al-Bābilī in Egypt. Al-Kūrānī, who had already belonged to the Sufi order of the Naqshabandiyya, was initiated into the Shaṭṭāriyya order as well by al-Qushāshī, and succeeded him as head of that order in Medina.[15]

Among al-Kūrānī's most prominent students was Muḥammad b. 'Abd al-Rasūl al-Barzanjī (1630–1691), who was born in al-Kūrānī's native town of Shahrazūr in Kurdistan. Al-Barzanjī, twenty-four years younger than al-Kūrānī, followed his master to Medina and studied with him there.[16] In 1682, an *istiftā'*, a request for a legal opinion, was sent from the *'ulamā'* of India to the *'ulamā'* of the Ḥaramayn, concerning the writings of Aḥmad Sirhindī (1564–1624). The letter was addressed particularly to Ibrāhīm al-Kūrānī, who asked al-Barzanjī to reply. The latter wrote an entire treatise, which received the full support of al-Kūrānī, in which he declared Sirhindī's ideas to be unbelief.[17]

Ibrāhīm al-Kūrānī had a special relationship with scholars from Sumatra, foremost among whom was 'Abd al-Ra'ūf al-Sinkilī (c. 1620–after 1693). 'Abd al-Ra'ūf lived in Medina for twenty-one years, between 1640 and 1661, and studied there with al-Qushāshī and al-Kūrānī. On his return to Acheh in northern Sumatra, he was designated *khalīfa* of the Shaṭṭāriyya order, which became very popular there. Following al-Kūrānī's teachings, he emphasized the search for inner mystical significance, without, however, exempting the believer from the duty of observing the *sharī'a*. The Shaṭṭāriyya was thus a reform Sufi order that combined mysticism with scripturalism, in contrast to the pantheistic mysticism that had prevailed in Acheh. Significantly, most of the leaders of the Padri reform movement in the late eighteenth century came from the Shaṭṭāriyya. For thirty years, 'Abd al-Ra'ūf exchanged letters with Ibrāhīm al-Kūrānī across the Indian Ocean. He rendered major works of Islam into Malay, including *Tafsīr al-Jalālayn*, as well as some of al-Kūrānī's own works.[18]

Another distinguished student of al-Kūrānī was al-Zayn b. Muḥammad 'Abd al-Bāqī al-Mizjājī (1643–1725). Members of the Mizjājī family were prominent scholars in their native town of Zabīd, the most important centre of learning in Yemen in the eighteenth century. Relations between the Kūrānī and the Mizjājī families continued into the next generation, when Abu'l-Ṭāhir Muḥammad (1670–1733), son of Ibrāhīm al-Kūrānī, became the teacher of 'Abd al-Khālik b. al-Zayn al-Mizjājī (c. 1705–1740).[19] The latter initiated Ma Ming-Hsin (1719–1781), who visited Zabīd on his pilgrimage to Mecca, into the Naqshabandiyya. Ma Ming-Hsin was the founder and spiritual leader of the "New Teaching," a reformist movement that swept Northwest China in the second half of the eighteenth century.[20]

Muḥammad b. Ibrāhīm al-Kūrānī was born in Medina and became the Shāfi'ī muftī there. He studied with his father and with the other leading scholars of the network, Ḥasan al-'Ujaymī, Aḥmad al-Nakhlī, 'Abdallāh al-Baṣrī and Muḥammad al-Maghribī.[21]

Muḥammad b. Ibrāhīm was the teacher of Shāh Walī Allāh (1702–1762), the leader of Islamic reformism in India in the eighteenth century. Shāh Walī Allāh came to the Ḥaramayn in 1731 and for fourteen months concentrated on the study of *ḥadīth* collections beyond the standard six books. He was particularly influenced by the *al-Muwaṭṭa'* of al-Mālik, and emphasized its importance when he taught *ḥadīth* in India, after his return from the Ḥaramayn. John Voll has pointed this out as yet another illustration of the cross-fertilization which took place between different traditions of Islamic scholarship, in this case those of the Ḥanafī in India and of the Mālikī in the Maghreb.[22] Shāh Walī Allāh himself mentioned in one of his writings that it was in the Ḥaramayn that he had visions of the Prophet and his two grandsons, al-Ḥasan and al-Ḥusayn, who ordered him to initiate his reform movement.[23]

Within the scholarly community of Medina, the most prominent student of Muḥammad b. Ibrāhīm al-Kūrānī was Muḥammad Ḥayāt al-Sindī, an Indian scholar who settled in Medina and died there in 1750. The eighteenth-century Muslim historian al-Murādī called Ḥayāt al-Sindī "the bearer of the banner of the *sunna* in Medina." Ḥayāt al-Sindī also studied with 'Abdallāh b. Sālim al-Baṣrī and Ḥasan b. 'Alī al-'Ujaymī.[24] But Ḥayat al-Sindī's greatest debt was to another *mujāwir* from India, Abu'l-Ḥasan Muḥammad b. 'Abd al-Hādī al-Sindī (d. 1726). Abu'l-Ḥasan himself studied with Ibrāhīm al-Kūrānī and with Muḥammad al-Barzanjī.[25]

A detailed analysis of the teachers and students of Ḥayāt al-Sindī by John Voll presents a microcosm of the world of learning that radiated out of the Ḥaramayn.[26] The network reached as far as the region of present-day northern Nigeria, where 'Uthmān dan Fodio (1754–1817) began his *jihād* in 1804. In 1786 'Uthmān dan Fodio had studied *ḥadīth* with his uncle Muḥammad Rāj, who made the pilgrimage some time before 1773 and studied in Medina with Abu'l-Ḥasan al-Saghīr, a student of Muḥammad Ḥayāt al-Sindī.[27]

Muḥammad Ibn 'Abd-Wahhāb

Ḥayāt al-Sindī, as a prominent scholar of *ḥadīth*, had at least two Ḥanbali students. One of them was Muḥammad b. Aḥmad al-Saffārīnī from Nablus (1702–1774), who met Ḥayāt al-Sindī when he made the pilgrimage in 1736. Before that, he had studied in Syria and Palestine with two great Sufi mentors, 'Abd al-Ghanī al-Nāblusī (1641–1731) and Muṣṭafā al-Bakrī (1688–1749). The Muslim historian al-Jabartī described al-Saffārīnī as a Sufi and an ascetic, but also as a radical "who defended the *sunna* and suppressed *bid'a*."[28]

Muḥammad Ibn 'Abd al-Wahhāb was introduced to Ḥayāt al-Sindī by 'Abdallāh b. Ibrāhīm b. Ṣayf, a Ḥanbali from an important Najdi family. 'Abdallāh b. Ibrāhīm believed in reform through education, as is suggested by the anecdote relating that he showed Ibn 'Abd al-Wahhāb a collection of books which he described as "weapons I have prepared for Majma'a" (his native town in Najd). Ibn 'Abd al-Wahhāb studied *ḥadīth* with Ḥayāt al-Sindī. It is said that one day Ibn 'Abd al-Wahhāb called the attention of Ḥayāt al-Sindī to those who arrived at the Prophet's tomb seeking intercession. Ḥayāt al-Sindī condemned the practice as non-Islamic.[29] This anecdote, according to John Voll, illustrates his argument that the study of *ḥadīth* in Medina "did not remain a quiet intellectual pursuit, [but] was utilized to provide a standard of judging current practices among Muslims."[30]

The brief period that Ibn 'Abd al-Wahhāb stayed in Medina, and in particular his study of *ḥadīth* with Ḥayāt al-Sindī, may have been a source of inspiration for him. Ibn 'Abd al-Wahhāb told his grandson 'Abd al-Raḥmān that it was only when he studied *ḥadīth* and *tafsīr* that he realized how far Muslims had strayed from belief in the unity of Allah (*tawḥīd al-uluhiyya*).[31] Ibn 'Abd al-Wahhāb's teachers in Medina, 'Abdallāh b. Ibrāhīm and Ḥayāt al-Sindī, represented the spirit of revivalism, which was then current in the Ḥaramayn. But they were quietists and could not have been responsible for Ibn 'Abd al-Wahhāb's militant docrines, and in particular his pronouncement of anathema on other Muslims (*takfīr*).

In his search for the sources of Ibn 'Abd al-Wahhāb's doctrines, Michael Cook found that he did not acknowledge any near-contemporary scholar as an authority. As he himself said in one of his epistles, "I did not know the meaning of 'there is no God but Allāh,' nor did I know the religion of Islam, before this blessing (*khayr*) which God vouchsafed to me. Likewise, not one among my teachers knew it." Ibn 'Abd al-Wahhāb insinuates here that he received the truth by revelation. Michael Cook concluded that the sources of his doctrines were literary and included especially the writings of the two great Ḥanbali scholars of the fourteenth century, Ibn Taymiyya and Ibn Qayyim al-Jawziyya.[32]

Indeed, Muḥammad b. Ismā'īl Ibn al-Amīr al-Ṣan'ānī (1688–c. 1768), a militant Yemeni reformist, thought that Ibn 'Abd al-Wahhāb was poorly educated, because he had not studied under the guidance of scholars; hence his naive interpretation, as al-Ṣan'ānī saw it, of the works of Ibn Taymiyya and Ibn Qayyim al-Jawziyya. Ibn al-Amīr was twenty-five years older than Ibn 'Abd al-Wahhāb, but we do not know whether there were personal contacts between the two. Ibn al-Amīr at first approved the activities of Ibn 'Abd al-Wahhāb, but he changed his mind after examining some of the latter's works.[33]

The Circulation of Reformist Ideas

Ibn al-Amīr al-Ṣan'ānī studied in the Ḥaramayn with Muḥammad b. Ibrāhīm al-Kūrānī, 'Abdallāh al-Basrī and Abu'l-Ḥasan al-Sindī. The latter, according to some sources, influenced al-Ṣan'ānī by directing him to the study of *ḥadīth*. It was after al-Ṣan'ānī had returned from Medina in 1720 that he began to call for a reform of society and government in Yemen.[34] A copy of his treatise on "the purification of the faith" (*Taṭhir al-i'tiqād 'an adran al-ilḥād*) was found bound together with a book by Ibn 'Abd al-Wahhāb, indicating that al-Ṣan'ānī's work, which condemned the veneration of tombs and asserted that people in Yemen, Syria and Najd were full of *shirk*, may have been studied by the Wahhābis.[35]

Reformist ideas circulated in and out of the Ḥaramayn. Ṣāliḥ al-Fullānī came to Medina from Fūtā Jallon in West Africa, which had experienced an earlier *jihād* movement in 1725. Al-Fullānī seems to have formulated his ideas during his studies in his native Mauritania and in Morocco. He came to Medina in 1774 and was one of the most infuential teachers there for thirty years, until his death in 1803. He opposed *taqlīd* and called for a strict adherence to the Koran and the *sunna*. Though he does not seem openly to have advocated *ijtihād*, he certainly was against partisanship of a single *madhhab*.[36]

Aḥmad Ibn Idrīs al-Fāsī (1749–1837) held similar views. When he came to Mecca in 1799 he met with the hostility of the *'ulamā'* there, because he preferred the text of the *ḥadīth* to the ruling of the *madhhab*. His views may have been formed during his studies between 1770 and 1797 in Fez, which was permeated with reformist ideas during the reigns of Sīdī Muḥammad b. 'Abdallāh (1757–1790) and his son Mawlay Sulayman (1793–1822).[37]

Ibn Idrīs stayed in Mecca after the Wahhābi conquest in 1803 and was treated with respect by the Wahhābīs. He conducted theological disputations with their *'ulamā'*, continued to follow his Sufi way, and even read Ibn 'Arabī, whose teachings were considered unbelief by the Wahhābīs. He left Mecca in 1803, after the Wahhābīs had been driven out, and returned only in 1817. After conducting acrimonious debates with the *'ulamā'*, he left Mecca again, or was expelled, in 1827, and he spent the last ten years of his life, until his death in 1837, first in Yemen and later in 'Asīr, which was then under the rule of the Wahhābīs.[38]

Ibn Idrīs preferred Yemen, because he was closer to its scholars, particularly Muḥammad b. 'Alī al-Shawkānī (1760–1834), in his attitude towards *madhhab* partisanship. Al-Shawkānī, the most celebrated Zaydi scholar of the eighteenth century, studied with Yemeni Sunni *'ulamā'*, members of the Mizjājī and Aḥdal families. He was also directly connected to our network through a certain 'Alī b. Ibrāhīm, a student of Muḥammad Ḥayāt al-Sindī. His debt to the study of *ḥadīth* in the Ḥaramayn is evident in his major book on *ḥadīth*, *Itḥāf al-kabīr bi-isnād al-dafātīr*, a collection of *asānīd* in which he relies heavily on the *asānīd* of al-Bābilī, Ibrāhīm al-Kūrānī, al-Nakhlī, 'Abdallāh al-Baṣrī and Muḥammad Ibn al-Ṭayyib (1698–1756).[39]

A Sufi Network

By the end of the seventeenth century, the Naqshabandiyya was firmly established in the Ḥaramayn and included among its affiliates most of the key figures in our network, such as Ibrāhīm al-Kūrānī, Aḥmad al-Nakhlī, Ḥasan al-'Ujaymī and Muḥammad Ḥayāt al-Sindī.[40] The eighteenth century saw a transition among *ṣūfi ṭuruq* from devotional paths, sets of *adhkār* and *awrād*, to corporate social organizations.[41] Pilgrims were initiated in the Ḥaramayn into new *ṭuruq*, and carried back to their homelands not only new ideas but also the nuclei for more cohesive and structurally organized *ṭuruq*.

A contemporary collection of biographies of scholars in Medina gives information about Sufi affiliation in only four or five entries. One may suggest that although almost all the scholars were affiliated with at least one *ṭarīqa*, few became famous primarily as mystics. One of them was Muḥammad b. 'Abd al-Karīm b. Ḥasan al-Sammān (1718–1776). He was initiated by Muṣṭafā b. Kamāl al-Dīn al-Bakrī (1688–1749) into the Khalwatiyya (also referred to as *al-ṭarīqa al-Bakriyya*). Although Muṣṭafā al-Bakrī himself had been initiated into several *ṭurūq* earlier in his life, he demanded from his disciples exclusive affiliation with his *ṭarīqa*. Indeed, the biographies of al-Sammān seem to emphasize the latter's full commitment to al-Bakrī's *ṭarīqa*.[42]

Al-Sammān's fame as a Sufi attracted distinguished visitors, such as the leading Moroccan scholar al-Tawūdī Ibn Sūda (in 1769),[43] and Aḥmad al-Tijānī, the founder of the Tijāniyya (in 1774). Al-Tijānī, who was actively searching for a devotional path, had already been initiated twice into the Khalwatiyya, by Muḥammad b. 'Abd al-Raḥman al-Azharī in Algeria and by Maḥmūd al-Kurdī in Cairo. According to al-Tijānī's biographer, he was directed to al-Sammān by the recluse *shaykh* Abu'l-'Abbās Sīdī Aḥmad b. 'Abdallāh al-Hindī, a resident of Mecca. Al-Tijānī communicated with al-Hindī without actually meeting him, through the medium of his servant. The Indian *shaykh* declared that al-Tijānī was the heir to his knowledge, secrets and gifts. He then directed him to al-Sammān, calling him "my successor as *quṭb*." From Mecca al-Tijānī continued to Medina, where he met al-Sammān. Although al-Tijānī refused to enter into a *khalwa*, al-Sammān taught him the holy names, thus reinforcing al-Tijānī's adherence to the Khalwatiyya.[44]

Two of al-Sammān's disciples spread a *ṭarīqa*, called al-Sammāniyya after him, to Sumatra and to the Sudan. 'Abd al-Ṣamad al-Palimbānī (c. 1703–c. 1788) spent most of his working life in Arabia, and was initiated by al-Sammān into his *ṭarīqa*, presumably the Khalwatiyya. 'Abd al-Ṣamad, in his turn, initiated students from Sumatra, who had come to study with him in Mecca, into the *ṭarīqa* that he named after his master, *al-ṭarīqa al-Sammāniyya*. On their return to Sumatra, they spread the new *ṭarīqa* in Palembang in south Sumatra. That the Sammāniyya became rooted in Sumatra already in the lifetime of its founder is demonstrated by the appearance there in 1781, only six years after al-Sammān's death, of a hagiography of him, and this hagiography mentions an even earlier account of miracles performed by al-Sammān.[45]

From his residence in the Ḥaramayn, 'Abd al-Ṣamad served as a guide and teacher to scholars in Sumatra. He maintained links with his homeland by correspondence, inspiring resistance to the Dutch through the messages he communicated thereby. In 1772 he wrote letters from Mecca on behalf of two returning pilgrims to three princes in Central Java. Two of the letters urged defence of the faith, while the third spoke of the virtues of a holy war. In 1774 he wrote a treatise on *Imān*, including a section on holy war. It became popular in Acheh and a century later inspired fighters against the Dutch in the Acheh war of 1873–1910. He also wrote an Arabic *ratīb*, a poetic composition for *dhikr* recitation. In 1818 a revolt broke out against the Dutch, set off by a scuffle between several returning pilgrims who were reciting a *ratīb* and a group of inquisitive Dutch soldiers. Perhaps this was a *ratīb* of the Sammāniyya.

Reform of *ṣūfī ṭuruq* in the eighteenth century was associated with a renewed interest in the doctrines of al-Ghazālī. Between 1779 and 1788 'Abd al-Ṣamad rendered into Malay the *Lubab ihyā' 'ulūm al-dīn*, an abridgement of al-Ghazālī's *Ihyā' 'ulūm al-dīn*. Like the Malay rendering of *Tafsīr al-Jalalayn* by 'Abd al-Ra'ūf, this work remained very popular. Both 'Abd al-Ra'ūf, the student of Ibrāhīm al-Kūrānī, and 'Abd al-Ṣamad, the student of al-Sammān, enriched the Islamic religious literature in Malay, thus contributing to the radicalization of Islam, as happened in several parts of the Muslim world in the eighteenth century.[46]

The Sammāniyya was introduced into the Sudan by Aḥmad al-Ṭayyib b. al-Bashīr, who had been initiated by al-Sammān in Medina. He returned to the Sudan in 1800 and spread the Sammāniyya there until his death in 1823. The Sammāniyya as a reformed *ṭarīqa*, organized on a wider geographical and societal scale and with a central hierarchical authority, expanded at the expense of the two older *ṭuruq*, the Qādiriyya and the Shādhiliyya, which had been adapted to the local parochial pattern of "holy families."[47] The Sammāniyya contributed to Islamic militancy in the Sudan through the affiliation of Muḥammad Aḥmad, the Mahdi. He was a member of the Sammāniyya for ten years (1861–1871) as a disciple of Muḥammad al-Sharīf, the grandson of Aḥmad al-Ṭayyib al-Bashīr.[48]

Some Characteristics of the Network

Tarājim a'yan al-Madīna al-munāwwara fi'l-qarn al-thānī 'ashar, an anonymous collection of biographies of scholars active in Medina in the twelfth century of the Muslim era, written after 1786 (1201), provides us with a rare opportunity to study that scholarly community. Out of more than 80 biographical entries, 24 concern *mujāwirūn*: 7 of these came to Medina from the Maghreb, 5 from Sind (India), 4 from Kurdistan, 3 from the central Ottoman Empire, 2 from Uzbekistan, and one each from Aleppo, West Africa and Daghestan. Evidently, scholars from the areas of the Maghreb, Sind, Kurdistan and the central lands of the Ottoman Empire, which made up "the intermediate region" between the "inner circle" and the farther lands of Islam, made a special contribution to intellectual life in the Ḥaramayn.

We can identify the *madhhab* affiliation of 73 scholars, among whom 47 were Ḥanafīs, 16 were Shāfi'īs, 8 were Mālikīs and 2 were Ḥanbalīs. Thirty of the Ḥanafīs belonged to seven families that produced at least four scholars each who held the offices of *qāḍī*, *nā'ib* and *mufti*. Six other Ḥanafīs came from Sind, and two were Uzbeks. Among the Shāfi'īs, five were members of Ibrāhīm al-Kūrānī's family, and four were members of the Samhūdī family. There were also three other Kurds and one Daghestanī. All the

Mālikīs were Maghribīs, except for the West African Ṣāliḥ al-Fullānī.

A comparison between Medina and Mecca suggests that more *mujāwirūn* preferred to study and teach in Medina, where the scholarly community seems to have been more cosmopolitan. This would be in line with a more general pattern noted by W. Ende:

> Many pious Muslims considered *mujāwara* in Medina, at the tomb of the Prophet and the resting-place of many of his companions, as even more meritorious than that in Mecca. This opinion was, among other things, influenced by the fact that apparently none of the Companions of the Prophet had expressed the wish to remain in Mecca as a *mujāwir* after having performed the smaller or greater pilgrimage.[49]

It is significant that Arab scholars from the countries of the "inner circle" — from Egypt (like al-Bābilī and Ḥasan al-Jabartī, 1698–1774), from Syria and Palestine (such as al-Saffārinī),[50] and many more from Yemen — studied and taught for many years in Mecca and Medina, but returned to their native countries.

Among the pilgrim-scholars from the farther lands of Islam, only one, Ṣāliḥ al-Fullānī, became a *mujāwir* and a teacher in the Ḥaramayn. Other pilgrims from the "outer circle" stayed for some time in the Ḥaramayn, went on to study in Zabīd or in Cairo, and returned to their homelands — to Southeast Asia ('Abd al-Ra'ūf and 'Abd al-Ṣamad), China (Ma Ming-Hsin), Agades (Jibrīl b. 'Umar) and Hausaland (Muḥammad Rāj). Some of them were inspired by the spirit of revivalism in the "inner circle," and they or their disciples (like 'Uthmān dan Fodio) became leaders of reformist movements.

Eyewitness Reports: Mecca under the Wahhābīs

The first eyewitness report on Mecca was by 'Alī Bey al-'Abbāsī, pseudonym of the Spanish (some say Jewish) traveller Domingo Badia y Leblich, who visited Mecca in 1807 dressed as an Arab. At that time Mecca was under the rule of the Wahhābīs, and the number of pilgrims was only a fraction of what it had been. Though it could accommodate over one hundred thousand souls, there were only some sixteen to eighteen thousand at that time. Almost two-thirds of the buildings in Mecca stood empty. These had been hostels for pilgrims, and in their absence the houses were not maintained and became half ruined. Scholarship in Mecca was poor; only a handful of *ṭalaba* gave lessons to an audience of a dozen in the main mosque. 'Alī Bey found the copies of the Koran produced in Mecca to be full of mistakes that revealed the ignorance of the copyists.[51]

John Lewis Burckhardt visited Mecca in 1814, after the city had been liberated from the Wahhābīs and was being ruled by a governor in the name of Muḥammad Alī. Mecca had begun to recover, but was still only a shadow of its former self. The city could have accommodated three times the number of its residents in 1814. Apart from Hijāzī Beduins who had settled in Mecca, all the other residents were foreigners or the descendants of foreigners, who adopted the local language and customs, except for the Indians, who continued to maintain their own as well. The following excerpts from Burckhardt's report speak for themselves:

> I think I have sufficient reason for affirming that Mecca is at present much inferior even in Muhammedan learning to any town of equal population in Syria or Egypt. It probably was not so when the many public schools or Medreses were built, which are now converted into private lodgings for pilgrims.[52]
>
> In the mosques, after prayers, chiefly in the afternoon, some learned olemas explain a few religious books to a very thin audience, consisting principally of Indians, Malays, Negroes and a few natives of Hadramaut and Yemen, who, attracted by the great name of Mekka, remain here a few years, until they think themselves sufficiently instructed to pass at home for learned men. The Mekkawys themselves, who wish to improve science, go to Damascus or to Cairo.[53]
>
> There is no public library attached to the mosque; the ancient libraries, of which I have already spoken, have all disappeared. Mekka is equally destitute of private libraries, with the exception of those of the rich merchants, who exhibit a few books to distinguish them from the vulgar; or of the olemas, of whom some possess such as are necessary for their daily reference in matters of law. The Wahhābys, according to a report, carried off many loads of books; but they were also said to have paid for every thing they took ... They told me that bookdealers used formerly to come here with the Hadj from Yemen, and sell

> valuable books ... There are no copyists at Mekka to replace the books that have been exported.[54]

These eyewitness reports illustrate the consequences of the Wahhābī conquest of Mecca in 1803. The holy city became deserted and impoverished, as the pilgrimage stopped almost completely, as well as the flow of annual gifts from Istanbul, Cairo and other Muslim capitals. The changing fortunes of the holy city and pilgrim centre were similar, it seems, to those of commercial cities in parallel circumstances. Commercial cities had a core of native inhabitants, but their prosperity depended on the floating population of traders. Among the latter, some became residents while others were seasonal visitors. But when conditions changed as a result of wars or the diversion of trade routes, the foreign traders, even those who had been resident for years or generations, deserted the commercial city, which was left only with its native inhabitants.[55]

Mecca had a floating population of scholars and pilgrims, as well as of those who provided them with services. 'Alī Bey's report about the poor scholarship in Mecca suggests that the leading *'ulamā'*, who considered the Wahhābīs sectarians or even heretics, had left the city. It seems that some of those who had made their living from catering to the pilgrims had also left Mecca.

We do not have similar eyewitness reports for Medina, which had been more cosmopolitan than Mecca. Perhaps Medina was not as heavily affected as Mecca by the Wahhābī conquest, allowing greater continuity with the recent past.

The rehabilitation of the foreign scholarly community was slow, but in 1826 Muḥammad b. 'Alī al-Sanūsī found some teachers of prominence in Mecca and Medina. Some of these were linked by scholastic and mystical chains (*salāsil*) to the great scholars of earlier generations. Ṣāliḥ al-Fullānī appears more often than others in these *salāsil*. The proportion of natives of Mecca among the scholars seems to have been larger than before the Wahhābī conquest, when many of the prominent scholars had been immigrants to Mecca or their descendants.[56]

The spirit of reform in the Ḥaramayn came to an end as a result of the conquest by the Wahhābiyya. In Egypt, the revival of the Khalwatiyya had run its course by the beginning of the nineteenth century, as a result of the upheavals caused by the French conquest and the rise of Muḥammad 'Alī. In Morocco, the reformist thrust ceased after Mawlāy Sulaymān, whose reign ended with a revolt of the anti-reform forces.[57] Elsewhere in the Islamic world, however, the reform movements of the nineteenth century that changed the character of Islam in the farther lands, and particularly in Africa, were directly linked to the networks of *ḥadīth* scholars and Sufis with their centre in the Ḥaramayn, as well as to the Khalwati *shaykhs* in Egypt and to the reformist milieu of Fez.

Notes

1. See the Introduction to N. Levtzion & J.O. Voll (eds.), *Eighteenth Century Renewal and Reform in Islam*, Syracuse 1987, pp. 3–20.
2. For Morocco, see N. Levtzion & G. Weigert, "Religious Reform in Morocco in the Eighteenth Century," *North African, Arabic and Islamic Studies in Honor of Pesach Shinar, Jerusalem Studies in Arabic and Islam*, XIII (1995), pp. 173–197.
3. C.R. Boxer, *The Portuguese Seaborne Empire, 1415–1825*, London 1969; R.B. Serjeant, *The Portuguese off the South Arabian Coast*, Oxford 1963; and N. Steensgaard, *The Asian Trade Revolution of the Seventeenth Century*, Chicago 1973.
4. M. Niebuhr, *Travels through Arabia and Other Countries in the East*, London 1792, pp. 153, 417–418.
5. Ashir Dan Gupta, "Trade and Politics in Eighteenth Century India," in D.S. Richards (ed.), *Islam and the Trade of Asia: A Colloquium*, Oxford 1970, 181–214.
6. G. Fisher, *Barbary Legend*, Oxford 1957; P. Mason, *Histoire de l'établissements et du commerce français dans l'Afrique barbaresque, 1560–1793*, Paris 1903.
7. Abu'l-Qasim al-Zayyānī, *Al-Turjamāna al-kubrā fi akhbār al-ma'mūr barran wa-baḥran*, Rabat 1967, pp. 58–60, 83–86, 379–380; 'Alī Ḥarazm, *Jawāhir al-ma'ānī wa-bulūgh al-amānī*, Cairo 1929, I, p. 39.
8. Niebuhr, *Travels through Arabia* (above, note 4), pp. 40–44, 177, 221, 236; on travelling by boat between Suez and Jedda see also al-Zayyānī, *al-Turjamāna al-kubrā* (above, note 7), p. 215.
9. J.O. Voll, "*Ḥadīth* Scholars and *Ṭarīqahs*: An *'Ulamā'* Group in Eighteenth Century Ḥaramayn and Their Impact on the Muslim World," *Journal of Asian and African Studies*, XV (1980), pp. 264–273, particularly p. 266.
10. Muḥammad Amīn al-Muḥibbī, *Khulāṣat al-athār fi a'yān al-qarn al-ḥadī 'ashar*, Beirut 1966, IV, pp. 39–42.
11. 'Abd al-Raḥmān al-Jabartī, *'Ajā'ib al-athār fi'l-tarājim wa'l-Akhbār*, ed. Ḥasan Muḥammad Jawhār et al., Cairo, 1957–1968, I, p. 177.
12. *Ibid.*, I, p. 213; Muḥammad Khalīl al-Murādī, *Silk al-durar fī a'yān al-qarn al-thānī 'ashar*, Baghdad 1301/1883f, I, pp. 171–172.
13. Al-Jabartī, *'Ajā'ib al-athār* (above, note 11), I, pp. 208–209; J.O Voll, " 'Abdallāh ibn Sālim al-Baṣrī and 18th-Century Ḥadīth Scholarship," paper presented to MESA meeting in Baltimore, November 1987.
14. Al-Muhibbī, *Khulāṣat al-athār* (above, note 10), IV, p. 207.
15. Al-Murādī, *Silk al-durar* (above, note 12), II, pp. 5–6; al-Jabartī, *'Ajā'ib al-athār*,

I, p. 171; A.H. Johns, *EI*², V, cols. 432–433, s.v. *Al-Kūrānī*, and col. 525, s.v. *al-Kushāshī*.

16. Al-Murādī, *Silk al-durar* (above, note 12), IV, pp. 65–66.
17. Y. Friedmann, *Shaykh Aḥmad Sirhindi: An Outline of His Thought and a Study of His Image in the Eyes of Posterity*, Montreal 1971, pp. 8, 96–101, 119.
18. A.H. Johns, "Islam in Southeast Asia: Problems and Perspectives," in C.D. Cowan & O.W. Wolters (eds.), *Southeast Asian History and Historiography*, Ithaca, N.Y., 1976, pp. 304–320.
19. J.O. Voll, "Linking Groups in the Networks of Eighteenth-Century Revivalist Scholars: The Mizjājī Family in the Yemen," in Levtzion & Voll, *Eighteenth Century Renewal* (above, note 1), pp. 69–92. When Niebuhr visited Zabīd in 1763, the town was in economic decline after its thriving commerce had shifted to Mokha. However, it was still full of religious scholars, who drained more than half of the town's revenues. See *Travels through Arabia* (above, note 4), pp. 282–284.
20. J. Fletcher, "Les voies (*turuq*) soufies en Chine," in A. Popovic & G. Veinstein (eds.), *Les Ordres mystiques de l'Islam*, Paris 1986, pp. 14–26.
21. Al-Murādī, *Silk al-durar* (above, note 12), IV, p. 27.
22. Voll, "*Ḥadīth* scholars" (above, note 9), p. 266. In the same period, the reformist Moroccan sultan Sīdī Muḥammad b. 'Abdallāh broadened the scope of *ḥadīth* studies by introducing the study of *ḥadīth* collections other than Mālik's *al-Muwaṭṭa'*. See Levtzion & Weigert, "Religious Reform in Morocco" (above, note 2).
23. Mohamed A. Al-Freih, "The Historical Background of the Emergence of Muḥammad Ibn 'Abd al-Wahhāb and His Movement," Ph.D. Dissertation, UCLA, 1990, pp. 333–334; and S.A.A. Rizvi, *Shāh Walī Allāh and his Times*, Canberra 1980, pp. 215–216, 225, 295, 396–397.
24. Al-Murādī, *Silk al-durar* (above, note 12), IV, p. 34.
25. *Ibid.*, p. 66.
26. J.O. Voll, "Muḥammad Ḥayāt al-Sindī and Muḥammad ibn 'Abd al-Wahhāb: An Analysis of an Intellectual Group in Eighteenth Century Madina," *Bulletin SOAS*, xv (1980), pp. 32–39.
27. 'Abdallāh ibn Fūdī, *Tazyīn al-waraqāt*, ed. and English transl. by M. Hiskett, Ibadan 1963, p. 38; transl., p. 95. Ḥayāt al-Sindī studied with Abu'l-Ḥasan al-Kabīr and taught Abu'l-Ḥasan al-Saghīr. The latter, the teacher of Muḥammad Rāj, was Abu'l-Ḥasan Muḥammad b. Muḥammad Ṣadīq al-Sindī. He was born in Sind in 1713, came to Medina in 1747, and died there in or after 1773. See *Tarājim a'yān al-madīna al-munawwara fi'l-qarn al-thānī 'ashar* (author unknown), ed. Muḥammad al-Tawunjī, Jedda 1984, p. 59.
28. Al-Muradī, *Silk al-durar* (above, note 12), IV, pp. 31–32; al-Jabartī, *'Ajā'ib al-athār* (above, note 11), III, pp. 106–110.
29. Ibn Bishr, *'Unwān al-majd fī ta'rīkh Najd*, Beirut, n.d., p. 17; 'Abdallāh Ṣāliḥ al-'Uthaymin, "Muḥammad ibn 'Abd al-Wahhāb: The Man and His Works," Ph.D. Dissertation, Edinburgh, 1972, pp. 68–74; Al-Freih, "Historical Background of Ibn 'Abd al-Wahhāb" (above, note 23), p. 337; M. Cook, "On the Origins of Wahhābism," *Journal of the Royal Asiatic Society*, Series 3, II (1992), p. 192.

30. Voll, "*Ḥadīth* Scholars," (above, note 9), p. 267.
31. Al-Freih, "Historical Background of Ibn 'Abd al-Wahhāb" (above, note 23), p. 338, quoting Ibn Ḥasan, *al-Maqamāt*, fol. 7.
32. Cook, "Origins of Wahhābism" (above, note 29), pp. 198–202.
33. *Ibid.*, p. 200.
34. Al-Freih, "Historical Background of Ibn 'Abd al-Wahhāb," p. 334 (above, note 23, quoting Qāsim Aḥmad, *Ibn al-Amīr wa-'aṣruhu*, n.d., p. 128, and 'Abd al-Raḥmān Ba'kar, *Musliḥ al-Yaman*, 1988, p. 70).
35. M. Cook, personal communication.
36. J.O. Hunwick, "Ṣāliḥ al-Fullānī of Futa Jallon: an Eighteenth-Century Scholar and *mujaddid*," *Bulletin IFAN*, XL (1978), pp. 879–885; idem, "Sāliḥ al-Fullānī (1752/3–1803); The Career and Teaching of a West African *'Ālim* in Medina," in A.H. Green (ed.), *In Quest of Islamic Humanism: Arabic and Islamic Studies in Memory of Mohamed al-Nowaihi*, Cairo 1984, pp. 139–154.
37. Levtzion & Weigert, "Religious Reform in Morocco" (above, note 2).
38. R.S. O'Fahey, *Enigmatic Saint: Aḥmad Ibn Idris and the Idrisi Tradition*, Evanston 1990, pp. 58–80.
39. Ḥusayn b. 'Abdallāh al-'Amrī, *The Yemen in the 18th & 19th Centuries: A Political and Intellectual History*, London 1985, pp. 106–114.
40. Voll, "*Ḥadīth* Scholars," p. 268.
41. Levtzion & Voll (eds.), Introduction to *Eighteenth Century Renewal and Reform* (above, note 1), pp. 9–10. In the older pattern of Sufism, scholars were affiliated with several *ṭuruq* simultaneously, as was the case with a scholar of Medina, Muḥammad Badr al-Dīn b. Naṣr al-Dīn al-Bukhārī al-Ḥanafī, born in 1752. He studied with Ismā'īl b. 'Abdallāh al-Uskudārī (c. 1707–c. 1768), who was *shaykh al-ṭā'ifa al-Naqshabandiyya* in Medina. He was initiated into the *al-ṭarīqa al-Bakriyya* by Muḥammad al-Sammān, and into the Naqshabandiyya by his father and also by al-Khawāja Raḥmatallāh al-Naqshabandī, by correspondence from India (*bi'l-murāsala min al-Hind*). He was initiated by Abū Sa'īd al-Ḥasanī in Medina into the Naqshabandiyya, the Qādiriyya and the Ḥusayniyya. See *Tarājim a'yān al-Madīna* (above, note 27), pp. 61, 109–110.
42. *Tarājim a'yān al-Madīna* (above, note 27), p. 95: "*akhadha al-ṭarīqa wa-awradahu wa-intafa'a bihi*," and al-Murādī, *Silk al-durar* (above, note 12), IV, pp. 60–61: "*waqāma 'alā waẓā'if al-awrād wa'l-adhkār*." On Muṣṭafā al-Bakrī's call for exclusivity, see G. Weigert, "The Khalwatiyya in Egypt in the Eighteenth Century," Ph.D. Dissertation, The Hebrew University of Jerusalem, 1989, pp. 107–108, quoting al-Jabartī, *'Ajā'ib al-athār* (above, note 11), IV, p. 66.
43. Al-Jabartī, *'Ajā'ib al-athār* (above, note 11), II, p. 243.
44. 'Alī Ḥarazm, *Jawāhir al-ma'ānī* (above, note 7), I, pp. 40–41.
45. This information about 'Abd al-Ṣamad is based on an unpublished paper by A.H. Johns, "Enriching the Language of the Tribe: The Works of Jawi 'Ulamā' in the 17–19 Centuries," presented to the Conference on Eighteenth Century Renewal and Reform in Islam, Jerusalem, 1985. Johns cited G.W.J. Drewes, "Directions for Travellers on the Mystic Path," *VKI: Verhandlingen van het koninklijk Instituut voot Taal-, Landen volkenkunde*, LXXXI (1977).

46. N. Levtzion, "The Eighteenth Century: Background to the Islamic Revolutions in West Africa," in Levtzion & Voll, *Eighteenth Century Renewal and Reform* (above, note 1), pp. 26–28.
47. Aḥmad 'Alī al-Bashīr, *Al-Adab al-ṣūfī fi'l-Sūdān*, Cairo 1970, p. 43; P.M. Holt, "Holy Families and Islam in the Sudan," *Princeton Near East Papers*, IV (1967).
48. Na'ūm Shuqayr, *Jughrāfiyya wa-ta'rikh al-Sūdān*, Cairo 1903–1904, III, 113–118.
49. W. Ende, *EI*[2], VII, s.v. *Mujāwir*, cols. 293–294.
50. Al-Murādī, *Silk al-durar* (above, note 12) has many references to Syrian scholars who studied for some time in the Ḥaramayn; see, e.g., III, pp. 63–64, 220–221.
51. *Voyages d'Ali Bey El-Abessī en Afrique et en Asie pendant les annees 1803, 1804, 1805, 1806 et 1807*, Paris 1814, II, pp. 392–398, 423.
52. J.L. Burckhardt, *Travels in Arabia*, London 1829, I, p. 389.
53. *Ibid.*, pp. 390.
54. *Ibid.*, pp. 392–4.
55. An example of a trading town that was deserted in the wake of a civil war and the diversion of its trade route was Salaga in the northern region of Ghana, toward the end of the nineteenth century; see N. Levtzion, *Muslims and Chiefs in West Africa*, Oxford 1968, pp. 26–48.
56. K. Vikor, "Sufi and Scholar on the Desert Edge: Muḥammad b. 'Alī al-Sanūsī (1787–1859)," Ph.D. Dissertation, University of Bergen, 1991, pp. 92–99.
57. Weigert, "The Khalwatiyya" (above, note 42), pp. 156–160, 186; Levtzion & Weigert, "Religious Reform in Morocco" (above, note 2).

XIII

The Dynamics of Sufi Brotherhoods

SHARI`A AND MYSTICISM IN THE PUBLIC SPHERE

Islamic religious law is the totality of God's commands that regulate the life of every Muslim in all its aspects. Islamic law is the most typical manifestation of the Islamic way of life, the core and kernel of Islam itself. Theology has never been able to achieve a comparable importance in Islam; only mysticism was strong enough to challenge the ascendancy of the Law over the minds of the Muslim, and often proved victorious.[1]

The *shari`a*, a God-ordained law, is entrenched in a deep-rooted public sentiment and forms the basis for the Muslim social order. Sanction of the religious law contributed to the formation of a Muslim public opinion that accorded the *shari`a* and the *`ulama'* near monopoly of legal and moral legitimization, and endowed the *qadi* with a degree of autonomy vis-à-vis the rulers. The *shari`a* was developed as an autonomous legal system by *fuqaha'* (jurists), who asserted their position as the sole interpreters of the Prophet's heritage.

Since their formation in the eighth and ninth centuries, the various legal schools not only represented different interpretations of the law but were also solidarity groups. Only the Hanbali school of law retained these characteristics over a long period; the other schools of law ceased to function as mobilizing social movements after the twelfth century, and this role was taken over by Sufi brotherhoods and related organizations.

Islamic orthodoxy emphasizes the distance between God and man, as comparable to that between a slave and his master: like a slave, a man can please God only by strictly observing his commands. Sufi mystics developed alternative ways of approaching God, through spiritual and physical exercises. Sufis therefore do not have to observe the precepts of the religious law, as do others.

Islamic mysticism began as a marginal esoteric movement, considered heretic by the jurists. The rupture between jurists and mystics reached a dramatic peak with the execution in 922 of al-Hallaj, who claimed to have reached

Reprinted by permission from *The Public Sphere in Muslim Societies*, edited by Miriam Hoexter, Schmuel N. Eisenstadt, and Nehemia Levtzion, the State University of New York Press

a complete union with God. But in the tenth and eleventh centuries more Sufis accepted the Islamic law as binding. Sufism became integrated into the mainstream of Islam, and before long religious leaders (*`ulama'*) were simultaneously Sufi shaykhs and legal scholars.

THE ORGANIZATION AND STRUCTURE OF EARLY SUFI BROTHERHOODS

Small communities of a master and his disciples (*murids*) replaced the loose master-disciple relationship of early Sufism. These entities continued to be known as *tariqa* (plural: *turuq*), but the literal meaning of "a devotional path" gave way to such terms as *brotherhood* or *order*.

Before the eighteenth century, however, brotherhoods did not have a central organization and were not actually self-supporting social organizations.[2] The loosely structured Sufi brotherhoods nevertheless became active in the public sphere, by allying themselves with more structured social organizations. In the countryside they became embedded in tribal or territorial units, which charismatic shaykhs were able to manipulate. In urban societies the brotherhoods were linked to voluntary organizations, like the *futuwwa*, the urban movement of young men. Later, in the Ottoman Empire, the Sufis were allied with the *akhi* association of young men and the trade guilds, as well as with *ghazis* (warriors on the frontiers of Islam) and the Janissaries.

For most Muslims the connection to Sufi brotherhoods was through the cult of saints (*awliya'*), which from the twelfth century on became central to the religious experience of Muslims. It was through the shaykh and the tomb, rather than through the *`alim* and the mosque, that Islam reached the common people. One was born and socialized around the shaykh's tomb and the *baraka* (divine blessing) that emanated from it, and each village, town ward, and tribe had its saint's tomb. Visitations to saints' tombs were the highlights of religious life, particularly for women, who went to the saint's tomb on Fridays, when the men went to the mosque for the Friday prayer.[3] By giving confidence to individuals, through the power of their protective amulets, the saints helped to maintain social stability.[4]

Sufis were deeply concerned with the life of the community. Shaykhs voiced the people's grievances and condemned tyranny and oppression. They played a part in conciliation and arbitration, and their houses were sanctuaries.[5]

Individual Sufis and brotherhoods oscillated between individualistic denunciatory piety and community-oriented legalistic world affirmation. Pious withdrawal from the world was characteristic of the more popular and less orthodox brotherhoods. The more legally *shari`a*-oriented brotherhoods were "this world" oriented. A positive attitude to "this world" also provided the framework within which political engagement became licit and spiritually acceptable.[6]

SUFIS AND THE STATE

Most *`ulama'* depended on the state, either because they held appointed positions or because they were associated with institutions supported by the state. On the other hand, Sufi shaykhs were not economically dependent on the rulers, because they received gifts and contributions from the people.

Not being dependant on the state, Sufis operated beyond the frontiers of *dar al-Islam*. From the tenth century on Sufi shaykhs lived among the infidel Turkish nomads of the steppes and were instrumental in converting them to Islam. Following the Mongol conquest and the destruction of the Muslim state, only the Sufi shaykhs of all men of religion continued to provide leadership to the Muslim communities. They also associated themselves with the Mongol rulers, and by the end of the thirteenth century had converted them to Islam.

The institutionalization of Sufism advanced when rulers began to endow hospices *(khanqahs)* for Sufis. The *khanqah* organized Sufism under the control of the state, aiming to foster the type of Sufism that conformed with the teachings of the *shari`a*.[7]

Besides the state-supported *khanqahs* there were completely independent, modest personal lodges *(zawiya* or *ribat)* of shaykhs. The *zawiya* served both as the residence of the shaykh and as a meeting place for members of the *tariqa*. The shaykh was buried in his *zawiya*, which then became a place of pilgrimage, with an annual festival.

Sufi lodges at strategic positions helped the expansion of Muslim commercial networks within and outside of *dar al-Islam*. In the fifteenth and sixteenth centuries a number of *tekkes* (lodges) were established on major roads in the Balkans to serve as inns. These inns accommodated poor scholars, military personnel, and wayfarers and received financial support from the central administration.[8]

Muslim rulers sought the favor of saints, built lodges and mausoleums for them, and made public pilgrimages to their tombs. Sufis justified royal patronage by their duty to guide the rulers.[9] Some sultans became *murids* of shaykhs, which implied a spiritual submission to the latter. When the shaykh `Izz al-Din b. `Abd al-Salam died, the Mamluk sultan Baybars (1260–1277) said: "Only now has my authority been consolidated,"[10] so powerful was the influence of the Sufi shaykh over the Sultan. From the Sufi viewpoint, the rulers hold power only through the grace *(baraka)* of the saint; indeed, powerful saints might be influential in making and unmaking kings.[11]

Association with the court brought deviant Sufi brotherhoods closer to orthodoxy in practice and in doctrine.[12] Compared to the problematic relations of the Chishti Sufis with the political authorities in India, the leaders of the Suhrawardiyya were always enthusiastically involved with Muslim rulers and accumulated great wealth and landed interests.[13]

When Christians invaded *dar al-Islam*, Sufis rallied rulers with the spirit of *jihad*. This was the case of one `Abdallah al-Yunini (*Asad al-Sham*) who joined Salah al-Din's campaigns, and of Ahmad al-Badawi, who called for *jihad* at the time of the Crusade of Louis X. In fifteenth-century Morocco al-Jazuli and his followers joined the *jihad* against the Portuguese. In the first half of the fourteenth century Sufis accompanied the Muslim armies in their advance southward into the Indian subcontinent.[14] Wandering dervishes, the *babas* from Central Asia, were the spiritual guides of the Turkish *ghazis* in the thirteenth and fourteenth centuries. Sufi shaykhs consecrated the *ghazis* as warriors in the cause of Islam.[15]

The Ottoman sultans tolerated socially deviant dervishes, who often also exhibited Shi`i-oriented beliefs and practices; but this attitude changed at the beginning of the sixteenth century, when the Ottomans were threatened by the Shi`i propaganda of the Safawids. Political pressure on suspected dervishes then increased, and dervish groups sought respectability by joining the ranks of the Bektashiyya brotherhood, which itself became more orthodox at that time, at least outwardly.[16]

The Janissaries became formally associated with the Bektashis at the end of the sixteenth century. The supreme Bektashi shaykh was appointed "colonel" of a Janissary unit, and eight Bektashi dervishes were assigned to Janissary units as chaplains. In formal parades the Bektashi shaykh marched in front of the *agha* of the Janissaries. The Janissaries adopted the uniform of the Bektashiyya and participated in their ceremonies. They were called "the children of Haji Bektash."[17]

Khalwati shaykhs were invited to Istanbul in the sixteenth century to join the fight against the heretics, particularly on the western frontier of the Balkans. Close relations between Khalwati shaykhs and Ottoman sultans continued until the middle of the seventeenth century, and for almost two centuries the Khalwatiyya had the largest number of *tekkes* and affiliates in the Ottoman capital.[18]

THE CONVERSION OF CHARISMA TO ECONOMIC AND POLITICAL POWER

In the seventeenth century the Ottoman central authority weakened in Anatolia, and people turned to religion in search of stability. In such circumstances Sufi shaykhs became influential by converting their charisma to economic and political power. But the Ottoman state never became weak enough to permit the rise of Sufi shaykhs to such powerful positions as in certain parts of Morocco.[19]

In the segmentary political and social system of Morocco, where the central authority is too far away to be effective, holy men who live near the tomb of a saintly ancestor provide the continuity and the stable framework for that political system. Their moral authority helps to guarantee political, legal, and ecological arrangements reached through their arbitration. The saints also play an important role by anchoring the local society in the wider system of Islam. For the local tribesmen, they represent the religion of the central tradition, and guarantee the tribesmen's incorporation into it.[20]

The situation in Sind seems to have been somewhat similar to that in Morocco. Since temporal authority was a distant force with which they had little contact, local tribes in Sind tended to follow Sufi *pirs*, whose power base was in the countryside. *Pirs* of important shrines possessed substantial land holdings and political power, and wielded great influence over the lives of the people. Like the saints of the Atlas in Morocco, *pirs* in Sind acted as "professional neutrals" to balance opposing interests. Indeed, the social order was based on the bond between *pir* and *murid*, because individuals felt more secure under the patronage of a powerful *pir*. It is significant, however, that both in Morocco and in Sind, individual shaykhs, not brotherhoods, wielded real power.

One of the most powerful individuals was the Naqshabandi shaykh `Ubaydallah Ahrar (1404–1490) in Samarqand, who converted the charisma of a Sufi shaykh to economic and political power. He exploited the decline of the authority of the Timurid sultans and gained almost absolute influence over the sultan Abu Sa`id (1451–1468), who was his *murid*. Ahrar also accumulated considerable land holdings, as a result of peasants selling their holdings to him in order to become his disciples and enter under his protection (*himaya*). Ahrar protected them from taxation, as well as other excessive and arbitrary burdens deemed contrary to Islamic principles, by threatening emirs with his spiritual powers. In typical Naqshabandi fashion, Ahrar reconciled his worldly engagements with a state of mind of being mentally disengaged from worldly matters. Wealth in the context of his spiritual world symbolized a favor bestowed by God.[21]

INITIATION AND *DHIKR*

Sufi congregations in hospices and around tombs attracted the common people. They sought access to the *baraka* of the shaykh, and to participate in the collective sessions of the *dhikr*. Such affiliates needed only the simplest form of initiation and a basic mystical training. They took the oath of allegiance (*bay`a*) and accepted the shaykh as teacher and leader, but continued their normal life. As the circle of devotees grew, Sufi brotherhoods became devotional movements where lay affiliates found relief from worldly anxieties.[22]

The most important part of Sufi liturgy is the *dhikr* (literally: the act of remembering). It is a litany tirelessly repeated, consisting of formulae containing the names of Allah. There are two modes of *dhikr*: the silent *dhikr*, known as *khafi* (hidden) or *qalbi* (by the heart) and the vocal *dhikr*, known as *jahri* (public) or *lisani* (by the tongue). The two modes are equally legitimate, and both have authoritative traditions;[23] but the silent *dhikr* was thought to be more respectable and was practiced by those who were more advanced along the spiritual path. The vocal *dhikr*, considered more popular and practiced in a collective ceremony, helped to induce a mystical experience in the ordinary man relatively quickly, through rhythmical exercises.

The silent *dhikr* was typical of the more orthodox *shari`a*-oriented brotherhoods. Mustafa al-Bakri (1688–1749), who inspired the reform of the Khalwatiyya in Egypt, adopted the vocal *dhikr* and presided over vocal *dhikr* ceremonies in Jerusalem, where participants would faint from excitement and exhaustion. His disciple al-Hifni conducted ceremonies of vocal *dhikr* in Cairo. These ceremonies became so popular he had to repeat them for days and nights to admit the many thousands who wanted to attend.[24]

One may speculate as to why Mustafa al-Bakri, whose reform of the Khalwatiyya was toward greater orthodoxy, changed to the more popular form of *dhikr*. The reason was probably that the vocal *dhikr* offered greater scope for the participation of common people in the rituals and helped to popularize the *tariqa* and win adherents. This move might be better appreciated in the wider context of the structural, organizational, and ritual changes that Sufi brotherhoods experienced in the eighteenth century.

STRUCTURAL, ORGANIZATIONAL, AND RITUAL CHANGES IN THE EIGHTEENTH CENTURY

In the eighteenth century, brotherhoods transformed from old patterns of decentralized diffusive affiliation into larger-scale organizations, more coherent and centralized. Led by charismatic shaykhs, the reformed Sufi brotherhoods cut across regional, ethnic, and political boundaries to mobilize wider popular support,[25] and they incorporated local saintly lineages. Local shaykhs, who had controlled the spiritual life of the common people, became regional representatives, *muqaddams* and *khalifas* in hierarchically structured organizations.[26]

Before the eighteenth century, Sufi shaykhs obtained initiation into several *turuq*, and often shifted their principal allegiance from one *tariqa* to another.[27] But Mustafa al-Bakri insisted that his own disciples be affiliated exclusively to the Khalwatiyya and ordered them to break their former allegiance to other *turuq* and shaykhs.[28] Exclusivity gave greater cohesion to the *tariqa*, and added to the commitment of its adherents. The Tijaniyya, an offshoot of the Khalwatiyya, adopted the concept of exclusive affiliation with even greater zeal. The Tijaniyya, in its turn, influenced rival *turuq* in the Maghrib and in West Africa, in particular the Qadiriyya, which also became more assertive and cohesive.[29]

The restructured Sufi brotherhoods reached out to the common people and mobilized popular support, thus contributing to the penetration of a more meaningful religious experience into the lower levels of Muslim society and spreading from the urban to the rural population.

In the countryside of West Africa, the growth of Islam from the seventeenth century brought about a new rural religious leadership. Unlike the urban scholars, who had been spokesmen of the merchants, the new leadership articulated the grievances of the peasants. They criticized the rulers and contributed to the radicalization of Islam, thus preparing the ground for the great reformist movements, better known as the *jihads*.[30]

MYSTICAL VERSE IN VERNACULAR LANGUAGES

Looking for common features of Sufi movements across the Muslim world I have observed that written Islamic literatures in the vernacular languages appeared simultaneously all over the Muslim world in the seventeenth and eighteenth centuries, and that the predominant literary genre in all the vernacular literatures was the mystical verse. This development is explained by the expansion of Islam to the countryside, where the knowledge of Islam could be disseminated to the illiterate peasants and herdsmen only in the vernacular languages.

The need to write down oral mystical poetry in folk idioms arose also with the growth in scale of the brotherhoods, whose leaders sought to communicate with affiliates living in remote communities. Poems in the vernaculars, which had earlier been transmitted and recited orally, were committed to writing in the Arabic script, and copies of the written texts were sent out to the literate representatives of the shaykh in different localities, who then recited these texts to an illiterate audience.

In India, Sufis turned to the regional idioms—Urdu, Sindhi, and Punjabi—for preaching and teaching because the sacred languages—Arabic and Persian—were inaccessible to the masses.[31] The discourse of the elite continued in Arabic and Persian, the classical languages of Islam, whereas the vernacular literature was important in building bridges to the common people.[32]

Muslim literature in China, written mostly in Chinese characters, developed from the middle of the seventeenth century. As elsewhere, mystical works were important. This literature was composed in an easy style, inclining toward the spoken language because it addressed the masses.[33]

The preaching of Imam Mansur in 1785 in the Caucasus is said to have been in simple language and directed to the peasants.[34] In the sixteenth and seventeenth centuries, a period of literary decline in Egypt, works of theology and law were written in bombastic style, but Sufi texts were composed in the simple down-to-earth language of the people.[35] Sufis all over the world then began to adapt their idiom and style to achieve efficient communication with the people they sought to mobilize.

The efficiency of preaching and exhortation in the vernacular to mobilize popular support is described in the case of `Uthman dan Fodio, the leader of the *jihad* in what is today Northern Nigeria: "Then we rose up with the

Shaykh, helping him in his mission work for religion. He traveled for that purpose to the east and west, calling people to the religion of God by his preaching and his poems *(qasidas)* in a non-Arabic language *(`ajami)*."[36] When `Uthman dan Fodio saw that his community was ready for the *jihad*, "he began to incite them to arms . . . and he set this in verse in his non-Arabic Qadiri poem *(qasida `ajamiyya Qadiriyya)*." This mystical verse had a hypnotic effect on devotees on the eve of the *jihad*.[37]

SUFI BROTHERHOODS IN THE PUBLIC SPHERE

Mysticism, an inward and individualistic mode of worship, is unlikely to create a social space. After the tenth century the esoteric form of piety, elitist in nature, gradually became the most popular mode of devotion in Islam, mainly through the contribution of brotherhoods. It was the brotherhoods that brought Sufism from the private to the public sphere, to play an important sociopolitical role in the communal and religious life of the Muslims for a period lasting seven centuries.

Before the seventeenth century most of the brotherhoods had been loosely organized and localized, and had not been self-supporting social organizations. Brotherhoods reached all social strata through the cult of saints. The *baraka* (grace) of the saints imbued individuals with confidence and helped maintain social stability. Commercial fairs and religious festivals took place around saints' tombs. Moreover, Sufism offered a social space of religious experience to women, who had hardly enjoyed any place in formal religious life.

The political authorities sought to control the activities of the Sufis by the endowment of hospices *(khanqahs)*, which organized Sufism under the control of the state and fostered *shari`a*-abiding Sufism. Some Sufi brotherhoods avoided the courtly scene and cultivated the ideal of ascetic poverty. But other brotherhoods were closely associated with rulers and accumulated great wealth. Even socially deviant dervishes were attracted to the rulers' courts, where they were pressured to conform to the *shari`a*. According to the Sufi vision of authority, rulers were entrusted with a temporary lease of power through the *baraka* of a saint. Muslim rulers thus sought the favor of saints, and sometimes became disciples of Sufi shaykhs.

Sufis, unlike other *`ulama'*, could function also outside the Muslim state, and Sufi lodges helped the expansion of Islam beyond the frontiers of *dar al-Islam*. Where the central authority was weak, people sought security with Sufi shaykhs, who transformed their charisma into economic and political power, gaining possession of substantial land holdings and wielding great influence over the lives of the people. Wealth represented a blessing bestowed by God, and such shaykhs managed to reconcile the possession of worldly assets with mental disengagement from this world.

Sufi brotherhoods being esoteric organizations, induction into them needed an initiation ceremony, not only for those wishing to become *murids* but also for those who only sought access to the blessing of the shaykh. A collective *dhikr* evolved to induce a mystical experience for the ordinary man in a relatively short space of time. With a much larger circle of devotees, brotherhoods became more a devotional than a mystical movement.

Sufi brotherhoods thus fulfilled multiple roles in Muslim societies; they provided moral guidance to voluntary associations, opened opportunities for release from the hardships of everyday existence, gave confidence to individuals, and helped sustain social stability. They also maintained lines of communications between the common people and the authorities.

Before the eighteenth century these brotherhoods had been localized and had influenced only their immediate communities. But in the eighteenth century Sufism experienced a radical change, when brotherhoods transformed from old patterns of decentralized, diffusive affiliations to larger-scale organizations, more centralized and coherent.

Changes in rituals emphasized the hierarchical and centralized nature of the reformed *tariqa* and the expanded role of the shaykh. Brotherhoods offered larger scope for the participation of the common people in their ceremonies, facilitating the recruitment of new adherents.

A new Muslim leadership emerged that articulated the grievances of the masses, criticized the rulers, and contributed to the radicalization of Islam. The discourse of the public sphere in Muslim societies addressed social and political issues, and in order to reach the illiterate it was written in the vernacular languages. In this way, written Islamic literatures in the vernacular languages developed simultaneously all over the Muslim world in the seventeenth and eighteenth centuries, with mystical verse as the predominant genre.

Reformed brotherhoods gave rise to movements of renewal and reform in the eighteenth century. One may be tempted to speculate that these reformed premodern movements could have led Muslim societies into the modern period with a sense of revival. But this process was truncated when leaders of these movements redirected their major efforts from internal reform to defending *dar al-Islam* against the invading European powers. Ultimately they were all crushed by the overwhelming military power of the Europeans.

NOTES

1. Schacht 1974, 393.
2. Karamustafa 1994, 88–89; Levtzion 1997.
3. Trimingham 1971, 232.
4. Ibid., 220–21, 234; Karamustafa 1994, 87–89.
5. Trimingham 1971, 27, 230, 237–38.

6. Algar 1976, 44; 1990, 152.
7. Fernandes 1988, vol. 1, 24.
8. Faroqhi 1976, 73-75; 1981, 99–101, 113; Norris 1993, 101–2, 109.
9. Eaton 1993, 94.
10. Quoted in Abu Zahra, 1953, 143.
11. Eaton 1993, 31, 83.
12. Eaton 1978, 45–48, 50–53; Ernst, 1993, 47.
13. Ansari 1992, 5, 30.
14. Eaton 1978, 284.
15. Trimingham 1971, 83; Faroqhi 1993, 197; Zarcone 1993, 71.
16. Ocak 1993, 249–51; Trimingham 1971, 83; Faroqhi 1981, 92; Karamustafa 1993, 243; 1994, 83–84, 94–95.
17. Birge 1937; Zarcone 1993, 71; Goodwin 1994, 148–52.
18. Trimingham 1971, 75; Zarcone 1993, 80; Clayer 1994, 65–67, 70.
19. Faroqhi 1993, 197, 205–6.
20. Gellner 1969, 41ff; 1981, 114–30.
21. What is offered here is a preliminary analysis of the role of Ahrar as a charismatic shaykh, based on Paul 1991; DeWeese 1993; Gross 1988; 1990.
22. Trimingham 1971, 27–28, 186, 199–200; Eaton 1978, xxxi.
23. See Gardet EI^2.
24. al-Jabarti (d. 1240/1825–1826) 1879–1880, vol. 1, 300; Weigert 1989, 109–11.
25. For a more detailed analysis see Levtzion 1997 and Levtzion and Voll 1987.
26. Clancey-Smith 1994, 41–45; Karrar 1992, x, 20; Algar 1990; Abu-Manneh 1990, 295; Hofheinz 1990, 28–29; Grandin 1990, 645.
27. Eaton 1978, xxxi–xxxii, 207; Winter 1982, 92, 97.
28. al-Jabarti, 1879–80, vol. 1, 295; vol. 2, 61; Weigert 1989.
29. Abun-Nasr 1965, 15–57; Martin 1969; Brenner 1988.
30. Levtzion 1987, 23–26.
31. Schimmel 1975, 131, 135, 163; Shackle 1993, 163, 265, 285–88; Roy 1984, 58; Eaton 1978, 91. It is significant that in the independent state of Bijapur, where, being far from the Mughal court, the influence of Persian culture was weaker, literature in Dakhni developed from the fifteenth century, more than two centuries before the appearance of Urdu literature.
32. Schimmel 1973, 48–50; 1976, xi, 11.
33. Aubin 1990, 496–97.
34. Bennigsen 1964, 195.
35. Winter 1982, 27.
36. Ibn Fudi (d. 1245/1829) 1963, 85.
37. Ibid., 51; see also Hiskett 1975.

BIBLIOGRAPHY
CHAPTER XIII

Abu-Manneh, B. "Khalwa and Rabita in the Khalidi Suborder," in *Naqshabandis*, edited by M. Gaborieau, A. Popovic and T. Zarcone, Istanbul: Institut Français d'Etudes Anatoliennes d'Istanbul, 1990, pp. 289–302.

Abu Zahra, M. *Ibn Taymiyya*. Cairo: Dar al-Thaqafa al'Arabiyya, 1953.

Abun-Nasr, J. *The Tijaniyya*. Oxford: Oxford University Press, 1965.

Algar, H. "The Naqshbandi Order: A Preliminary Survey of its History and Significance," *Studia Islamica*, No. 44, 1976, pp.123–52.

Algar, H. "A Brief History of the Naqshabandi Order," in *Naqshabandis*, edited by M. Gaborieau, A. Popovic and T. Zarcone. Istanbul: Institut Français d'Etudes Anatoliennes d'Istanbul, 1990, pp.13–9.

Ansari, S. *Sufi Saints and the State Power: the Pirs of Sind, 1843–1947*. Cambridge: Cambridge University Press, 1992.

Aubin, F. "En Islam Chinois? Quells Naqshabandis," in *Naqshabandis*, edited by M. Gaborieau, A. Popovic and T. Zarcone. Istanbul: Institut Français d'Etudes Anatoliennes d'Istanbul, 1990, pp. 491–572.

Bennigsen, A. "Un movement populaire au Caucase au 18e siècle: la guerre sainte du sheikh Mansur, 1785–1791," *Cahiers du Monde Russe et Soviétique*, Vol. 2, 1964, pp.159–205.

Birge, J.K. *The Bektashi Order of Dervishes*. London: Luzac, 1937.

Brenner, L. "Concepts of Tariqa in West Africa: the Case of the Qadiriyya," in *Charisma and Brotherhood in African Islam*, edited by D.C. O'Brien and C. Coulon. Oxford: Clarendon, 1988, pp. 32–52.

Clancey-Smith, J.A. *Rebel and Saint: Muslim Notables, Populist Protest, Colonial Encounter (Algeria and Tunisia, 1800–1904)*. Berkeley: University of California Press, 1994.

Clayer, N. *Mystiques, état et société: les Halvetis dans l'aire balkanique de la fin du 15e siècle à nos jours*. Leiden: Brill, 1994.

DeWeese, D. "Review of Jurgen Paul," *Journal of Asian History*, Vol. 27, 1993, pp. 66–7.

Eaton, R.M. *Sufis of Bijapur: Social Roles of Sufis in Medieval India*. Princeton: Princeton University Press, 1978.

Eaton, R.M. *The Rise of Islam and the Bengal Frontier, 1204–1760*. Berkeley: University of California Press, 1993.

Ernst, C.E. "An Indo-Persian Guide to Sufi Shrine Pilgrimage," in *Manifestations of Sainthood in Islam*, edited by G.M. Smith and C.E. Ernst. Istanbul: Isis Press, 1993, pp. 43–67.

Faroqhi, S. "The Tekke of Haci Bektaş, Social Position and Economic Activities," *International Journal of Middle East Studies*, Vol. 7, 1976, pp. 183–205.

Faroqhi, S. "Seyyid Gazi Revisited: The Foundation as Seen through Sixteenth Century Documents," *Turcica*, Vol. 13, 1981, pp. 90–122.

Faroqhi, S. "Sainthood as Means of Self-Defense in Seventeenth-Century Ottoman Anatolia," in *Manifestations of Sainthood in Islam*, edited by G.M. Smith and C.E. Ernst. Istanbul: Isis Press, 1993, pp. 193–208.

Fernandes, L. *The Evolution of a Sufi Institution in Mamluk Egypt: the Khanqah*. Berlin: Klaus Schwarz Verlag, 1988.

Gardet, L. "Dhikr," *EI²*.

Gellner, E. *Saints of the Atlas*. Chicago: Chicago University Press, 1969.

Gellner, E. *The Muslim Society*. Cambridge: Cambridge University Press, 1981.

Goodwin, G. *The Janissaries*. London: Saki Books, 1994.

Gross, J.A. "The Economic Status of a Timurid Sufi Shaykh: a Matter of Conflict or Perception," *Iranian Studies*, Vol. 21, 1988, pp. 84–104.

Gross, J.A. "Multiple Roles and Perceptions of a Sufi Shaykh: Symbolic Statements of Political and Religious Authority," in *Naqshabandis*, edited by M. Gaborieau, A. Popovic and T. Zarcone. Istanbul: Institut Français d'Etudes Anatoliennes d'Istanbul, 1990, pp. 109–21.

Hiskett, M. *A History of Hausa Islamic Verse*. London: School of Oriental and African Studies, 1975.

Hofheinz, A. "Encounters with a Saint: al-Majdhub, al-Mirghani, and Ibn Idris as Seen through the Eyes of Ibrahim al-Rashid," *Sudanic Africa*, Vol.1, 1990, pp. 19–59.

Ibn Fudi, *'Abdallah. Tazyin al-Waraqat*. edited and translated by M. Hiskett Ibadan: Ibadan University Press, 1963.

al-Jabarti, 'Abd al-Rahman b. Hasan. *'Aja'ib al-'Athar fi 'l-Tarajim wa 'l-Akhbar*. Cairo: Bulaq, 1879–1880.

Karrar, A.S. *The Sufi Brotherhoods in the Sudan*. Evanston: Northwestern University Press, 1992.

Karamustafa, A.T. "The Antinomian Dervish as Model Saint," in *Modes de transmission de la culture religeuse en Islam*, edited by H. Elboudrari. Cairo: Institut Français d'Archéologie Orientale du Caire, 1993, pp. 241–60.

Karamustafa, A.T. *God's Unruly Friends: Dervish Groups in the Islamic Later Middle Period 1200–1550*. Salt Lake City: University of Utah Press, 1994.

Levtzion, N. "Eighteenth-Century Sufi Brotherhoods: Structural, Organizational and Ritual Changes," in *Islam: Essays on Scripture, Thought, and Society, A Festschrift in Honour of Anthony H. Johns*, edited by P.R. Riddle and T. Street. Leiden: Brill, 1997, pp.147–60.

Levtzion, N. and Voll, J.O. *Eighteenth Century Renewal and Reform in Islam*. Syracuse: Syracuse University Press, 1987.

Martin, B.G. "Notes sur l'origine de la tariqa des Tijaniyya et sur les débuts d'al-hajj 'Umar," *Revue des Etudes Islamiques*, Vol. 37, 1969, pp. 267–90.

Norris, H.T. *Islam in the Balkans: Religion and Society between Europe and the Arab World*. Columbia: University of South Carolina, 1993.

Ocak, A.Y. "Kalenderi Dervishes and Ottoman Administration from the Fourteenth to the Sixteenth Centuries," in *Manifestations of Sainthood in Islam*, edited by G.M. Smith and C.E. Ernst. Istanbul: Isis Press, 1993, pp. 239–55.

Roy, A. *The Islamic Syncretistic Tradition in Bengal*. Princeton: Princeton University Press, 1984.

Paul, J. "Forming a Faction: The himaya system of Khwaja Ahrar," *International Journal of Middle East Studies*, Vol. 23, 1991, pp. 533–48.

Schacht, J. "Law and the State," in *The Legacy of Islam*, edited by J. Schacht and E.C. Bosworth. Oxford: Clarendon Press, 2nd edition, 1974, pp. 392–403.

Shackle, C. "Early Vernacular Poetry in the Indus Valley: its Contexts and its Character," in *Islam and Indian Religions*, edited by A.L. Dallapicola and S. Zingel-Ave Lallemant. Stuttgart: Steiner, 1993, pp. 259–89.

Schimmel, A. *Islamic Literatures of India*. Wiesbaden: Harrassowitz, 1973.

Schimmel, A. *Classical Urdu Literature from the Beginning to Iqbal*. Wiesbaden: Harrassowitz, 1975.

Trimingham, J.S. *The Sufi Orders in Islam*. Oxford: Clarendon Press, 1971.

Weigert, G. "The Khalwatiyya in Egypt in the Eighteenth Century." Ph.D dissertation, The Hebrew University of Jerusalem, 1989.

Winter, M. *Society and Religion in Early Ottoman Egypt: Studies in the Writings of 'Abd al-Wahhab al-Sha'rani*. New Brunswick: Transaction Books, 1982.

Zarcone, T. Mystiques, P*hilosophes, et franc-maçons en Islam: Riza Tevfik, penseur ottoman (1868–1949), du soufisme à la confrérie*. Istanbul: Librairie d'Amérique et d'Orient, 1993.

XIV

Resurgent Islamic Fundamentalism as an Integrative Factor in the Politics of Africa and the Middle East[1]

Studies of the resurgence of Islamic fundamentalism, otherwise called the Islamist movements, brought the debate about Orientalism back to public attention. Those who postulate a cultural essence that underlies and unifies Islamic history are considered to be neo-Orientalists. It is significant, however, that there is a convergence between the view of the so-called neo-Orientalists and that of the Islamists, who insist on the monolithic universality of Islam.[2]

The politicization of Islam in the 1980s and 1990s must be explained in terms of social, political and economic context.[3] Algeria's armed Islamist insurgency arose from political exclusion, economic misery and social injustice. Likewise, the violent clashes in the poor quarter of Imbaba in Cairo should be explained by the living conditions there, which might have caused even more violence.[4] In other words, we should pay careful attention to political and economic conjunctures, national particularities and local histories.[5]

For Muslims, history is of great significance, particularly the period of the Prophet and his Companions, known as the days of the *salaf*, and the following three centuries, when Muslims ruled the world and Islamic civilization was more advanced than other civilizations. I have researched the simultaneous

---

[1] This chapter was first presented to the Conference on "Islam and the West: the African Perspective", Evangelische Akademie Loccum, 21–23 October 2002.

[2] S. Zubayda, "Is Iran an Islamic State" in *Political Islam: Essays from Middle East Report*, edited by J. Beinin and J. Stork, Berkeley: University of California Press, 1997, p. 103; H.I. 'Ali, "Civil Society and Democratization in Arab Countries with special reference to the Sudan" in *Islamic Area Studies Project – Islamic Area Studies working paper series no. 12*, Tokyo, Japan, 1999, p. 2.

[3] S. Carapico, "Introduction to Part One" in *Political Islam*, 1997, p. 31.

[4] Beinin and Stork, "Introduction" in *Political Islam*, 1997, p. 17.

[5] R. Vitalis, "Islam and the Struggle for the State in the Middle East" in *Political Islam*, 1997, p. 102.

emergence of renewal and reform movements throughout the Muslim world in the eighteenth century, which has some parallels with the recent resurgence of Islam as a worldwide phenomenon. In other words, the universality of Islamic militancy cannot be accidental, and should also be viewed as derived from an historical process, based on legal, ideological and cultural foundations.[6]

The Public Sphere

The relationship between state and society is a favorite topic in the study of Islam. Our contribution to this discourse consists of analysing the concept of public sphere, which in Islamic societies may be taken as replacing the Eurocentric term, civil society. The public sphere is defined as the autonomous space between the official and private spheres. The most important institutions of the public sphere in pre-modern societies were the *sharīʻa* courts, the *muḥtasib* and the marketplace, the *waqf*, the *madrasa*, Sufi brotherhoods and craft associations.

Papers collected in *The Public Sphere in Muslim Societies*, edited by Hoexter, Eisenstadt and myself, demonstrate the existence of a vibrant public sphere that was of crucial importance in shaping the dynamics of pre-modern Muslim societies. The papers dispute the concept of "Oriental despotism" and the notion of a total separation and estrangement of the society from its rulers. In reality, the autonomous institutions of the public sphere placed limits on the absolute power of the ruler.

Institutions of the public sphere in pre-modern Muslim societies remained vital until the end of the eighteenth century. But from the beginning of the nineteenth century these institutions faced the challenge of Western influence, modernity and the nation state. The power of the *sharīʻa* courts was eroded. *Waqf* endowments were appropriated by the modern state, and the religious institutions lost financial autonomy. The craft guilds were destroyed by capitalist penetration. The *ʻulamā'* lost their monopoly in the field of education to Western-style schools. Modernist movements attacked Sufi brotherhoods as one of the principal reasons for the decadence of Islam. The modern state further undermined the autonomy of those institutions, and the vacuum created in the public sphere has been filled by the Islamist movements.

Religion is a good source for political ideas: its symbols are indigenous and easily recognized. The Islamist movements win public support because they articulate the authentic values of Islam that are close to the heart of every

---

[6] A. Khurshid, "The nature of the Islamic resurgence" in *Voices of Resurgent Islam*, edited by J.I. Esposito, Oxford: Oxford University Press, 1983, pp. 222–5, 203.

Muslim.[7] From an historical perspective, religion emerged as a banner under which the oppressed and dispossessed rallied in periods of economic and social hardship. Where it was, or is, the official state religion (the Ottoman Empire, Saudi Arabia, Pakistan and Iran), Islam is a legitimating ideology for the ruling class and constitutes part of the state mechanism. Unofficial Islam, on the other hand, has throughout history frequently expressed popular protest, and often assumed unorthodox, sectarian, or mystical (Sufi) forms in order to challenge the centre's religious and political legitimacy.[8]

The declared political target of all Islamist movements is to rebuild Islamic societies and states on the foundations of the *sharī'a.* However, the *sharī'a* as interpreted and articulated by modern Islamists is not the same as that elaborated by the *'ulamā'* over the centuries. Most radical Islamists did not originate from the circles of the *'ulamā'.* They oriented themselves to a broad public, rather than to a restricted circle of scholars. To many *'ulamā'*, the language and modes of thought of the Islamists appear un-Islamic, as they mix passages from the Koran with discussions of current affairs. The resurgence of Islam involves a broader awareness of the social and political dimensions of the faith, and calls on believers to be more active participants in public life.[9]

The Islamists developed networks of voluntary organizations that dispensed charity, looked after the needs of the poor, built mosques and ran schools and clinics. They provided services that the state was unwilling or unable to undertake. They created a new autonomous public sphere that challenged state power. Funding for these social services came partly from public contributions, but also from businessmen who favoured the Islamists' economic programmes of tax cuts, deregulation and economic incentives for business development. In Syria, the Islamic opposition to the Ba'th Party in the early 1980s developed out of the *sūq*, where religious institutions and the trading economy came together. The Islamic movement expressed the worldview of the *sūq* against the radical policies of the Ba'th. In Algeria, the "commercial bourgeois" were important financial contributors to the Islamic Salvation Front (FIS) party, because of its programme of tax cuts, deregulation, and economic incentives for business development. It is significant that the propaganda of the pro-Islamic Refah Party

---

[7] J. Crystal, "Civil Society in the Arabian Gulf" in *Civil Society in the Middle East*, edited by Augustus Richard Norton, Leiden: Brill, 1995, ii, pp. 259–86, 275; C. Tripp "Islam and the Secular Logic of the State in the Middle East" in *Islamic Fundamentalism* edited by A. Sidahmed and A. Ehteshami, Boulder: Westview Press, 1996, pp. 51–69.

[8] R. Margulies and E. Yildizoglu, "The resurgence of Islam and the Welfare Party in Turkey" in *Political Islam*, 1997, pp. 144–5.

[9] R.W. Heffner, "Public Islam and the problem of democratisation", *Sociology of Religion*, 62, 4 (2001), pp. 491–514.

in Turkey was not concerned with Allah, but with social and economic issues like privatization, unemployment, prices, salaries and wages.[10]

Al-Ikhwān al-Muslimūn (the Muslim Brotherhood) in Egypt was the first organized movement of Islamists. Having emerged between the two world wars, in the age of liberalism, it continued the discourse of the modernists by demonstrating the viability of Islam in the modern world. It used a somewhat apologetic tone, unlike the affirmation of Islam's authenticity by contemporary Islamists. Even today, the mainstream of the *Ikhwān* is committed to broad-based social reforms, and not to seizing political power.

By the end of the 1980s, a broader range of intellectuals and professionals had become involved in the reaffirmation of the Islamic tradition and the Islamization of daily life. With its greater political activism, the non-violent mainstream of Islamic fundamentalism attracted a broader group of people.[11] From the universities, student activists moved on to join the professional associations. The victory of the Islamic trend in the professional associations indicates the growing alienation of the educated middle class both from the ruling elites and their secular opposition, and the emergence of the Islamic trend as the only credible political alternative to the Egyptian regime. The Muslim Brothers are the only independent political force with broad-based mass support. Since the mid–1970s, when its leaders renounced the use of violence, the Brothers have been working towards Islamic reform through institution building, persuasion, and increased participation in legal, mainstream channels of public life.

Support for the Brothers crosses class and generational lines, but their recruitment efforts have been particularly successful among recent secondary school and university graduates – doctors, engineers, pharmacists, lawyers and other professionals – in large cities and provincial towns. Islamic schools, health clinics and community centres created by the Muslim Brothers have provided employment for young doctors, teachers and other professionals. Islamist leaders are close in age to new graduates and are familiar with the same deprivations. Muslim Brothers and more militant groups have indoctrinated the youth with the idea that the reform of society is a religious duty incumbent on every Muslim. They are imbuing the educated youth with a new sense of civic obligation, and a new perspective on their own capacity to effect social change. The Mubarak regime may be able to contain the activity of armed Islamic groups through increased intimidation and repression, yet it is far less equipped

---

[10] Margulies and Yildizoglu 1997, p. 150.

[11] J.O. Voll, "Fundamentalism in the Sunni Arab World: Egypt and the Sudan," in *Fundamentalisms Observed* edited by M.E. Marty and R. Scott Appleby, Chicago: University Of Chicago Press, 1991, pp. 386–7.

to stem the Islamic trend's social and ideological incorporation of new groups at the grassroots level.[12]

In Jordan, the tolerance of the Hashemite regime encouraged moderation in the Muslim Brotherhood, which supported the king in moments of crisis.[13] Even the Hizballah decided to participate in the parliamentary elections of August and September 1992, and scored a brilliant victory.[14]

In Morocco, the pragmatic and moderate Islamic Party for Justice and Development opted for dialogue and a degree of consensus. In September 2002 the party participated for the second time in the general elections, seeking to increase its representation, but was concerned that a landslide that might generate reaction among the pro-Western elite, similar to the events in Algeria more than ten years earlier. Leftist and liberal observers acknowledge the Islamists' superior election campaign organization, financing and tactics, which together with public sympathy, strengthened by communal involvement, gave them an advantage in free elections.[15] Government policy is therefore an important factor in determining the nature of the political discourse, and the resorting to violence by Islamist movements depends to a large extent on the way that a government deals with Islamist activists. It was under the oppressive regime of Nasser that Sayyid al-Qutb developed an ideology that became the banner of the extreme Islamist movements that branched off from the *Ikhwān*. They advocated withdrawal from society and the formation of a new, alternative, believing society that would eventually supplant the unbelieving one.[16]

Heated debates took place among the extreme Islamists as to whether, and under what conditions, it was permissible to declare Muslims to be infidels and therefore legitimate targets for *jihād*. Differences among Islamists also revolve around whether an Islamist society should precede, or succeed, an Islamist state. Answers to such questions chart different political strategies, and determine the role of Islamists in the public sphere.

---

[12] C.R.Wickham, "Islamic Mobilization and Political Change: the Islamist Trend in Egypt's Professional Associations" in *Political Islam*, pp. 120–24,133.

[13] M. Boulby, *The Muslim Brotherhood and the Kings of Jordan, 1945–1953*. Atlanta, GA: Scholars Press, 1999.

[14] V. Langohr, "Of Islamists and Ballot Boxes", *International Journal of Middle East Studies*, 33 (2001), pp. 591–610.

[15] Wickham 1997, p. 129.

[16] Voll 1991, pp. 381–2.

The Challenge of Islam to the West

Of all world religions, Islam has had the greatest political success, with the creation of a worldwide empire shortly after the rise of the new faith. The success of Muslims contrasts with the historical experience of the Jews, who had no state of their own for long periods, and with the early history of the Christians, who were persecuted during their first three centuries. Jews await messianic redemption, whereas for Christians the Kingdom of God is in heaven. Muslims, on the other hand, seek to establish the Kingdom of God on earth, here and now, through the implementation of the law of God, the *sharīʻa*. This is the task of the Muslim state, which therefore has a sacred religious mission.

The basic political concepts of Islam were formulated during the period of political success, and they bear the mark of a triumphant religion. Thus, the political ascendancy of Islam is so deeply inherent in the mind of Muslims that periods of decline are viewed as deviations from the natural course of history, and as temporary aberrations that must be reversed. Indeed, there was a point at which contemporary Muslims believed that history had returned to its natural course. The 1973 oil boycott by OPEC, a predominantly Muslim organization, shocked the industrialized West. The 1960s was the period of the "Cold War" between Egypt and Saudi Arabia over hegemony in the Arab world; between Nasser's Egypt with its adherence to Arab nationals and socialism, and Saudi Arabia with its Islamic orientation. The defeat of Nasser in 1967 and the flow of petrodollars to Saudi Arabia after 1973 helped to shift the emphasis in the Arab world to Islam.[17] Although oil politics lost their momentum, the moral boost reasserted Muslim identity and authenticity.

The Islamic concept of international relations, also formulated during periods of military expansion, is embedded in the *shariʻa*, and divides the world into two: *dār al-Islām*, where the law of Islam is supreme under Muslim rule, and *dār al-ḥarb*, lands still under the rule of infidels. Muslims are obliged to exert every effort to extend *dār al-Islām* at the expense of *dar al-Ḥarb*. The Arabic word for exertion is *jihād*, a term that became a synonym for holy war. *Jihād* is central to the theory of international relations as the instrument for implementing the expansion of Islam throughout the rest of the world.

Whatever political entities exist in *dār al-ḥarb* are necessarily temporary and lack any legitimacy. In theory, the Muslim state cannot even make valid treaties with these political entities. Hence, the conduct of the Muslim state in the international arena is unilateral, not bilateral. The Ottoman Empire, the last great Muslim power, put this theory into practice. The Ottoman sultan accepted European ambassadors at his court, but did not send ambassadors to Europe until the nineteenth century. The change came about when the Ottoman Empire

---

[17] A. Sidahmed and A. Ehteshami, "Intruduction" in *Islamic Fundamentalism*, 1996, pp. 1–15.

was forced to sign the Treaty of Karlovic with the Habsburg Empire and the Republic of Venice in 1699, and to recognize the existence of legitimate political entities in *dār al-ḥarb*. Thus the perpetual *jihād* gave way to permanent co-existence. In modern times, Muslim states operate within a world order based on Western diplomatic code and agreements, the same world order that sanctioned imperialism and colonialism, and which continues to favor the rich industrialized nations.

The challenge to the West began with Nasser, from a secular position of non-alignment. But Mu'ammar al-Qadhafī of Libya, who considered himself Nasser's successor, challenged the West from a militant Islamic position. Radical Islamist movements claim that full restoration of Islam is not possible within the existing world order.[18] For Khumeinī, the United States was the symbol of evil, the leader of a distorted illegitimate world order that must be destroyed. Ṣaddām Ḥusayn came to power as the leader of the secularist Ba'th Party. But when he challenged the West in 1991, he resorted to Islamic rhetoric.

The attack on the United States of 11 September 2001 turned the spotlight onto the non-state Islamic terrorist challenge to the West. The worldwide terrorist network was made up of *mujāhidūn* from many Muslim nations who had originally volunteered for the cause of Islam in Afghanistan. They had been supported and armed by the United States to resist the Soviet Union. Many of them later went on to fight for the cause of Islam in Bosnia and Chechnya. They were joined by members of extremist Islamist groups, mainly from Egypt, who had earlier been supported by Saudi Arabia, and were recruited by Sadat in the battle against the Nasserites and leftists. The Islamist movement broke with the Egyptian regime after Sadat's autocratic tendencies were clearly manifested, and when the promises of economic prosperity failed to materialize and the peace treaty with Israel was signed.[19]

Saudi Arabia's pro-Western policy supports the existing world order because it serves the economic and political interests of the royal house. This policy, however, is in conflict with the doctrines of the Wahhābiyya movement that gave birth to the kingdom. The eighteenth-century Wahhābiyya, the most radical Islamic movement in pre-modern times, followed the teachings of the fourteenth–century Ibn Taymiyya, whom contemporary radicals Islamists adopted as their spiritual mentor.

The Islamic discourse is the only legitimate one in Saudi Arabia, but the threat to the regime is from radicals who point to the contradictions between realities and the doctrinal principles of the Wahhābiyya. Hence, whenever a clash between Islamic and Western values is apparent, the royal house tips the scales towards Islam in order to perpetuate the alliance between the religious

---

[18] D. George, "Pax Islamica: An Alternative New World Order" in *Islamic Fundamentalism*, 1996.

[19] Beinin and Stork, "Introduction" in *Political Islam*, 1997, pp. 9, 11.

establishment and the political elite. This alliance goes back to the eighteenth-century concordat between the Shaykh Muḥammad Ibn ʻAbd al-Wahhāb, who gave his name to the Wahhābiyya movement, and the Emir Saʻūd, who gave his name to the kingdom of Saudi Arabia. Because the authority of the established *ʻulamāʼ* is still acknowledged in charting rules of social behaviour, any criticism of the royal family is presented as being against Islam itself.[20]

Pragmatism and Accommodation in Islam

The Wahhābi-Saudi case illustrates the accommodation of a radical Islamic movement to practical realities. Pragmatism and accommodation in Islam find expression in the political concept that any authority is better than anarchy, and that any effective government is legitimate. This concept had evolved as early as the first century of Islam, in the wake of the traumatic civil war that brought about the great schism between the Sunna and the Shīʻa.

Pragmatism and accommodation helped Sunni Islam to attain two of its greatest historical achievements: the end to schisms in Sunni Islam after the split with the Shīʻa, and the spread of Islam across continents and over cultural barriers. All Muslims in the outer lands of Islam are Sunnis, and they accepted Islam not as a result of a military conquest, but through a long and peaceful process of accommodation.

Ijmāʻ, or the general consensus, is one of the four principles of jurisprudence in Sunni Islam. *Ijmāʻ* is reached through a process by which an innovation (*bidʻa)* becomes a *sunna*, or orthodoxy, after it has been practised for generations, with the tacit consensus of the *ʻulamāʼ*. This process might be conceived as a legal mechanism guided by pragmatism. Yet almost everything that was endorsed through *ijmāʻ*, such as the visitation of saints' tombs, is controversial. For centuries, these rulings were challenged by the radicals of every generation. Indeed, Muslim radicals may be defined as those who strictly adhere to the ideals of Islam, and reject pragmatism and accommodation.

Perhaps the most important concept that evolved out of the general consensus is that a Muslim does not become *kāfir*, an infidel, even if he commits a grave sin. But extreme radicals claim that Muslims can be declared infidels, and that *jihād* against them is therefore permitted. Sayyid al-Qutb developed the view that contemporary Muslim societies, particularly which of Egypt, live in the *jāhiliyya* because they follow man-made laws and not the divine law. According to al-Qutb, there is no contemporary state that is ruled by the law of Islam, and therefore the whole world is *dār al-ḥarb*, and *jihād* is the

[20] M.G. Nehme, "The Islamic-Capitalist State of Saudi Arabia: The Surfacing of Fundamentalism" in A.S. Moussalli, *Islamic Fundamentalism: Myths and Realities*. London: Ithaca Press, 1998, pp. 291, 292, 294, 298.

only recourse.[21] The *jihād*, which had originally been an instrument for expanding the land of Islam at the expense of the land of the infidels, was transformed, in the ideology of the modern radicals, into an Islamic revolution against the infidels within.

The process by which pragmatism mitigates radical movements has been repeated also in Iran. The approved arena of Islamic politics has featured a continual struggle between different factions of political clerics and their supporters, who represent a spectrum from radicals to pragmatists. Radicals wish to carry on the revolutionary momentum, and advocate exporting the revolution to other countries. They call for uncompromising opposition to the United States and to Western influence. The conservatives, who comprise the mainstream of Iranian clerics, seek to reinforce Islamic values and religious morality, including censorship of art, culture and the media. The third group, the pragmatists who won the presidential and parliamentary elections, support reform and foreign investment, which also implies a conciliatory attitude towards the West.[22]

Africa

In Africa, one may also observe radicalism contained by pragmatism. The drive for reform in West Africa was initiated in the 1950s by those known as Wahhābis, graduates of al-Azhar, who criticised the worship of saints. They provoked a violent and bloody confrontation with the Sufi brotherhoods.

The Wahhābī movement in Mali, like Islamist groups elsewhere, established a range of institutions, such as mosques, modernized Muslim schools, clinics, pharmacies and cultural centres. Funding has come from contributions of local communities or individuals, migrant workers, and foreign Arab and Muslim sources. Yet the most important source of funding, in Africa as in the Middle East, is wealthy merchants. Acts of piety enhance the prestige of merchants and raise their commercial credability. They perform the pilgrimage to Mecca, and dispense charity by building mosques and financing other religious activities. Thus they benefit the reform movement.[23]

In Nigeria in the 1950s there were violent clashes between adherents of the Qādiriyya, which was associated with conservative "establishment" Islam, and the Tijāniyya, which had developed in reaction to the perceived elitist bent of

---

[21] Y. Choueiri, "The Political Discourse of Contemporary Islamist Movements" in *Islamic Fundamentalism*, 1996, pp. 19–33.

[22] Zubaida 1997, p. 112.

[23] L. Brenner, "Constructing Muslim identities in Mali" in *Muslim Identity and Social Change in Sub-Saharan Africa*, edited by Louis Brenner, Bloomington: Indiana University Press, 1993, pp. 59–78, 67, 74, 70.

the Qādiriyya. The reformists in Nigeria, represented by the Izala movement, provoked friction and physical confrontation with the Sufis that often resulted in loss of life and damage to property. In 1980, the violence of Maitatsine, the fundamentalist prophet, and his followers in Kano shocked Muslims of all persuasions. The widespread destruction that resulted from these disturbances forced a reconsideration of questions of religious differences. The state security apparatus became more meticulous in monitoring religious organizations and banned open-air preaching, which affected the Izala more than other religious organizations.[24]

Since the early 1980s there have been periodic clashes between Muslims and Christians in Nigeria, which may be related to the growing militancy among Muslims, particularly the call for the implementation of the *sharī'a*, which would change the status of non-Muslims. The Christians became alarmed, and also more violent.

In the Ivory Coast, riots represented the revival of rivalries between the mainly Muslim north and the predominantly Christian south. Muslims in the Ivory Coast, who comprise about half of the population, are mainly migrants from neighbouring countries, particularly Burkina Faso. The succession dispute after Felix Houphouet's death in 1993 was between the Catholic Henri Konan Bedie and the Muslim Alassane Ouattara. The former became interim president, and harassed Outtara's supporters. Muslim officers were purged from the army and the civil service. In 1994, Bedie legislated a citizenship bill that created a dual system favourable to the Christians of the south. People of the north complain of being treated as second-class citizens, and have been determined to defend their rights.[25]

Facing the common enemies of secularism and Christianity, there has been, since the late 1980s a tendency towards reconciliation between the rival Islamist and Sufi shaykhs. In the process, radicalism has lost much of its violent and sectarian connotations in West Africa, and a consensus has grown among the different groups about the orthodox tradition of Islam. This culture of tolerance caused praying styles to lose a good deal of their significance. Old adversaries joined together in organizations sponsored by governments. Reformist schools co-exist and co-operate with the religious or *zāwiya*-operated schools, to compete with secular education. Koranic schools improved their appearance

---

[24] M. Sani Umar, "Changing Islamic identity in Nigeria from the 1960s to the 1980s: From Sufism to Anti-Sufism" in *Muslim Identity and Social Change in Sub-Saharan Africa*, pp. 154–78.

[25] L. Kaba, "Islam in West Africa: Radicalism and the New Ethic of Disagreement, 1960–1990" in *The History of Islam in Africa*, edited by N. Levtzion and R.L. Powels, Athens: Ohio University Press, 2000, pp. 189–208.

with tables, blackboards and modern equipment and the curriculum was expanded to cover non-religious subjects.[26]

With independence, Islam became politically marginalized, as the new political elite opted for a secular order. Only in Senegal did Muslims play a significant role, because Léopold Senghor's political interests converged with those of the Sufi brotherhoods. These brotherhoods, particularly the Mourides, successfully adapted to modern conditions. The urban Mourides have developed a viable associative organization, which reflects the understanding that the brotherhood's commercial community thrives best within its own networks. Mouride ritual in this case serves as the bond of a commercial association. The successful Mouride entrepreneur appears to have taken on something of the social function of the rural shaykh, who provides for the material existence of his clientele.[27]

Yet the Mourides' traditional leadership is challenged from two sides in the town: from the brotherhood's more successful traders, who can be very much richer than the shaykhs, and from the new generation of Western-educated urban disciples. As the state opened schools in Mouride areas and Mouride parents were encouraged to enrol their children. The outcome was an assertive Mouride presence in the university, in the form of militant Mouride students with an active association (a *dāi'ra*), a programme of proselytism among the young, and an ideological restatement of the Mouride faith. Aḥmadou Bamba is represented as the pioneer of the struggle against Western decadence. The young Mourides are against pop music, the use of drugs and Western dress. Mouride defence of African cultural pride is a powerful attraction to the young. A Mouride reform movement defends the Brotherhood from the attacks of the reformists. Bamba, who had created an independent African Sufi movement, also represents the refusal to subordinate to the Arab world, which Mourides claim distinguishes them from the Senegalese Tijāniyya and Qādiriyya, who defer to Fez or Baghdad.[28]

Sudan

Sudan, an Arab-African state, is the only Sunni country that has experienced a genuine Islamic revolution. Ḥasan al-Turābī, who emerged as the leader of the country's Islamist movement, advocated the reformation of the Muslim Brotherhood in the Sudan as a popular, potentially mass, political association.

---

[26] Ibid., pp. 202–4.

[27] D.B. Cruise O'Brien, "Charisma comes to town: Mouride urbanization, 1945–1986" in *Charisma and Brotherhood in African Islam* edited by D.B. Cruise O'Brien and C. Coulon, Oxford: Oxford University Press, 1988, pp. 135–6, 141.

[28] Ibid., pp. 136, 144, 146, 153.

He opted to cooperate with President Ja'far al-Numayrī when the latter called for national reconciliation in 1978. With the new openings that this provided, the Brotherhood laid the foundations for the National Islamic Front (NIF) and for the emergence of the Islamists as an effective, if still relatively small, political force.

The September Laws of 1983, enacted by Numayrī, were considered by al-Turābī to be only the first step, however imperfect, in the actual Islamization of society. Following the military coup of 1989 led by General 'Omar Bashīr, the revolutionary government soon became identified with the NIF, and al-Turābī emerged as the major articulator of the ideology and programme of the new regime.

The Bashīr government actively suppressed all opposition, and the human rights record of the regime has been widely condemned.[29] It has tried to control all social, political and cultural activities through "popular committees" that are entitled to forbid "non-Islamic" behaviour in the streets, in living quarters and in places of work. The explanation was that the function of such organizations is based on the traditional Islamic duty "to enjoin justice and forbid evil".[30]

Conclusion

The modern state completed the destruction of pre-modern institutions in the public sphere of Islamic societies that had already been eroded under the impact of modernization and Western influence. The Islamists filled up the public sphere, and through their communal welfare projects also took over many functions of state institutions. The debate among Islamists was whether they should first work to create an Islamic society, or should seize state power in order to impose change from above, as the Sudanese regime has done. The reaction of governments may to a large extent determine both the nature of the political discourse and the level of violence.

Sunni Islam has always inclined towards pragmatism, which contemporary Islamists strongly reject, because they dismiss all compromises. These Islamists continue a long radical tradition in Islam, epitomized in the figure of the fourteenth-century Ibn Taymiyya, whom contemporary Islamists consider their spiritual mentor. The radicals reject legal constructions that developed out of the *ijmā'*, which represents a process of compromise and accommodation. The most extreme radicals also reject the basic concept that there is no *takfīr* of Muslims. By addressing Muslim governments as infidels, extreme radicals legitimize a

---

[29] J.O. Voll, "The Eastern Sudan, 1822 to the present" in *The History of Islam in Africa*, edited by N. Levtzion and R.L. Powels, Athens: Ohio University Press, 2000, pp. 153–167.

[30] Haydar 1999, p. 14.

jihād against Muslim societies and a total attack against the world order by every means, including international terrorism.

Is there any comfort in our analysis that Muslim radicals might accommodate to other systems and values, or at least be partially pragmatic? Does this depend also on the reaction of the international community? Is there a way to fight international terrorism other than by force? Scholars can hardly propose answers to these questions, which are political in nature. We can only suggest that politicians be more attentive to the nuances of scholarly analyses of society, history, religion and culture.

Bibliography

'Ali, H.I. "Civil Society and Democratization in Arab Countries with special reference to the Sudan" in *Islamic Area Studies Project - Islamic Area Studies Working Paper Series no. 12*, Tokyo, Japan, 1999.

Beinin, J. and Stork, J. "Introduction" in *Political Islam: Essays from Middle East Report*, edited by J. Beinin and J. Stork, Berkeley: University of California Press, 1997.

Boulby, M. *The Muslim Brotherhood and the Kings of Jordan, 1945–1953*. Atlanta, GA: Scholars Press, 1999.

Brenner, L. "Constructing Muslim identities in Mali" in *Muslim Identity and Social Change in Sub-Saharan Africa*, edited by L. Brenner, Bloomington: Indiana University Press, 1993.

Carapico, S. "Introduction to Part One" in *Political Islam: Essays from Middle East Report*, edited by J. Beinin and J. Stork, Berkeley: University of California Press, 1997.

Choueiri, Y. "The Political Discourse of Contemporary Islamist Movements" in in *Islamic Fundamentalism* edited by A. Sidahmed and A. Ehteshami, Boulder: Westview Press, 1996, pp. 19–33.

Crystal, J "Civil Society in the Arabian Gulf" in *Civil Society in the Middle East*, edited by A.R. Norton, Leiden: Brill, 1995.

George, D. "Pax Islamica: An Alternative New World Order" in *Islamic Fundamentalism* edited by A. Sidahmed and A. Ehteshami, Boulder: Westview Press, 1996.

Heffner, R.W. "Public Islam and the problem of democratisation", *Sociology of Religion*, 62, 4 (2001), pp. 491–514.

Kaba, L. "Islam in West Africa: Radicalism and the New Ethic of Disagreement, 1960–1990" in *The History of Islam in Africa*, edited by N. Levtzion and R.L. Powels, Athens: Ohio University Press, 2000, pp. 189–208.

Khurshid, A. "The nature of the Islamic resurgence" in *Voices of Resurgent Islam*, edited by J. I. Esposito, Oxford: Oxford University Press, 1983, pp. 218–229.

Langohr, V. "Of Islamists and Ballot Boxes", *International Journal of Middle East Studies*, 33 (2001), pp. 591–610.

Margulies R. and E. Yildizoglu, "The resurgence of Islam and the Welfare Party in Turkey" in *Political Islam: Essays from Middle East Report*, edited by J. Beinin and J. Stork, Berkeley: University of California Press, 1997.

Nehme, M.G. "The Islamic-Capitalist State of Saudi Arabia: The Surfacing of Fundamentalism" in A.S. Moussalli, *Islamic Fundamentalism: Myths and Realities*. London: Ithaca Press, 1998, pp. 275–302.

O'Brien, D.B. Cruise. "Charisma comes to town: Mouride urbanization, 1945–1986" in *Charisma and Brotherhood in African Islam* edited by D.B. Cruise O'Brien and C. Coulon, Oxford: Oxford University Press, 1988.

Sidahmed, A. and Ehteshami, A. "Intruduction" in *Islamic Fundamentalism* edited by A. Sidahmed and A. Ehteshami, Boulder: Westview Press, 1996, pp. 1–15.

Tripp, C. "Islam and the Secular Logic of the State in the Middle East" in *Islamic Fundamentalism* edited by A. Sidahmed and A. Ehteshami, Boulder: Westview Press, 1996, pp. 51–69.

Umar, M.S.. "Changing Islamic identity in Nigeria from the 1960s to the 1980s: From Sufism to Anti-Sufism" in *Muslim Identity and Social Change in Sub-Saharan Africa*, pp. 154–78.

Vitalis, R. "Islam and the Struggle for the State in the Middle East" in *Political Islam: Essays from Middle East Report*, edited by J. Beinin and J. Stork, Berkeley: University of California Press, 1997.

Voll, J.O. "Fundamentalism in the Sunni Arab World: Egypt and the Sudan," in *Fundamentalisms Observed* edited by M.E. Marty and R. Scott Appleby, Chicago: University of Chicago Press, 1991, pp. 345–402.

Voll, J.O. "The Eastern Sudan, 1822 to the present" in *The History of Islam in Africa*, edited by N. Levtzion and R. Powels, Athens: Ohio University Press, 2000, pp. 153–167.

Wickham, C.R. "Islamic Mobilization and Political Change: the Islamist Trend in Egypt's Professional Associations" in *Political Islam: Essays from Middle East Report*, edited by J. Beinin and J. Stork, Berkeley: University of California Press, 1997.

Zubayda, S. "Is Iran an Islamic State" in *Political Islam: Essays from Middle East Report*, edited by J. Beinin and J. Stork, Berkeley: University of California Press, 1997.

XV

The Role of Sharī'a-Oriented Sufi *Ṭuruq* in the Reform Movements of the 18th and 19th Centuries[1]

In the nineteenth century, Muslim movements resisted the expansion of European powers in several areas: the Padri movement in Indonesia against the Dutch; 'Abd al-Qādir in Algeria and *al-ḥājj* 'Umar in West Africa against the French; the Mahdī in the Sudan against the British (and Egyptians); Sayyid Aḥmad Brēlwī in India against the British (and the Sikhs); Imam Shāmil in the Caucasus against the Russians; and the Sanusiyya in the Sahara and around Lake Chad against the French and Italians.

The origin of all these movements goes back to the eighteenth century, when they emerged not in reaction to a threat from the European West, but out of the internal dynamics of Islam, and were aimed at reform and renewal. They developed within the Sufi *ṭuruq* (sing. *ṭarīqa*), denoting the way to the divine reality (*ḥaqīqa*), which in the eighteenth century experienced a radical restructuring, achieving greater cohesion and reaching out to mobilize followers both in urban and rural milieus. These reformed Sufi movements were the most dynamic – perhaps the only dynamic – Muslim forces under charismatic leadership. When their countries were invaded by colonial powers, these movements redirected their major efforts from internal reform to defending *dār al-Islām*. Because they forced the colonial powers to stretch their military resources, they feature prominently in colonial records. All of the movements were eventually crushed by the military superiority of the Europeans. The inroads of colonialism put an end to the process of reform and renewal, and derailed Muslim societies from a trajectory of socio-moral reconstruction.

---

[1] This paper was prepared for the IV International Conference on Islamic Legal Studies: *Law and Sufism*. Murcia (Spain), 7–10 May, 2003.

Ḥadīth and Taṣawwuf in the Ḥaramayn: The Seventeenth and Eighteenth Centuries

During this period, an awareness of the discrepancy between the ideals of Islam and the realities of Muslim life created a cyclical drive for renewal (*tajdīd*). The annual pilgrimage provided the Muslim world with a physical as well as a symbolic centre, and sustained a measure of unity and conformity within the diversity of regional forms of Islam. There is enough evidence to suggest that the number of pilgrims increased significantly in the eighteenth century.[2]

In the Ḥaramayn, teachers and students of different legal schools came together and were engaged in the study of *Ḥadīth*, which is common to all schools of law, rather than of *fiqh*, which is particular to each school. The intellectual creativity that made the Ḥaramayn the focus for Islamic revivalism was the outcome of the convergence of different traditions of *Ḥadīth* studies and different streams of Sufism – from India, North Africa and Egypt. The fusion of *Ḥadīth* and *taṣawwuf*, of the exoteric and esoteric sciences, freed scholars from the fetters of *taqlīd* and reoriented Sufism towards a more rigorous observance of the *sharī'a*.[3]

In a Ph.D. dissertation on Ibrāhīm al-Kūrānī, my student Atallah Copty argued that it was Aḥmad al-Qushāhshī (1583–1661) who contributed to the merging of the study of *Ḥadith* and *taṣawwuf* in the Ḥaramayn. Al-Qushahshī, a native of Medina, and his Egyptian contemporary, Muaḥmmad al-Bābilī (1591–1666), who had spent ten years in Mecca, are credited with the creation of a widespread scholarly network. Their own students, and their students' disciples, later appear in the *asānīd* of prominent scholars from all over the Muslim world. But the most influential in the network was Ibrāhīm al-Kūrānī (1616–90), a *Shafi'ī* from Kurdistan. In analysing the transmission of *Ḥadith* in the circles of Ibrāhīm al-Kūrānī, Copty underlined the search for shorter *asānīd* that take the student in fewer stages to the Prophet. This is in line with the tendencies of the reformed *ṭuruq* to shorten the number of mystical steps needed to come closer to the Prophet. Copty also pointed out that al-Kūrānī adopted the *kashf*, or mystical unveiling, to assert that a certain *Ḥadīth* is *ṣaḥīh*, thus enriching the repertoire with more authentic traditions.[4]

Abū'l-Ṭāhir Muḥammad, the son of Ibrāhīm al-Kūrānī, was born in Medina and studied with his father and with other leading scholars in the network. Abu'l-Ṭāhir was the teacher of 'Abd al-Khāliq b. al-Zayn al-Mizjājī (*c.*1705–

---

[2] Levtzion and Weigert 1998, pp. 260–61.
[3] Voll 1980, p. 266.
[4] Copty, 2005.

40), a member of a prominent family of scholars. 'Abd al-Khāliq al-Mizjājī appears in the Naqshabandiyya *silsila* of Ma Ming-Hsin (1719–81), the leader of the "New teaching", a reformist movement in China. Abū'l-Ṭāhir also taught Shāh Wālī Allāh (1702–62) when the latter spent 14 months in the Ḥaramayn. Muaḥammad Ḥayāt al-Sindī (d. 1750), another student of Abu'l-Tāhir, was the teacher of Muḥammad Ibn 'Abd al-Wahhāb, the founder of the Wahhābiyya, which shows that even the most radical reformist belonged to the same scholarly network.

Sharī'a and *Ṭasawwuf*

The spirituality of Sufi *ṭuruq* is profoundly Sunni, and is firmly rooted in orthodox Islam. The obligation to observe conventional cultic practice is stressed by all the great masters. For Sufis, the *sharī'a* is the starting point, and *ṭarīqa* shows the way. There were, however, Sufis who believed that when they reached an advanced stage on the path to God they were relieved of the obligation to observe the precepts of the *sharī'a.* Another deviation from orthodoxy was practised by *turuq* that were loosely organized, bound neither by a discipline nor by the religious law of Islam, and profoundly influenced by indigenous beliefs and practices. When Sufi *ṭuruq* recruited adherents from among the lay population, their deviation became ever more dangerous. The mystical-intellectual component of the *ṭuruq* increasingly gave way to appealingly simplistic and populist rituals.

In spite of this, the *sharī'a* orientation of most Sufis was not in doubt throughout history. But *sharī'a*-minded Sufism achieved its most lasting impact in the eighteenth century, when Sufi *ṭarīqa*, led by charismatic shayks, became more cohesive and centralized.

The Attitude to This World and to Political Involvement

Sufism oscillated between an individualistic renunciation of this world and a community-oriented, legalistic world-affirmation.[5] The *sharī'a*-oriented *ṭuruq* were clearly on the side of this world. A positive attitude towards the present world was important in two of the oldest *ṭuruq*. In India, the Suhrawardīs mingled enthusiastically with Muslim rulers, and accumulated great wealth and

---

[5] Karamustafa 1994, pp. 29–30, 96, 98.

landed interests.[6] The Shādhiliyya in Egypt shunned mendicancy and a renunciation of the world, and insisted that its members should lead active and economically productive lives. They were by no means averse to worldly riches and were not ascetic.[7]

The Naqshabandiyya, with its positive attitude to this world and to activism in social, political and economic life, recognized that the Islamic ideal required a combination of outward activity with inward tranquillity. They therefore adhered to the principle of "solitude within society" (*khalwa fī jalwa)*, so that a person could be inwardly alone with God and concentrated on his reality, while outwardly immersed in the transactions and relationships that sustain Muslim society.[8] In Central Asia, the Naqshabandiyya stressed mystical attainments at the same time as actively participating in ordinary life, both in terms of attracting followers and of securing a firm organizational and financial foundation for the *ṭarīqa.*[9] 'Ubaydallāh Aḥrār (1401–90), the towering Naqshabandī shaykh in Central Asia, used to say: "Having worldly engagements is not in contradiction with being mentally disengaged from worldly goods." In the context of the spiritual world, wealth symbolized a favour bestowed by God.[10]

Al-Tijānī lived in Fez in comfort, without any manifestations of asceticism. He opposed withdrawal from this world, and promised access to Paradise for his adherents without requiring that they forsake their possessions. This positive attitude to worldly affairs attracted rich merchants and senior officials to the *ṭarīqa.*[11] Al-Sanūsī forbade begging, and insisted on a work ethic in his *ṭarīqa.* All brethren had to do manual labour for the benefit of the lodge, either in building, agriculture or training in various handicrafts.[12]

The Political Potential of Sufi *Ṭuruq*

With a positive attitude to this present world, political engagement became legitimate and spiritually acceptable, and prepared the reformed Sufi *ṭuruq* to be more actively involved in social and political life. The key to the political

---

[6] Nizami 1957, p. 109; Ansari 1992, p. 5
[7] Winter 1982, p. 90.
[8] Weismann 2001, p. 46.
[9] Deweese 1988, pp. 79–81.
[10] Gross 1988, pp. 90, 104.
[11] Levtzion and Weigert 1995, pp. 193–4; Radtke 1996, p. 342.
[12] Vikor 1991, p. 180.

potential of the Sufi *ṭuruq* is their independent organization and charismatic leadership. As pious and religious organizations, distant from the existing political order, they could be transformed into political movements under certain external circumstances. Sufi *ṭuruq* became vehicles for social mobilization, with the potential to communicate and articulate discontent.

In Indonesia, Bengal and West Africa, Islam expanded from the towns into the countryside and won adherents among the peasants. This process broadened the popular basis of Sufi shaykhs, and contributed to the radicalization of Islam. The political potential of Sufi *ṭuruq* was realized in these peripheral countries of the Muslim world, where political structures were more fragile. The militant movements of the periphery seem to have been radical manifestations of the undercurrents of religious change and revivalism in the central Muslim lands.

Under the leadership of the powerful ʻUbaydallāh Aḥrār, the Naqshabandiyya developed a tight organization, based on relations of personal and economic dependency, which served Aḥrār's interests in defending conformity with Islamic law. The political objectives of Mawlānā Khālid (d. 1827) were the most ambitious and pronounced of any figure in the Naqshabandiyya since Aḥrār. During the long history of the Naqshabandiyya, only the Khālidiyya developed into a structured hierarchical organization. Khālid constructed a network of *khulafā'*, each with a carefully delineated geographic area of responsibility.[13]

Al-Sanūsī (b. 1787 and active in Cyrenaica; see below) may be seen as an organizer of great capability as well as a scholar. This is perhaps the most original aspect of his work.[14] In creating new institutions and new hierarchies, the emergent *ṭuruq*, mainly in Muslim Africa, introduced new patterns of loyalties that tended to transcend tribal and social boundaries.[15]

Ijtihād and the Mystical Dimensions of the *Sharīʻa*

The concept of the mystical unveiling (*kashf*) of the inner meaning of the Koran and the *Ḥadīth* not only mitigated the potential contradiction between mysticism and *sharīʻa*, but made Sufi scholars more confident in providing legal responses.

The Egyptian scholar ʻAbd al-Wahhāb al-Shaʻrānī (d. 1565) himself experienced *kashf*. He travelled the mystical path until, in a waking state (*yaqẓatan*), he beheld the very source of the *sharīʻa*, the Prophet Muḥammad.

---

[13] Algar 1990b, pp. 129–30, 145.

[14] Vikor 1991, p. 266.

[15] O'Fahey 1990, pp. 7–8.

He had heard from the shaykh Aḥmad al-Zawāwī (d. 1517) about his own encounter with the Prophet: "We recite the *tasliya* on behalf of the Prophet so often that he then sits with us while we are in a waking state and we keep company with him as the *saḥāba* did. Then we question him about matters of our religion and about *Ḥadīth*s, which are held to be weak in the opinion of our religious scholars. Subsequently we base our behaviour on his words."[16]

Al-hājj 'Umar al-Tijānī, who was deeply influenced by al-Sha'rānī, claimed that an experienced mystic knows far more than those who have spent many years in the study of the law, because he possesses inspired knowledge.[17] The knowledge of a mystic, who encounters the Prophet while he is awake, is superior to that of all others, and he becomes an infallible authority for interpreting the law.[18] This mystical approach to the *sharī'a* opened wider the gates of *ijtihād*, and encouraged the rejection of following one's *madhhab*. Indeed, it was because of his mystical understanding of the Koran and the Sunna that Ibn Idrīs rejected *taqlīd* and the *madhāhib*.[19]

The disciple of Ibn Idrīs, Muḥammad b. 'Alī al-Sanūsī, also sought to eliminate *taqlīd*, and insisted that every Muslim is obliged to exercise a measure of *ijtihād*, or at least to try to do so, but he argued within the traditional framework of *usūl al-fiqh*. He seems to have maintained the distinction between Sufism and exoteric knowledge more clearly than his master and other scholars.[20] Mawlānā Khālid's understanding of the *sharī'a* was that of a *faqīh* rather than a Sufi. His letters are remarkable for the paucity of specifically Sufi themes, and his library contained very few Sufi books and a large collection of *fiqh*.[21]

Ibn 'Arabī and *Sharī'a*-oriented *Ṭuruq*

Rejection of Ibn 'Arabī's teaching, and particularly of *waḥdat al-wujūd*, is counted among the characteristics of the reformist *sharī'a*-oriented *ṭuruq*.[22] Ibn 'Arabī's mysticism dominated Sufism throughout the late middle ages of Islam. Ibn 'Arabī came to be known as *al-shaykh al-akbar*, because he offered erudite

---

[16] Radtke et al. 2000, pp.16–18.
[17] Martin 1976, p. 95.
[18] Radtke 1996, pp. 338–9, 359–60; Radtke et al. 2000, p. 8.
[19] O'Fahey 1990, p. 209; Radtke et al. 2000, p. 28.
[20] Vikor 1991, p. 265; Dallal 1993, p. 358.
[21] Algar 1990b, pp. 137–8.
[22] Levtzion and Voll 1987, p. 9; O'Fahey and Radtke 1993, p. 57.

and challenging explanations of all the basic issues of Islamic theory and practice.[23] Yet the Sufi principles formulated by Ibn 'Arabī were vulnerable to charges of heresy, ranging from Ibn Taymiyya (1328) and al-Simnānī (d. 1336), to the seventeenth century Kadizadelis, an anti-Sufi movement in the Ottoman Empire that derided Ibn 'Arabī as *al-shaykh al-akfār*,[24] and to the eighteenth-century Wahhābis.

But there were also prominent orthodox scholars who supported Ibn 'Arabī. Mullā 'Abd Allāh Ilāhī (d. 1491), a disciple of Aḥrār, who was the first major propagator of the Naqshabandiyya in Turkey, popularized Ibn 'Arabī's ideas in works in Arabic, Persian and Turkish. Al-Sha'rānī was a famous and prolific defender of Ibn 'Arabī, as well as of al-Qushāshī and his disciple Ibrahīm al-Kūrānī.[25]

Others were ambivalent concerning Ibn 'Arabī, as shown by the scholars who followed his ideas without referring to him by name. In the same text, or in two texts by the same author, one can find ideas borrowed from Ibn 'Arabī as well as a denunciation of him, for reasons of spiritual opportunism or political prudence. It is said of 'Ubaydallāh Aḥrār that he used to stop commenting on Ibn 'Arabī's *Fuṣūṣ* when visitors arrived.[26] The thoughts of Bāqī Bi'llāh (1564–1603), who founded the Naqshabandiyya in India, were based on Ibn 'Arabī's *waḥdāt al-wujūd*, but he was very critical of the excesses of the eccentric followers of this doctrine. He attempted to make the followers of *waḥdat al-wujūd* adhere to the *sharī'a*. It was his disciple, Sirhindī (1564–1624), who developed the concept of "the oneness of witness" (*waḥdat al-shuhūd)* to replace Ibn 'Arabī's "the oneness of being" (*waḥdat al-wujūd*), or "All is from Him" in opposition to "All is He".[27]

The Naqshabandiyya was rather ambivalent towards Ibn 'Arabī, who had a stronger following in the Khalwatiyya. 'Ali Qarābāsh (d. 1658), founder of the Karābāshiyya branch of the Khalwatiyya, was the author of a commentary on the *Fuṣūs*. Muṣṭafā Kamāl al-Dīn al-Bakrī, who inspired the Khalwatiyya reform in eighteenth-century Egypt, belonged to the Qarābāshiya branch, and the influence of Ibn 'Arabī is shown in the writings. There are frequent references to Ibn 'Arabī in works of the Tijāniyya, an offshoot of the Khalwatiyya.[28]

[23] Chittick, x, p. 317.
[24] Zilfi 1988, pp. 37–8.
[25] Chittick, x, p. 322.
[26] Chodkieicz 1993, pp. 204–6.
[27] Chittick, p. 318.
[28] Zarcone 1993, p. 81; Chodkieicz 1993, pp. 209, 212–14.

Ibn ʻArabī's mysticism engendered religious tolerance among Sufis who lived in mixed societies, and blurred meaningful lines between religions. Indeed, militant reformism was encouraged by the growth of Muslim identity in regions where Muslims lived in symbiosis with non-Muslims. In India, for example, Aḥmad Sirhīn reacted against Akbar's syncretism. The *jihād* movement of Sayyid Aḥmad Brēlwī was directed against the Sikhs. Khālid agitated against the Christians. In Northern Nigeria, ʻUthmān dan Fodio called for the *hijra* to draw a line of separation between the faithful and the infidels.

W.C. Chittick has presented a revisionist understanding of Ibn ʻArabī's teachings in relation to the *sharīʻa*-minded Sufis. He put forward pairs of concepts that designate the extreme limits of various spectra within which Muslims understand their religion and put it into practice. Whereas Ibn ʻArabī Sufism stresses the first term in the following complementary pairs, *sharī'a*-minded Sufis stress the second: *furqān* and Koran, *kashf* and *ʻaql*, mercy and wrath, *ḥaqīqa* and *sharīʻa*, intoxication (*sukr*) and sobriety (*ṣaḥw*), intimacy (*uns*) and awe (*hayba*), meaning (*maʻnā*) and form (*ṣūra*), spirit and letter.[29]

The Naqshabandiyya and the *Jihād* of Sayyid Aḥmad Brēlwī

Of all the Sufi *ṭuruq*, the Naqshabandiyya is more clearly identified with the Sunni tradition of Sufism, which consistently opposed antinomian Sufism and marginal cults. In Samarqand, the Naqshabandi shaykh `Ubaydallāh Aḥrār (1404–90) converted the charisma of a Sufi shaykh into economic and political power. He exploited the decline in authority of the Timurid sulṭāns and gained almost absolute influence over the Sulṭān Abū Saʻīd (1451–68), who was his *murīd*. Ahrar also accumulated considerable landholdings, as peasants sold their property to him in order to become his disciples and enter under his protection (*ḥimāya*). In typical Naqshabandi fashion, Aḥrār reconciled his worldly involvement with a state of mind of being mentally disengaged from worldly affairs. Wealth in the context of his spiritual world symbolized a favor bestowed by God. The dissemination of the Naqshabandiyya through the *salāsil* emanating from ʻUbaydallāh Aḥrār made the Naqshabandiyya an important element in the shared culture of three major Sunni regions – Central Asia, India and the Ottoman Empire.[30]

---

[29] See Chittick's two revisionist articles in the *Encyclopaedia of Islam.*

[30] Paul 1991, pp. 533, 543; DeWeese 1993, pp. 66–7; DeWeese 1996, p. 200; Algar 1990a, p. 16.

It was in recognition of his services to the cause of orthodox Islam that Sirhindī was acclaimed as *mujaddid al-alf al-thānī.* Even in his lifetime, his influence spread as far as Afghanistan and Central Asia. After his death, it extended still further through his descendants and disciples, who propagated a new branch of the movement, known as Naqshabandiyya-Mujaddidiyya.

Shāh Walī Allāh (d. 1762) updated the activist elements of the Naqshabandiyya-Mujaddidiyya. He sought to reform and purify religious beliefs and practices from Hindu influence and other accretions. He lived after the decline of the Mughal Empire, and his goals were to restore a traditional system that was falling into disarray and decay, and to prop up and revive a Muslim way of life threatened with disappearance.

Shāh 'Abd al-'Azīz (1746–1824) continued his father's work as a scholar and teacher, compiling large collections of legal rulings (*fatwā*s) that could serve as a comprehensive resource for Muslims engaged in the socio-moral reconstruction of society. His declaration that India under British rule was *dār al-ḥarb* laid the legal and theological foundations for *jihāds*.

Some consider the militant movement of Sayyid Aḥmad Brēlwī (1786–1831), a *murīd* of Shāh 'Abd al-'Azīz, to be in line with the Naqshabandiyya-Muhjaddidiyya. But Sayyid Aḥmad charted his own way, and later other Naqshabandis considered his followers to be their adversaries, and to have formed a distinct *ṭarīqa* bordering on infidelity (*kufr*). After he had served between 1810 and 1817 in the army of the Nawāb Amīr Khān, Sayyid Aḥmad went to Delhi where, roused by the religious and political degradation of his co-religionists, he embarked on a missionary tour as a religious teacher and reformer. He agitated for a pure and simple form of religion, free from superstitious innovations and the exaggerated veneration of prophets and saints, and based on the true faith on the Koran and Sunna alone.

As early as 1818, Sayyid Aḥmad initiated his two devoted disciples – Isma'īl Shahīd and 'Abd al-Ḥayy, the nephew and son-in-law of Shāh 'Abd al-'Azīz, respectively – into his own Sufi *ṭarīqa*, which became known as *Ṭarīqa-i Muḥammadiyya*, and seems to have been a reformulation of the Naqshabandiyya-Mujaddidiyya. It was Isma'īl Shahīd (1779–1831) who wrote the major reformist-oriented literature of Sayyid Aḥmad's movement. Followers of the movement stressed their distinct identity from other Sufi *ṭuruq* by ostentatiously avoiding practices of other Sufis, which they considered contrary to the *sharī'a*. They condemned the cult of dead saints and the reverence for living spiritual guides. They denounced the *rābiṭa*, or the contemplation of the image of one's shaykh, which was central to the Naqshabandiyya. In modern scholarship, Ismāʻīl Shahīd is credited with pioneering what later became known as the *ahl-i Ḥadīth* movement.[31]

The reputation of Sayyid Aḥmad spread far and wide, and thousands of Muslims adopted his views. In 1821 he went to the pilgrimage with more than 600 disciples. On his return in 1824, he began preparations for a *jihād*. The ultimate goals of his reformist movement were to overthrow British rule and to oust the Sikhs from the Panjab. In 1826 he occupied Peshawar and established a *sharīʻa*-oriented state, but he was killed in battle with the Sikhs in 1831.[32]

The Naqshabandiyya-Mujaddidiyya-Khālidiyya and the *Jihād* of Imām Shāmil

In the Ottoman Empire, the government pursued a mild policy *vis-à-vis* the non-orthodox *ṭuruq* until the reign of Bayazīd II (1481–1512). The situation changed at the beginning of the sixteenth century, after the rise of the Safawids in Persia, and the flow of Shīʻī-Ṣafawī propaganda since 1502. As the Ottomans were involved in fierce battles with Iran, political pressures on the non-orthodox *ṭuruq* increased.[33]

As a politically active *ṭariqa* concerned with the community and its moral and religious well-being, the Naqshabandiyya was favoured by the Ottomans in their efforts to weaken heretical and potentially rebellious elements in Anatolia. But it was only with the arrival of the Mujaddidiyya, and later the Khālidiyya branches, that the Naqshabandiyya became of greater significance in the politics of the Ottoman Empire.[34] The Khālidiyya seems to have been the driving force behind the eradication of the Janissaries and the abolishing of the Bektashis. Some of the central *zawāyā* of the Bektashiyya were handed over to the Naqshabandis.[35]

Damascus became an important centre of the Naqshabandiyya-Mujaddidiyya when Murād al-Bukhārī settled there, after he had travelled extensively and developed close relations with the Sulṭān Muṣtafā II (1695–1703), who granted him properties in Damascus. The Naqshabandiyya, led by the Mūradī family,

---

[31] Gaboriau 1999, pp. 452–67; Buehler 1999, p. 479.

[32] Inayatullah; Rizvi 1970, p. 75; Algar 1990a, p. 35; Bazmee Ansari.

[33] Ocak 1993, pp. 249–51.

[34] Abu-Manneh 2001, p. 8; Algar 1990b, p. 130.

[35] Abu-Manneh 2001, p. 69.

benefitted from official Ottoman patronage, and was a vehicle of political integration and mobilization in favor of the state.[36]

Mawlānā Khālid was born in the Shahrazūr region in Kurdistan. He went to the *ḥajj* in 1805, and in 1808 traveled to Delhi and was initiated into the Naqshabandiyya by Shāh Ghulām ʻAlī (d. 1824), whose Naqshabandi *silsila* traces its lineage through Mīrzā Maẓhar Jāni-i Janān, Sayyid Nūr Muḥammad Badā'ūnī, and Khwāja Sayf al-Dīn, the son of Sirhindī. After his return from India in 1811, Khālid settled in Sulaymaniyya. He became influential, and princes of the ruling family joined his *ṭarīqa*. Among the *khulafā'* ordained by Khālid were former shaykhs of the Qādiriyya, which highlighted tensions between the two *ṭuruq*. Because the Qādirīs were closer to the local rulers, Khālid was forced to flee from Sulaimaniyya in 1820. In Baghdad, the *walī* Dāwūd Pāshā, who had been his *murīd*, also turned against him, and he left Baghdad for Syria.

During the years 1811–20, Khālid's representatives spread the *ṭarīqa* in Turkey, Syria, Palestine, Iraq, Daghestan and other regions. Both in Istanbul and in Damascus, Khālid and his deputies succeeded in arousing religious feelings among the population. They extended their influence beyond the urban centres to the lower classes in the countryside.[37]

Khālid used devotional practices in *ṭarīqa* to unify the Naqshabandiyya-Mujaddidiyya-Khālidiyya into a centralized and disciplined organization. The *rābiṭa* binds the heart of the *murīd* with that of the shaykh by keeping the shaykh's image in the *murīd*'s mind, even in the latter's absence. All Naqshabandīs agree that the *rābiṭa* is between the *murīd* and his immediate spiritual guide, but in order to strengthen his personal authority Khālid insisted that all *murīd*s would concentrate on his own image and not on that of their immediate shaykh. He also introduced the practice of 40 days *khalwa* to replace the much longer process of *ṣuḥba*, in order to train more *khulafā'* and to accelerate the expansion of the *ṭarīqa*.[38]

Khālid believed that the *umma* had gone wrong and he sought to restore it to the right path, reflecting the period of the Prophet and his Companions. He had a clear sense of socio-political mission, derived from the Naqshabdiyya's emphasis on the *sharīʻa* and from his realization of the dangerous juncture at which the Muslim world stood. He demonstrated the centrality of the *sharīʻa*, not with the purpose of elucidating its inner aspect and meaning, as both

---

[36] Schatkowski -Schilcher 1985, pp. 119, 165.

[37] Abu-Manneh 2001, pp. 20–21, 67.

[38] Abu-Manneh 1990, pp. 291–3.

Sirhindīand Shāh Walī Allāh had done in their differing ways, but rather through *ṭarīqa* to secure its supremacy in Muslim society.[39]

The militancy of the Khālidiyya found expression in the Caucasus. In parts of Chechnya and Daghestan, Islam, as brought by the Tatars of Crimea, had been accepted only by the representatives of the upper classes, while the masses remained untouched by Islam until the eighteenth century, maintaining their ancestral rites and beliefs. The preaching of Imām Manṣūr, who led a *jihād* in the years 1785–91, addressed the peasants in simple and direct language. His most durable work was the Islamization of the population of the North-west Caucasus, preparing the way for the Naqshabandi preachers and for the *jihād* of Imām Shāmil.[40]

Followers of Khālid spread the *ṭarīqa* in Daghestan and Chechnya in the early years of the nineteenth century. Shaykh Ismāʻīl al-Kurdemīrī, a follower of Khālid, was active in Shīrwān in the 1810s. With the progress of the Russian occupation, many of the local rulers submitted to Russian rule, so that the traditional political establishment was increasingly discredited. In this context, the message of the renewalist Naqshabandiyya *ṭarīqa* had strong popular appeal, and the movement grew under the leadership of Muḥammad al-Yarāghī, a student of Shaykh Ismāʻīl. Al-Yarāghī's first concern was to establish respect for and adherence to Islamic law and to reform local practice.[41]

Hamid Algar asserts that the directives of Mawlānā Khālid consistently guided the political activities of the Khālidī Naqshabandī shaykhs in Daghestan and Chechnya, and it was there that the Khālidiyya survived in its purest and most integral form. The *jihād* of Imām Shāmil, from 1832 to 1859, had an important internal dimension. He created a territory where the *sharīʻa* was supreme, and eradicated various local dynasties that had been associated with practicing the local customary law.[42]

The Khalwatiyya in Egypt

The Khalwatī tradition initially had strong links with the cult of ʻAlī, and was suspected of leaning toward the Shīʻa. According to Katib Celebi (d. 1657), the Khalwatīs also played on the social and entertainment aspects of Sufi

---

[39] Abu-Manneh 2001, p. 23; Algar 1990b, pp. 129–30, 137–8; Algar 1990a, pp. 29, 32.

[40] Bennigsen 1964, p. 195.

[41] Algar 1990b, pp. 123–52.

[42] Algar 1990b, p. 145.

associations in *tarīqa* in order to attract a larger following. In his view, the Khalwatis in particular had an increasingly vulgar side.[43] Orthodox *'ulamā'* of Istanbul accused the Khalwatīs of moving too far from the *sharī'a* towards popular Islam, and considered them to be disseminators of *bid'a* and of *ghulāt* ideas and practices.

Yaḥyā al-Shīrwānī (d. 1464) was the author of *wird al-sattār*, the principal liturgy of the Khalwatiyya, and with him that the Khalwatiyya first became identified as a distinguished *ṭarīqa*. He was the first Khalwatī shaykh to send *khulafā'* to spread the *ṭarīqa* in the Ottoman Empire. He warned against those who claimed that a person who reached the Sufi *ḥaqīqa* had no need of the sharī'a.[44]

Before his accession, Bayazīd II (1481–1512) was the governor of Amasya, where he established close relations with the Khalwatī shaykh Celebi Khalīfa. In 1490, seven years after Bayazīd had become sulṭān, he invited the shaykh to Istanbul. He came with about 100 disciples and created the first Khalwatī *tekke*. The sulṭān permitted him to send *khulafā'* to different parts of the empire. It was the beginning of a long period of close relations between the Khalwatīs and the Ottoman sulṭāns, which also involved a process by which the Khalwatiyya moved towards greater orthodoxy. The Khalwatīs served the Ottoman Sulṭāns Selim I and Sulaymān in their policy of consolidating the Sunna and fighting heretics.[45]

Muṣṭafā b. Kamāl al-Dīn al-Bakrī (1687–1748) was initiated into the Khalwatiyya by 'Abd al-Latīf al-Ḥalabī, himself a disciple of 'Alī Karābāsh (d. 1658), founder of the Karābāshiyya branch. Before his death in 1708, al-Ḥalabī appointed al-Bakrī as his *khalīfa*. Al-Bakrī studied the books of Ibn 'Arabī with al-Nabulsī, who initiated him into the Qādiriyya and the Naqshabandiyya. Al-Bakrī travelled extensively, and everywhere performed nightly *dhikr* ceremonies. The disciples had to wake up to read *wird al-saḥar* (composed by al-Bakrī himself) until dawn.[46]

During his first visit to Cairo in 1720, al-Bakrī initiated Muḥammad Salīm al-Ḥifnī (1689–1768) into the Khalwatiyya, and the two became allied by a spiritual bond. Al-Ḥifnī continued to teach at al-Azhar until 1736, when he

---

[43] Zilfi 1988, p. 169; Chelebi 1957, pp. 43–4.

[44] Weigert 1989, pp. 47–8.

[45] Clayer 1994, pp. 65–7; Weigert 1989, p. 58.

[46] The section on Muṣṭafā al-Bakrī and the revival of the Khalwatiyya in Egypt is based on the Ph.D. dissertation of my late student Dr. Gideon Weigert, "The Khalwatiyya in Egypt in the Eighteenth Century", The Hebrew University of Jerusalem, 1989.

visited al-Bakrī in Jerusalem. For four intensive months he followed the different stages as a *murīd*, until he reached perfection. Back in Egypt, al-Ḥifnī propagated the Khalwatiyya intensively. It is said that by the time al-Bakrī settled in Egypt in 1747, the number of followers of the Khalwatī exceeded 100,000. Al-Ḥifnī appointed scores of *khulafā'* from among his Egyptian disciples, whom he sent to spread the *ṭarīqa* in all parts of Egypt. The mobility of scholars to and fro between town and village added to the intensity of the *tarīqa*'s expansion Al-Ḥifnī was appointed to the office of shaykh *al-Azhar* in 1757, succeeding the first Khalwatī shaykh *al-Azhar*, 'Abdallāh al-Shubrāwī. He therefore combined the highest office in the hierarchy of the *'ulamā'* with the headship of a *ṭarīqa*. The son of a rural family, he lived in a modest and secluded manner as an ascetic Sufi. He distributed the numerous gifts he received from all parts of the Muslim world among his brethren in the *ṭarīqa* and also to the poor.

Before 1737, the Khalwatiyya in Egypt had been marginal and of little significance in absolute as well as relative terms, compared with the growth of other Sufi *ṭuruq*.[47] Its two branches, the Demirdāshiyya and the Ghulshaniyya, had adherents mainly among the Turks and some members of the upper classes. With al-Ḥifnī, however, the Khalwatiyya became, in the words of al-Jabartī (d. 1825), "a truly Egyptian *ṭarīq*."[48] Such was al-Ḥifnī's prestige, and the political influence of Khalwatī, that it is said that during his lifetime nothing of importance could have happened in Egypt without his prior knowledge and approval.[49] In terms of orthodoxy, al-Jabartī described the Khalwatiyya as "the best of the Sufi *ṭuruq* (*khayr al-ṭuruq*)".[50] In the second half of the eighteenth century, all but one who held the office of *shaykh mashā'ikh al-Azhar* were Khalwatīs.

Al-Ḥifnī's principal successors as the leading shaykhs of the Khalwatiyya in Egypt were Maḥmūd al-Kurdī (1729–80) and Aḥmad al-Dardīr (1715–86), who helped to spread the influence of the Khalwatiyya beyond Egypt. Ahmad al-Dardīr, who was from Upper Egypt, became the chief Muftī Mālikī of Egypt. Hence his closer relations with scholars and Sufis from Morocco, and the generous gift he received from the Moroccan Sulṭān, Sīdī Muḥammad. Like many of the Khalwatī shaykhs he had his roots deep in Egyptian society, and defended the poor of Cairo against depredations from the Mamluks and the Ottoman authorities.

---

[47] de Jong 1987, p. 123.
[48] Al-Jabartī 1390 AH, i, p. 301.
[49] Al-Jabartī 1390 AH, i, p. 304.
[50] Al-Jabartī, 1390 AH, i, p. 295.

Although it was al-Ḥifnī who brought about the revival of the Khalwatiyya in Egypt, he attributed all his achievements to to his master al-Bakrī, or in the words of al-Jabartī, it was al-Bakrī "who built the pillars of this *ṭarīqa*".[51]

Building on the work of Gideon Weigert, we shall attempt to identify the new elements that al-Bakrī introduced to the Khalwatiyya. Generally speaking, al-Bakrī followed traditional Khalwatī rituals, mainly those of the Karābāshiyya branch. When initiating changes, he sought legitimacy either by seeking guidance from shaykhs of past generations, or by correspondence with living shaykhs. Like many Sufi shaykhs, al-Bakrī was affiliated to several *ṭuruq*, but later he insisted that his own disciples should be affiliated exclusively to the Khalwatiyya and must break any allegiances to other *ṭuruq*. This was not easily implemented, and even some of his senior disciples did not completely sever former affiliations.

But al-Bakrī's most radical innovation was the change of the *dhikr* from silent (*khāfī*) to vocal (*jahrī*) mode. He presided over *dhikr* ceremonies in Jerusalem, where participants fainted from excitement and exhaustion. In Cairo, al-Ḥifnī conducted *dhikr* ceremonies that became so popular that he had to repeat them day and night. During his sojourn in Jerusalem in 1710, al-Bakrī visited the holy places in Hebron and Nabī Mūsā. During these visits he and his followers strictly observed orthodox rules. Thus the popular elements in the movement were controlled by al-Bakrī's emphasis on close adherence to the *sharī'a*. Hence, al-Bakrī's heritage as elaborated by al-Ḥifnī in Egypt, brought about the development of a cohesive, *sharī'a*-oriented *ṭarīqa* that allowed greater scope for participation by the common people, but could also accommodate leading orthodox scholars.

The reformist thrust of the Khalwatiyya in Egypt was exhausted when, at the end of the eighteenth and the beginning of the nineteenth century, there was deterioration in the behaviour of shaykhs and the heads of *ṭuruq*. Many of them exploited their religious and social position to become rich. During the French occupation, as the ruling elite sought refuge in neighbouring countries, the *'ulamā'*, and in particular Sufi shaykhs, emerged as the only local leadership trusted by the population. The French employed them in the different divans they created. Muḥammad 'Alī also relied on the *'ulamā'* at the beginning of his rule. But after he had consolidated his power, Muḥammad 'Alī turned to reduce the influence of the Sufi shaykhs, and took away their economic resources by abolishing the *iltizām* and confiscating the large *awqāf*. He finally brought all Sufi *ṭuruq* under a central leadership controlled by the political authorities. This

---

[51] Al-Jabartī 1390 AH, i, p. 166.

explains the end of the revivalism of the Khalwatiyya and of other Sufi *ṭuruq* in Egypt.[52]

But even during the eighteenth century, when Khalwatī shaykhs exerted great influence, their political and social activism did not manifest itself in Ottoman Cairo, close to the centre of power. Rather, the political, even revolutionary, potential of the reformist thrust of the Khalwatiyya can best be appreciated though its radiating influence in many directions, but mainly in the Maghrib .

Typical of the Khalwatiyya was a fragmentation and splitting into numerous subsidiary *ṭuruq*. But changes in the ritual and practices of newly created *ṭuruq* were often only minimal. The new *ṭuruq* continued their association with the Khalwatiyya because of the prestige of the *ṭarīqa*, whose name was a guarantee of respectability. They continued to observe Khalwatī practices. A testimony to the persistence and continuity of rituals within the dispersed and fragmented Khalwatī network is the fact that a manual of the Tijāniyya in West Africa has the same rules concerning the *khalwa* as those expressed in a poem written by a member of the Demirdāshiyya in Cairo three centuries earlier.[53]

The Influence of the Khalwatiyya on Reformist Sulṭāns and *'ulamā'* in Morocco

Biographies of *'ulamā'*, and the flourishing of travel accounts of the *riḥla* literature, indicate a significant growth in scale of the pilgrimage in the eighteenth century. Many of the *'ulamā'* of Fez who made the pilgrimage visited Cairo on their way to Mecca. In Cairo they met the Khalwatī shaykhs, who were the leading Sufis and *'ulamā'* at that time.

Aḥmad b. 'Abd al-'Azīz al-Hilālī al-Sijilmāsī (d. 1761) received an *ijāza* from Muṣṭafā al-Bakrī He also studied *Ḥadīth* with al-Ḥifnī. Back in Fez, he often quoted to his students *Hadīth*s that he had learned from al-Ḥifnī. Aḥmad b. Muḥammad al-Ṣaqalī (d. 1763–74), the leading sufi in Morocco in the middle of the eighteenth century, was initiated by al-Ḥifnī into the Khalwatiyya. Al-Ḥifnī gave him permission to propagate the *wird*. On his return to Fez, al-Ṣaqalī taught his disciples the mystical litanies he had learned from al-Ḥifnī. Al- Ṣaqalī passed on his Khalwatī *silsila* to 'Abd al-Wahhāb al-Tāzī (1688–1792), who was the teacher both of Ibn Idrīs and al-Sanūsī. But al-Tāzī was also initiated into the Khalwatiyya directly by al-Ḥifnī himself, and studied with Maḥmūd al-

---

[52] de Jong 1978.

[53] Triaud 1988, p. 55; Clayer 1994, pp. 31, 35; see also Zarcone 1993, pp. 79, 81.

Kurdī. Muhammad b. al-Ṭayyib al-Qādirī (1711–73), the author of *Nashr al-mathānī*, likewise received an *ijāza* from al-Ḥifnī. In his biography of al-Ḥifnī, al-Qādirī paid tribute to al-Ḥifnī's contribution to the Maghrib in the two fields of *Ḥadīth* and *taṣawwuf*. The *qāḍī* Ibn Sūda (d. 1795), the senior scholar in Fez, met Maḥmūd al-Kurdī and other Khalwatī shaykhs. In Medina, Ibn Sūda met Muḥammad b. ʻAbd al-Karīm al-Sammān, who had been initiated into the Khalwatiyya by al-Bakrī.[54]

Through their influence on leading Moroccan *ʻulamā'*, the Egyptian Khalwatiyya contributed to the reformist thrust in Fez under the two sultans Sīdī Muḥammad (1757–90) and his son Mawlay Sulaymān (1792–1822). Sīdī Muḥammad encouraged the study of *Ḥadīth*, and asserted that all four schools of law were equal. His reforms were directed against what he perceived as social malaise and a deplorable religious and moral situation. In 1788, Sīdī Muḥammad sent a copy of his controversial royal decree to the *ʻulamā' of* Cairo, seeking their approval to overcome local opposition to his reforms. He was initiated into the *sharīʻa*-oriented Nāṣiriyya, to which also the leading *ʻulamā'* , such as al-Ṣaqalī and Ibn Sūda, were affiliated.

The *ʻulamā' closest* to the Sulṭān Mawlāy Sulaymān – Sulaymān al-Ḥawwāt (1747–1816), Ḥamdūn b. al-Hājj (1760–1817) and Muḥammad al-Ṭayyib Ibn Kirān (1758–1812) – were of the same age as Ibn Idrīs, and like him, students of Ibn Sūda. In 1806 Mawlāy Sulaymān replied to a letter sent out by the Wahhābī ruler Saʻūd b. ʻAbd la-ʻAzīz. The reply, drafted by Ibn Kirān, praised the asceticism of the Wahhābīs and their efforts to purify the religion and accepted the ban on reprehensible customs associated with the visiting of saints' tombs, but rejected the Wahhābīs' condemnation of the *shafāʻa* of saints and the ban on al-Jazūlī's *Dalā'il al-Khayrāt.* The reply pleaded against the *takfīr* of Muslims. This response to the Wahhābīs reflected the spirit of reform in a milieu based on Sharīfian legitimacy and imbued with Sufi mysticism.

The Raḥmaniyya: An Offshoot of the Khalwatiyya in Algeria

Muḥammad ibn ʻAbd al-Raḥman al-Azharī (1713–93) was initiated into the Khalwatiyya by al-Ḥifnī, and like his master he merged *taṣawwuf* and *fiqh*, *sharīʻa* and *ḥaqīqa*. His association with the great Khalwatī shaykhs in Cairo

[54] This section is based on a joint article with my late student Gideon Weigert: Levtzion and Weigert 1995. We have been well served by two excellent studies on the reformist sulṭāns: El-Mansur 1990 and Harrak 1989. Neither El-Mansur nor Harrak was able to identify the influence of the Khalwatiyya in Fez.

contributed to the social recognition of his personal piety and learning. When he returned from Cairo to Kabylia in 1769, he established a *zāwiya* and a school. News of the homecoming Azharī and the new ideas brought back from the Mashriq soon spread, and attracted learned men from Algiers, Constantine and Bougie. By the 1790s, the *zāwiya* had evolved into a prestigious center of learning.[55]

In the writings of al-Azharī and his immediate successors, until the middle of the nineteenth century, there is no record of the name Raḥmaniyya, and they referred to themselves as Khalwatīs. There were only a few minor changes in ritual from those laid down by Muṣṭafā al-Bakrī for the Khalwatiyya. But in the different social environment of Algeria, the Raḥmaniyya became quite distinct from the urban Khalwatiyya in Egypt.

Before the coming of al-Azharī, local marabouts dominated the spiritual life and allegiance of the mountain population of Kabylia. The rapid expansion of the new *ṭarīqa* may be explained by the strategy of incorporating local saintly lineages into the expanding network that he created, and making the marabouts local representatives of the *ṭarīqa* or *muqaddam*s. The emergence of the Rahmaniyya as a ramified Sufi *ṭarīqa* thus drew in large part upon the older tradition of veneration for local holy men (and women), upon which were superimposed corporate and hierarchical principles. In this way the Bāsh Tārzī family, with its prior religious credentials, was crucial in the dissemination of the Raḥmaniyya in Constantine.[56]

The orthodoxy of the Raḥmaniyya *ṭarīqa*, and its distinct character apart from the Khalwatiyya, was affirmed by the Prophet's appearance to Muḥammad b. ʻAbd al- Raḥman on seven different occasions. The recitation of the "seven dreams" was performed during weekly Sufi meetings, and in religious festivals and pilgrimages. Adepts of the Raḥmaniyya were permitted to belong to other *ṭuruq* concurrently, which helped its growth into a mass association. In keeping with the spirit of the reformed Sufi *ṭuruq*, a sound knowledge of the law was a requisite for a Rahmaniyya *muqaddam*. An examination of the diplomas conferred upon notables of the Raḥmaniyya reveals that they were indeed well-versed both in the fundamentals of jurisprudence and in the esoteric doctrines of classical Sufism. Schools and libraries were attached to most Raḥmaniyya centers, and the *ṭarīqa* was considered an important medium for educational activities.

The Raḥmaniyya's expansion, coherence and activism generated the opposition of the old guard of *ʻulamā' and* Sufi shaykhs, who accused al-Azahrī

---

[55] The section on the Raḥmaniyya is based on Clancy-Smith 1993 and 1994.

[56] Clancy-Smith 1993, pp. 150, 162; Clancy-Smith 1994, pp. 42–3.

of *bid'a* and even of acts of infidelity. The Ottoman authorities restricted his movements and confined him to the vicinity of Algiers.

While there is little hint of millenarian anticipation in al-Azharī's original teachings, after his death – and above all after the French conquest – millenarian expectations grew. Several Raḥmaniyya *zawāyā* served as cores for Mahdist-led revolts, which were either led or supported by Sufi notables. By the end of the nineteenth century, it commanded the largest following among both men and women of all the *ṭuruq* in Algeria, and the French referred to the Raḥmaniyya as "l'église national algérienne".[57]

The Tijāniyya and the *Jihād* of *al-ḥājj* 'Umar in West Africa

Aḥmad al-Tijānī was born in 1737/38. He moved to Fez in 1757/58. He experimented successively with the litanies of the major Sufi *ṭuruq* of Morocco – the Qadiriyya, Shādhiliyya, Nāṣiriyya and the Tayyibiyya – but soon forsook them, expressing disappointment with the established *ṭuruq*. He did not stay long in Fez, but returned to 'Ayn Madi, and in the following years travelled back and forth between the desert recluses and the towns of the region like Tlemcen. He seems to have studied Sufi topics in the desert and exoteric, non-mystical knowledge in the towns. In 1772/73 he went on pilgrimage. On the way he met al-Azharī, who initiated him into the Khalwatiyya. He was reinitiated in Cairo by Maḥmūd al-Kurdī. In 1774 in Medina, Aḥmad al-Tijānī met al-Sammān, who reinforced his adherence to the Khalwatiyya. His attachment to the Khalwatiyya was therefore quite different from his earlier discontent with other Sufi *ṭuruq*. On his return to the Maghrib in 1774, he initiated his first disciples into the Khalwatiyya. The Tijāniyya represented a departure from the Shādhilī tradition to which all other Moroccan *ṭuruq* belonged.

In 1782 al-Tijāni returned to the fringes of the desert, where he had his greatest mystical experience. The Prophet appeared to him "while he was awake", and taught him a litany that enunciated a new independent way direct from the Prophet, who also instructed al-Tijānī to sever relations with other *ṭuruq* and chains of authority, and to assert the exclusivity of the Tijāniyya. This implied a break with the Khalwatiyya, although elements of the revived Khalwatiyya remained embedded in the doctrines and rituals of the Tijāniyya, including the principle of exclusivity. Al-Tijānī introduced only minor changes to the rituals and doctrines of the Khalwatiyya, in *ṭarīqa*, to present it as a new

[57] Clancy-Smith 1993, p. 158; Clancy-Smith 1994, pp. 44–5.

independent *ṭarīqa*. He introduced the silent *dhikr* and did not permit visitation of saints' tombs during the popular *mawāsim*. In 1796 he left the Algerian Sahara for Fez, where he was well received by Mawlāy Sulaymān, and was given a house and a pension. Some scholars, like Ibn Kirān, denounced his claim to direct revelation from the Prophet.[58]

The revolutionary potential of the Tijāniyya found expression in West Africa, with the *jihād* of *al-hājj* 'Umar Tāl al-Fūtī, but not in Sharīfian Morocco or in French Algeria, where the Tijāniyya remained loyal to the authorities, largely in opposition to the Qādiriyya and its leader 'Abd al-Qādir. In Mecca, during the pilgrimage (1828–30), *al-hājj* 'Umar was initiated into the Tijāniyya by Muḥammad al-Ghālī, who appointed him *khalīfa* of the Tijāniyya in West Africa, and commissioned him to spread the *tarīqa*. Muḥammad al-Ghālī was linked to the Khalwatiyya through Maḥmūd al-Kurdī (1715–80), who had also initiated Aḥmad al-Tijānī.

This *jihād* was among the latest in a series of militant Islamic movements in West Africa, all carried out by Torodbe scholars aided by Fulbe pastoralists. Among all the leaders of the *jihād*s, only *al-hājj* 'Umar employed the *ṭarīqa* structure for organizational and political purposes. 'Uthmān dan Fodio was a Qādirī, and mystical experiences were milestones on his road to the *jihād*, but Sufism served no organizational purpose.[59] His *jihād*, launched in 1852, was aimed at the creation of an extensive *dār al-Islām* at the expense of the non-Muslim Bambara states of the Middle Niger and the Sahel. He then became entangled in a conflict with the Muslim state of Hamdullahi in Massina, which developed into a full-scale war. 'Umar was killed in battle in 1864, and his successors – sons and a nephew – were involved in internal disputes and kept busy subduing endless revolts. From the days of *al-hājj* 'Umar himself, the Tijānīs resisted the French advance up the Senegal river until their state was eliminated by the French, and their leader Aḥmad al-Kabīr, son of *al-hājj* 'Umar, performed the *hijra* eastwards.

The Sammāniyya in the Sudan and Indonesia

Muḥammad b. 'Abd al-Karīm al-Sammān (1717–75) was initiated into the Khalwatiyya by Muṣṭafā b. Kamāl al-Dīn al-Bakrī, during one of his four pilgrimages. Indeed, the biographies emphasize al-Sammān's commitment to al-Bakrī's *ṭarīqa*. Al-Sammān visited Egypt in 1760, where he presided over

---

[58] Vikor 1991, pp. 60–3; Levtzion and Weigert 1995, pp. 192–3.
[59] Brenner 1987, p. 58.

Khalwatī *dhikr* ceremonies in Mashad al-Ḥusayn.[60] Two of his disciples spread a *ṭarīqa*, called al-Sammāniyya after him, into Sumatra and the Sudan. In both countries, the Sammāniyya contributed to Islamic revivalism.

Aḥmad al-Ṭayyib al-Bashīr was initiated by al-Sammān in Medina. He returned to the Sudan in 1800, and spread the Sammāniyya until his death in 1823. The two older *ṭuruq* in the Sudan, the Qādiriyya and the Shādhiliyya, had been adapted to the local parochial pattern of holy families. The Sammāniyya, on the other hand, represented a reformed *ṭarīqa*, a corporate social organization with a central hierarchical authority, on a wider geographical and societal scale. The Sammāniyya therefore expanded at the expense of the older *ṭuruq.*[61]

The Sammāniyya was at the back of the most important militant movement in the Sudan, that of the Mahdiyya, in the second half of the nineteenth century. Members of the family of the immediate ancestors of Muḥammad Aḥmad, the future Mahdi of the Sudan, were *murīds* of Aḥmad al-Ṭayyib al-Bashīr. Muḥammad Aḥmad himself was a member of the Sammāniyya for ten years (1861–71), as a disciple of Muḥammad al-Sharīf (d. 1908), the grandson of Aḥmad al-Ṭayyib al-Bashīr. He studied with him for seven years and received permission to teach independently as a shaykh of the Sammāniyya. He eventually quarrelled with Muḥammad al-Sharīf, and transferred his allegiance to another Sammāni shaykh, al-Qurashī w. al-Zayn (d. 1878). The Mahdī's Khalīfa 'Abdullāhī also had Sammānī connections. His grandfather 'Alī was the head of the Sammāniyya in Dārfūr, and his father Muḥammad Karrār is said to have been initiated into the Sammāniyya by a student of Aḥmad al-Ṭayyib.[62]

'Abd al-Ṣammad al-Palimbānī (*c.*1703–*c.*1788) spent most of his working life in the Ḥaramayn. He was initiated by al-Sammān into the Khalwatiyya (or al-Bakriyya, as it was known). 'Abd al-Ṣammād, in his turn, initiated students from Sumatra who had come to study with him in Mecca into the *ṭarīqa* that he named after his master, *al-ṭarīqa al-sammāniyya.* On their return to Sumatra, they spread the Sammāniyya in Palembang in south Sumatra.

From Medina, 'Abd al-Ṣammād seems to have played the role of advisor, guide and teacher to scholars in Sumatra. He maintained links with his homeland by correspondence. The messages he communicated in different ways were militant, and inspired resistance to the Dutch. In *taṣawwuf* he adhered to the teachings of al-Ghazālī, and rendered into Malay an abridgement of *Iḥya' 'ulūm al-dīn* of al-Ghazālī.[63]

---

[60] Weigert 1989, pp. 107–8, 207; al-Jabarti 1390 AH, I, p. 417.

[61] Al-Bashīr 1970, p. 43; Holt 1967.

[62] O'Fahey 1999.

[63] Azra 1999, pp. 682–4.

The Shaṭṭāriyya and the Padri Movement in Indonesia

The Shaṭṭāriyya was established in the late fifteenth century in India. It was known especially for its emphasis on meditative techniques. Its leader, Muḥammad Ghawth (1502–63), was persecuted because of ecstatic statements that he made about his spiritual status. The persecution suppressed the most extravagant claims of ecstatic Sufism, and in the generations that followed, the Shaṭṭāriyya became characterized by a conspicuous conformity with *sharī'a*-based norms of behaviour. Shaṭṭārī Sufis increasingly focused on obligatory *sharī'a* worship and on Koranic and *Hadīth* studies. Wajīh al-Dīn 'Alawī (1504–89) a disciple of Muḥammad Ghawth, established his conservative credentials by asserting that prophecy is always superior to sainthood. Within this *sharī'a* orientation, Shaṭṭārī Sufis continued to develop specialized mediations. Also, the teachings of Ibn 'Arabī, although perhaps restricted to capable students, was retained as the basic theoretical framework for mystical Islam by nearly all the masters of the Shaṭṭāriyya.[64]

Indian Sufis brought the Shaṭṭāriyya to the Haramayn, where it was adopted by Aḥmad al-Qushāshī, the teacher of al-Kūrānī. 'Abd al-Ra'ūf al-Siṇkilī (1615–93) from Acheh in Indonesia came to Medina in 1642, where he was initiated by al-Qushāshī into the Shaṭṭāriyya. After al-Qushāshī's death in 1661, al-Siṇkilī continued his studies with Ibrāhīm al-Kūrānī. He maintained a close relationship with al-Kūrānī after his return to Acheh, seeking his advice on several occasions. Al-Siṇkilī himself authored works on *fiqh*, and wrote a complete *tafsīr* in Malay. At the centre of his teachings was the harmony between the legal and mystical aspects of Islam, and that only by total obedience to the *sharī'a* can a genuine experience of *ḥaqīqa* be attained. As a disciple of al-Kūrānī he was not adverse to Ibn 'Arabī, although he reformulated *waḥdat al-wujūd* to emphasize the transcendence of God.[65]

Before he left Medina, al-Siṇkilī was designated as *khalīfa* of the Shaṭṭāriyya *ṭarīqa*, which he disseminated in Indonesia, where the Shaṭṭāriyya represented a reformed Sufi *ṭarīqa* that combined mysticism with close conformity to the Scriptures, as against the pantheistic mysticism that had prevailed in Acheh.[66]

The Padri reform movement began in the regions around the centre of the Shaṭṭāriyya, and most of the Padri leaders came from the Shaṭṭāriyya. In the late eighteenth century the area surrounding the Shaṭṭāriyya centre of Kota Tua in Agam experienced commercial stimulation and a new influx of wealth,

---

[64] Ernst 1999, pp. 416–35.
[65] Azra 1999. pp. 678–80.
[66] Johns 1976, pp. 304–20.

occasioned by the coffee trade of the neighbouring hill villages. Individuals who had done well in trade could afford to make the pilgrimage. More people from this small region went to Mecca, and on their return exposed their villages to fresh currents from the wider Muslim world.[67]

Around 1784, Tuanku Nan Tua presided over the Shaṭṭāriyya in Kota Tua, which attracted thousands of students. With the rapid growth of commercial agriculture in the area, Tuanku Nan Tua became personally involved in commerce, and became known as the "patron of traders". Such involvement led to a renewed interest in Islamic law to endorse the successful pursuance of commercial ventures, because the old local customs did not cover the needs of traders.[68]

In 1803 a small group, including a former student of Tuanku Nan Tua, Hājji Miskīn, returned from Mecca, convinced of the need for a more explicit adherence to the fundamentals of Islam. Soon Padri leaders established control over certain villages, which were reorganized as separate communities. Popular religious customs were forbidden in these communities, Islamic practices were enforced, and the inhabitants wore distinctive clothing. The Padri villages became engaged in *jihād* against non-observant villages and the local monarchy. By 1819, just before the Dutch returned to establish their rule, the Padri seemed poised to gain full control over the Minangkabau region. The early renewalist *jihād* developed into the Padri war of 1821–38, a war of anti-imperialist resistance.[69]

The Tradition of Ibn Idrīs

We now come to the last Sufi tradition that generated reform movements, mainly in Muslim Africa. These movements drew their inspiration from Aḥmad ibn Idrīs al-Fāsī

His major affiliation was to the Khaḍiriyya, which had been founded in Fez by the *sharīf* ʻAbd al-ʻAzīz al-Dabbāgh (d. 1720). Al-Dabbāgh claimed that al-Khaḍir had revealed to him the ultimate meaning of Sufism. Al-Dabbāgh initiated ʻAbd al-Wahhāb al-Tāzī, who in his turn initiated Ibn Idrīs. Ibn Idrīs claimed that he had taken his prayers, the kernel of the Idrīsī devotional way, from al-Khaḍir in the physical presence of the Prophet. Ibn Idrīs boasted that his *sanad*, from al-Tāzī through al-Dabbāgh to al-Khadir, was among the most

---

[67] Dobbin 1983, pp. 125–7.

[68] Dobbin 1983, p. 125; Keddie 1994, p. 474.

[69] Voll 1999, p. 534.

exalted of the short *asānīd* because al-Khaḍir had met the Prophet, and took from him the *ṣaḥaba*. Likewise, al-Dabbāgh took from al-Khaḍir the *tābi'iyyun* from the *ṣaḥāba.*[70]

But al-Tāzī had multiple affiliations. We have already mentioned that he was initiated into the Khlawatiyya by al-Ḥifnī and Maḥmūd al-Kurdī, and it is likely that al-Tāzī introduced Ibn Idrīs also to the Khalwatiyya, as Ibn Idrīs listed both his Moroccan Shādhilī and Egyptian Khalwatī *silsila*s.

The years that Ibn Idrīs studied in Fez, between 1769 and 1798, were the days of the reformist Ṣulṭāns Sīdī Muḥammad (1757–90) and Mawlāy Sulaymān (1792–1822). Ibn Idrīs studied with Ibn Sūda and with other leading scholars of the Qarawiyyin, among those who had been influenced by the Khalwatiyya. In the late eighteenth century, Fez was the intellectual and religious background to the teachings of Ibn Idrīs.

Aḥmad ibn Idrīs came to the Ḥaramayn on the eve of the Wahhābī conquest of the holy cities. Responding to the challenge presented by the Wahhābī movement, Ibn Idrīs sought to preserve the inner (*bāṭinī*) aspect of Islam, which was rejected completely by the Wahhābīs. At the same time, he vigorously condemned the accretions that had debased the *ṭuruq*. He sought to bind believers together through full adherence to the law, along with an emotionalized Islam based on devotion to the Prophet. His chief disciples claimed to perpetuate his way, but at the same time to have received heavenly directions to found their own distinctive ways. All the new *ṭarīqas* created by his disciples were moved by missionary fervor to augment their membership.

Ibn Idrīs was an outspoken teacher and preacher, unafraid to state his views on current political and religious issues of the day, but there is no evidence that he was an activist in any organizational sense. He laid the foundation for a revivalist tradition in Islam that gave birth to leaders of holy wars, men who established religious states, and a number of important centralized *ṭuruq*. Ibn Idrīs attracted disciples from areas where Islam was still relatively unstructured, and he sent some of them back to those regions as missionaries. He thus initiated a practice that was to be particularly characteristic of the *ṭuruq* within the Idrīsī tradition.

---

[70] The section on Ibn Idris is based on O'Fahey 1990. But see also O'Fahey and Radtke 1993, p. 69 and Radtke 1996, p. 334.

The Sanūsiyya: From Piety to Structural Organization

Ibn Idrīs regarded Muḥammad 'Alī al-Sanūsī as his chosen student, and believed that al-Sanūsī reached "an equal rank with ourselves and he is a true likeness of us."[71] They seem to have been of the same mould, although one generation apart, as both of them were informed by the religious and intellectual milieu of eighteenth-century Fez.

Muḥammad b. 'Alī al-Sanūsī was born in 1787. In late 1808 or early 1809 he moved to Fez to study at the Qarawiyyin, and stayed there until 1830. He studied with Ibn Kirān, who wrote the reply on behalf of Mawlāy Sulaymān to the Wahhābīs. Al-Sanūsī's views, as he formulated them in the Hijāz twenty years later, evidently had their roots in mid-eighteenth century Fez. Al-Sanūsī was initiated into the Nāṣiriyya by Muḥammad b. Muḥammad al-Madanī, a close companion of the Ṣūltān Mawlāy Sulaymān, who studied in Egypt with Murtadā al-Zabīdī and Aḥmad al-Dardīr. He criticized the current situation of the rural Sufi *ṭuruq*, and rejected *taqlīd* in favour of *ijtihād*.[72]

Al-Sanūsī became associated with Aḥmad al-Tijānī, who was then resident in Fez, and studied Koran with al-Tijānī: "He told me that he had taken it from the Prophet, asleep and awake … He honoured me by letting me take the Koran from him, by this noble *sanad*."[73] The spiritual content of al-Sanūsī's Sufism seems to have come entirely from Ibn Idrīs. The path of Ibn Idrīs, however, was much more clearly mystical, as his mentor al-Tāzī was exclusively known for his Sufi teachings rather than for any exoteric knowledge. Al-Sanūsī brought Sufism closer to the *sharī'a*, to the world of the exoteric, non-mystical Islamic scholarship.

Al-Sanūsī was not a political thinker or leader. His interests and activities were fully centred on the religious and scholarly world. The organization that was to have such a profound impact on the political future of the central Sahara and the desert edge was a pious one. Thus the history of the Sanūsiyya is the history of the transformation of a religious structure into a political one, through its merging with the ethnic identity of the Saharan Bedouins. Al-Sanūsī's reform was the combination of ideas and organization, of theory and practice, in the desert edge region.

Al-Sanūsī sought a region where he could develop his new organization with as little conflict as possible, a "virgin region" untouched by rival Sufi ṭarīqas. The Bedouins of Cyrenaica were quite well aware of Sufis and holy men, and

[71] O'Fahey 1990, pp. 131–2.

[72] The section on the Sanūsiyya is based on Vikor 1991.

[73] Ibid., pp. 63–4.

had some important shrines, but there was no Sufi organization present. Al-Sanūsī established a structure of lodges, independent of the tribes. The centre had direct control over the local lodges, without an elaborate structure, without imposing an authority over the tribes and without intervening directly in their affairs. It did only what was necessary to maintain a strongly cohesive religious structure, its own *ṭarīqa* of learning and piety.

The development and the structure of the *ṭarīqa* was clearly the conscious work of al-Sanūsī himself. He built alliances with the tribes and factions in Cyrenaica. He organized the *ṭarīqa* with a great degree of centralization and control from the centre. He based himself on the model of the holy men who already existed among the Bedouins of the area – which he knew from his homeland – but transformed and restructured it.

The sons of al-Sanūsī extended the influence of the *ṭarīqa* far into the Sahara, to Lake Chad. Since 1871, French politicians considered the Sanūsīs to be partners in a conspiracy with the Turks that was directed against France. By 1900 the Sanūsīs had collided with an advancing French military expedition near Lake Chad. Because they were a genuinely mystical, but not a military organization, the poorly armed and weak Sanūsīs could not hope to sustain effective resistance to the French, and were driven north into Cyrenaica. By 1911 they were involved in a desperate struggle, in alliance with the Ottomans, against the Italian invaders of Libya.

Conclusion

In this chapter we have traced the history of manifestations of Muslim resistance to colonial expansion back to an earlier stage of renewal and reform within Sufi *ṭuruq*, which occurred almost simultaneously in all parts of the Muslim world in the eighteenth century. This was the culmination and crystallization of undercurrents from the sixteenth and seventeenth centuries that reinforced the *sharī'a* orientation of Sufi *ṭuruq*.

Two major Sufi streams charted the map of renewal movements – the Naqshabandiyya and the Khalwatiyya, with their ramifications. From Aḥrār in Central Asia to Sirhindī and the Mujaddidiyya, the Naqshabandiyya made inroads into the Ottoman Empire with the Khālidiyya, and into the Caucasus. Whereas the Naqshabandiyya's influence was in this northern crescent, the Khalwatiyya made its impact on Muslim Africa, west and south of Egypt.

If the nineteenth century saw the rise of militant movements, and the eighteenth century experienced the restructuring of *sharī'a*-oriented Sufi *ṭuruq*, it was, in the seventeenth century that Muslim scholars had begun to break out of the combination of legal *taqlīd* and mystical pantheism. Sirhindī in India and al-Qushāhī in Medina, followed by Ibrāhīm al-Kūrānī, advanced the merging of *Ḥadīth* and *taṣawwu*, which became a prescription for *sharī'a*-oriented *ṭuruq*. Indian scholars were important in the Ḥaramayn as a result of the growth of the pilgrimage, during which they encountered Sufis and *muḥaddithun* from North Africa, Egypt and Kurdistan. Pilgrims from the farthest lands of Islam – Indonesia, Africa and China – were initiated in the Ḥaramayn into new *ṭuruq*, and carried back to their homelands new ideas and the nuclei for more cohesive and structurally organized Sufi organizations. It was in those countries at the periphery of the Muslim world that the evolutionary process of Islamization reached a stage that called for a radical departure from past traditions, which could be achieved only through revolution.

References

Abu-Manneh, B. "'Khalwa and Rābiṭa in the Khālidī suborder", in Gaborieau, Popovic and Zarcone (eds), *Naqshabandis*. Istanbul and Paris, 1990, pp. 289–302.

Abu-Manneh, B. *Studies on Islam and the Ottoman Empire in the Nineteenth Century*. Istanbul, 2001.

Algar, H. "A brief history of the Naqshabandi order", in Gaborieau et al., *Naqshabandis*, pp. 13–19.

Algar, H. "Political aspects of Naqshabandi history", in Gaborieau et al., *Naqshabandis*, pp. 123–52.

Ansari, S. *Sufi Saints and State Power: The Pirs of Sind, 1843–1947*. Cambridge: Cambridge University Press, 1992.

Azra, A. "Opposition to Sufism in the East Indies in the Seventeenth and Eighteenth Centuries", in *Islamic Mysticism Contested*, edited by F. de Jong and B. Radtke. Leiden: Brill, 1999, pp. 665–86.

al-Bashīr, A. 'Alī. *Al-Adab al-Ṣufi fī'l-Sūdān*. Cairo, 1970.

Bazmee Ansari, A.S. "Al-Dihalawī Shāh Walī Allāh", *Encyclopaedia of Islam* – CD Edition 2001.

Bennigsen, A. "Un mouvement populaire au Caucase au 18e siècle: la guerre sainte du sheikh Mansur, 1785–1791", *Cahiers du Monde Russe et Soviétique*, II (1964), pp. 159–205.

Brenner, L. "Muslim Thought in Eighteenth-Century West Africa: the Case of Shaykh 'Uthmān b. Fūdī" in N. Levtzion and J.O. Voll (eds), *Eighteenth-Century Renewal and Reform in Islam*. Syracuse, 1987, pp. 39–42.

Buehler, A.F. "Charismatic versus scriptural authority: Naqshabandi response to deniers of mediational Sufism in British India", in de Jong and Radtke, *Islamic Mysticism Contested*, pp. 468–91.

Chelebi, K. *The Balance of Truth*, trans. by G.L. Lewis, London: Allen and Unwin, 1957, pp. 43–4.

Chodkiewicz, M. "Quelques remarques sur la diffusion de l'enseignement d'Ibn 'Arabi'", *Mode de Transmission de la Culture Religieuse en Islam*. Cairo, 1993, pp. 201–24

Chittick, W.C. "Taṣawwuf " in Encyclopaedia of Islam, x, pp. 317–24

Chittick, W.C. "Taṣawwuf and Waḥdat al-shuhūd" in Encyclopaedia of Islam, xi, pp. 37–9.

Clancy-Smith, J.A. "The man with two tombs: Muḥammad ibn 'Abd al-Raḥmān, founder of the Algerian Raḥmāniyya, *c.* 1715—1798", in *Manifestations of Sainthood in Islam*, edited by G. Martin Smith and C.E. Ernst. Istanbul, 1993, pp. 147–69.

Clancy-Smith, J.A. *Rebel and Saint: Muslim Notables, Populist Protest, Colonial Encounters (Algeria and Tunisia, 1800–1904)*. Berkeley: University of California Press, 1994.

Clayer, N. *Mystiques, état et société: les Halvetis dans l'aire balkanique de la fin du 15e siècle à nos jours*. Leiden: Brill, 1994.

Copty, A. "Ibrāhīm Ibn Ḥasan al-Kūrānī al-Shārazurī (1025–1101/1616–1690) and his Intellectual Heritage: Hadīth and Sufism in Medina in the 17th Century", Ph.D. dissertation, Hebrew University of Jerusalem, 2005.

Dallal, A. "The origins and objectives of Islamic revivalist thought, 1750–1850", *Journal of the American Oriental Society*, 133/iii (1993), pp. 341–59.

DeWeese, D. Review of Jurgen Paul, *Journal of Asian History*, 27 (1993), pp. 66–7.

DeWeese, D. "The Masha'ikh-i Turk and the Khojagan: rethinking the links between the Yasavi and Naqshabandi Sufi traditions", *Journal of Islamic Studies*, 7:2 (1996), pp. 180–207.

Dobbin, C. *Islamic Revivalism in a Changing Peasant Economy: Sumatra 1784–1847*. London and Malmo: Curzon Press, 1983.

El-Mansour, M. *Morocco in the Reign of Mawlay Sulayman*. Wiesbach: Menas Press, 1990.

Ernst, C.E. "Persecution and circumspection in Shatari Sufism", in de Jong and Radtke, *Islamic Mysticism Contested*, pp. 416–35.

Gaboriau, M. "Criticzing the Sufis: The debate in early nineteenth-century India", in de Jong and Radtke, *Islamic Mysticism Contested*, pp. 454–67.

Gross, J. "The economic status of a Timurid Sufi Shaykh: A matter of conflict or perception", *Iranian Studies*, 21 (1988), pp. 84–104.

Haar, J.G.J. Ter. "The Naqshabandi tradition in the eyes of Aḥmad Sirhindī", in *Naqshabandis*, edited by M. Gaborieau et. al., pp. 83–93.

Harrak, F. "State and Religion in Eighteenth-Century Morocco: The religious policy of Sīdī Muḥammad ibn 'Abdallāh, 1757–1790", Ph.D. dissertation, School of Oriental and African Studies (SOAS), University of London, 1989.

Holt, P.M. "Holy families and Islam in the Sudan", *Princeton Near East Papers*, 4 (1967).

Inayatullah, Sh. "Sayyid Aḥmad Brēlwī, *Encyclopaedia of Islam* (CD Edition 2001)

al-Jabartī, 'A. al-Raḥmān. *'Aja'ib al-athār fi'l-tarājim wa'l-akhbār*. Cairo, 1390.

Johns, A.H. "Islam in Southeast Asia: Problems and Perspectives", C.D. Cowan and O.W. Wolters (eds), *Southeast Asian History and Historiography: Essays Presented to D.G.E. Hall.* Ithaca: Cornell University Press, 1976, pp. 304–20.

De Jong, F. *Turuq and Turuq-linked Institutions in Nineteenth-century Egypt.* Leiden: Brill, 1978.

De Jong, F. "Mustafa kamal al-Din al-Bakri (1688–1749): Revival and reform of the Khalwatiyya?", in N. Levtzion and J.O. Voll (eds), *Eighteenth-Century Renewal and Reform in Islam.* New York: Syracuse University Press, 1987, pp. 117–32.

Karamustafa, A.T. *God's Unruly Friends: Dervish Groups in the Islamic Later Middle Period, 1200–1550*. Salt Lake City: University of Utah Press, 1994.

Keddie, N.R. "The Revolt of Islam, 1700 to 1993: Comparative considerations and relations to imperialism", *Comparative Study of Society and History*. 1994, pp. 463–87.

Levtzion, N. & Voll, J.O. *Eighteenth-Century Renewal and Reform in Islam*, New York: Syracuse University Press, 1987.

Levtzion, N. and Weigert, G. "Religious Reform in Eighteenth-century Morocco", in, *North African, Arabic and Islamic Studies in Honor of Pessah Shinar*, published as *Jerusalem Studies in Arabic and Islam*, 19 (1995), pp. 173–97.

Levtzion, N. and Weigert, G. "The Muslim holy cities as foci of Islamic revivalism in the eighteenth century", in *Sacred Space: Shrine, City, Land*, edited by B.Z. Kedar and R.J. Zwi Werblowsky. New York: New York University Press, 1996, pp. 259–77.

Levtzion, N. "Eighteenth-Century Sufi Brotherhoods: Structural, Organizational and Ritual Changes", in *Essays on Scripture, Thought and Society. A Festschrift in Honour of Anthony H. Johns*, edited by P.G. Riddell and T. Street. Leiden: Brill, 1997, pp. 259–77.

Martin, B.G. *Muslim Brotherhoods in Nineteenth-century Africa.* Cambridge: Cambridge University Press, 1976.

Nizami, K.A. "The Suhrawardī silsilah and its influence on medieval Indian politics", *Medieval Indian Quarterly*, 3 (1957), pp. 109–49.

Ocak, A.Y. "Ḳalenderī dervishes and Ottoman administration from the fourteenth to the sixteenth centuries" in Smith and Ernst, *Manifestations of Sainthood in Islam*, pp. 239–255.

O'Fahey, R.S. *Enigmatic Saint: Ahmad ibn Idris and the Idrisi tradition.* London and Evanston: Northwestern University Press, 1990.

O'Fahey R.S. and Radtke B. "Neo-sufism reconsidered", *Der Islam*, 70I (1993), pp. 52–87.

O'Fahey, R.S. "Sufism in suspense: the Sudanese Mahdi and the Sufis", in de Jong and Radtke, *Islamic Mysticism Contested*, pp. 267–82.

Paul, J. "Forming a Faction: The *ḥimāyat* system of Khwaja Ahrar", *International Journal of Middle East Studies*, 23 (1991), pp. 533–48.

Radtke, B. "Sufism in the 18th Century: An attempt at a provisional appraisal", *Die Welt des Islams*, 36 (1996), pp. 326–64.

Radtke et al. *The Exoteric Ahmad Ibn Idris: A Sufi Critique of the Madhahib and the Wahhabis*. Leiden: Brill 2000.

Rizvi, S.A.A. "The Breakdown of Traditional Society", *Cambridge History of Islam*, edited by P.M. Holt, A.K.S. Lambton and B. Lewis. Cambridge, 1970, pp. 67–96.

Shatkowski Schilcher, L. *Families in Politics: Damascene Factions and Estates of the 18th and 19th Centuries*, Stuttgart: F. Steiner, 1985.

Triaud, J.L. "Khalwa and the career of sainthood: An interpretative essay", *Charisma and Brotherhoods in African Islam*, edited by C. Cruise O'Brien and C. Coulon. Oxford 1988, pp. 53–66.

Vikor, K. *Sufi and Scholar on the Desert Edge: Muhammad ibn `Ali al-Sanusi (1787-1859)*. Evanston: Northwestern University Press, 1995.

Voll, J.O. "A History of the Khatmiyya tariqah in the Sudan", Ph.D. dissertation, Harvard 1969.

Voll, J.O. "Muhammad Hayya al-Sindi and Muhammad ibn 'Abd al-Wahhab; An analysis of an intellectual group in eighteenth-century Medina", *Bulletin SOAS*, 38 (1975), pp. 32–9.

Voll, J.O. "Hadith scholars and tariqahs: an 'ulama' group in the eighteenth-century *haramayn* and their impact in the Muslim world", *Journal of Asian and African Studies*, XV (1980), pp. 264–73.

Voll, J.O. *Islam: Continuity and Change in the Muslim World.* Boulder: Westview Press, 1982.

Voll, J.O. "Foundations for Renewal and Reform: Islamic Movements in the Eighteenth and Nineteenth Centuries", *The Oxford History of Islam*, edited by J. Esposito, Oxford: Oxford University Press, 1999, pp. 509–47.

Weigert, G. "The Khalwatiyya in Egypt in the Eighteenth Century", Ph.D. Dissertation, The Hebrew University of Jerusalem, 1989.

Weismann, I. *Taste of Modernity: Sufism, Salafiyya, and Arabism in Late Ottoman Damascus*. Leiden, Brill, 2001.

Winter, M. *Society and Religion in Early Ottoman Egypt: Studies in the Writings of 'Abd al-Wahhab al-Sha'rani.* New Brunswick: Transaction Books, 1982.

Zarcone, T. *Mystiques, philosophes, et franc-maçons en Islam: Riza Tevfik, penseur Ottoman (1868–1949), du soufisme à la confrérie*. Istanbul, 1993.

Zilfi, M.C. The Politics of Piety: The Ottoman Ulema in the Postclassical Age (1600–1800). Minneapolis, MN, Bibliotheca Islamica, 1988.

Index

The editors wish to thank Michael Barak for preparing the index.